Alan Shipnuck

Hootie, Martha,

THE BATTLE FOR AUGUSTA NATIONAL

and the

Masters of the Universe

Simon & Schuster

New York   London   Toronto   Sydney

SIMON & SCHUSTER
Rockefeller Center
1230 Avenue of the Americas
New York, NY 10020

For information regarding special discounts for bulk purchases,
please contact Simon & Schuster Special Sales at
1-800-456-6798 or business@simonandschuster.com

Designed by Elliot Beard

Manufactured in the United States of America

10 9 8 7 6 5 4 3 2 1

Library of Congress Cataloging-in-Publication Data is available.

ISBN 0-7432-5500-3

For my parents, who have taught me so much about so many things.

And for Olivia, who kept me motivated.

ALSO BY ALAN SHIPNUCK

Bud, Sweat, & Tees

Contents

THE BATTLE FOR AUGUSTA NATIONAL

At the Point of a Bayonet

"MR. JOHNSON, THIS IS the first Masters that you're presiding over as chairman—I just wonder how it feels personally, and what responsibility you feel to both the past and the future?"

"Well, it is a great honor to be in this position, and I feel a great responsibility to preserve the traditions and the customs established by Bob Jones and Cliff Roberts. I guess that is the main concern that I have."

With those words, William Woodward (Hootie) Johnson was officially introduced to his public. He had been named Augusta National Golf Club's fifth chairman on May 1, 1998, but it was nearly a year later—on Wednesday of Masters week in April 1999—that he first commanded the stage, at the annual press conference conducted by the club chairman on the eve of the tournament. For the better part of half an hour Johnson was questioned about such mundane matters as the tournament's revamped qualifying criteria and proposals to speed up the pace of play. His responses were authoritative and informed with the proper reverence. At one point Johnson was asked if he was "nervous" about how his tenure as chairman would be remembered, given that for his first Masters he was unveiling significant changes to four holes and a well-groomed layer of rough framing the fairways—a noteworthy departure from Bobby Jones's vision of the course. "Well, anything having to do with Augusta National is a heavy responsibility and one that we always give careful thought to," said Johnson. "It is a national treasure. It is something precious and something to be preserved."

Near the end of the Q&A session Christine Brennan raised a hand. Since the debut of her weekly column in *USA Today* in 1998, Brennan had emerged as one of the most prominent sportswriters in the country. Her Olympic background—including two books about figure skating— had provided her with an opportunity to write often about women's sports, and she was never shy about crusading for her sisters. The 1999 Masters was Brennan's first sojourn to the manly world of Augusta National; she was not imbued with the reflexive deference to this famous club that is typical of so many sportswriters covering the tournament. Earlier in the week Brennan had read a clip about Augusta National's aversion to publicly discussing its membership; without identifying herself, Brennan said to Johnson, "We were talking yesterday"—reporters, that is—"trying to get the numbers straight. If you wouldn't mind telling us how many African Americans there are at Augusta National and how many women members? And if there are no women members, why aren't there?"

"Well, that's a club matter, ma'am, and all club matters are private," Johnson replied.

"Are there women members?"

"That's a club matter, ma'am, and all club matters are private."

The next question was about the recent course renovations, and the press conference petered out shortly thereafter.

"I've heard reporters saying that there were chuckles in the room when I asked those questions," Brennan says. "I think that's how they want to remember the moment. As I recall, there was complete silence. Awkward silence. But afterward, some of my buddies came up and punched me on the arm and they were like, 'Way to go, you've been at the Masters exactly one day and you're already causing trouble.' That didn't bother me. What bothered me was, Why didn't anyone else follow up? Was it so unique a question, so out of left field, that they couldn't see it was a legitimate issue?"

Brennan's acidic column came out the next day, April 8, 1999, the first round of the sixty-third Masters. It began, "I made a right turn off the main drag in Augusta the other day and ended up in 1975. Or perhaps it was 1940. It was hard to tell." She recounted her exchange with Johnson, then quoted him saying, "It is something precious and something to be preserved." Brennan's kicker: "He was talking about the golf course and the tournament. And, hopefully, nothing else."

Brennan's initial clash with Johnson would grow into a scab that she would pick over and over in the years to come. At her second Masters, in what was otherwise a valentine to 2000 champion Vijay Singh, Brennan wrote, "He became only the second person of color, joining [Tiger] Woods, to win at this lily-white bastion of still mostly segregated golf, where today, in the year 2000, amazingly enough, there still are only three black members and no women." In a shrill pretournament piece the following year, Brennan made note of "the behavior of our host this week, good old Augusta National. No club this visible is doing more to promote the advancement of poor, beleaguered white men in golf than this one. It's a secret how many black and female members Augusta National has in total, but it's fairly certain there are no more than three black members, and no women members."

At the U.S. Open two months later, in a column slamming Tiger Woods for his lack of an overt social conscience, Brennan again made mention of the absence of women members at Augusta National.

By the time the 2002 Masters rolled around, even Brennan was tired of hearing Brennan rag on Augusta National. "I had become a cliché—I had become a joke in my profession," she says. "I decided it was time to give it a rest." In fact, Brennan skipped Augusta altogether. But on Monday of Masters week, while at home in Washington, D.C., she cracked open the May/June issue of *Golf for Women*, a sister publication of *Golf Digest*. Contained within its glossy pages was an article by Marcia Chambers entitled "Ladies Need Not Apply."

Chambers was the author of a groundbreaking 1990 report for *Golf Digest* about the legal and ethical challenges facing exclusionary private clubs. Her interest in the topic led to the book *The Unplayable Lie: The Untold Story of Women and Discrimination in American Golf*. She had been installed as a contributing editor at *Digest* in the early nineties, becoming the conscience of the Golf Digest Companies, whose chairman and editorial director, Jerry Tarde, likes to brag in print about his membership at Pine Valley, perhaps the most macho of the country's all-male golf clubs. "Ladies Need Not Apply" was a meticulously researched, 4,500-word screed about the exclusionary membership practices of Augusta National and the Royal and Ancient Golf Club of St. Andrews, the tweedy Scottish ruling body that runs the British Open. Chambers's piece would be nominated for a National Magazine Award, but with *Golf for Women*'s petite four hundred thousand circulation, it failed to register with the public at large. Brennan, however, was intrigued by one tidbit buried on the fifth page of the story: In a roundup of Augusta National's tiny tribe of black members, Chambers mentioned Lloyd Ward, who had just become the CEO of the United States Olympic Committee. The Olympics is one of the few places in sports where women and men are on a level playing field, and Brennan was stunned that the USOC's highest-paid official would belong to an all-male club. She picked up the phone and called Ward.

ON APRIL 11, 2002, Martha Burk traveled from her home in Washington, D.C., to Austin, Texas, to spend the weekend at the home of her son Mark, who was hosting a family get-together. En route she grabbed a copy of *USA Today*. Burk's father and two sons are avid golfers; with the Masters beginning that day, she knew it would be a topic of conversation, and, as always, she wanted to have all the answers. When Burk opened the paper to the sports section the top of the front page screamed "Augusta Faces Push for Women." When she turned the page, Brennan's column called out to her. Both pieces cited Chambers's article in *Golf for Women*, but *USA Today* was able to advance the story thanks to Ward, who had violated the basic tenet of Augusta National membership. Like mobsters and professional caddies, Augusta National members live under a code of *omerta;* it is verboten to speak publicly about the family business. Yet here was Ward, on page one of the *USA Today* sports section, saying, "I want to have influence from the inside. I want to talk to members of Augusta and say, quite frankly . . . you've got to have a broader membership, and that includes women." He added, "Inclusion does not just mean people of color. It should be extended to that broader base that includes women."

As the chair of the National Council of Women's Organizations (NCWO), Burk has devoted her professional life to fighting gender discrimination. These stories of Augusta National's grass ceiling resonated deeply with her. Four days later Burk was plopped in front of the TV at her son's home, studying the final round of the Masters. At one point she turned to her daughter-in-law Kim and said, "You know, I found out that this club discriminates against women. And we're going to change that."

Later in the telecast, Hootie Johnson appeared, to conduct the awkward ceremony in which the Masters champion is presented with a green jacket, the iconic symbol of Augusta National membership. Burk got a hoot out of Johnson's drawl, which is thicker than U.S. Open rough. Adopting an over-the-top southern accent, she said, "Hootie Johnson, ah'm a-gonna wraaaht yew uh letter!"

IN LATE APRIL the NCWO's all-female executive committee convened for its bimonthly meeting. Near the end of the session Burk said, "By the way, I learned about this golf club that doesn't allow women members. Why don't we write them a letter?" The women murmured their assent. As Burk would later say, "It was such a small deal we didn't even vote on it." Letter writing is a common practice of the NCWO, designed to create dialogue, apply pressure, or both. Burk and her organization write a handful of such letters every month.

In the weeks after her executive committee meeting Burk pecked out a draft of a letter to the chairman of Augusta National and circulated it for comment. "People helped tweak it—a word here, a word there," she says. The finished letter was dated June 12. A full two months had passed since the Masters. "My best guess is that we sent it registered mail," Burk says. "I'm sure it wasn't overnight, because we don't like to spend that kind of money. There certainly wasn't any sense of urgency, which should be obvious because it took me a while to get it done."

The scarlet letter ran exactly nine sentences:

The National Council of Women's Organizations (NCWO) is the nation's oldest and largest coalition of women's groups. Our 160 member organizations represent women from all socioeconomic and demographic groups, and collectively represent over seven million women nationwide.

Our member groups are very concerned that the nation's premier golf event, the Masters, is hosted by a club that discriminates against women by excluding them from membership. While we understand that there is no written policy barring women, Augusta National's record speaks for itself. As you know, no woman has been invited to join since the club was formed in 1932.

We know that Augusta National and the sponsors of the Masters do not want to be viewed as entities that tolerate discrimination against any group, including women. We urge you to review your policies and practices in this regard, and open your membership to women now, so that this is not an issue when the tournament is staged next year.

Our leadership would be pleased to discuss this matter with you personally or by telephone. I will contact you in the next few weeks.

In hindsight, Burk says, "I regret only one line in the letter. Where I wrote 'so this is not an issue next year,' in my mind, I meant 'as it already has become this year.' I wish I had completed the sentence on paper. But I think it's important to point out that I was accused of putting a deadline on this, which you will see is inaccurate if you read the letter carefully."

Weeks went by without a word from Johnson. Burk was hardly put out. Her letters often engendered blow-off form replies, or no response at all. "I have always assumed the reason we didn't hear from Hootie right away was because he doesn't read the mail every day," Burk says. "I never thought he was down there plotting an offensive."

A COUPLE OF DAYS after receiving Burk's letter, Johnson had lunch in his hometown of Columbia, South Carolina, with his friend and mentor Bob McNair, the former governor of the Palmetto State. They have known each other since the late 1950s, when Johnson was a callow twenty-five-year-old who had been talked into running for a seat in South Carolina's House of Representatives, and McNair, an older, wiser member, took him under his wing. "We didn't talk about it at length, but Hootie did mention that he had received this letter and he intended to put the matter to rest," says McNair. "His thing was that he wanted to make his case clear. He didn't want to crack the door for further debate. Looking back now, it's worth a chuckle, but at the time Hootie didn't anticipate much of a public reaction." McNair's avuncular advice, shaped by a lifetime of public service, was not to underestimate the power of a determined activist.

Johnson continued to stew on Burk's letter, chatting up his best friend and frequent hunting companion Hugh McColl, a fellow Augusta National member. Johnson's foray into politics had been brief; after one two-year term as a state representative, he dedicated his professional life to growing his daddy's small-town bank. Johnson would turn Bankers Trust into a southeastern power, and in 1985 he merged it with McColl's North Carolina NationsBank. A series of further mergers, some of them bloody, made Johnson a multimillionaire and left him as the chairman of the executive committee of the country's biggest financial institution, Bank of America, with McColl entrenched as its CEO. Though Johnson would be described by *The Charlotte Observer* as McColl's "hatchet man," theirs has always been a relationship of mutual respect. "Hootie is my closest friend in the world," says McColl. "If he asks a question, I give him an answer. We have a saying: I have an opinion unencumbered by the facts."

McColl declines to discuss the specifics of his advice on how to handle Burk's letter, but it's not hard to guess its tenor. Through the years McColl has been described by *Fortune* variously as a "combative," "bombastic," "pugnacious" "scorched earth operator," not to mention "a ruthless taskmaster who chews up everything in his path." *Time* chimed in too, calling him "a tiny stick of dynamite . . . with a big mouth and a short fuse." And if Johnson ever needed a military analogy—involving, say, a bayonet—he could certainly count on it to be supplied by McColl, a former Marine who kept a crystal grenade on his desk and who once celebrated a business victory by reenacting the raising of the flag at Iwo Jima with some of his loyal boardroom lieutenants.

Johnson sought further opinions on how to proceed from his kitchen cabinet of fellow members. As a kingmaker in South Carolina politics,

Johnson had earned a reputation as a fearless visionary who was "stubborn as a mule," according to a man he helped elect to South Carolina's General Assembly, I. S. Leevy Johnson. But Hootie's indecisiveness on how to handle Burk can be traced to a public relations fiasco from the previous year. One of the most treasured perks of winning the Masters has always been the lifetime invitation to play in the tournament, and the fossilized past champs have long been a beloved part of the Masters firmament, even as they struggle to break 90. In May 2001, Johnson ordered a bluntly worded letter to be sent to a handful of past champions, strongly encouraging them to hang up their spikes so as to spare the Masters their ragged play. The insult to these proud men was later codified, as the Masters set an age limit of sixty-five for its participants. The revocation of the lifetime exemption led to howls of protest among the players and sharp criticism in the press, as much for the unfeeling manner in which it was handled as for the merits of the decision. Thus chastised, Johnson proceeded with caution after receiving Burk's letter.

"People think this was a knee-jerk reaction," says an Augusta National employee, "but the Chairman spent three weeks carefully deliberating a response." (Like Sinatra and Mao, Johnson is referred to as the Chairman by his supplicants.) At the urging of his inner circle, Johnson agreed that the club should seek the counsel of a Washington, D.C., public relations consultant who moved in the same circles as Burk and was familiar with the politics of protest. After some fishing around, the consultant rendered his verdict: Burk was deemed "an attack activist," says the club insider. "The recommendation was that we fight back, that we set the agenda on the debate."

As June melted into July, Johnson pecked out a draft of a press release, aided by the consultant. It was then circulated among his camp for comment and further tweaking. The final version ran to three pages and would be e-mailed to eighty media outlets across the country. Its tone was somewhere between defiant and foaming-at-the-mouth rabid:

We have been contacted by Martha Burk, Chair of the National Council of Women's Organizations (NCWO), and strongly urged to radically change our membership. We want the American public to be aware of this action right from the beginning. We have advised Dr. Burk that we do not intend to participate in such backroom discussions.

We take our membership very seriously. It is the very fabric of our club. Our members are people who enjoy each other's company and the game of golf. Our membership alone decides our membership—not any outside group with its own agenda.

Dr. Burk's letter incorporates a deadline tied to the Masters and refers to sponsors of the tournament's telecast. These references make it abundantly clear that Augusta National Golf Club is being threatened with a public campaign designed to use economic pressure to achieve a goal of [the] NCWO.

Augusta National and the Masters—while happily entwined—are quite different. One is a private club. The other is a world-class sports event of great public interest. It is insidious to attempt to use one to alter the essence of the other. The essence of a private club is privacy. Nevertheless, the threatening tone of Dr. Burk's letter signals the probability of a full-scale effort to force Augusta National to yield to [the] NCWO's will.

We expect such a campaign would attempt to depict the members of our club as insensitive bigots and coerce the sponsors of the Masters to disassociate themselves under threat—real or implied—of boycotts and other economic pressures.

We might see "celebrity" interviews and talk show guests discussing the "morality" of private clubs. We could also anticipate op-ed articles and editorials.

There could be attempts at direct contact with board members of sponsoring corporations and inflammatory mailings to stockholders and investment institutions. We might see everything from picketing and boycotts to t-shirts and bumper stickers. On the internet, there could be active chat rooms and email messaging. These are all elements of such campaigns.

We certainly hope none of that happens. However, the message delivered to us was clearly coercive.

We will not be bullied, threatened or intimidated.

We do not intend to become a trophy in their display case.

There may well come a day when women will be invited to join our membership but that timetable will be ours and not at the point of a bayonet.

JULY 9, 2002, was a quiet Tuesday around the NCWO headquarters. When a FedEx deliveryman came knocking, Burk signed for a slender package herself and immediately popped it open. Inside was a letter on Augusta National letterhead, in which Johnson had dashed off a pithy three sentences to Burk: "As you are aware, Augusta National Golf Club is a distinctly private club and, as such, cannot talk about its membership and practices with those outside the organization. I have found your letter's several references to discrimination, allusions to the sponsors and your setting of deadlines to be both offensive and coercive. I hope you understand why any further communication between us would not be productive."

Says Burk, "I thought the tone was pretty cold, but I put the letter aside. It didn't make a strong impression because we sometimes get dismissive responses like that. But not ten minutes after getting the letter, my phone rang. It was the first reporter calling, about the press release that had just been issued by the club. I had no idea what he was talking about. The timing was such that I have often wondered if Hootie was tracking the FedEx, ensuring that it was delivered before he unleashed his statement to the world."

The reporter on the other end of the phone line was Doug Ferguson, the industrious golf writer for the Associated Press. When Burk pleaded ignorance, Ferguson faxed her Johnson's statement.

"The response is insensitive at best and confrontational at worst," Burk told Ferguson. "I and my groups are making a good-faith effort to urge the club to be fair, to not discriminate against women and basically to come into the twenty-first century. We were trying the olive-branch approach, but he's unwilling to talk."

Burk went on to say that the NCWO's next step would be to contact the Masters' corporate sponsors. "I hope they'll respond positively," she said, in what sounded like a warning. As for Johnson's excruciatingly detailed forecast of a public campaign against the club, Burk said, slyly, "He's certainly given us a good blueprint."

Before the day was out, Johnson's defiance and Burk's resolve were burning up the AP wire. The battle had been joined for the soul of Augusta National.

TWO

To Shoal Creek, and Beyond

WHAT SET OFF HOOTIE JOHNSON? It's tempting to think that his sharply worded press release was an idiosyncratic response from a singular personality, but Johnson's fighting words were seventy years in the making. Augusta National's timeless atmosphere comes with strings attached, as today's green jackets are forever beholden to the past. Founder Bobby Jones has been dead for thirty-three years but still haunts the letterhead, with the title President in Perpetuity. His cofounder, Clifford Roberts, also lives on more than a quarter century after his death, as Chairman in Memoriam. Is it any wonder, then, that a challenge to the club's very identity would spark more than a form letter in response?

To understand where Johnson was coming from it is necessary to survey the long history of Augusta National, which has largely been defined by four men: Jones, an icon of American sport whose desire for privacy led him to Augusta, where he could fulfill his dream of building a championship golf course in his native South; Roberts, a starstruck Wall Street financier who willed Jones's dream into creation and whose obsessive-compulsive personality shaped the Masters and the club's autocratic leadership culture; Dwight Eisenhower, who made twenty-seven trips to Augusta National during his presidency, cementing the club's status as a cloistered refuge for the ruling class; and longtime member Hall Thompson, who tried to replicate the Augusta mystique at his own club, Birmingham's Shoal Creek, but who unwittingly brought to the fore long-festering issues of discrimination and inclusion in golf. Thompson's bigoted comments on the eve of the 1990 PGA Championship at Shoal Creek—"we don't discriminate in every other area except the blacks"—led to a period of painful self-examination in the golf world. That controversy still resonated twelve years later when a letter from the National Council of Women's Organizations landed with a thud on the desk of the chairman of Augusta National Golf Club. For better or worse, the legacies of these four key green jackets guided Johnson as he answered Burk's challenge with his poison pen.

DURING AMERICA'S JAZZ AGE—when Jay Gatsby threw the best parties and the only thing that traveled farther than Charles Lindbergh was a Babe Ruth home run—no figure was more glamorous than Bobby Jones. Competing only as an amateur, he was the picture of the golfing gentleman, with a wardrobe as stylish as his swing, and accomplishments on the course matched by those in academia. (Jones held degrees in engineering, literature, and the law from universities such as Harvard and Georgia Tech.)

Though he would win thirteen major championships by the time he was twenty-eight, tournament golf was exquisite torture for Jones. He often sweated off a dozen pounds or more during an event, and after playing he would repair his body and psyche with an ice bath and a couple of stiff drinks. When he won the Grand Slam in 1930, sweeping the United States and British Amateur and Open titles, his overriding emotion was relief, not joy; having produced the perfect finale, Jones could finally retire to his law practice.

But before the ticker tape had been swept from Broadway, he set out to realize another dream: building a world-class golf course in the South. Two of the defining tournaments of Jones's career, the U.S. Open and the U.S. Amateur, had never been conducted below the Mason-Dixon Line. Jones pined to bring an important championship to the South, but he also had personal reasons for wanting his own course. He was mobbed every time he teed it up in a friendly game, even at his home course, Atlanta's East Lake, and he needed a place to escape to. It was this vision—to both advance the game and fashion a private retreat—that led to his unlikely partnership with Clifford Roberts, who was another kind of American success story.

Charles DeClifford Roberts Jr. was born in 1894 in Morning Sun, Iowa, and had an austere childhood working on the family farm. Though he had only an eighth-grade education, Roberts was driven and disciplined, and determined to reinvent himself. He had grown up reading the biographies of great men, and after hustling his way to Wall Street success, he set out to emulate their dashing lifestyle. He took an apartment on Park Avenue and joined Knollwood Country Club in Westchester County, and in this rarified air he soon made the acquaintance of the great Bobby Jones, who played an exhibition at Knollwood in the mid-twenties. Roberts journeyed to New Jersey for the 1926 U.S. Amateur at Baltusrol Golf Club, and after Jones lost in the final, Roberts was one of a small group who consoled him over drinks in the clubhouse.

Though they came from wildly different backgrounds, Jones and Roberts had plenty to talk about. Both enjoyed playing winter golf in Augusta, Georgia, an industrious, growing burg 150 miles east of Atlanta that had a much milder climate during the cold months. They had mutual friends in Augusta, including Tom Barrett, who would become mayor. In 1930, Roberts suggested to Jones that he build his dream course there, and offered to handle the financing.

Jones collaborated on the design with the great Scottish architect Alister MacKenzie. Both abhorred the brutally penal style of golf that had taken hold in the United States, on courses like Oakmont and Pine Valley. Jones wanted a wide-open canvas that would encourage artistic expression, the kind of freewheeling golf he loved playing en route to three British Open championships. His model was the quirky, fabled links of the Old Course in St. Andrews, Scotland, where MacKenzie had been employed to survey and map the course.

Construction on Augusta National began in February 1932 and took just seventy-six working days, thanks in part to Jones's and MacKenzie's minimalist approach. (There were only twenty-two bunkers in the original design.) Upon completion, MacKenzie, no stranger to hyperbole, declared Augusta National to be the "world's wonder inland course."

Jones and Roberts dreamed of a club as grand as the course. The business plan called for 1,800 members, each paying an initiation of $350, with dues of $60 a year. A second eighteen, designated as the "Ladies Course," was to be built once the membership rolls hit a thousand. This track was planned with the wives in mind. They were accorded playing privileges at the club for an extra $15 a year. Tennis courts, outdoor squash, a bridle path, and a couple dozen houses lining the course were also in the plans, as was a new clubhouse.

To fill out the membership, Roberts enlisted Wall Street moneymen, and Jones cherry-picked from the glamorous social and business circles that he moved in. Yet when Augusta National opened in January 1933, during the nadir of the Great Depression, Jones and Roberts were more than 1,700 members short of their goal.

Augusta National's early money struggles may have been a blessing, because they helped define what the club would become. Frivolities like the squash courts were never built. The fairways were not lined with private houses, as had been planned. By necessity, Augusta National Golf Club became exactly that—a wonderful course, and little else. Hoping to generate interest in memberships, as well as a positive cash flow, Jones and Roberts dreamed up a professional tournament for the club to host, recognizing that they possessed a surefire means for attracting international interest—Bobby Jones, who would come out of retirement to tee it up for the first time since the 1930 U.S. Amateur. The first Augusta National Invitational Tournament was held in 1934. Had the club succeeded in landing a U.S. Open, as it tried to do, the United States Golf Association would have come in and run the show by its rules. But Augusta National's decision to throw its own invitational assured autonomy. Five years after its debut, the tournament was renamed the Masters, a more regal title that hinted at the grandeur that was to come.

Augusta National was prime grazing land for cattle and turkeys while it was closed for the duration during World War II. By 1945, it was

time to get back to business, and that year one of the club's more significant developments quietly occurred, when Eddie Barber, a magnate of
the eponymous steamship line, gave Roberts $25,000 to build a cabin for
lodging members. The accommodations would be open to all green jackets, with the caveat that Barber would have first dibs when he was at the
club. The idea sparked a building craze adjacent to the 10th tee, and in
the ensuing years, members would finance eight more cabins, giving the
club a total of ninety-four beds on-site. The club, already a couple of degrees removed from the town, became even more insular with its own accommodations. It was like a casino—once on the property, there was
never any reason to leave.

In 1948, a special guest was given the keys to the Bobby Jones
cabin—Dwight D. Eisenhower, who brought along his bride, Mamie.
The general was friendly with one of Augusta National's most influential
members, Bill Robinson, the publisher of the *New York Herald Tribune*.
Eisenhower had mentioned that he and Mamie were looking to take
their first vacation in a decade, and Robinson, with Roberts's blessing,
suggested Augusta National.

The Eisenhowers fell hard for the place, staying eleven days. At the
end of his stay Ike borrowed a green jacket and posed for a picture, which
he inscribed to the chairman: "For Clifford Roberts—who did so much
to make our visit to Augusta National the most delightful vacation of our
lives." Soon enough Eisenhower had a green jacket of his own.

Ike had arrived at an important time in Roberts's life, as the chairman
was being forced to confront Jones's physical decline. In 1948, Jones was
diagnosed with syringomyelia, a rare disease in which fluid-filled cavities
form inside the spinal cord, destroying it over a period of years. It was,
and remains, all but incurable, with progressive symptoms that are crip-
pling and ultimately fatal. Jones would gradually waste away in the public eye.

As Jones's health faded, Roberts immersed himself in Eisenhower's affairs. Ike would eventually execute a power of attorney that gave Roberts
discretion over all of his investments, as well as make him an executor of
his will. In Jones and Eisenhower, Roberts had befriended two of the
most admired men in the world. His was the truest kind of friendship, in
that he wanted nothing in return. Basking in their refracted glory was

more than enough. When Eisenhower decided to run for president in 1952—with plenty of encouragement from his high-powered friends from the National—Roberts dedicated himself to amassing a war chest for the campaign. Naturally, he tapped the endless reserves of the Augusta National membership, especially W. Alton (Pete) Jones, the chairman of Cities Service Co. As Roberts recalled in a Columbia University oral history about Eisenhower, "I used to go over to Pete's office or he'd come over to my office, and he'd give me $25,000 at a time in currency. Then I'd have to figure out how I could get it into the treasury of one of the various committees that were working for General Eisenhower's election. I had a lawyer check into it, and it was very evident that through this operation Pete and I were skirting around the fringes of the law—and still, despite the laws that were on the books about campaign funds . . . nobody ever went to jail for violating them, so neither Pete nor I worried too much." Roberts's solution for laundering the money was to give it to other supporters in chunks of a couple thousand dollars and have them contribute it under their own names. He calculated that in this manner, Pete Jones contributed a quarter of a million dollars.

The influence of the green jackets on Eisenhower took place primarily behind closed doors, but the intimate connection would become clear enough. The day after Ike was elected the thirty-fourth president of the United States, handily defeating Adlai Stevenson, he flew to Augusta National on a plane chartered by Roberts. It was estimated that 250,000 people lined the roads along the twenty-mile drive from the Augusta airport to the club, hoping to catch a glimpse of Eisenhower. Almost overnight, Augusta National was on the lips of the electorate from coast to coast.

Eisenhower's frequent trips to the club while in office only made the place more aggressively private, yet, at the same time, his publicized golf outings turned him into the game's most important popularizing figure since Jones in the 1920s. (During his reelection campaign, a sardonic bumper sticker became popular: BEN HOGAN FOR PRESIDENT. IF WE'RE GOING TO HAVE A GOLFER, LET'S HAVE A GOOD ONE.) The president became such a part of the Augusta National firmament that a tree along the 17th fairway was nicknamed in his honor, because he frequently clipped it with his errant drives. When the club built a par-3 course in 1958, the best fishing spot was named Ike's Pond. Roberts, meanwhile, was such a frequent visitor to the White House that Eisenhower reserved the Red Room for the chairman's exclusive use, and kept a toothbrush and pair of pajamas for him in the closet.

In his memoir *Mandate for Change,* Eisenhower wrote of his fellow green jackets, "These were men of discretion, men who, already successful, made no attempt to profit by our association. It is almost impossible for me to describe how valuable their friendship was to me. Any person enjoys his or her friends; a President needs them, perhaps more intensely at times than anything else."

WHILE IKE WAS SPRINKLING stardust on Augusta National, the Masters was simultaneously emerging as golf's most exciting tournament, thanks to the game's luminaries. Beginning in 1949, the tournament enjoyed a breathtaking run of Hall of Fame winners: Sam Snead, Jimmy Demaret, Hogan, Snead, Hogan, Snead (in a playoff over Hogan). In 1956 this most photogenic of courses was finally introduced to the public in the first Masters telecast, and within three years the tournament had the biggest purse in professional golf ($75,400).

It was bitter irony that the Masters and Augusta National were flourishing as Jones's physical condition continued to deteriorate. (He would die in 1971.) With his cofounder increasingly enfeebled, Clifford Roberts grew into an all-powerful force in the life of the tournament and the club. He ruled unilaterally, but there was little squawking among the membership, given the effectiveness of Roberts's leadership. The preeminent golf writer Herbert Warren Wind once called Roberts "a relentless perfectionist with one of the best minds for management and significant detail since Salmon P. Chase"—Abraham Lincoln's secretary of the treasury and the sixth U.S. chief justice.

Roberts's specific vision for Augusta National, and his relentless pursuit of perfection, led to endless improvements for the Masters. (It was his idea that the members should wear green jackets during the tournament, so as to be easily identifiable should fans have any questions.) In 1960, the Masters pioneered a new scoring system, in which a player's progress was measured in relation to par rather than with cumulative strokes, which made it far easier to follow the action. It was also at the Masters that tee-to-green gallery ropes and pairings sheets for spectators were first introduced.

Roberts set the standard for how to efficiently run a tournament on the ground, but shaping the presentation of tournament golf on the airwaves was one of his most profound influences. The first Masters telecast in 1956 was a success largely because of Roberts's broad vision. CBS had planned to concentrate only on the 18th hole, but as an inducement to increase the coverage Roberts cut the rights fee that the network paid the club from $10,000 to $5,000, with the caveat that the savings go toward installing a second transmission station near the 15th hole.

With Augusta National's coffers swollen from the sellout Masters crowds, Roberts wanted from CBS not money but perfection, a far scarcer currency. Following every Masters, Roberts would send the network suits a dreaded, detailed critique of the coverage, and helpfully explain how they would do better the next time around. Though Jones's body was giving out, he still had a voice, and he helped ensure the purity of the Masters telecasts. Having played golf for free throughout his career, Jones abhorred any hint of commerce in the presentation of the Masters. Commercials were limited to four minutes per hour, when three or four times that many was common. CBS announcers were contractually forbidden to discuss prize money or estimates of crowd size, and God forbid they try to shill for other network programming.

The club was able to get its way because Augusta National and CBS operated on one-year contracts. This arrangement minimized CBS's financial exposure in the first, tenuous years televising the Masters, but as the tournament took off, Augusta National gained tremendous leverage. If CBS did not prostrate itself to the chairman's demands, Roberts could simply jump to one of the other networks.

The unmatched quality of the telecasts was proof that the scare tactics worked. But for CBS, being beholden to Augusta National would lead to considerable complications during an eventful Masters week in 2003.

REFLECTING ON THE SUCCESS of the Masters, Roberts once said, "I never thought it would be possible in a little tank town such as Augusta."

Tank town is an old-fashioned phrase for the nondescript settlements that were found along railroad lines, dotted with tanks to dispense water for railroad engines. It was not a flattering term. Roberts was also known to refer to the Masters' host city as "the village."

The condescending air came straight from Park Avenue, and Roberts was surely not alone in his views. The vast majority of Augusta National's original seventy or so members were New Yorkers, and as the club grew to two hundred members, and then three hundred, no more than 10 percent hailed from Augusta. The rest were the royalty of the corporate, political, or golf worlds, and they were drawn from more cosmopolitan places. Though few locals have been welcomed as members, the overwhelming majority of Augustans love the Masters and are thrilled to be a part of it, however peripherally. The club is held in such high esteem it has picked up an article—around town it is always referred to as *the* Augusta National, just as one talks about the Vatican, or the White House. The Masters is beloved because it generates dollars for the city, along with prestige. This was obvious as early as 1939, when the *Augusta Chronicle* carried the headline "Businessman Stresses Value of Golf Event." It is easy to understand the excitement—Augusta was a town in need of good news.

In the late-nineteenth century, Augusta boasted the second-largest inland cotton exchange in the country, and it was a thriving resort area for snowbirds escaping northern winters. The cotton industry unraveled sometime shortly after World War I, about the time the tourists collectively decided to stay on the train a little while longer in favor of Florida, a sunnier, cheaper alternative. These days Augusta gets by on a healthy medical industry, an expanding service sector, and light manufacturing—the two largest employers in that sector are golf cart makers E-Z-Go and Club Car. The Masters is as important as ever to the financial health of the city; in recent years it has been estimated that tournament week brings more than $100 million to Augusta, what locals call a thirteenth month of income, or Christmas in April. Hotels quadruple their rates, and the price of steak doubles overnight. Schools close down for Masters week, allowing students to become part of the workforce or families to pack up and leave town. The scarcity of hotel rooms has led to the local tradition of families renting their homes to visiting fans or (more commonly) corporations, for up to $15,000 for the week, depending on the location and number of bathrooms. The income is tax-free, thanks to a loophole in the tax code pushed through in part by Georgia politicians.

The dark side to the Masters' success is that Augusta's black population has felt largely disenfranchised from the spoils. No one rents a house during Masters week in the Terri—local shorthand for the Negro Territory, a dated designation for the 130-block neighborhood in the south part of town. A Terri philosopher named Sonny Hill says of Augusta National and the Masters, "They take that whole entire thing out there and pave it over with cement, ain't twenty-nine people in this town gonna miss church come Sunday. The people of Augusta built this thing up from nothing, and I'll tell you quite honestly, folks out there at the National don't give diddly back."

Barbara Gordon, the editor and publisher of *The Metro Courier*, an Augusta weekly centered on the black community, adds, "People all over the country watch the Masters, but black folks here pay little or no attention to it. They have other problems. There's another world here beyond those manicured greens and the azaleas—and it isn't nearly as pretty. This place is one of the most racist little cities I've ever seen in my life, and I mean that sincerely."

Augusta has never been shy about its Confederate heritage. There is a white marble monument on Greene Street adorned with statues of four Civil War generals—Lee, Jackson, Cobb, and Augusta's William Talbot Walker—and a famous inscription: "No Nation Rose So White and Fair/None Fell So Pure of Crime."

Augusta National was built in the shadow of this monument, and the attitudes of its pioneering members reflected the time and place in which they were raised. When Roberts was ten, his father wrote to his mother saying he had traded the contents of the family store for a 160-acre farm, forty-five acres of cotton "& a family of Negroes." Among the green jackets was Lester Maddox, an avowed segregationist who was elected governor of Georgia, and Freeman Gosden, the voice of Amos in the wildly popular radio show *Amos 'n' Andy*. At his peak, Gosden made $100,000 a year performing six times a week, in the voice of an uneducated black

man from the country. (He wore blackface for the 1930 big-screen min-
strel *Check and Double Check*.) At the 1951 Masters, Gosden was invited
into the tower behind the 18th hole to commentate for CBS Radio, to
perform as both Amos and Andy:

"Say, dat's a pretty good shot dere, Amos, by Mister Mangrum."

"Sho is, Kingfish."

"And we'd like all our friends out dere to come see dis here Masters."

"We sho do."

The civil rights movement of the fifties would slowly begin to affect
prevailing attitudes on race. In 1957, in the wake of the landmark
Supreme Court decision *Brown v. Board of Education*, striking down seg-
regated schools, President Eisenhower sent the 101st Airborne to Little
Rock, Arkansas, to assist nine black students in enrolling at Central
High School. This sparked outrage throughout the South—even the
Augusta Chronicle printed a scolding editorial—and inspired Clifford
Roberts to tighten up Augusta National's membership policies. "The
chairman suddenly realized the potential public relations disaster for
Eisenhower if a black man applied for membership to the National and
was turned down," Curt Sampson writes in *The Masters*. Sampson quotes
Roberts from the Columbia oral history, "We had to get busy in a hurry
and change our procedure around entirely, so that no one was ever
turned down." This contradicted earlier statements that the invitation-
only policy was enacted to spare the feelings of the many Bobby Jones
fans who might have applied and been rejected. In the oral history
Roberts bragged of how he stonewalled questions about the makeup of
Augusta National's membership, recalling the story of having once been
asked by a reporter if the club had any Jewish members.

"I can't answer that question, because that is not one of the questions
that an invitee is expected to tell us about," Roberts said.

Interviewer: "So you were completely in the clear, in terms of membership requirements?"

Roberts: "We were completely in the clear to our own satisfaction,
put it that way."

Augusta National remained all-white into the 1990s, like many golf
and country clubs across America. Though African Americans were not
welcome as members, they were integral to the life of the National. Res-

idents of the Terri worked as caddies, busboys, cooks, waiters, shoe-shiners, and a host of other jobs, and intimate relationships developed between the help and many of the members. Roberts took on club steward Bowman Milligan as his manservant, and the "large, strong, and fine-looking black man" (Cliff's words) would awaken the chairman every morning, tuck him in at night, and attend to him in the hours in between. Roberts left Milligan $5,000 in his will and devoted four paragraphs to him in his club history, *The Story of Augusta National Golf Club*, measures of his esteem.

However, it was another passage in Roberts's book that crystallized the popular perception of race relations at Augusta National. The subject of the anecdote was Claude Tillman, one of club's earliest employees. Before arriving at the National in 1934, Tillman had been employed by Thomas Barrett Jr., the mayor of Augusta and one of the club's earliest members. As Roberts wrote, "Tom Barrett's war injuries were credited with bringing on a fatal illness, and during that time he told me that he wanted me to have Claude. He apparently made a stipulation to that effect, because Tom's widow, Louise, placed a Christmas wreath around Claude's neck, tied a card to it bearing my name, and sent Claude to me . . . I passed along my gift to the club by placing Claude in charge of the kitchen."

This image of human chattel was appalling—all the more so because *The Story of Augusta National Golf Club* was published in 1977, and Roberts still felt no compunction about telling the story so long after the civil rights movement had changed the world outside Magnolia Lane.

That Augusta National's membership was all white, and the club employees who served them all black, was striking to many of the visitors to the club. More disconcerting was that the Masters also remained segregated between the ropes. Until 1983, Masters competitors were forced to use the club's all-black caddie corps, not their own traveling professional bag toters. In his autobiography, *Just Let Me Play*, Charlie Sifford, one of the first successful black touring pros, quotes Roberts as saying, "As long as I live, there will be nothing at the Masters besides black caddies and white players." Those close to Roberts have disputed the accuracy of the quote, but no matter. Given the circumstantial evidence, Roberts's critics were all too happy to believe that he had said it.

In an era of tumultuous social change, Augusta National and its prized tournament came under renewed scrutiny. In April 1969, Jim Murray, the *Los Angeles Times* columnist who would later win a Pulitzer Prize, wrote a scathing critique of the Masters under the headline "As White as the Ku Klux Klan." Murray was outraged that more than two decades after Jackie Robinson's debut with the Dodgers, the Masters' color barrier had not been broken, and he implored the green jackets to make a special exception and invite Sifford. Alas, it wasn't quite that simple. Though the tournament was still billed as an invitational, the field was largely filled through automatic qualifying criteria, none of which Sifford met. The only subjective invitations doled out by the club were limited to international players, because Bobby Jones had always wanted the Masters to be a world stage. No American pros, including African Americans, were given special consideration from the Masters. (In those days, past champions were also allowed to vote in one player, but neither Sifford nor any other black players got the nod.)

Sifford remains bitter that he never got to play in the Masters; he told Sampson, "I didn't want any help. All I wanted was a chance to play. Them motherfuckers kept me out." But Jones had long been openly rooting for him. In 1968, the president of Augusta National sent Sifford a letter assuring him that he would be welcome if he qualified, adding, "I for one would be particularly happy to see you realize this ambition."

The Masters' lily-white tradition received even more attention in 1973, when, just weeks before the tournament, eighteen members of the House of Representatives sent a telegram to Roberts: "We are writing to express our very deep concern over the fact that a black touring professional will not be competing in the Masters this year and that after 37 years the color barrier will still not be broken." The congressmen beseeched the club to take "affirmative action" and invite Lee Elder, at the time thirty-first on the PGA Tour money list.

Roberts professed to being "a little surprised as well as being flattered that eighteen congressmen would be able to take time out from trying to solve the nation's problems to help us operate a golf tournament." In his written response, he noted his respect for Elder and pointed out that Elder would have earned an automatic invitation to the Masters had he prevailed in a playoff against Lee Trevino at the previous year's Greater

Hartford Open. (A PGA Tour victory came with a ticket to Augusta beginning in 1972, five years after Sifford won the GHO.) However, the chairman was unwilling to play favorites, even for the legislative branch. "If we were to make an exception in favor of Mr. Elder or any other golfer who had failed to qualify," Roberts wrote, "we might quite properly be condemned by all of the other golfers including the growing number of black players who are making a career of tournament golf."

Elder finally put the matter to rest in April 1974, sinking an eighteen-foot birdie putt on the 4th playoff hole to trump Peter Oosterhuis and win the Monsanto Open. He was going to Augusta. Said Roberts, "The only quarrel I have with Lee is we're sorry he didn't do it sooner." Elder would qualify for five of the next six Masters, but the integration of the tournament was not the end of Augusta National's problems with race.

IN GOLF'S LONG HISTORY of exclusion, there is plenty of shame to go around. In 1943, the PGA of America added an article to its constitution, stating that only "professional golfers of the Caucasian Race . . . shall be eligible for membership." The bylaw was vigilantly enforced until 1961, when the PGA of America's marquee event, the PGA Championship, was slated to be played at Brentwood Country Club (which was, ironically, an almost entirely Jewish club that had been founded because of prevailing discrimination). When Stanley Mosk, California's attorney general, started making noises about refusing to allow the tournament to go forward because the so-called Caucasian Only clause violated the state constitution, the PGA Championship was abruptly moved to the City of Brotherly Love, Philadelphia. That bit of misdirection did not quell the controversy, and the Caucasian Only clause was soon excised. But even though golf's racism was no longer spelled out in black and white, the sentiment lingered for decades to come.

In June 1990, Augusta National member Hall Thompson was interviewed by his hometown *Birmingham Post-Herald,* but not about the Masters. Thompson had founded Shoal Creek Golf Club, and the superb Jack Nicklaus design was about to host the PGA Championship, which, like the Masters, is now considered one of golf's four major championships. In discussing Shoal Creek's membership practices, Thompson said, "We have the right to associate or not to associate with whomever we choose. The country club is our home and we pick and choose who we want. I think we've said we don't discriminate in every other area except the blacks." He added that inviting African Americans to join a country club is "just not done in Birmingham." He wasn't kidding. It would come out that at the city's seven major country clubs, the roughly 6,000 members included only two blacks.

Almost overnight "Shoal Creek" became shorthand for discrimination in golf. Thompson's remarks had not even made the front page of the *Post-Herald*, but they sparked a firestorm that engulfed the PGA Championship. Civil rights groups threatened to picket the tournament, and corporate sponsors—including IBM, Honda, Toyota, and Lincoln-Mercury—pulled more than $2 million in advertising from the ESPN and ABC telecasts. Toyota went so far as to recommend that its endorsers, including Lee Trevino, not wear the company logo during the tournament. The story spilled off the sports page and onto A1, and into prime time. Golf's dirty little secret could no longer be ignored, and the damage control proceeded at warp speed.

Nine days before the tournament was to begin, a deal was brokered between Shoal Creek and the Southern Christian Leadership Conference—the same organization that had organized sit-ins at Birmingham's segregated lunch counters—in which the club agreed to accept its first black member. Louis J. Willie, the president of a local insurance company, didn't even have to pay the $35,000 initiation fee. The PGA of America quickly adopted language preventing future PGA Championships from being played at clubs with discriminatory membership practices. This was significant given that the next two editions of the tournament were slated for all-white clubs: Crooked Stick in Carmel, Indiana, followed by Bellerive in St. Louis. Those clubs' mad scramble to find qualified minority members was repeated throughout the country. (African Americans of a certain station have an in-joke about being members of "the class of 1990," because that was when so many were invited to join prestigious country clubs.) The United States Golf Association, which conducts the U.S. Open, adopted antidiscrimination language similar to the PGA's, which led to the almost immediate desegregation of future Open sites Hazeltine, in Chaska, Minnesota (1991);

Baltusrol, in Springfield, New Jersey (1993); Oakmont (Pennsylvania) in 1994; and Shinnecock Hills in Southampton, New York (1995).

It was remarkable how one unguarded comment from a Birmingham tractor salesman could so profoundly change the face of the country's most private clubs. When the PGA Tour—which conducts the weekly events for touring pros and is unaffiliated with the PGA of America, an organization of club pros—took a hard look at its schedule, its brass was aghast to discover that seventeen of its host clubs were all-white. In the wake of Shoal Creek, the Tour adopted a stringent antidiscrimination policy that stated, "Host Facility represents and warrants that the membership practices and policies do not discriminate on the basis of race, sex, religion, or national origin." (Gays and the handicapped would have to fend for themselves.) Further, the Tour said that "in the event a golf club indicates that its membership practices and policies are nondiscriminatory but there is information that raises a question as to such practices and policies (e.g., all-white membership), the staff is authorized to require on a case-by-case basis that as a condition of hosting an event, the applicable golf club take appropriate action to encourage minority membership."

The forceful action of the golf establishment was widely hailed as an important step in eradicating institutionalized racism. "This is a watershed in the social dynamics of America," said Arthur Ashe, the tennis legend and social crusader.

However, not every club was willing to play ball by reforming exlusionary membership policies. Rather than tweak its membership, Butler National, an all-male enclave in Chicago, gave up the Western Open after having hosted the event for seventeen straight years. It was a much bigger deal that the Cypress Point Club renounced its spot in the Pebble Beach National Pro-Am. Cypress had been part of the three-course rotation ever since 1947, when the tournament was known as the Bing Crosby Clambake. Cypress's elite membership of 250 contained a handful of women but no minorities. The club's defiance was stunning, but perhaps unsurprising given its fierce exclusivity. Cypress, Pine Valley, and Seminole are three of the four sacred corners of the shawl that wraps private-club golf in the United States. The fourth is Augusta National, which had been put in an awkward position by Shoal Creek.

The PGA of America, the USGA, and the Tour have to balance the interests of diverse staffs as well as corporate partners and charitable interests. Augusta National is beholden to no one, and could play by its own rules. One thing was immediately clear—no carefully worded antidiscrimination statement would be forthcoming. But would the club bow to pressure and take its first black member? Augusta National certainly didn't have to alter its membership to continue putting on the Masters. But a complicating factor was that it is recognized as an official event on the PGA Tour. It was never threatened, but the Tour could have withheld recognition of the Masters, which would have devalued the tournament.

What would Cliff do? The parlor game raged in Augusta, and elsewhere. The fiery former chairman had been dead for thirteen years, his ashes scattered at a secret spot on the golf course, yet his specter still hovered over the club. Hord Hardin, the club's third chairman, was running the show when Shoal Creek erupted. Hardin was a St. Louis native with no-nonsense Midwestern sensibilities. He had been president of the USGA in 1968–69, so he had a background in building consensus, not running his own fiefdom. And yet he was acutely aware of maintaining Roberts's legacy. (Hardin's successor, Jack Stephens, would say, "Cliff is our bible.")

Hardin died in 1996, but a member of his immediate family agreed to be interviewed for this book on the condition that he remain anonymous. "There was some talk of canceling the Masters," he says. "Based on our conversations, I can tell you that he would have canceled the tournament before he would have jeopardized the club. He felt strongly that Augusta National stood for more than just the Masters."

Yet, according to Hardin's relative, the idea of a black man in a green jacket was not as radical as many assumed. "They had already approached a couple. One guy turned them down—somebody you would know and the country would recognize. I remember distinctly [Chairman Hardin] saying to me, 'I got a major problem here—we were already working on it, and now Shoal Creek has blown us out of the water.'"

In the end, Hardin decided not to put up a fight, and fifteen years after Lee Elder's Masters debut, Augusta National had its first black member, Ron Townsend, who at the time was the head of the Gannett Media

Group's television division. As Hardin said in a statement, "We concluded at least a year ago that there were more black people playing golf, more black people climbing the business ladder, more climbing the scientific and educational ladders, and we realized that there were people in that group who would enjoy being with the people we have as members. I don't want to create the impression that all of our members are enthusiastic about this. Shoal Creek perhaps expedited something that we would have liked to do in our own way. The ideal way, to my mind, would have been that we would bring in a black with no announcement, just as we bring in all of our members. And then, two or three years down the road, someone would come up to me and say, 'You mean you got a black member and he's been in two years and you never told anyone?' "

That would clearly have been preferable. The club's commitment to diversity was viewed largely with skepticism, because it had come at the point of a bayonet. The key line in Hardin's statement was *I don't want to create the impression that all of our members are enthusiastic about this*. Augusta National was not used to being told what to do. In the wake of Shoal Creek, future challenges to the club's membership would meet with greater resistance.

RACIAL DISCRIMINATION wasn't golf's only bugaboo at the dawn of the nineties. The propriety of all-male golf clubs was also becoming an issue, thanks in large part to two high-profile politicians. In the spring of 1990, Sam Nunn, the influential senator from Georgia, created a stir when he resigned from the Beltway power spot Burning Tree Golf Club, citing "personal reasons." Those reading the tea leaves in Washington, D.C., interpreted the move as a preemptive strike to thwart criticism should Nunn make a run for the presidency in 1992. Nunn grew so tired of the speculation that at one point he snapped, "Maybe I should rejoin Burning Tree—then maybe somebody would believe me [that I'm not running]."

Burning Tree, founded in 1924, has long catered to the Washington elite, extending honorary memberships to presidents and vice presidents and the occasional congressional bigwig. Dan Quayle was a regular at the club during his days as vice president, but post–Shoal Creek, his presence led to increased sniping in the press. In December 1990, Quayle was defiant when questioned about the club. "I've played there before and I'll play there again," he told the AP. Headline writers across the country denounced the vice president's insensitivity: "Quayle's Position on Discrimination Insults Women" (*St. Petersburg Times*); "Keeping Women Subpar" (*The Boston Globe*); "Fair Play on the Fairway" (*St. Louis Post-Dispatch*).

Part of what makes Burning Tree such an inviting target is its aggressive antiestrogen stance. Not only are women not allowed to be members, they aren't allowed to set foot on the grounds, except for a designated day in December when they can visit the pro shop to Christmas-shop for their husbands. This rigid separation of the sexes is not uncommon at the two dozen all-male clubs in the United States. When Jack Nicklaus played Pine Valley on his honeymoon, his dutiful bride, Barbara, was famously forced to wait in the car. Then again, at least Pine Valley maintains a certain decorum, with jackets required for dinner. Burning Tree is a place where the boys let it all hang out. Stories are legion of our nation's leaders playing a round of golf in nothing but boxer shorts and spikes (and lots of sunblock). Of course, at Preston Trail, in Dallas, that's considered overdressed. The club has enacted the Mickey Mantle Rule, in honor of the baseball legend who was a member: You have to wear *something* in the grillroom.

Considering the endless farting and scratching of its all-male brethren, Augusta National is positively enlightened. There are no restrictions on when female guests can play the course, and they are welcome in the clubhouse and dining room. But absent a Hall Thompson to spark a far-reaching controversy, the idea of a woman member was simply not taken seriously for most of the club's history. As Chairman Hord Hardin told *Golf Digest* in 1990, "We love women, but we don't want any fussin' with them."

THE ADDITION of one black member at Augusta National had potent symbolism, but it did not entirely expunge the legacy of the fifty-seven years of segregation that preceded it, as the club would learn in a graphically public way. In October 1992, Billy Payne, the president and CEO of the Atlanta Committee for the Olympic Games, held a press conference behind the 10th tee at Augusta National, announcing his intention to bring golf back to the Olympics in 1996 after a ninety-two-year absence. "It's been a well-known fact that the Atlanta Committee for the Olympic Games has always said we want to make a permanent contribution to sports," Payne said. "Historically, we've always believed that with the tradition of golf in our area, with the great Bobby Jones coming from Atlanta, that golf would be a logical sport to champion." Augusta National was the dream venue, and, in a bit of an upset, the club threw open its arms, offering to host the Games, which would include both men's and women's competitions.

Chairman Jack Stephens joined Payne at the press conference, and he was inevitably asked how a club with no female members and only one minority could presume to represent the Olympic ideal. "We're trying to send a message that we're for both men and women's golf," Stephens said. "We have no prohibition for any member or any type of member, and that's always been the policy of the club."

Stephens and Augusta National picked up an important endorsement from Ladies Professional Golf Association commissioner Charlie Mechem: "Our feeling is that the way to advance the cause for equality is precisely to go to places where women haven't been allowed to go before."

Others took a dimmer view of the club's involvement. Within a month of Payne's press conference, the Atlanta City Council had passed an "Anti-Augusta National" resolution. Council member Jabari Simama said, "There are certain institutions and places in this state that are symbols of the Old South and a period many of us have worked our entire lives to eradicate. To award this particular golf course with an Olympic venue would send out the wrong message to many blacks and minorities who have suffered and still suffer at the hands of institutionalized racism."

Things got even nastier when Rev. Timothy McDonald, the executive director of Concerned Black Clergy, threatened pickets at an upcoming International Olympic Committee meeting. Of the battle over

Augusta National, he warned, "This is going to get worse before it gets any better."

In fact, within a couple of months the notion of an Augusta National Olympics was dead. (Payne's consolation was a subsequent invitation to join the club.) It was an embarrassing episode for Augusta National, and the soft-spoken Stephens's pique was evident.

"It's puzzling to me," he said. "It was my understanding from the beginning . . . that the IOC had accepted Augusta National's composition of membership, that everyone knew what we are. We've offered them the venue. The rest is up to them."

For the second time in three years, this most private of clubs had endured a brutally public examination of its membership practices. The Olympics debacle made it clear that Augusta National's traditions, and its insular customs, were ill-suited to the complexities of the outside world. On membership matters, the days of appeasement were now over. The people of Augusta were similarly embittered. In the delirium that accompanied the prospects of Olympic golf in Augusta, city officials estimated that the two-week event would have an economic impact of $165 million. Kissing that windfall good-bye was a wake-up to the Augusta citizenry that any attack on the National would be felt in its pocketbook. The next time a muckraker came to town threatening the green jackets he, or she, could expect a hostile reception.

AT AUGUSTA NATIONAL, the nineties were bracketed by Shoal Creek and the elevation of Hootie Johnson, who in 1998 became the club's fifth chairman. He seemed the perfect choice to lead the club into the twenty-first century. Tiger Woods's epic victory at the 1997 Masters had made diversity the hot topic in golf, and Johnson's credentials on the subject were impeccable. In the initial burst of publicity about the new chairman, seemingly every story touched on his admirable past in South Carolina, in which Johnson had been a high-profile advocate of inclusion. He was also well attuned to matters of symbolism and public perception; in the divisive battle over flying the Confederate flag in front of the capital building in his hometown of Columbia, Johnson was an outspoken critic of the flag-wavers.

"He's by far the most liberal person I've ever heard of being a member," said Robbie Williams, the coauthor of *Gentlemen Only*, a book about her decades as the wife of a (now deceased) Augusta National member. "I'd put him in the top five among members who would not qualify as sexist or chauvinistic."

THREE

Hootie & Martha

WILLIAM WOODWARD JOHNSON and Augusta National were born in the same town and the same year, 1931. Four years later, around the time little W. W. had been dubbed "Hootie" by a playmate at William Robinson Grammar School, he attended the second Masters with his mother, who, he says, thought it would be a "novelty" to check out Bobby Jones's little invitational. The Johnsons were well integrated into Augusta's golf culture. Hootie's dad, Dewey, was a crack three handicap, and he taught Hootie and his brother, Wellsman ("Bubba"), the game at Augusta Country Club, the family-friendly outpost that abuts its more famous neighbor.

When Hootie was eleven his father—who began his banking career out of high school as a lowly runner—headed a group of investors who purchased the Bank of Greenwood, and the family moved to the eponymous mill town in western South Carolina. It was in this rural hamlet that Hootie's life took on all the flourishes of the Norman Rockwell oeuvre. At Greenwood High School he grew into a devilishly handsome football star, and the son of the bank president soon began going steady with one of the most popular girls in school, Pierrine Baker, the raven-haired daughter of a local surgeon and the granddaughter of one of

Greenwood's most progressive mayors. "These people were like royalty," says local historian Ann Herd Bowen, who sat in front of Johnson in Miss Sunbeam Andrews's algebra class. "Hootie was Greenwood's golden boy." His exploits were chronicled in the high school's student newspaper, *HI-TYPE*, as obsessively as Paris Hilton items adorn Page Six. In the October 29, 1948, edition, a starry-eyed young woman wrote a poem about Johnson that began, "There is a boy in our twelfth grade English class / Who is the secret hero of each lass / One look at him and you will know why / Because you see he's just cute as pie!" Other notices in *HI-TYPE* mentioned his "sharp yellow shirt" as well as a new haircut.

Johnson also induced heavy breathing in the football writers at the *Greenwood Index-Journal*, who described him as the "blond wheelhorse of the Emerald backfield." The star tailback led Greenwood High to state championships in 1947 and '48, and during his career he scored forty-three touchdowns, including two runs of ninety yards or more. The mythmakers at the *Index-Journal* nearly ran out of superlatives for Johnson in a 1948 dispatch: "The crazy-legged youngster ripped and tore through and around Saluda for long gains, scored one TD by snaring a Saluda pass and reeling off a brilliant 35-yard run, and set up three other scores by eating up huge gobs of yardage for the Emeralds."

Johnson was as ornery as he was elusive—during the 1946 season he was kicked out of two games for fighting. Johnson's leather-helmeted toughness came courtesy of Greenwood High's legendary coach, J. W. "Pinky" Babb, who over thirty-nine years would ring up a 336–81–25 record. Babb was a taskmaster obsessed with the old-fashioned fundamentals of his idol Vince Lombardi, and he forged his teams every August in a two-week boot camp in the hills outside Clayton, Georgia. The boys stayed in spartan cabins illuminated only by candlelight and had to endure endless drills in the searing heat. One of Johnson's contemporaries, fullback Sonny Horton, once said, "Coach Babb would practice us to death, and the only water break we got was when it rained."

This brand of macho discipline brought out the best in Hootie. Two decades after graduating from Greenwood High he told South Carolina's *The State* newspaper, "Coach Babb just makes a boy want to play. He's probably the greatest competitor I've ever known and also the poorest loser. I don't mean that he's a poor sport—Coach Babb is a gentleman in the best sense of the word, but he doesn't like to lose. I cherish the days I spent with him. He had a greater influence on my life than any other person other than my mother and father." Johnson was a pallbearer at Babb's funeral and to this day maintains a correspondence with Pinky's widow, Elizabeth.

The old-school lessons learned on the gridiron were complemented by Johnson's parents, who drilled into their son the coda that with great privilege comes great responsibility. Dewey and his wife, Mabel, were community leaders with an activist bent; he raised the money to build the town's YMCA, and she was a charter founder of the Greenwood Woman's Club and was involved in a variety of charities. Old-timers around Greenwood fondly recall Mabel's annual lunch on Valentine's Day for the little old ladies at the church, widows who otherwise would have been alone. "My parents trained me in humanistic ways," Hootie says. "To be thoughtful of other people's feelings, and considerate of their ideas and their circumstances in life. I don't want to sound like I'm putting any of my old friends down, because I played football with them, but I mean, it was a textile town, and there were a few doctors and lawyers and bankers and most everybody else worked in the mill. That's just how it was, and my father let us know that we were very fortunate to have what we had." After school, when he wasn't at football practice, Hootie dutifully worked at the bank, depositing checks and performing other clerical duties.

Dinner conversation in the Johnson household often veered into politics. Dewey was a color-blind Democrat, an unrepentant Roosevelt booster who was fond of saying that the New Deal had saved the South. Dewey's convictions were never clearer than during the 1948 presidential election, in which South Carolina's governor, Strom Thurmond, ran a segregationist campaign as a third-party Dixiecrat. Thurmond easily carried South Carolina, but Dewey cast his vote for Truman.

Hootie took his small-town worldview to the big time, accepting a football scholarship to the University of South Carolina after a pitched recruiting battle. He didn't exactly fit in with his teammates, and not only because he married Pierrine while still an undergrad. "Hootie was the wealthiest kid on the football team," says Tom Price, the sports editor of *The Gamecock* student newspaper in the early 1950s. "Most of those boys were World War II vets on the GI bill, as was I. Hootie had an apartment on the top floor of the Cornell Arms, a big apartment building across from campus. That was a bit unusual. And he drove a shiny new Kaiser. That was unusual, too."

And yet Johnson earned acclaim as a team player willing to do the dirty work. Talented upperclassmen limited Johnson's playing time until his junior year, and he lost his starting job late that season because of fumbling problems and an inability to catch balls out of the backfield, which some reports have attributed to his poor eyesight. Hootie, however, was not the quitting type. During spring ball he volunteered to move to fullback, and in his senior year, in 1952, he earned the Jacobs Blocking Trophy, given to the best collegiate blocker in the state. "Hootie just loved to run people over," says his old USC quarterback, Johnny Gramling.

Following graduation, Johnson (and his bride) moved back to Greenwood to help his father grow the bank, but Dewey had a touch of Joseph Kennedy in him, and he was forever pushing Hootie to be politically active. In the fall of 1956, twenty-five-year-old Hootie ran for a seat in the South Carolina legislature. What inspired this sudden ambition for public office? "Nothing," Johnson says. "I was drafted. There were two big mill operations that were headquartered in Greenwood. The head men from both came into my daddy's office one day to say that they weren't satisfied with the people who were running for office. I was only twenty-five, but they said, 'We'd like Hootie to run. Everybody knows him, everybody likes him.' So my daddy does like that"—here Johnson performs an exaggerated head nod—"I'm way down at the other end of the bank, I run up there, and he tells me I'm running for state office. I about fell over. So I went home and told my wife—this was a small town, so you would go home for lunch—and she has more sense than I do, so she says go back after lunch and tell your father you are happy to do it this time, but you're only going to do one term, and then they'll have to find someone else."

The football hero/political novice swept to victory in the election, receiving 170 more votes in Greenwood County than Strom Thurmond did in his U.S. Senate race. Two months after Johnson was elected, Augusta National member Dwight D. Eisenhower called for the passage of a civil rights bill in his State of the Union address, but none of the ensuing turmoil filtered down to Representative Johnson. As promised, he served only one uneventful two-year term, and then dedicated himself to his daddy's bank. Of his stint in public office, Johnson says, "It was a valuable experience if for no other reason than it gave me a better understanding of how the real world works." He would soon begin applying those lessons: Instead of the compromises and quagmires of elected office, Johnson settled into the role of a backroom dealmaker.

MARTHA BURK was born in October 1941 and grew up in the Houston suburb of Pasadena. Her father, Ivan, an oil company engineer, put a roof over her head but never a glass ceiling. "He encouraged me to be competitive, to do my best and to use the intelligence I had," she says. Burk's mother, Dorothy, offered her own inspiration. She had a college degree, unusual for a woman born in 1914, and was a savvy businesswoman who ran the family clothing store, though her real passion was golf. "She was not your typical grandmother who sat home and cooked all day," says Martha's son Mark Talley. "She'd take us golfing all day, and then we'd eat out at night. I think my mother was influenced by her as much as by her father."

As a girl, Martha often accompanied her mom to Houston's Quail Hollow Country Club, and it was there that she spotted her first case of sex discrimination, urging Mom to demand better tee times than those set aside for women by the club. If this has eerie overtones of a future struggle, Burk's childhood nickname borders on the unbelievable—her two younger brothers called her "Hootie," a moniker she didn't shed until she was twelve. (As Burk would later say of the antagonist who shares the nickname, "The difference between me and Mr. Johnson is that I outgrew it.") Martha was a brilliant student, but whatever her budding feminist sensibilities, she shared a dream with most of the other girls in her school: "Everybody wanted to be a cheerleader," she says, including her. Burk never got to wave the pom-poms; her laser focus on academics led her to graduate high school at sixteen. Science was her strongest subject, and she fancied a career as a marine biologist. But this was the 1950s, and Burk's counselors steered her toward teaching and nursing. She enrolled at the University of Houston and chose psychology as a major, what she felt was an acceptable compromise.

Burk was dismayed to discover that many of the other women on campus were less interested in academics than in finding Mr. Right. "My first-year roommate's parents had given her one year to find a husband," Burk says. "I found that quite bizarre." And yet the cheerleading aspirant was not immune to the peer pressure of the times. Burk wed Ed Talley in 1960, while still an undergrad. The young couple settled into the Dallas suburb of Colleyville, where Ed, a pharmacist by trade, established a small chain of drugstores. By the time Burk was twenty-five she had two young sons and was busy doing what she calls "the soccer-mom thing."

"She was just like any other mother: she took us to practice and games and school activities," says Mark. Of course, not every mom of that era offered to coach her son's Little League team. No one else had been interested in the job until Burk volunteered. "Then men started coming out of the woodwork," Burk says. "It was like, 'My God, we can't have a woman coach.'"

It was this incident and a hundred other little ones that gradually led Burk to question her lot in life. "The most radicalizing experience of my life was being a stay-at-home mother," she says. "It's an unhealthy model, for the kids and the mother. It's forced isolation for women in that situation. I knew there was something wrong with this picture."

This widespread malaise among American housewives was first chronicled in Betty Friedan's *The Feminine Mystique*, published in 1963. Burk went back to school shortly thereafter. In 1968 she earned a master's in psychology (with a minor in computer science) from the University of Texas's Arlington campus, and four years later she had a Ph.D. in experimental psychology from the same school. (Her dissertation was on game theory.)

Armed with her doctorate, Burk applied for a teaching position at the University of Dallas, only to be asked to take a clerical typing test. "I found it odd, but not as supremely insulting as I would now," she says. "Like many other women then, I did not have a feminist consciousness at that point."

Gradually that consciousness was raised, a process Burk describes as "drip, drip, drip." After taking a teaching position at UT-Arlington, in the study of management, she decided to use public records to compare her salary with that of her male counterparts. "I found out that I was making substantially less than the men," she says. "I complained about it to the chair, and he said he was going to make me a better offer. The better offer he made me was to double my workload for double the present pay."

Burk unceremoniously quit. At loose ends, she thought about running for city council "until I realized I wasn't going to get any support because people considered me too radical." She funneled her passion into a special program funded by the National Science Foundation for those she calls "women who were underemployed or out of the workforce. It was an amazing group. I had women with medical degrees working in film kiosks, women who were gas chromatographers rolling enchiladas in restaurants. My job was to help them get enough self-confidence to go after the jobs they were capable of."

In terms of gaining financial independence, Burk practiced what she preached. In the late seventies she "decided to teach myself to program a microcomputer and write some software," she says. Her Talley Special Education Management System (which helped school districts comply with federal reporting requirements) and Exam Builder (for automated student testing) were picked up by Radio Shack and "just kept selling," Burk says. With her boys out of the house—Mark, now thirty-eight, sells oil drilling parts in Tulsa, Oklahoma, while Ed, forty-one, owns an electronics business in Austin, Texas—Burk and her husband drifted apart, eventually divorcing in 1985 after a quarter-century of marriage. She says that her budding feminism "absolutely" led to the divorce and today speaks affectionately of her ex-husband, whom she calls "a good guy."

Financially secure from her software programs but looking for a new challenge, Burk moved to Wichita, Kansas, to work as a consultant to the company that had published her software. It was in this quiet corner of the Midwest that the fuse would be lit on her political activism.

By 1965, Hootie Johnson, thirty-four, was the youngest bank president in South Carolina—Dewey had died four years earlier—and through a series of shrewd mergers and acquisitions the Bank of Greenwood had morphed into Bankers Trust. Dewey's dream had always been to take his bank statewide. Hootie had more than exceeded this vision; Bankers Trust not only covered South Carolina but was beginning to grow into a regional power. To facilitate the wheeling and dealing, Hootie and Pierrine and their four daughters relocated to South Carolina's capital.

Entrenched in Columbia's ruling class, Johnson began to dabble in the politics of South Carolina, the first state to secede from the Union in advance of the Civil War, and, in the wake of the civil rights movement, the last to integrate. Johnson saw the tumultuous racial politics of the day in the black-and-white moral terms of his father: Electing African Americans to public office was simply the right thing to do. Johnson quickly grew into what his friend and mentor Robert McNair, South Carolina's governor from 1965 to 1971, calls "one of the most enlightened, progressive citizens in the history of the state."

In 1970, Johnson threw his weight behind a handful of African American candidates, coining a slogan ("the home team") that explicitly linked them to the rest of the Democratic slate. When the votes were tallied, Herbert Fielding and I. S. Leevy Johnson had been elected to South Carolina's General Assembly, becoming the first blacks to take a state office since Reconstruction. Says I. S. Leevy Johnson, "I can still hear those campaign radio ads in my head, and they would always end, 'Paid for by the Democratic Party of South Carolina, Hootie Johnson, treasurer.' Those were the days of a lot of empty rhetoric, but Hootie walked the walk. He put his name on the line for us." (And that name was always Hootie. Regardless of the setting, W. W. Johnson has always preferred to be addressed by his lifelong nickname. "He thought it made him more approachable," says I. S. Leevy Johnson.)

Hootie's cresting profile led future Clinton acolyte Vernon Jordan to offer Johnson a post on the board of directors of the Urban League, making him its first white member from the Deep South. Elliot Franks, the executive director of the Urban League's Columbia chapter, wasted no time putting Johnson to work. "One of the things we were struggling with was finding employment opportunities for young African American women," says Franks, "and Hootie devised a training program to place these women at Bankers Trust. They were trained in mathematics and customer service, and they were placed in the bank as tellers. Understand, these were different times, turbulent times. But these women were not hidden in a back room somewhere, but placed at the front of the bank, where they dealt with customers, handled money, and were treated just like the other tellers. That was a very strong statement, and Hootie was the one who made it. Following his lead, all four major banks in town adopted the program." With Johnson pulling the strings, Bankers Trust would become the first bank in the state to have an African American on its board of directors, and, later, the first to have a woman on the board.

Johnson is also credited with helping to desegregate higher education in South Carolina in the 1970s. Jim Clyburn, presently serving his fourth term as a U.S. congressman—Johnson chairs his finance committee—was part of a task force charged with making it happen. "Hootie's idea," says Clyburn, "was to establish a system where if you wanted to pursue a certain discipline you had to go to certain schools. For example, to receive a doctorate of education, you had to go to South Carolina State, which was a historically black college. It was a simple, elegant idea, but a lot more revolutionary than it sounded. If you were a white University of South Carolina undergrad and didn't want to leave the state to get that degree, you had to go to a black school. That was a big, big, big deal, and yet, over time, it worked. To me, for all his many accomplishments, it is this desegregation that is Hootie's legacy. Quite frankly, it was all about Hootie, and among prominent white businessmen, he has to be considered the biggest supporter of African Americans in the history of the state of South Carolina."

Part of what made Johnson such a fearless pioneer was his belief in his decision making. "When he thinks he's right, why, the devil won't change his mind," says John C. West, South Carolina's governor from 1971 to 1975 and a friend of Johnson's going back to their days in the legislature. "Hootie simply doesn't give in to pressure, and that's one of his leadership traits that we all admire."

I. S. Leevy Johnson puts it more bluntly: "Stubborn as a mule. And that's coming from a friend."

An offshoot of Johnson's stubbornness is that he does not liked to be challenged, and long before Martha Burk, his unyielding manner led to a few public dustups. A onetime finance chairman for South Carolina

Democrats, Johnson parted ways with the party over his role in the 1978 reelection campaign of Senator Thurmond, whose conversion to the Republican Party in 1964 began the seismic shift in the South's political landscape. Johnson's relationship with Thurmond was grounded more in friendship than in politics, and in Johnson's universe, loyalty is among the most prized of attributes. Despite the protest of other Democratic leaders, he refused to dissociate himself from Thurmond's campaign. "So they kicked me out of the Democratic Party just like that," Johnson says, "and I've been an independent ever since."

The truth, according to Clyburn, is a bit more complicated: "I recall quite vividly, during a meeting a young lady raised the issue, saying she thought that Hootie's public support for Strom was improper. Hootie resigned his post because of this one voice of dissent, and he did so in a huff. I always thought that was disappointing."

Johnson's single-mindedness can lead to impressive results. For years he was on the board of trustees at Converse College, in Spartanburg, South Carolina, an esteemed all-female university from which one of his daughters graduated. In the mid-nineties Johnson got it in his head that South Carolina should become the first university in the country with a business school named after a woman. He began an ardent pursuit of Darla Moore, a South Carolina native who made her fortune on Wall Street. Twenty-five million dollars later, the Moore School of Business was born.

Johnson's backroom maneuvering was equally effective in the banking world. In 1985, he instigated a merger between Bankers Trust and North Carolina Nations Bank, which was run by McColl, his best friend and fellow Augusta National member. In 1998, Johnson was the architect of the deal in which NCNB swallowed Bank of America, and he took over as chairman of the executive committee. This new financial institution, which kept the name Bank of America, became the largest in the country, with assets at the time of $570 billion, which is a long way from the Bank of Greenwood. And yet it was McColl, the blustery former Marine, who was the star of a *Time* cover story, not Johnson. Both men preferred it that way.

Johnson also moonlighted as the chairman of the South Carolina Ports Authority from 1968 to 1981, and typical of his visionary leadership, he pushed through a $68 million bond measure that spurred the reinvigoration of Charleston's dilapidated port into what is now the fourth-largest container port in the United States. "Hootie is part of the cadre who opened up South Carolina for business," says Fred Monk, the former financial editor at *The State*. "He was a driving force for everything that is happening today. When BMW chose Spartanburg as the site of its new plant in 1992, that was the capstone of forty years of undeniable progress, and Hootie Johnson was one of the most important and forceful people in the state during those years."

And yet, in *South Carolina: A History,* the definitive account of the Palmetto state published in 1998 by historian Walter Edgars, Johnson didn't rate a single mention across 716 pages. No doubt Hootie was pleased. He has often struggled with the high-wire act of being an intensely private man who has lived an exceedingly public life. In the late 1990s, Johnson gave $250,000 to the Cultural Council of Richland and Lexington Counties, an umbrella organization of arts groups. The endowment funded a recently opened children's museum and continues to provide seed money for a variety of projects. "He has never wanted any fanfare," says Dot Ryall, the director of the Cultural Council. "Some people say that, then call and yell at you when their name is left out. Hootie is sincere. We had put him up for the Forbes Award, which is national recognition for businessmen who make extraordinary contributions to charity, and somehow he got wind of it and he insisted we pull the nomination. That was just so typical of Hootie. His presence is always felt, but he likes to be unseen. Course that would change, wouldn't it?"

THE WICHITA THAT WELCOMED Martha Burk was ground zero in the abortion wars. In June 1986, a pipe bomb was detonated in front of the local Women's Health Care Services clinic, ripping an eight-foot hole in the building and blowing debris into a creek 150 feet away. The blast occurred late at night, sparing any human carnage, but it capped years of explosive debate and constant protesting and counter-protesting. In the wake of the bombing, the owner of the clinic, Dr. George Tiller, continued to inflame passions with incendiary rhetoric. In assessing who bears responsibility for such an attack, he said, "It goes right to the White House, which aids and abets this sort of anarchy. That's what we are talking about—anarchy right here in Wichita." In the ensuing years, Tiller grew into a high-profile abortion advocate, and thus a target for the extremist element in the pro-life movement. In 1993, he survived a shooting in front of his clinic.

Burk rode into battle in this messy milieu, becoming president of the Wichita chapter of the National Organization for Women. She worked on child-care issues and fought to gain equal representation for women on various state boards and commissions. The bloodiest battle was in the Kansas legislature, where Burk and her charges helped to defeat proposals that would have restricted abortion. "I won't say I ever had an overt death threat," Burk says, "but I certainly watched my back. A lot. I did worry about physical violence because . . . there are people who are violent and murderous around this issue."

In full-time advocacy, Burk found the missing purpose in her life. In Ralph Estes, she found the perfect postmodern sensitive guy as a mate. Estes was an accounting professor at Wichita State, not to mention an ardent feminist, the former president of the Texas chapter of the ACLU, and a onetime auditor at Arthur Andersen, a stint that had left him with deep suspicions of the corporate world. (In 1996, he would write the book *The Tyranny of the Bottom Line*.) They had actually met previously in 1968, when Estes was a professor of accounting at UT-Arlington. "I was trying to develop a program to rate college football teams," he says. "I didn't want to do the programming, so I put the word out I was looking for an assistant. Martha was recommended to me as a bright young woman who was finishing her master's in psychology.

"My first impression? She smelled like a dog. Literally. She had been washing her dogs earlier in the day. I also thought she was very bright and very charming, but she was married and had two kids and so that was the end of that. From 1973 until 1986 we had no contact."

With his gentle manner and soothing voice, Estes comes across as a left-leaning Fred Rogers. Martha calls him Ralphie, while he opts for flashier adjectives: "She's good-looking, sexy, fun, brilliant, tenacious, tough, but soft, too," Ralphie says. "She's the woman of my dreams."

They were married in 1986, the same year the Tiller clinic was bombed. Estes encouraged and nurtured Burk's budding devotion to the woman's movement. "I can't say it was me or the circumstances, but it was like a flower opening up and blossoming," Estes says. "When I began to see her as a public figure in Wichita, as head of the NOW chapter and as a feminist activist, I thought this woman really needs and really deserves the bigger stage that is not available here . . . If we wanted to be effective we had to come to Washington and found a nonprofit organization."

In 1990 they took the plunge, moving to D.C. and dreaming up the Center for the Advancement of Public Policy, which they ran out of their Du Pont Circle town house. Burk claimed the title of president, and she created a sassy newsletter, the *Washington Feminist Faxnet*, to use as a bully pulpit to mobilize support. The *Faxnet* began with a circulation of fifty and eventually grew to ten thousand. When the Clinton administration considered extending diplomatic recognition to the Taliban as Afghanistan's official government in the mid-nineties, she spurred a letter-writing campaign in opposition, citing the regime's repressive treatment of women. This was just one of a broad variety of causes that Burk advocated, from protecting Social Security and Title IX to promoting the Equal Rights Amendment to railing against rap lyrics that she considered misogynistic. Some of Burk's causes were counterintuitive: From her other soapbox, as an occasional columnist in *USA Today*, Burk created a stir by arguing that women should not always get custody of their children in a divorce. "The idea was that children should be a more equal responsibility, and if so, then men should get custody of their children as often as we women do," says her friend Heidi Hartmann, president of the Institute for Women's Policy Research.

What helped Burk catch the attention of her audience was the distinctive down-home manner she brought to D.C.'s uptight political community. "She has all these folksy sayings, like, 'That dog just don't hunt,' " says Hartmann. In person, Burk's Texas twang and girlish giggle soften her delivery; she knows that those whom she refers to as "so-called strident feminists" are easier to tune out. "I have always believed in dancing at the revolution," Burk says. "I try to remember that in all my work. We have to keep our sense of humor and our sense of balance."

"She's funny, irreverent," says Sandra Talley, who keeps in touch with her former sister-in-law. "She's a real kick to sit around with over a six-pack."

When Burk wants to let down her hair she and Ralph take their thirty-four-foot trawler for a spin around Chesapeake Bay. Burk refurbished the boat herself, refusing to allow her better half anywhere near the teak. "My husband is a man of many talents," she says, "but staining and painting are not among them. I decided to banish him from that." So Estes would sit dockside and read while his wife did the dirty work. Says Estes, with a laugh, "Guy comes along, says, 'Wish I could get my wife to do this.'"

Burk christened the boat *Alice Paul,* after one of her favorite feminist heroes. Paul was an advocate for women's suffrage and was fond of marching in front of the White House armed with signs that said, "Mr. President, How Long Must Women Wait for Liberty?" Woodrow Wilson decried her "unladylike" behavior and eventually had her arrested, but Paul was unrelenting, and by 1918, President Wilson was publicly supporting women's right to vote. Two years later the Nineteenth Amendment was adopted.

Burk does most of her sailing with the Seafarer's Yacht Club, which is another expression of her open mind. Founded in 1945, the Seafarer's is the oldest African American yacht club on the East Coast, and Burk is one of the few whites who tags along. She laughs at the highfalutin sound of her one private club affiliation. "Actually, it's more like the broken-down boat club," Burk says.

HOOTIE JOHNSON is a man of confounding contradictions. He championed the removal of the Confederate flag from atop the South Carolina capitol building but staunchly defends his favorite lunch spot a couple blocks away, the exclusive Palmetto Club, which made national headlines in the late 1980s for its all-white membership. He is credited as one of the driving forces behind Augusta National admitting its first black member post–Shoal Creek—"because it was the right thing to do," he says—but Johnson is also comfortable with his membership at Columbia's Forest Lake Country Club, an old-money enclave that has no blacks among its one thousand members. (Until very recently, Forest Lake did not have any Jewish members, either; Johnson, as you probably could have guessed, is a past recipient of the B'nai B'rith outstanding citizen award.) He also plays out of a country club closer to his home, Spring Valley, a more open-minded place that was founded mostly by new money who couldn't get into Forest Lake.

The short drive between Forest Lake and Spring Valley is a metaphor for Johnson's journey between the Old South to the New, from the culture of exclusivity to the politics of inclusion. That Johnson can travel back and forth between these worlds seems only natural to him, if not to everybody else. "I don't think it's a contradiction at all," Johnson says. "You know, it can be kind of nuts. I have stood up for doing the right thing my whole life, but not to be a member at Forest Lake because it doesn't have any Jews? I don't run that place. To suggest it's a contradiction to my moral integrity, I'm offended. All you have to do is look at the details of my life to know what I stand for."

Those close to Johnson understand the divide between his public and private worlds. "There's something we call 'old hat' in South Carolina," says Congressman Clyburn. "This state is very traditional when it comes to gathering places. People tend to want to socialize with certain types of people. Yet we expect to be judged by our public lives, not what we do in private. Looking from afar, it might seem inconsistent, but that's how we are."

And what does Johnson reveal of himself in private, at the exclusive hideaways he prefers, where he can mingle with people exactly like himself? In these settings, the statesmanlike pillar of the community turns into a trash-talking, fun-loving character. Golf is Johnson's enduring passion, and he is a strong player, with a low round of 73 at Augusta National, though recent knee surgeries have curbed much of his power. To his golf buddies, Hootie is a cutthroat competitor who negotiates strokes so bloodlessly he rarely loses a match, the stakes of which are typically a $2 Nassau, or $5 when he's feeling frisky. Phillips McDowell, a Columbia investment maven who is president of Forest Lake Country Club, says, "When you arrive on the tee, the bet has already been arranged. There are no negotiations."

McDowell likes to tell the story of a game at Augusta National in which he was down fifteen dollars to Johnson after eighteen holes. "I said, 'Let's play the back nine double or nothing.' Hootie said, 'No, how about we play number eight and nine for five dollars apiece?' Of course, that way he would come out ahead no matter what happened."

McColl, who claims never to have beaten Johnson on the golf course, says, "We always joke that his handicap is whatever the eighteenth hole is rated. He always seems to make sure he has a stroke on the last hole."

Besides taking money from his friends on the golf course, Johnson's other primary diversion is pheasant hunting. He has been to England in pursuit of grouse, and to Spain to chase red-leg partridges, but even in these pastoral settings he's known to shoot off his mouth. "Very frequently we shoot at the same bird, at the same time," says McColl. "He has a classic line, 'Did you shoot?' Meaning he was the one who bagged the bird. That's a famous Hootie-ism."

This brand of jocularity is classic male bonding. In *Golf in the Kingdom*, author Michael Murphy explains the appeal of the game, writing, "Men lovin' men, that's what golf is." This holds true for Johnson's other leisure activities as well. "Most of our hunting trips is really just riding around in the back of a pickup truck talking, with intermittent shooting," says McColl. "Hootie is very, very good company. He is very interested in history, very interested in world events, very interested where this country is heading. He's the best-read person I know. His recall of American and European history is tremendous. Even if you never killed a bird, you could have a great time hunting with him. Of course, it's more fun when you bag at least one more bird than he does."

These days Johnson does much of his shooting at the Oakland Club, in Pineville, South Carolina, what Governor McNair calls "the Augusta National of quail hunting." Hootie is one of only twenty-one members from around the world who share the Oakland Club's twenty-five thousand acres. A club representative says that the estimated time to clear the wait list for membership is fourteen years.

Johnson has had a hand in preserving the club's sterling reputation. "The Oakland Club had always been controlled by northerners, and it was running down," says Governor McNair. "It was not the wonderful place it had been. In the late eighties, Hootie got himself elected president, and very quickly the membership went from passive to activist. He changed managers and improved the quality of everything—the horses, dogs, grounds, everything."

At the Oakland Club jackets are required for dinner in the rustic white clubhouse, and imagining Johnson in this idyll it is hard not to think of Charlie Croker, the protagonist of Tom Wolfe's *A Man in Full*, a meditation on tensions between the Old South and the New. Croker's only escape from mounting real-world pressures is to retreat to Turpmtine, his twenty-nine-thousand-acre quail-hunting spread. "It wasn't sufficient to be rich enough . . ." Croker thinks to himself at one point, in mid-hunt. "No, this was the South. You had to be man enough to deserve a quail plantation. You had to be able to deal with man and beast, in every form they came in, with your wits, your bare hands, and your gun."

BY THE END of her first decade in D.C., Martha Burk had established herself as one of the leading feminist voices in the capital, her networking greatly enhanced by an active role in the National Council of Women's Organizations. (She had become a member as president of the Center for the Advancement of Public Policy.) The NCWO was established in 1983 as a backlash from the defeat of the Equal Rights Amendment and the policies of President Reagan. Its purpose was to bring together a broad spectrum of women's-rights groups to create a stronger unified voice. In April 2000, Burk was voted chair of the NCWO, a job she accepted without pay.

Her home away from home became the NCWO office, on the tenth floor of the Woodward Building, on NW 15th Street, which also houses the Washington Area Bicyclists Association and the National Association for Multicultural Education. The spartan office has just enough room for two desks and a fax machine. The humble surroundings are in sharp contrast to the impressive numbers the NCWO claims: some 160 member groups, representing a total of over 7 million women. "You get more bang for the buck if you're 160 groups rather than just one," Burk says. "We are a strong coalition, though we're not a rich coalition. Our wealth is not in money. It is in our numbers and our dedication to what we do." Prominent mainstream organizations such as NOW, Planned Parenthood, the YWCA, and the League of Women Voters fall under the NCWO's umbrella, as do fringe outfits such as the National Association of Orthopaedic Nurses and Digital Sisters, Inc., which was founded "to promote and provide technology education and enrichment for young girls and women of color."

Like any club or organization, the NCWO has its membership policies. Only nonprofit groups can join, and those whose purpose is to elect candidates from a single party are verboten. On the membership form, all applicants must "subscribe to the core policies listed in the NCWO Policy Agenda. While not all member organizations work actively in all of these concerns, all do agree not to work in opposition to them." The Policy Agenda includes supporting ratification of the Equal Rights Amendment, protecting Social Security, and supporting affirmative action, among many other topics. (Golf club memberships do not rate a mention, but probably would fall under the auspice of "supporting the principles of the National Women's Equality Act for the 21st Century.") As its name indicates, the NCWO does discriminate on the basis of gender. According to the membership form, applicants must be "an organization composed predominantly of women." However, if a group with a small number of male members joins the NCWO, the men are accepted as part of the bargain. Burk claims there are about ten thousand male members of her club.

With an annual budget of $300,000, the NCWO's only means for spreading the word is through the free press. A sampling of Burk's press clippings hints at the breadth of her success. She was quoted in articles carrying the headlines "Women's Coalition Urges Cheney to Promote ERA Support" (*U.S. Newswire*, August 1, 2000); "Bush Proposal on Social Security Would Hurt Women Worst" (*The Washington Post*, August 11, 2000); "National Women's Groups Protest Choice of Moderators in Presidential Debate" (*PR Newswire*, October 10, 2000); "Since Sept. 11, Bush Has Forged New Alliances with Feminists" (Knight-Ridder wire services, February 3, 2002). Elsewhere, Burk weighed in on everything from congressional resistance to ergonomics legislation ("From secretaries to nurses to needle trades workers, repetitive-motion injuries hurt American families") to Washington D.C.'s courtship of a prize fight featuring convicted rapist Mike Tyson ("Big businesses are always wanting to bring something like this in despite the social costs.")

In the summer of 2002, one of the top items on Burk's agenda was advocating for President Bush to ratify the international women's "Bill of Rights" treaty, known as CEDAW (Convention on the Elimination of All Forms of Discrimination Against Women), which only three other nations have not signed—Afghanistan, Iran, and the Sudan. To the cynic who wonders whether such a symbolic act would improve the life of women in this country, Burk says, "Widespread change almost always begins with a symbolic victory. Rosa Parks was symbol. Jackie Robinson was symbol. You can't tell me symbols aren't important."

In June 2002, while working on the CEDAW, Burk made time to attack another symbol, sending a letter to the chairman of Augusta National.

HOOTIE JOHNSON was invited to join the club in 1968, via a letter from Bobby Jones that remains one of his most treasured possessions. But at the time, the enfeebled Jones was only three years from the grave. The Augusta National that Johnson joined was defined not by the preeminent golfing gentleman but rather by his fastidious cofounder, Clifford Roberts.

Johnson got along famously with the chairman, as they dined at each other's homes and frequently teed it up together. "At our [members-only] parties, we play foursome against foursome," Johnson says. "One year I was partnered with Cliff and two other fellows. At eleven, he and the other two guys hit their second shots into the pond. I was about fifteen yards off the green, to the right. Well, they were all counting on me, and I knew it. Unfortunately, I chipped my ball clear across the green and into the water. He didn't say anything to me for the rest of the round. It was one of my worst moments here at the club."

Roberts forgave his friend sufficiently to make him a vice president of Augusta National in 1975, a largely ceremonial position that nonetheless stamped Johnson as a potential successor. Hootie redoubled his close study of Roberts's domineering leadership style. "I kinda liked it," he says. "Actually, I liked it a lot. The club ran pretty well."

In May 1998, twenty-one years after Roberts committed suicide on the grounds of Augusta National, Johnson became the club's fifth chairman. The three who served in between were little more than caretakers, paralyzed by the legacy they were sworn to uphold. Johnson immediately began imposing his will on the club as Roberts had before him, and he wasn't shy about invoking the so-called benevolent dictator as his guiding light. In a press conference Johnson was asked, "What would you think of getting some past champions together on Wednesday morning for a competition?"

"I would not think of it at all," Johnson said.

And why not?

"I don't have to give you a reason," the chairman snapped. "Mr. Roberts would not give you a reason."

Johnson's unprecedented era of change began in June 1998, when he announced a series of significant modifications to the golf course, including the lengthening of the 2nd and 17th holes and the reshaping of the 11th green to bring the pond more into play. (Many of the initiatives enacted under Johnson had been percolating for years, but it was Hootie who pulled the trigger.) In March 1999, just a month before Johnson was to preside over his first Masters as chairman, he announced another stunning modification to the course: Augusta National had framed its fairways with rough, akin to a beard being airbrushed onto the *Mona Lisa*. Said Johnson, "We've been thinking about the 2nd cut for a good little while. The move has been made primarily to put a greater premium on accuracy off the tee." The 2nd cut was just an inch and a half tall, hardly the ankle-length snarl sometimes found at the U.S. Open. But it was just long enough to preclude crisp contact, and losing just a little bit of spin made it hard for players to attack Augusta National's devilish greens, which demand pinpoint approaches.

Along with the June 1998 announcement that trees had been planted to narrow the fairways on the 15th and 17th holes, the addition of rough was a marked departure from the vision of Bobby Jones and Alister MacKenzie, who wanted a wide-open course to encourage bold shotmaking, not a penal design that stifled creativity. The evolution of Augusta National was greeted unfavorably by many players. Said two-time Masters champion Seve Ballesteros, "Why would you change the face of a beautiful woman?"

The reviews were far harsher in 2000, when the fairways were narrowed even further, dramatically changing the sight lines on many tee shots. Only one lone eagle was made during each of the final two rounds, a stunning lack of action for a tournament that had long been celebrated for its back-nine pyrotechnics. (In 1992, thirty-four eagles were made during the week.) There was much talk about Bobby Jones spinning in his grave, for he had loved the do-or-die, risk-reward nature of his course, writing in the early 1950s, "We have always felt the make-or-break character of many of the holes on our second nine has been largely responsible for rewarding our spectators with so many dramatic finishes." When charisma-free Vijay Singh plodded his way to the 2000 Masters title, it seemed to confirm that the course changes had robbed Augusta National of much of its distinctiveness. Six-time Masters champ Jack Nicklaus loosed a Rumsfeldian rant: "Do they do things here that I wouldn't do? Yes. Is this the Augusta we played? No. Is this the Augusta we won on? No, not even close. Does it take away the flavor of Augusta? Yes. Is it what Bobby Jones had in his mind? No way. Not even close. But does it matter what I think? No, it doesn't."

Having been on the front lines of desegregation in South Carolina, Hootie Johnson was unmoved by a little whining from pro golfers, no matter how famous. For the 2002 Masters he unveiled the full-Ivana, a head-to-toe cosmetic surgery on the fabled links in which three hundred yards were added, fairways were regraded, bunkers were relocated and expanded, and more trees were planted. "What we hope to do is to keep up with the game of golf today," the chairman said. "And the guys are hitting it longer and they're in better condition and the equipment is better. We're attempting to strengthen the golf course and stay in tune with the times."

Stay in tune with the times? The appeal of Augusta National has always been its timelessness, as a place where golf goes back to the future. Of the revamped course, Greg Norman said, "I don't like to see this because I like to step up on the tee and say, 'Well, Gene Sarazen did this or Byron Nelson did this,' and feel the same nostalgia and history under my feet. When you change [the course], you change all that."

Tighter and more penal, Augusta National was increasingly resembling a U.S. Open setup, and this split personality conjured up imagery of a dismemberment. "It's kind of like a cadaver they keep whacking away at," said Tom Weiskopf, a four-time Masters runner-up who has become an eminent course architect. "Pretty soon, the course we knew won't be recognizable."

What emboldened Johnson's critics was that once again he appeared to be contradicting Jones's written instructions. In his memoir *Golf Is My Game*, Jones wrote, "It is our feeling that there is something wrong with a golf course which will not yield a score in the 60s to a player who has played well enough to deserve it. We are willing to have low scores made during the tournament and it is not our intention to rig the golf course so as to make it tricky."

It's no small irony that Johnson was being criticized for being too forward-thinking. His reinvention of the golf course was just one of his assaults on the past, as he also blew off one of the Masters' most hallowed traditions, in which champions are extended lifetime invitations to compete in the tournament. Following the 2001 Masters, Johnson ordered impersonal letters be sent to a handful of aging past champs whose performance had become increasingly erratic, urging that "your participation as a player in the 2001 Masters should be your final one." Johnson subsequently rescinded the lifetime invitation altogether, setting an age limit of sixty-five that was to take effect in 2004. Gay Brewer, the 1967 champ, felt so disrespected by this double whammy that he boycotted the 2002 tournament in protest, and other past champs openly vented their displeasure. Johnson ultimately reversed himself and reinstituted the lifetime exemption in the days before the 2003 Masters, but he remains stubbornly unrepentant. "The letter was a mistake," Johnson was quoted as saying in the April 2003 *Golf Digest*. "It would have been better to make a phone call. But the decision was not a mistake."

Johnson's aggressive refashioning of Augusta National and the Masters did not stop with the golf course and past champs. In November 1998, the chairman announced that the club had donated $3 million to charity, two-thirds going to Augusta-area organizations and the other mill to the First Tee Foundation, a nonprofit founded in 1997 with the mission to bring golf to underprivileged kids, particularly in urban settings. The club had been giving out millions in charity for years, but, "I did decide that it should go public," Johnson said. "We had everything to gain and nothing to lose." In November 1998, ten days after the charitable donations were made public, Johnson announced that the Masters was overhauling its qualification criteria. Beginning in 2000, the World Ranking would be the primary factor in determining who was invited to the tournament.

Subsidizing the First Tee and embracing the World Ranking may seem unrelated, but Augusta National's ground-level involvement with both organizations demonstrates how this exclusive private club of three hundred men was growing into a powerful force at every level of the game, with its bold new chairman assuming the role of a de facto commissioner of golf.

The $1 million given to the First Tee was not an aberration—the Masters is one of its founding partners, along with the PGA and LPGA tours, the PGA of America, and the USGA, and the dollar amount has been matched every year since 1998. The Masters is also a member of the First Tee's oversight committee, which approves its budget and business plan. This means that the golf experience of millions of American kids is in some small way shaped by the boys from Augusta. Club officials take great pains to emphasize that it is the Masters, not Augusta National, that has this very public role with the First Tee. But for all practical purposes, the two entities are interchangeable. Augusta National Inc. owns the trademark to the Masters Tournament, and, per the First Tee, the tournament's designated representative is Jim Armstrong, who is the general manager of Augusta National Golf Club, where his boss is Hootie Johnson.

A parallel situation exists with the World Ranking, which, since the Masters' embrace, has become the most important measuring stick in golf, affecting the makeup of virtually every important international tournament. The Masters is on the Ranking's governing board, represented by Augusta National member Will Nicholson. The complicated statistical formula used to determine the World Ranking is not static; it was overhauled in September 2001 for greater efficiency and sensitivity. Any policy change at the World Ranking is voted on by the governing board—and each member can suggest such changes—which means that

Augusta National, Inc. has a say in the livelihood of professional golfers across the globe. "I think there is a great deal of merit in taking the position that Augusta National is really like an association," Reed Mackenzie, then president of one of golf's official ruling bodies, the USGA, said in 2002, "and that when they speak on matters relating to golf it has an impact beyond their borders, and beyond what they are doing simply as a golf club."

As Augusta National's influence was increasingly felt in every corner of the golf world, Hootie Johnson quickly grew into one of the most powerful figures in the game. A month before the 2002 Masters, he engaged in his brashest saber rattling yet, saying, "If technology brings about change in the next several years like we've seen in the past several years, then we may have to consider equipment specifications for the Masters."

Johnson's solution was to float the idea of a so-called Masters ball, which would be designed to make it fly a bit shorter, thus sparing Augusta National from having to be torn up and rebuilt every few years. It was a potentially revolutionary idea, establishing Hootie Johnson as the commissioner of a third-party ruling body, setting policy that would have a dramatic effect at every level of the game. It was a measure of Johnson's and Augusta National's power that a half-baked notion such as the Masters ball was given serious consideration.

Said Luke Reese, the general manager of Wilson Golf, "I think if the Masters wants to make sure its course is going to be played a certain way, then they'll say, 'Here's the design specs,' and we'll all do it. They can do whatever they want. The Masters is bigger than any of us."

The debate about the Masters ball, the flap over the past champs, and the sharp critiques of the course redesign combined to make the 2002 tournament one of the most contentious ever, and the chairman of Augusta National was as much a focus as any of the players. Hootie even got some extra TV time when Tiger Woods won his second straight Masters. Usually, the previous year's champion presents the ceremonial green jacket to the new winner, but rather than have Woods dress himself, Johnson did the honors. The image was beamed around the world, including to Austin, Texas, where the chair of the NCWO was watching with her family.

As Johnson's reach kept expanding, the golf world was left to collectively hold its breath—after four years of near constant controversy, what mischief would Hootie find next? The suspense didn't last long. Two months after the 2002 Masters, the chairman received a letter from Martha Burk.

FOUR

Traction

On Wednesday, July 10, 2002, the world awakened to the image of Hootie Johnson's bayonet. *USA Today*, the *L.A. Times*, *Chicago Tribune*, and *The Atlanta Journal-Constitution* were among the many papers that played his press release about the National Council of Women's Organizations on the front page of the sports section. (It made A1 of the *Augusta Chronicle*.) Among the most interested readers were the 290 or so Augusta National members who had not been privy to Johnson's deliberations on how to respond to Martha Burk's letter and were thus unaware of the gathering storm. "I read about it in the paper, like everybody else," says Minneapolis-based Wheelock Whitney, the former owner of the Minnesota Vikings, who has been an Augusta National member since 1965. "It was a surprise, to say the least."

The initial blast of news coverage created strong first impressions of the story's protagonists. Doug Ferguson's widely distributed AP dispatch described Johnson as "defiant" and described his public statement as "surprisingly long and angry." The *Houston Chronicle* called it "long, strong and ominous," while the *Chicago Tribune* tabbed the press release as "an angry lightning bolt from the Masters mountaintop." Virtually every account quoted Johnson's diffident "not at the point of a bayonet" line, which immediately entered the lexicon.

If Johnson was largely portrayed as a grumpy old man who had inexplicably blown his cool, then Burk was depicted as the clueless muckraker who had lucked into a juicy controversy. One passage buried deep in Ferguson's story would resonate for months. (The gang from *Crossfire* made a big deal of it when Burk appeared on the show in September.) Wrote Ferguson, "Burk suggested that if Augusta National does not have female members, the Masters should move to a club that does. 'The Masters, in my mind, is not tied at the hip to this club,' she said. 'An event of this profile could be held somewhere else.' "

This nonsensical notion betrayed Burk's lack of a golf background as well as the cursory nature of her research prior to sending her letter to Johnson, allowing many to discount the message and focus on the messenger. *The Orange County Register*'s golf writer, John Reger, typed, "That has to be the most idiotic statement I have ever heard and makes me believe Burk is more interested in press clippings than actual change."

Alan Tays, in a column for *The Palm Beach Post*, wrote, "I believe Burk has won the triple crown here. This is the stupidest, most uninformed and most arrogant comment I've ever heard. Who died and left Burk and her ilk in charge of Augusta National or the Masters?"

Months later, Burk was still smarting at the vitriol. "I made a mistake, so shoot me," she says. "What's the big deal? My area of expertise is sex discrimination, not golf. I saw Jesse Jackson say the same thing in a press conference, and no one called him an idiot and ridiculed him for not knowing about golf. That showed a little sexism right there.

"Would I have preferred not to have made that mistake? Of course. Would it have changed the tenor of the initial coverage? Without a doubt. But in the grand scheme of things, it is utterly irrelevant."

Perhaps chastened by the tone of the first morning's newspaper stories, Burk sounded a conciliatory note when she appeared on CNN on the afternoon of July 10. Asked by anchor Daryn Kagan why she had sent Johnson the letter, Burk took pains to downplay her role in the burgeoning controversy. "Actually, I didn't start this," she said. "This was already news when I learned of it."

Later, Kagan said, "Martha, let's look at some of [the Masters'] sponsors. We are talking about mainstream American companies: Coca-Cola, IBM, Citigroup. You are going to target these companies and say what?"

"Well, I don't want to use the word target. I think we are probably going to have a discussion with the sponsors. Mr. Johnson"—in another showing of restraint, Burk initially resisted using the chairman's colloquial nickname—"has made it very clear he doesn't want to talk to us. I wanted to have a calm, relaxed dialogue with him to see if I could make him see the light. He sent me a letter that said, basically, Get lost, lady. So the alternatives that are left to me are to talk to you, the media, and possibly talk to the sponsors, to see if we can get them to look at their public image in relation to underwriting an event that is held at a facility that discriminates."

Burk was not the only person meeting the press on July 10. It was a quirk of the calendar that PGA Tour commissioner Tim Finchem had scheduled a press conference for that portentous day, at the site of the Ford Senior Players Championship. Finchem is the second most powerful man in golf, behind Tiger Woods, and he gave an early indication that the conservative golf establishment would mobilize to protect a member of the fraternity. "I won't quarrel with [Johnson's] statement that the policies of a club are the club's prerogative," said Finchem, who is a triple threat in spin, as before joining the Tour he was a high-school debate champion, a lawyer, and a political operative for President Carter. "I don't think it's for us to be concerned with. There are men's clubs around the country, and the Tour chooses to organize our tournaments at clubs that allow women members. We don't have a contractual obligation with Augusta National, but we do have a long-term recognition of the Masters. We have no plans to change that recognition in any way, shape or form."

Others were also scrambling for cover, employing the same nimble logic as Finchem. "Our sponsorship is of the Masters golf tournament, a one-week, public event that is viewed and enjoyed annually by millions of sports fans in every corner of the globe," Coca-Cola spokesman Ben Deutsch said in the hours after Johnson's comments were released. He added that it would be "inappropriate" for Coke to comment on Augusta National's policies.

Jack Nicklaus, reached by *The Atlanta Journal-Constitution*, said, "That's not my issue. That's Hootie's issue. I'm a member at the club, obviously, but I'm just a member . . . The club has its policies, and I'm not [involved] in the policies of the club. I'm just a member." Conditioned by decades of being muted, other green jackets contacted by the media parroted Nicklaus's I'm-just-a-member defense, or refused to speak altogether.

Few other figures of note in the golf world were commenting, in part because Johnson's press release had landed the week before the British Open. Most marquee players, and numerous golf dignitaries, were en route to Scotland, and thus unable to add their two cents. A few no-name players were milling around following their practice rounds at the low-wattage Greater Milwaukee Open, but there were few reporters on hand to question them. The smattering of national golf writers who were not on a busman's holiday playing golf in Great Britain were at the U.S. Women's Open. (Ferguson's initial AP story had a dateline of Hutchinson, Kansas, where Prairie Dunes Golf Club was hosting the Open.)

The debate was also quieted because Augusta National had released Johnson's fighting words on a Tuesday. It is axiomatic in golf circles that nothing big ever happens on Tuesday. That's because all three weekly sources of golf news—*GolfWorld, Golfweek,* and *Sports Illustrated*'s Golf Plus—go to the printers on Monday evening, with subscribers receiving their copies by Wednesday or Thursday. All three magazines landed in mailboxes during the first couple of days of coverage, but there was, eerily, nary a word about Augusta National in these pillars of the golf press.

Scores of newspaper columnists eagerly charged into the breach. The Hootie and Martha spat was tailor-made for wags of every stripe. The columns broke down into two warring camps: those who felt that the club was entitled to its (constitutionally protected) right of association, and the others who argued that as host to a very public tournament and a driving force in the game, Augusta National had a moral imperative to open its doors to all segments of society. Both sides had strong arguments that touched twenty-first century hot-button issues, which made the debate all the noisier.

Tays's visceral, over-the-top column ran on the front page of sports in the *Palm Beach Post*, under the headline "Don't Like Sexism at Augusta? It's a Private Club, So Stay Out." Wrote Tays, "Antidiscrimination is a noble-sounding goal, but in practice it's a myth. The person who turns you down for a date is discriminating against you because of your looks or your personality. The developer who won't sell you that big house is discriminating against you because of your income.

"Welcome to the real world. Privacy is basic to human nature. We choose our friends, our mates, our fellow club members. If you don't like it, form your own club. Tell the guard at the gate not to let me in.

"I may not like it, but I respect your right to do it."

Burk's supporters generally dealt not in polemics but in bone-dry recitations of their version of the facts. *The Washington Post* had reported Johnson's initial press release with wire copy in a corner of the second page of Sports, but a day later its golf writer and media critic Len Shapiro surveyed the issues, writing, "[E]very April, Augusta becomes all-inclusive, allowing the public to pass through its gates and onto the golf course to witness the Masters, the first major championship of the season. As such, the club leaves itself open to the sort of criticism directed its way recently by the Washington-based National Council of Women's Organizations . . .

"The timetable [for admitting female members] ought to be now, just as the timetable to have the club open its doors to African Americans should have been accomplished many years sooner than the early 1990s. Now there are six African Americans in the all-male 300-member club. Many make up a Who's Who of corporate America, who belong to a club with exclusionary rules many of their stockholders never would tolerate in the companies or businesses they run."

There were countless variations on these themes, but all the pontificating was doing little to advance the story. By the end of the first week the narrative of the Augusta National membership controversy was showing signs of petering out. Even Burk was unsure how to proceed. "We are not going to do anything from the hip like Hootie did in his missive to the media. We haven't decided what yet, but there will definitely be a next move." If the story was to gain any traction it would need a compelling new angle to capture the public's attention.

TIGER WOODS spent the week before the British Open outside Dublin, luxuriating at the K Club, Ireland's cushiest hotel. Woods has long made a pre-Open pilgrimage to the linksland along with his close friend Mark O'Meara (a spokesman for the Irish golf industry) and a rotating cast of hangers-on. In 2002, David Duval, the defending British Open champ, and Scott McCarron got the nod. This heavyweight foursome teed it up at the K Club's rather pedestrian course, which will host the 2005 Ryder Cup, and they also worked in rounds at Portmarnock, the European Club, and Mount Juliet, traveling in a helicopter that was parked conspicuously in the middle of the manicured formal garden behind the hotel. The trip, however, was as much about blowing off steam as it was about golf. Had you strolled past room 679 on the afternoon of July 12, the open front door would have revealed a shirtless Duval sharing a game of cribbage with a friend, as well as a bottle of Wild Turkey. Later that day a solitary figure was spotted casting a line on one of the lakes that dot the K Club's front nine; the scruffy, dressed-down Woods got a couple of bites.

One thing Woods and his buddies didn't catch was the news back in the States. The K Club offered no American newspapers or TV channels, and the nascent Augusta National controversy meant little to the Irish media or citizenry. Says McCarron, "We were fishing and golfing all day, and eating all night, with maybe a little more fishing thrown in. We didn't hear a thing. They didn't have anything in the papers, but we didn't really read any of the papers anyway. We had our cell phones off. It just didn't register over there. We wouldn't have known what was going on at Augusta unless the fish told us . . . and they didn't."

Tiger and the boys left the K Club on the afternoon of Sunday, July 14. Less than forty-eight hours after arriving at the tournament site—Muirfield, in Gullane, Scotland—Woods was ushered into the media center for his traditional pretournament press conference. When asked how much his client knew about the ongoing Augusta National developments, Woods's agent, Mark Steinberg, says, "It was discussed briefly in anticipation of the press conference." He declines to answer more specific questions.

What Woods may or may not have known was that he was walking into an ambush six years in the making.

At his first professional tournament, the 1996 Greater Milwaukee Open, Woods was featured in a provocative ad campaign for Nike, with whom he had signed a $40 million deal just days earlier. The ad carried the freighted message, "There are golf courses in the United States that I cannot play because of the color of my skin / I'm told that I'm not ready for you / Are you ready for me?" The backlash within the stodgy golf world was immediate. *Washington Post* columnist James K. Glassman asked a Nike spokesman which courses a three-time U.S. Amateur champ and budding Tour pro could not play because of the color of his skin, and the Swoosh mouthpiece conceded that no such place actually existed, asserting that the statement was not to be taken literally. Woods also sent a mixed message with his choice of attire: in the commercial he was wearing a shirt bearing the logo of Lochinvar Golf Club, a men-only club in Houston where his coach, Butch Harmon, had been director of golf. USGA executive director David Fay called attention to this untidy detail.

Earl Woods would later tell his son's biographer, John Strege, that this first splashy introduction "missed Tiger's personality to a degree." Indeed, even at the age of twenty, Woods was a middle-aged white guy at heart, like his budding best friend, O'Meara, a middle-aged white guy with two kids and a bald pate that years of endorsing Rogaine would not cure. The tone of the campaign was more in keeping with Earl's bluster than Tiger's true nature. Just as the fuss was dying down, Earl told *Sports Illustrated* in December 1996, in a story naming his son Sportsman of the Year, "Tiger will do more than any other man in history to change the course of humanity." Writer Gary Smith pressed Earl on the point—was he really saying that Tiger would have more impact than Mandela, or Gandhi, or Buddha?

"Yes, because he has a larger forum than any of them. Because he's playing a sport that's international. Because he's qualified through his ethnicity to accomplish miracles. He's the bridge between the East and the West. There is no limit because he has the guidance. I don't know yet exactly what form this will take. But he is the Chosen One. He'll have the power to impact nations. Not people. Nations. The world is just getting a taste of his power."

The ruckus over Earl's hyperbole was just dying down when the April 1997 GQ hit newsstands, with Tiger on the cover. In the accompanying article, the Chosen One was quoted telling sophomoric, off-color jokes about lesbians and ruminating on the mythical size of black men's genitalia. Woods was deeply wounded by the ensuing maelstrom, which confirmed for him that unguarded candor was simply too risky for an aspiring cross-cultural icon. As he labored to make the rocky adjustment to superstardom, Woods increasingly sought the counsel of "M," his cutesy nickname for Michael Jordan, a fellow Nike spokesman. Woods's choice of mentors was telling—M was a transcendent athlete but also an unabashed mercenary who drew criticism throughout his career for his unwillingness to address social issues. Jordan's defining epigram came in 1990, when his fellow North Carolinians beseeched him to support a moderate black Democrat named Harvey Gantt in a Senate race against the race-baiting incumbent, Jesse Helms. Jordan declined to enter the fray, saying, "Republicans buy sneakers too." Helms won a narrow election, and in time Woods mastered the art of Jordan's bland political disengagement.

It is certainly okay for an athlete to think about nothing other than the game he plays. Nicklaus was never criticized for his stance, or lack thereof, on the Vietnam War, and Woods's many defenders often complain that Tiger is singled out simply because of the color of his skin. This misses the point: Woods positioned himself as an agent of change with that first Nike ad campaign, and his father's grand pronouncements only heightened expectations.

So, back in the drafty press tent at the 2002 British Open, so many chickens came home to roost that Woods may as well have been Harlan Sanders. While the first fourteen questions put to him were almost exclusively about his pursuit of the Grand Slam, the fifteenth was about Augusta National, and Woods never saw it coming. His biggest fan,

Doug Ferguson of the AP, would later offer a rare critical word, describing Woods as "unprepared and uncomfortable."

Question from the press corps: "Tiger, the issue of women not being allowed to be members at [private] clubs was raised last week at Augusta. What is your position on that?"

A: "You know, it's one of those things where everyone has . . . they're entitled to set up their own rules the way they want them. It would be nice to see everyone have an equal chance to participate if they wanted to, but there is nothing you can do about it. If you have a group, an organization, that's the way they want to set it up, it's their prerogative to set it up that way."

Q: "If it also applied to other groups, African Americans, Asians, whatever, would you feel the same way?"

A: "Yes, I would. It's unfortunate that it is that way, but it's just the way it is. There are clubs that have segregated, whether it's sex or race, one of those two issues, and . . . or even age, those are issues and those are things that have happened and will continue to occur and they will continue to exist for a long period of time."

Q: "With your stature in the game, do you think you can force the change?"

A: "I've done my part so far trying to get more kids who haven't been able to have access to the game, that's what my foundation is all about, so I have . . . I'm trying to do my share in my sector where I'm really focused on, and it's not easy. A lot of these clubs that's what they believe and that's what they've believed for a long period of time. It's not easy."

The media outrage was immediate. Here was the issue that Woods and Nike had handpicked—exclusionary membership policies at private clubs—and Tiger was all but giving the thumbs-up to segregation, to use his own loaded word. The New York tabloids had an informal contest to see which could act the most indignant. The back cover of the *Post* screamed "Hypocrite!" with a subhead that shouted "Two-faced Tiger Says Augusta Has 'Right' to Ban Women." Inside, the story was adorned with the head "He's a Hypocrite with Gutless Stance." In case anyone had missed the point, Mark Cannizzaro went on to write in the accompanying story, ". . . his comments yesterday are deplorable and utterly hypocritical based on the man he sells to the public." Cannizzaro also asked, "When there was slavery, was that just the way it was?"

In the *Daily News* the headline was "Tiger Talks Tame Game," and one of America's most high-profile columnists, Mike Lupica, wrote, "Tiger Woods is the establishment in golf right now. He is never going to say anything controversial about anything. He doesn't want to be Arthur Ashe. He just wants to beat Jack Nicklaus. . . . He didn't have much to say because he doesn't have much to say."

The fallout from the Woods's British Open comments was twofold. Suddenly, Augusta National was on the radar screen of the media tastemakers in Manhattan. (On CBS *Evening News*, Dan Rather solemnly opined that, "Woods's reputation lost a bit of its sparkle this week after he declined to take a stand against one form of country club discrimination.") At the same time, Woods gave Martha Burk another point of entry on the issue, and in blasting the world's most famous athlete she found an emboldened voice. Gone was the conciliatory, almost defensive tone of her first statements. Now, for the first time, Burk was on the offensive. The day after Woods's press conference, in a live, prime-time appearance on MSNBC, she said, "Well, I wish Tiger had been stronger. Obviously, if Lee Elder"—Burk had obviously been doing her golf homework—"and others had not knocked down the door for Tiger, he wouldn't be where he is. And a certain responsibility comes with that." Two days later Burk appeared on ABC News, saying, "Tiger is wrong. There's a lot you can do about that. I think he has a special responsibility and opportunity because he is listened to more than any other athlete."

She also zinged Woods in numerous newspapers. One line appeared more than once: "If more people in the past had taken a position of not speaking out, Tiger Woods might be a caddie at Augusta and not a player." Ouch.

How much the story had grown since Hootie Johnson's press release was obvious in its treatment by the nation's newspaper of record. In the July 10 edition of *The New York Times*, the news of Johnson's opening salvo was buried on the fourth page of sports. Eleven days later it landed on one of the paper's most valuable pieces of real estate, the front page of the SundayStyles section. Burk was the star of a 1,500-word think piece that ran under the headline "It's Still a Man's, Man's, Man's World." "For all my respect for him, Tiger is naive," Burk said in the story. "We will not take the view that some have: Tiger has spoken and now it's over. It is not over."

Indeed, it was just beginning.

ON JULY 30, after more than a week of consultation with her kitchen cabinet at the NCWO, Burk sent a letter to the CEOs of the Masters' three sponsors, Citigroup, Coca-Cola, and IBM. "It was time to move beyond just Augusta National," she says, "and make it clear that this fight was not about golf but about sex discrimination, and to highlight that some of this country's most powerful businessmen and corporations were condoning it."

The formally worded letters all began with an introduction to the NCWO, and then Burk cut to the chase. "We are writing to request that [company name here] suspend sponsorship of the Masters Golf Tournament, since it is owned, controlled, and produced by Augusta National Incorporated, an organization that discriminates against women by excluding them from membership. While some would try to argue that they are separate, Augusta National Incorporated in fact owns and does business at the Masters Golf Tournament, and benefits directly from sponsorships. Since it is not a separate entity, the tournament cannot be moved to a club that does not discriminate. Sponsoring the Masters legitimizes the discrimination engaged by Augusta National."

Though the wording of the letters was largely the same, there were a few interesting nuggets buried in each. To Coke CEO Douglas Daft, Burk made a pointed reference to a high-profile 2000 class-action lawsuit in which Coke paid a record $192 million to settle a complaint brought by 2,200 black employees who had alleged that racial discrimination within the company had led to a pay gap in which whites earned on average $26,000 a year more than blacks.

From a long career in advocacy Burk knew that large, publicly traded corporations are paranoid about being associated with even the whiff of scandal or controversy. That was one of the lessons of Shoal Creek, when advertisers pulled more than $2 million worth of advertising from the telecast of the PGA Championship. As Burk highlighted in her letters, IBM was among the companies that got cold feet, releasing a statement at the time that said, "When we learned that this tournament was being played at a club that was exclusionary, we decided it was not an appropriate vehicle for our advertising. Supporting even indirectly activities which are exclusionary is against IBM's practices."

There was not a similar rush to judgment with Augusta National. As Burk would gleefully point out, that might have been because Louis V. Gerstner, IBM's chairman, was a member of Augusta National, as was Weill, the man who built Citigroup into the world's largest financial institution, with more than a trillion dollars in assets. (It is not a coincidence that the Masters' sponsors have close ties to the club, as Augusta National chooses the companies, not CBS—an arrangement that dates to the 1950s, when the tournament was sponsored by American Express and Travelers Insurance at a time when both were run by members.)

On August 15, IBM became the first of the Masters' sponsors to respond to Burk. Though she had addressed her letter to CEO Samuel Palmisano, the reply came courtesy of Rick Singer, the director of worldwide sponsorship marketing. Its corporate-speak couldn't have been blander or more hollow. "Thank you for your letter expressing the NCWO's views on the Augusta National Golf Club," Singer began. "We have followed the discussion as reported in the media and certainly hope that a resolution satisfactory to all parties will take place. . . . IBM is proud of its longstanding commitment to diversity and support for a broad range of organization dedicated to the advancement of women and girls in business, technology and science, and you can be sure that this record—part of the heritage and fabric of our company—will be sustained.

"We do not view our sponsorship of the Masters tournament as contradictory to this commitment."

A week later Citigroup responded with an even more milquetoast letter, from Leah Johnson, director of public affairs. "Thank you for your recent letter to Mr. Weill," it began. "Citigroup has long had strong policies and practices concerning diversity. . . . With regards to your comments regarding the Masters Golf Tournament, we have communicated our views privately to the management of the tournament. We believe that such a dialogue is the most constructive approach to this issue."

Coca-Cola never publicly responded to Burk. The conflicted feeling of its management was predictable, given the company's close ties to Augusta National. The president and CEO of Coca-Cola Bottling, Claude Nielsen, belonged to the club, as did two high-profile members of Coke's board of directors—Warren Buffet, the billionaire investor, and former Georgia senator Sam Nunn. In fact, Coke's ties to Augusta National stretch back to the nascent years of the club, in the outsized personage of Robert Winship Woodruff, one of National's most influential early members.

In 1923, Woodruff took over as president of a small, debt-ridden soda company, and over the next sixty-one years he turned Coca-Cola into one of the world's most recognizable brands. "The Boss," as Woodruff was widely known, had known Bobby Jones's family since the early 1920s, when Woodruff ran a Cleveland-based truck manufacturing company for which Jones's father did some legal work. Woodruff would become such a staple of Bobby's gallery that after Jones holed the final putt at the 1930 U.S. Amateur at Merion to clinch the Grand Slam, he handed his ball to Woodruff.

Woodruff and Jones (and by extension Clifford Roberts) became golf buddies, hunting companions, and eventually business partners. In the years following World War II, Woodruff set up for Jones and Roberts the Joroberts Corporation, to own and operate Coca-Cola bottling plants in Great Britain, South Africa, and Central and South America. Joroberts was a club within a club, reproducing Augusta National's power structure and roster. Jones was the president and secretary of Joroberts, while Roberts was vice president and treasurer. Almost all of the thirty stockholders belonged to Augusta National, including Dwight Eisenhower and his son John. In 1955, Woodruff furthered the cross-pollination between Coca-Cola and Augusta National by naming his fellow green jacket Bill Robinson as president of Coke. Later Robinson served as chairman of the board.

With all of this history, it's no surprise that in the summer of 2001, Coke leapt at the chance to become a Masters sponsor for the first time, when Cadillac bowed out after thirty-two years. The Masters was to be part of a larger strategy by the company to increase its sponsorship in athletic events. (In 2002, about 25 percent of Coke's staggering $1.7 billion marketing budget was sports-driven.) The Masters, however, hardly fit the profile of other big investments like soccer's World Cup or the National Hot Rod Association. Says one Coca-Cola executive, "Internally, the Masters was largely seen as a vanity project for upper management. It's a stodgy, old man's sport, and we're supposed to be all about youth and fun and excitement. When you get to the activation level with the Masters, where's the payoff? You hardly get any ad time during the telecast, and you can't even put your logo on the cups at the tournament. From a prestige standpoint, it's nice, but nobody here believes it made much difference in sales, or the bottom line."

Still, Coke's first Masters, in 2002, was the biggest social event to happen to the Atlanta-based company since the 1996 Olympics, with hundreds of top employees and VIP guests cavorting during a week of bottomless hospitality.

The close ties between Coke and the club were helpful as the membership controversy was beginning to ferment. Coke's PR department received a heads-up forty-eight hours before Johnson's "point of a bayonet" press release went out, allowing the flaks to put together a cogent response. As Burk stepped up her efforts to pressure the company, Coke quietly began discussions with Hootie Johnson on how they were all going to get out of this PR mess. Some of these details spilled out in a shortish story on the front page of The Atlanta Journal-Constitution on September 4. A fuller picture was provided in interviews with a Coke executive who was actively involved in dealing with Augusta National. He would speak only on the condition on anonymity. (Or perhaps "on the condition of paranoia" is more accurate. The executive warned, "I don't want a paper trail of anything that can be traced back to me. Do not leave me voice messages at work. Do not use my e-mail address . . .")

Despite having three Augusta National members among its top officers, "there was no predetermined outcome to how we would handle this," says the Coke insider. "There were no edicts coming from on high.

It was a fluid situation and we were constantly weighing the pros and cons."

As Burk hammered away at Coke, the pressure was mounting within the company to cut its ties with the Masters. "Everybody in upper management is still scarred by the discrimination lawsuit, and there is a tremendous desire to be seen as a company that does the right thing," says the Coke source. "The climate of fear was winning out."

THE CORPORATE SPONSORS were not the only ones feeling the heat. In early August a most interesting posting appeared under the diary section of tigerwoods.com. (In recent years Woods has increasingly eliminated pesky reporters from his life, controlling the dissemination of news through his Web site.) Woods started by defending the honor of his girlfriend, Elin Nordegren, a Swedish stunner who had been working as a nanny for Tour player Jesper Parnevik when she began dating Tiger a year earlier. "Apparently, some nude photos are making the rounds on the Internet that some claim are of my girlfriend," Woods wrote. "Although she has done some swimsuit modeling, she has never posed nude, nor does she have any intent to do so." From there he segued, awkwardly, into the Augusta National membership controversy. Whereas Woods's remarks at the British Open had been spontaneous and candid, his Web posting had the feel of a press release from his agents at International Management Group. "Everyone has to understand that Augusta isn't quick to change things," Tiger wrote. "No matter what I or the press says, they do things at their own pace, such as allowing the first black golfer to play or join the club, and they won't buckle to outside pressure. Would I like to see women members? Yes, that would be great, but I am only one voice."

Tim Finchem added to the chorus two weeks later, in a letter to Martha Burk dated August 20. She had written to him on July 30, saying, "We understand that the Masters is not an 'official' part of the PGA Tour. However, the PGA's recognition of the tournament, and counting the prize money toward a golfer's season earnings, is a close enough relationship to warrant the same scrutiny given clubs hosting tournaments that are part of the PGA Tour. To do less in the case of Augusta National renders the PGA Tour's nondiscrimination policy hollow, and indeed has the appearance of a double standard. Simply put, recognizing the Masters legitimizes the discrimination engaged in Augusta National."

Finchem had been strangely silent ever since his initial comments the day after Hootie Johnson's press release. Now, finally, he was addressing the issue head-on, but his mealymouthed comments were oblique to the point of transparency. "We understand and appreciate your position that women should be admitted to Augusta National as members," Finchem wrote in his opening paragraph. "As you indicate in your letter, the Masters Tournament is not an event cosponsored by the PGA Tour. You are correct that the PGA Tour requires that host clubs of our cosponsored events, with whom we have contractual relationships, maintain membership policies under which membership is not restricted on the basis of race, religion, sex, or national origin. However, since the PGA Tour does not cosponsor the Masters and does not have a contractual relationship with the Masters as it has with its cosponsored events, we are unable to require Augusta National to implement our host club policy with respect to the Masters . . ."

No doubt smirking, Finchem typed one final line: "I trust this letter is responsive to the questions raised in your correspondence."

His disingenuousness was breathtaking. Finchem's contention that the Tour does not have a contractual relationship with the Masters may be true in a narrow, Clintonian way: He and Hootie Johnson don't sit down every year and sign documents spelling out all the ways the Tour recognizes the Masters, but that recognition is deeply ingrained in Tour policy. Money earned at the Masters counts toward the Tour's official season and career money lists, and the tournament winner is granted a precious five-year exemption to the Tour. (A victory at a "regular" event brings only two years' worth of playing privileges.)

After reviewing Finchem's letter, Burk saved some of her best invective for the commish. Noting that he was a point man in the Tour's nondiscrimination policy in the wake of Shoal Creek, Burk said, "He is a person willing to sell his principles—and sell them awfully cheap. It's like, 'I and Hootie Johnson are above anybody's influence or sense of fairness. We are in a world of our own and we are going to stay in it.' It's palpable arrogance."

Finchem refused to defend his letter's inconsistencies, as Tour spin doctors rebuffed all interview requests for the commissioner and repeatedly referred reporters back to the letter. The institutional defensiveness was no doubt driven in part by the inconvenient fact that two members of the eight-man Tour policy board were members at Augusta National—Richard Ferris, former CEO of United Airlines, and Charles Knight, the chairman of Emerson Electric.

Finchem was lucky that he dashed off his letter when he did. A week and a half later, the PGA Tour's wishy-washy position was overshadowed by the most stunning event yet in a story that continued to pick up momentum.

ON AUGUST 30, Hootie Johnson made his first public statement since he had whipped out his bayonet. This press release, too, was e-mailed to media outlets around the country.

"As we predicted several weeks ago, the NCWO has launched a corporate campaign against the Masters Tournament and Augusta National Golf Club to force Augusta National to immediately invite women to join our Club. We are sorry, but not surprised, to see these corporations drawn into this matter but continue to insist that our private club should not be 'managed' by an outside group. Augusta National is NCWO's true target. It is therefore unfair to put the Masters media sponsors in the position of having to deal with this pressure. Accordingly, we have told our media sponsors that we will not request their participation for the 2003 Masters. This year's telecast will be conducted by the Masters Tournament."

In the long, twisty timeline of the Augusta National membership controversy, this is one of the two or three most important events. The average golf fan, who up till this point had barely been paying attention, suddenly had something to capture his or her imagination—an entire Masters with no commercials! By kissing off millions of dollars in sponsorship revenue and agreeing to shoulder a few million more in television production costs, Johnson made an emphatic display of the club's—or, at the very least, *his*—resolve to fight on. (Augusta National could certainly afford Johnson's determination; back-of-the-envelope calculations put its annual Masters take at $25 million or more, thanks largely to the gate and pricey merchandise sales.) And by placing a spotlight on a telecast that was more than seven months away, the chairman guaranteed that Augusta National would remain in the news at least until the 2003 Masters. But most striking was how his bold stroke changed the tenor of the debate. In the preceding six weeks Johnson and the club had receded largely from view, as Tiger, the sponsors, and the PGA Tour took their turn in the barrel. Now the chairman was deliberately drawing fire in his and the club's direction.

Moreover, in a twenty-first-century sports world increasingly driven and defined by money, Johnson was suddenly placing principle above the almighty dollar. This was a strange, novel concept, and plenty of people, reporters among them, applauded Johnson for putting his money where his mouth is, as dropping the sponsors furthered the club's ability to control its membership free of outside pressure. A noisier contingent took a dimmer view: Hootie Johnson was willing to spend millions of dollars to keep women out of his club. This was such a sexy story that it made page A1 of *The New York Times*, above the fold. In the days after the sponsors were fired, the chairman busted off the sports page and began making cameos in editorials everywhere from *The Atlanta Journal-Constitution* to *Advertising Age*, and he was spotted streaking across the gray expanse of the business page. "Hootie shocked me, and I think he shocked everybody else," says Burk. "When Augusta National's sex discrimination gets an extensive treatment in *BusinessWeek*, it's not just a little golf story anymore."

In the week or two immediately after the sponsorship announcement, the media coverage of the membership controversy lost all of its nuance and became little more than a shouting match. Burk's detractors may have been a minority, but they were growing increasingly shrill. Prior to the dropping of the sponsors, *GolfWorld* had been cautious in reporting the burgeoning controversy; now its editors decided this was a cover story. In a back-page column that served as an exclamation point to the Johnson cover, *GolfWorld*'s top writer, John Hawkins, railed against the "pure tokenism, even farcical symbolism" of Burk's campaign, writing, "In her search for unconditional equality in a discrimination-free world, NCWO chairman Martha Burk, who wouldn't know a five-wood from a dogwood, has chosen to drive her soapbox up Magnolia Lane and park it next to the world's most arcadian golf tournament. A more frivolous crusade you will not find."

In *The Atlanta-Journal Constitution*, Furman Bisher, an octogenarian who is one of the deans of the golf press, defended his favorite tournament in a column that began, "Well, I see Martha Burk has resorted to blackmail, taking a page out of the Jesse Jackson manual . . ."

However, the majority of the sporting press fingered Hootie as the bad guy, and their rhetoric was just as over-the-top as his defenders'. A day after Bisher's column, *The Atlanta Journal-Constitution* ran a counter-point in which Jeff Schultz called Johnson "arrogant, pig-headed, obstinate, archaic, racist, sexist, probably a few other 'ists' I can't think of right now," with "Neanderthal" thrown in for balance. In the Cleveland *Plain Dealer*, Bud Shaw wrote, "Johnson's reaction—to hold a tournament with no commercials—doesn't mark him as a man of high principle. He just looks more out of touch and spiteful."

For the first time, reductionist southern stereotypes began to fly. Johnson's drawl and his South Carolina roots were all held against him as evidence of the backwardness of Augusta National, but nothing quite captured the imagination of the sophisticates in the press like his nickname. It's likely that tenor of the press coverage of the membership controversy would have been markedly different if Augusta National's chairman was known simply as William Woodward Johnson. But Hootie was the most wonderfully evocative name this side of Buttafuoco, and it became more than just a moniker; in certain hands *Hootie* was an indictment, or a putdown. On the front page of sports in *The Miami Herald*, Linda Robertson began a column writing, "The first indication that there is something seriously backward about the Masters golf tournament is the nickname of its chairman, William 'Hootie' Johnson." She went on to disparage the "comical archaism" of this "misguided Southern gentleman," saying "the green jackets [will] someday possess a resonance similar to the 'Colored Only' signs of the segregation era."

This kind of vitriol was not uncommon. It was as if reporters had been biting their tongues for weeks, just waiting to go off on Johnson, and the defiance he showed in dropping the sponsors finally afforded the opportunity. The Portland *Oregonian* called the chairman "a Bull Connor for the plaid-pants set," while Bill Plaschke, in a column on the front page of the Sports section in the *L.A. Times*, likened Augusta National to a "private club still fighting the Civil War. Strip away tradition and legend and Augusta National becomes just another overgrown Southern backyard patrolled by good ol' boys in Wal-Mart blazers."

Needless to say, this was not the kind of press hallowed Augusta National was used to receiving. "The characterizations have been outrageous," said longtime member Hugh McColl in an interview. "I've seen things in the paper that are just crazy. Just because they haven't heard of Hootie's nickname they think he's a country boy who doesn't know what he's doing. If you don't mind me saying so, it's either ignorance or just plain snobbery among the Eastern elites in the press."

Johnson's second bombshell press release was also used as an opportunity to revisit his initial handling of Burk's private letter. His "point of a bayonet" statement in July was so unexpected and unprecedented that it had been hard to render a verdict on its merits. Was it a gross overreaction that instantly created a controversy where none had previously existed, or was it a courageous, principled manifesto against the forces of political correctness? Now his opening gambit was being viewed through the lens of the press release that followed. Taken together, these two hawkish moves were seen by many not only as tactical blunders but also evidence of a haughty cluelessness by the chairman.

The New York Times's Pulitzer Prize–winning columnist Dave Anderson had long enjoyed a friendly working relationship with Johnson, including private chats in the chairman's office during Masters week. In a September 1 column, Anderson parted ways with Hootie. It was akin to another Johnson, Lyndon Baines, losing Cronkite on Vietnam. Under the headline "Augusta Compounds Its Mistake," Anderson wrote, "Slowly, stubbornly, Augusta National is evolving into a little green planet revolving around itself. It's a fight Johnson can't win. The more punches he throws and the more he resists having a female member, the more stubborn he, the Masters and Augusta National appear."

On the front page of sports in *The Dallas Morning News*, Kevin Blackstone wrote, "All NCWO boss Martha Burk did was pen a private letter to Johnson a few months ago seeking a dialogue on her group's concern about Augusta's membership. Johnson responded by spitting at Burk's feet."

Still, the hard-liners at Augusta National were as strident as the club's critics. Asked if, on second thought, Johnson's approach should have been less confrontational, green jacket Hugh McColl barks, "Augusta National speaks with only one voice, that of the chairman's. But the answer to your question is HELL NO!"

THE ONLY PEOPLE HAPPIER than newspaper columnists about Johnson's decision were the Masters' sponsors, who were now off the hook. At Coca-Cola, the upper management had been growing increasingly uneasy, and the executive who agreed to speak for this book intimates that the company was on the verge of withdrawing its sponsorship. Johnson's announcement, then, was akin to a man who quit before he could be fired. When the announcement came, "The overriding feeling here [at Coke] was relief," says the source. "We had been put in a no-win situation, so it was much easier to have Hootie make the decision for us."

With Citigroup and IBM also out of the picture, all eyes were now on CBS. The Tiffany Network was the only public company still attached to the 2003 Masters, and as such Johnson had made CBS an easy target. The day after the chairman relieved the sponsors of their burden, Burk announced that she would be contacting CBS to have "a conversation" about dropping its telecast of the Masters. Burk was so busy with the ensuing media attention that she didn't get the letter out until September 18. It was addressed to the president of CBS Sports, Sean McManus. Burk's rhetoric had grown more forceful in the six weeks since she had approached the Masters' sponsors. "We are writing to request that CBS Sports suspend broadcasting the Masters Golf Tournament in 2003 if the Augusta National Golf Club continues to discriminate against women by excluding them from membership. The tournament is an event that is produced by and held at a facility owned by a for-profit corporation that is flaunting its practice of sex discrimination. In the year 2002, when women occupy prominent positions in every walk of life, it is astonishing that CBS would even consider such a broadcast.

"Press reports indicate that not only will CBS fail to realize a profit on a broadcast without sponsors, but the network will actually lose money. This makes CBS an active underwriter of an organization that discriminates against half of its viewers.

"Both Viacom and CBS have corporate policies against discrimination and in support of fairness and diversity. We know that the viewing public, the stockholders of Viacom, and consumers of other products and services owned or controlled by Viacom would applaud a decision by CBS not to showcase an organization that has become emblematic of discrimination against women."

Two months in the public eye had made Burk not only more emboldened, but more sophisticated, too. Instead of just leaking the text of her letter, the next day she sent around a full-blown press release, tacking on the gratuitous quote, "The broadcast would be a two-day commercial for the good-old-boy way of life."

At CBS, Burk's demand was met with a shrug. The network had been at the beck and call of the lords of Augusta for nearly half a century, and there was never any doubt that the telecast would come off as scheduled. One of the network's top on-air golf talents agreed to speak for this book, but in a sharp reversal of form for a TV announcer, he didn't want any publicity, for fear of running afoul with the network suits. "There was not the hand-wringing and internal debate that you might imagine. There wasn't a lot of anguish. We felt all along that the Masters is one of the world's great sporting events, and, if you will, news events, and we have an obligation to report what happens. Golf fans across the world should not be penalized because of the misguided crusade of one Washington lobbyist."

McManus's dismissive reply was just a formality. On September 19, he wrote, "I very much appreciate you sharing your position on CBS's broadcasting of the Masters Tournament. However, as a sports television programmer serving millions of men and women who eagerly anticipate and watch the Network's Masters broadcast each year, CBS will cover the Masters as it has done for the past 46 years. To not do so would be a disservice to the fans of this Major Championship. Please do not hesitate to stay in touch with our organization on issues that you find of importance."

The back and forth with CBS, and the giddy prospect of four days of the Masters uninterrupted by commercials, just added more mojo to a story that was getting juicier by the day. The only voice that had not yet been heard in what was becoming a great national debate was that of the cloistered Augusta National member. That was about to change, as the club had now been set up for a kind of public examination that would have been unthinkable only a couple of months earlier.

FIVE

Members

IN THE FALL OF 2002 there was an odd feeling in the air—it wasn't much fun to be an Augusta National member. The green jacket, for so long the most lusted-after symbol of success in the golf and business worlds, had suddenly become a black shawl, wrapping its wearer in unprecedented grief and embarrassment. Martha Burk's constant scoldings were bad enough, but a torrent of negative publicity surrounding the membership began in early September. It all started with Jack Welch, the iconic, recently retired CEO of General Electric, whose passion for golf had been exhaustively documented, as had his ties to Augusta National. (In his autobiography, which came out in early 2001, Welch included a photo of himself and some buddies in Amen Corner.)

Before the myriad fin de siecle scandals had besmirched America's business elite, Welch, sixty-eight, was the most celebrated of the 1990s relics, the superstar CEO. He was a media-friendly, hard-charging, ball-busting rainmaker who inspired hagiographies such as *Jack Welch and the GE Way: Management Insights and Leadership Secrets from the Legendary CEO*. But the legendary CEO began generating titillating headlines in March 2002, when word leaked out that he had left his wife for Suzy Wetlaufer, forty-four, a top editor at the *Harvard Business Review*. They had become involved when Wetlaufer interviewed Welch for the nation's most influential business management publication in late 2001. Apparently blinded by passion, Wetlaufer did not see the massive ethical conflict in publishing the interview until Welch's abandoned wife, Jane, phoned to question her impartiality, among other things. Wetlaufer then had the interview killed, which is how the affair became public. In the ensuing uproar a handful of *HBR* staffers quit in protest, Wetlaufer left the magazine, Welch and his wife separated, incredulity ripped through both the journalism and business worlds, and the tabloids were atwitter for months. (Sample headline from the *New York Post*: "$450M Jack Pot—GE Tycoon's Scorned Wife Seeks Half His Fortune.")

The story took another turn on September 5, 2002—less than a week after Hootie Johnson dropped the Masters' corporate sponsors—when Jane Welch filed divorce papers that included her estranged husband's lavish retirement package from GE, the details of which were largely unknown to the company's shareholders. There were plenty of big-ticket items like unlimited use of the company's Boeing 737, and helicopter and limousine service, but it was the little things that created such a stir. Welch's former employer was footing the bill not only for a palatial New York City apartment within the Trump International Hotel and Tower on Central Park West, but also his dry cleaning, fresh flowers, and newspapers. Welch had always held himself up as a paragon of corporate virtue, and the revelation that he was feeding at the trough like so many other disgraced CEOs filled the business press with indignant railing.

What landed Welch on the sports page was the news that GE was also paying for his membership at Augusta National. Burk immediately began pounding the point that thousands of hoodwinked female employees and investors of GE were paying for a membership to an all-male club. Further, she announced that she would be sending around a letter to other Augusta National members who served as CEOs of publicly traded companies. "We want to know how many of them are in the Jack Welch category where shareholders are paying for the membership," she said. (Welch eventually announced that he would pay his own way at Augusta National, and for most of the other perks, too.)

The Welch affair was still gurgling when the club got more unwelcome publicity. *Sports Illustrated*, in the Golf Plus section of the September 16 issue, broke the news that among the new members for the fall of 2002 was the richest man in the world, Bill Gates, and the football coach at Hootie Johnson's alma mater, South Carolina's Lou Holtz. (Johnson and Holtz are golf buddies who even share the same barber.) Gates's long-awaited invitation only turned up the heat on Burk's campaign to link corporate dollars to Augusta National, but it was Holtz's membership that created more buzz. The timing of the news couldn't have been worse. Holtz was under fire for his underachieving team, which was coming off a sloppy loss to the hated Georgia Bulldogs, dropping the Cocks' record below .500 for the first time since 1999. Worse still, a scandal was beginning to brew involving alleged NCAA violations in loaning a football player a $62,000 SUV. (No penalties have been announced by the NAACP.)

Burk instantly pounced on Holtz, pointing out that the state of South Carolina was paying his salary, which meant, by her logic, that taxpayers were indirectly subsidizing his membership. "It is absolutely the wrong kind of symbolism for an individual who represents a public university in a major way to belong to a club that discriminates against women," Burk said.

The headlines generated by Holtz and Welch were anathema to the Augusta National way. As it says in the annual report to members, "The club wants no publicity except with respect to the Masters Tournament" and "it is expected that [members] shall actively discourage any form of publicity pertaining to the Club." Holtz was still fending off critics—"I'm not going to talk about Augusta," he told reporters, "but I don't want to hear 'no women,' because my wife has played there"—when another lightning bolt hit. On September 13, Hootie Johnson had a coronary artery bypass, an aortic aneurism repaired, and an aortic valve replaced. Augusta National reverted to form, refusing to release any details, even the names of the doctors involved or the site of the surgery. The only public statement came from club spokesman Glenn Greenspan: "He's fine and resting comfortably. A full recovery is expected."

Burk took the high road, expressing sympathy for Johnson and his family, but the irresistible joke was that Martha had given Hootie heart trouble. Others within the club were no doubt feeling a few chest pains, too. Their embattled leader was wounded, and two high-profile members were covered in scandal. But misery loves company, and Johnson, Welch, and Holtz were about to be joined in the spotlight by three hundred or so friends.

ON SEPTEMBER 17, Michael McCarthy was hunched over a fax machine at the *USA Today* offices in midtown Manhattan, awaiting a special delivery from the golf journalism gods. McCarthy is a husky fellow with longish hair that is slicked back on the sides. He looks like the paper's resident rock-n-roll writer, but since 1999 he has actually been a mainstay of the Money section. With Johnson having kissed away millions of corporate dollars, and with Burk turning the screws on some of the country's highest-profile business leaders, the *USA Today* brass had decided in early September to bring in a reporter who could make sense of the dollars involved. A Deep Throat had warned McCarthy to guard the fax machine and to be on the lookout for what was being billed as a comprehensive list of the Augusta National membership. "There was a great sense of anticipation, just wondering if this was the real thing," McCarthy recalls. "Everybody loves a mystery, and this was one of the last great mysteries. It had been rumored, it had been written about, but nobody had ever gotten their hands on the actual list."

Eventually the fax machine belched out four pages, unadorned by an Augusta National logo or any other distinguishing mark. The names were arranged alphabetically by state, Alabama to Wyoming, followed by a smattering of international members, who were organized by country. Within each state or country the names were listed alphabetically, and a few cities of interest were broken out on their own—Augusta, Atlanta, New York City, and Washington, D.C. The only information given was a formal name and a corresponding city, and nothing else. The first entry on this list read simply: "Crawford T. Johnson III, Birmingham." Because of the dearth of identifying details, some famous names were not immediately recognizable. For instance, the notorious Mr. Welch, whose autobiography was entitled *Jack*, and who owns homes in multiple glamorous locales, was listed as John F. Welch, and his place of origin was rather arbitrarily given as Fairfield, Connecticut.

With his business background, McCarthy was immediately able to size up the list. "It was a who's who of the who's who, a roll call of the Fortune 500. These were the corporate leaders of today and ten to fifteen years ago." As for the origin of the fax, McCarthy will say only that it came from "a confidential source." Even with the list in his hands he was not positive of its authenticity. "It looked legit," McCarthy says. "It felt right. Now the challenge was to confirm the names."

He immediately faxed the list to USA Today's headquarters in McLean, Virginia. Julie Ward, deputy managing editor of sports, had been overseeing the paper's coverage of Augusta National, and she had been tipped off by McCarthy to expect the fax. Ward is a creature of the sports department, where she has spent two decades, including a brief stint in the mid-eighties as USA Today's golf editor. She does not have McCarthy's business background. As she pulled the pages out of the fax machine, she says, "My first thought was, Who are these people?" Her next thought: "Who else has the list?"

EARLY ON THE AFTERNOON of September 17, David Markiewicz arrived at the main offices of The Atlanta Journal-Constitution. Like McCarthy, he was traveling on two passports, a mainstay of the business page who dabbled in sports. Upon arriving at work, Markiewicz was handed a fax. He had no clue it was coming. After a cursory inspection of the four pages, Markiewicz knew immediately what it was. "It had the ring of truth," he says. But that was all it had. The list was identical to the one USA Today had received, and both faxes had come through without revealing the name or number of the sender.

Markiewicz immediately took the fax to business editor Mark Braykovic, who was about to step into a meeting with other top editors. By the time that meeting had adjourned, "the interest in the list had spread like wildfire," says Markiewicz. "Our feeling was that this could be a big story, and that we had to move on it. There were obviously questions about the authenticity that had to be checked out. There was also the competitive aspect. We didn't know who else had the list."

Turns out Martha Burk had one, too, and that she had been sitting on it since late August or early September. (She says she doesn't recall the exact date of arrival.) "I wasn't expecting it," Burk says. "It just showed up one day." The list was organized in the same manner as the other two, but it may have come from a different source, or perhaps the sender had taken less care to cover his or her tracks. Burk's fax, intriguingly, had a banner at the top of the page, listing a number with a 407 area code and an unusual company name. Woodward in heels she ain't: Burk tried to track the origin of the fax, but the business name on the banner was a dead end, leading to a company in Australia, and even armed with the Florida phone number she could not make headway into the sender's identity. (Burk says now that she can't remember either the number or the company name.) "I had no idea who sent it, and to this day I still don't," she says.

No one else received a roll call of the membership. The race was on in the newsrooms of *USA Today* and *The Atlanta Journal-Constitution*. Neither newspaper knew that the other had the list—"They did? Wow, I didn't know that," McCarthy says months later—but both suspected that the names would soon leak out. The papers immediately mobilized massive resources in an effort to confirm the names. *The Atlanta Journal-Constitution* eventually deployed an army of twenty reporters; *USA Today* put twenty-three pairs of boots on the ground.

Both papers were grappling with the same basic questions. For starters, how current was the list? It was easy enough to carbon-date, using two golf icons whose invitations to Augusta National had come with unusual publicity. Arnold Palmer had become a member in 1999. He was on the list. Jack Nicklaus had been extended membership in 2001. He was not on the list. Therefore the roll call was from either 1999 or 2000.

There were also ethical concerns, at least in one newsroom. Says an *Atlanta Journal-Constitution* writer, "Our people were always very worried about the legality of just printing the list wholesale. Just because someone faxed it to us, did we have the right to print it? What if it had been stolen?"

USA Today took a more liberal point of view. "Our feeling was that the controversy was so far advanced that any person on the list had to be considered a public figure," says Ward. *USA Today*'s lawyers signed off on the reasoning.

Both papers immediately began trying to contact the men on the list, or a family member or representative. Old news accounts, corporate résumés, and published lists of the various Masters committees were also used for ID purposes. It was slow going, to say the least. "It wasn't like we could call up Augusta National for confirmation," says Markiewicz. "It's already a secretive place, and all the publicity had only made the members more wary of reporters." After a day of fact-checking, the *Atlanta Journal-Constitution* brass decided it would be impossible to nail down every member. They began to focus on confirming a critical mass of bold-faced names.

On September 20, *The Atlanta Journal-Constitution* struck first, rushing into print its partial list of sixty-eight names. On page A1, under the headline "Who's Who at Augusta National," Markiewicz and Glenn Sheeley cowrote an accompanying story about the membership, making no allusion to the secretive fax that had tipped them off. Some names in the piece were already familiar to those who had been following the membership controversy: Holtz, Welch, Sam Nunn, Lloyd Ward, Jack Nicklaus, Arnold Palmer, Warren Buffet. At the end of the story the paper ran a compendium of names, broken into categories of emphasis: Atlanta, Augusta, Other Georgians, Business, Sports, Politics. Among the most interesting names: former secretary of defense Melvin Laird; former secretary of state George Shultz; former secretary of the treasury Nicholas Brady; Armory Houghton Jr., a sitting congressman from New York; Roger Penske, the race car magnate; John Harris, the 1993 U.S. Amateur champion; Nelson Doubleday, the former owner of the Mets; Billy Payne, the driving force behind the 1996 Atlanta Olympics; Dessey L. Kuhlke, an Augusta banker whose brother, W. B., was on the Augusta city commission; Peter Coors, of the eponymous beer maker; and Ken Chenault, the chairman and CEO of American Express.

In its story *The Atlanta Journal-Constitution* made the point that men running public companies would be vulnerable to Burk's broadsides. That went double for Representative Houghton, the only elected official on the list. He had been invited to join the club not because of his position on welfare reform but rather because his family founded, and he is a former CEO of, Corning, Inc. (His brother, James, the current chairman and CEO, is also a member.) Representative Houghton refused to speak to *The Atlanta Journal-Constitution*, but his spokesman said that the congressman was "ultimately . . . sure that Augusta will have women members" and that Houghton "has been in touch with the leadership at Augusta, and he's working with the organization."

Meanwhile, a spokesman for Coors Brewing Company made the point that Peter Coors's membership at Augusta National was not a company issue. "It's entirely personal, entirely private. There's no corporate relationship whatsoever with the golf club. Peter's position on diversity is reflected in the practices and policies of Coors Brewing Co., and those policies and practices have been widely applauded. Why would you drag our products into this controversy?"

Though they had been scooped, sort of, the folks at *USA Today* were not overly distraught to see *The Atlanta Journal-Constitution*'s story. "They obviously wanted to do something fast, and we wanted to do something comprehensive," says Julie Ward. The *Journal-Constitution*'s partial list guaranteed that *USA Today* would go whole hog, and the paper stepped up its efforts to reach the members for confirmation. "We tried hard to contact everybody," says McCarthy. "We didn't get 100 percent, but I think we got pretty close." Not so, says Ward: "Most of them would not comment. In the end the list was the primary source."

USA Today did comb through a database of obituaries in search of deceased members who were on the list, a legitimate concern given Augusta National's elderly membership. "We were very cognizant of making sure there would be no dead people on our list," says Ward. Good thinking. Wherever possible, the paper also added the ages of the members and their corporate affiliations.

On September 27, *USA Today* dropped its story on the front page of sports, under the headline "Privacy Becomes Public at Augusta." The story, written by McCarthy and Eric Brady, bragged, "USA Today has obtained a copy of the long-secret membership rolls for the club that hosts the Masters, one of golf's four major championships. The names on that list tell the tale of an old boys club, emphasis on old: The average age is 72. More than a third are retired. And they come mainly from the country's old-line industries: banking and finance, oil and gas, manufacturing and distributing." Nine members were on the Fortune 400.

The paper delicately acknowledged the difficulties in fact-checking, writing, "*USA Today* attempted to contact each man on the list. Of the ones reached, almost every one toed the club line, which is this: Club chairman William 'Hootie' Johnson speaks for the club." *USA Today* did score a coup, getting Representative Houghton to speak on record, perhaps because, as the paper noted, he was up for reelection in less than two months. "You can't have an issue like this hit the papers and be an ostrich," Houghton said. "I don't know what [Hootie] is thinking. I'm sure he's considered women members. It's probably an issue of timing."

The accompanying list of 295 members was garnished with a short introduction: "The Augusta National Golf Club membership list obtained by USA Today covers a time frame within the last two years. The membership list is fluid and changes as members resign, die or leave the club. USA Today did not include those identified as former or deceased members."

Examining the list brought the thrill of leafing through a forbidden diary. Beyond the fascination of seeing golf's best-kept secret laid bare, there were a couple of interesting tidbits within the agate. While The Atlanta Journal-Constitution had added Jack Nicklaus to its roll call, even though he wasn't part of the faxed membership list, USA Today overlooked the six-time Masters champ. This oversight may account for the two-year window the paper cited, when in fact its list could have been three years old. There was also an interesting sidelight involving member Howard Blauvelt, a retired oil man from Virginia. Blauvelt's son, Harry, is a longtime member of USA Today's sports department, and within the paper the old man's membership is well known. Yet for its compendium USA Today listed Howard Blauvelt's age as "N/A." Asked why she didn't just lean into the next cubicle and ask Harry how old his dad was, Ward offers one careful sentence: "Harry was not involved in any way on the membership project."

These niggling details didn't reduce the magnitude of USA Today's scoop. When it came time for the Associated Press sports editors to hand out their 2002 award, USA Today's work on exposing Augusta National's membership took the coveted first prize for news among papers with a circulation over 250,000. "We were pretty fried about that," says Atlanta Journal-Constitution golf writer Glenn Sheeley, "because that was sloppy journalism, and it was reckless. They said, 'Well, we tried to confirm the names on the list.' Hey, thanks for trying!"

*   *   *

IT IS IMPOSSIBLE to overstate how violated Augusta National's closeted membership felt after being outed in such spectacular fashion. "That's the most unfortunate thing that's happened in all of this," says Wheelock Whitney. "The club has always valued its privacy, and for all of us to be exposed so publicly was very unfortunate."

With all the buzz surrounding the publishing of the list, editors everywhere were screaming at their reporters to get a comment from an Augusta National member. Locating these most private of men was as easy as 411, as a surprisingly high number of their home telephone numbers were in the phone book, or available through online databases.

A call to Boone Knox, one of the most prominent Georgia members, was answered by his wife, Georgeann. "You might not hear back from him," she said, the edge in her voice a stark contrast to the peachy drawl that came with it. "We're not rude people, but ever since the membership became public, we have been overwhelmed. The phone has not stopped ringing." It rang again a couple of days later, and this time Boone answered. "I'd like to help you, but we need to reduce the hype," he said. "The less said the better."

Another call, to Bev Dolan in Florida, was even less successful. Dolan grew up in Augusta, with a kid named Hootie Johnson. Ring, ring: "Mr. Dolan, I do not want to talk to you about club policies but rather your boyhood friend, Hoot—"

"I have no comment about Augusta National," Dolan said. "The club speaks with one voice."

"I understand, sir. I only want to ask you about what Hootie was li—"

Dolan interrupted by growling, "What part of 'no' don't you understand, hoss?" before slamming down the phone.

After making a similar appeal to Ed Douglass, another member who grew up with Hootie, Douglass was searching for the right evasive words when a feminine voice piped up in the background, urging, "Just hang up on him! Just hang up!" Which he did, dutifully.

ON SEPTEMBER 28, a day after the membership list appeared in *USA Today*, Martha Burk sent out a new batch of letters, asking the recipients for statements that reconciled their corporate or public positions on workplace diversity with Augusta National's practice of excluding women. This time her pen pals were Representative Houghton, Senator Nunn, Lloyd Ward, Sandy Weill, Motorola CEO Christopher Galvin, and J. P. Morgan Chase CEO William Harrison. Burk said that Galvin and Harrison were chosen because their companies were scheduled to be honored the following month by the Business Women's Network at the Women and Diversity Leadership Summit in Washington. In her letters to them she wrote that the "public is demanding corporate accountability that goes beyond mere financial performance." In her missive to Ward, Burk wrote that his membership at Augusta "sends a message to the public" that the USOC's "statements and policies on nondiscrimination are not taken seriously by the leadership, and indeed give the impression that the organization approves of Augusta's exclusion of women."

The publication of the complete membership list opened another flank in Burk's battle to convince the public that, she says, "This is not about golf—it's about keeping women out of the halls of power. You don't get invited to join Augusta because you're a good golfer, and I hear most of those guys aren't very good at all. You get invited because you are a leader in the business world. Keeping women out of the club is just another manifestation of the glass ceiling."

Burk was never more mercilessly on message than in pounding this point, and there is some interesting anecdotal evidence to support her case. Way back in 1994, *Fortune* wrote an article entitled "Augusta: The Course CEOs Love Best." In Welch's autobiography, Augusta National has a cameo in an anecdote that makes explicit this nexis of golf and big business. "Golf even got me a GE board member," Welch writes in *Jack: Straight from the Gut*. "About three years ago, *Golf Digest* put out a list of CEO golfers and ranked Scott McNealy of Sun Microsystems at No. 1. Somehow, I was right behind him. Scott sent me a challenge: 'If I'm going to be No. 1, I want to be sure I'm No. 1. Jack, you name the place—anytime, anywhere, *mano a mano*, and we'll settle it once and for all.'

"I called him the moment I saw the message. We set a date, and Scott was generous enough to come to Nantucket that summer for a 36-hole match, which I won. Within two weeks, Scott sent me a trophy inscribed with the words 'Welch Cup.' I beat him again at Augusta the following year over 36 holes to keep the trophy." With an admiration and respect forged on the battlefield, Welch asked McNealy to join his board.

With Augusta National's membership now available for inspection, it was easy to connect the dots on the high-powered business opportunities shared among members. Hootie Johnson and Joe T. Ford were on the board of directors of the Stephens Group, the investment house founded by the chairman emeritus, Jackson Stephens, while Stephens's son Warren is on the board at Alltel, where Ford recently retired as CEO. Weill is on the board at AT&T, where Ray Robinson is president of the Southern Region. Sam Nunn and Roger Penske are on the board at GE, where Jeffrey Immelt has succeeded Welch as CEO. Lloyd Ward is on the board at J. P. Morgan Chase, where William B. Harrison is CEO. George Schultz is on the board of the Bechtel Group, the international construction conglomerate that boasts two eponymous members: Riley Bechtel, the current chairman and CEO, and Stephen Bechtel Jr., the former president of the company. There are numerous other examples. Do all of these men, with their strong business credentials, deserve the seats they've been given on the various boards? Absolutely. Does being a member of Augusta National make it easier to get such a plum position? Without a doubt.

BURK WAS NOT the only source of pressure on the club. On September 29, a day after her letters were sent, *The New York Times* ran one of its meatiest pieces to date on the membership controversy, nearly two thousand words beginning on the front page of Sports. Under the headline "Some at Augusta Quietly Seeking Change," the *Times* reported that interviews with "about a dozen members" had revealed fissures within the club, and that "several members said they intended to seek a face-saving middle ground, one that might mean welcoming one or two women as members either before or shortly after the Masters next April." The story went on to quote the members, anonymously, of course: " 'We ought to be left to make our own policy,' one member said, 'but there is a line painted in the sand now.' When asked if Johnson should have been less combative in his response to Burk, the member said: 'It didn't work that way, and the world is poorer for it.' "

According to Tom Wyman Jr., one of the key sources for the story was his father, a retired Bostonian who had held top positions at Nestlé, Polaroid, Pillsbury, and CBS. (Tom Wyman was the chairman and CEO at CBS from 1980 to 1986.) Even within the conservative corporate culture, the elder Wyman had been a progressive. While at Polaroid he worked to create opportunities for blacks at the company outpost in South Africa. Wyman was also attuned to the thorny issues surrounding all-male private clubs: In the mid-1970s he resigned in protest from New York City's Harvard Club over its refusal to admit women. (He rejoined years later when women were welcomed.)

Wyman's worldview had been passed on to his three sons, and during a family trip to Augusta National in February 2002, the four Wymans had a long heart-to-heart about their ideological problems with the club. Says Tom Jr., "We all sat by the fireplace in the men's bar, underneath a group photo of the membership. You've never seen so much homogeneity in your life. It bothered my dad, and us, that the club was so hostile to so many different segments of society."

In their minds that included women, and this, too, was discussed. "It is shocking when you're there—the lockerroom, the grillroom, the driving range, there's just one star after another of the business world," says Tom Jr. "It is where the business elite congregate. Talk about an example of where the glass ceiling is still at work in this country."

By the end of the trip, the boys did the unthinkable: They told their dad that this would be their last family get-together at Augusta National, barring a seismic shift in its landscape. "As much as we loved playing the golf course," says Tom Jr., "we really weren't comfortable there, and we didn't want to come back."

All of this was top of mind for Tom Wyman as Hootie thundered into battle with Burk. Says another son, Michael, "Dad disagreed with the policy, but he was irate about how Hootie handled the issue. I mean, he was livid. He was embarrassed to be associated with the situation."

In late August, Wyman had written a letter to Johnson asking him to rethink his hard-line stance. "Hootie's response was so snotty," says Tom Jr. "Instead of calling my dad to discuss the matter, or responding in a civil, genteel matter, he wrote a curt letter and attached like fifty letters from other members, all of them saying, basically, Give 'em hell Hootie."

The *Times*'s first story about the dissension among the members, in which Wyman had anonymously aired his long-festering grievances, was widely picked up and expounded on by other media outlets. Given the overheated climate, it seemed only a matter of time until a member publicly broke ranks. On October 4, Augusta National suffered its most high-profile betrayal since Lloyd Ward had popped off in *USA Today* six months earlier: Sandy Weill, the billionaire financier who built Citigroup, ordered his director of public relations, Leah Johnson, to send a conciliatory letter to Burk. "He has expressed his views to the Augusta National Golf Club and will continue to engage in what he hopes will be a constructive dialogue on this issue, toward an objective that he believes we share with your organization," Johnson wrote.

It was an important bellwether, regardless of the slipperiness of the language. (The *Augusta Chronicle* played the news on A1.) Why Weill? A cynic would point out that his company had just launched a unit called "Women and Company" specifically to target female investors, but his background offers more context. Weill was born to an immigrant family in Bensonhurst, the scrappy Brooklyn neighborhood that has birthed so many American dreams. In his rise through the WASPy, rarified air of the American business world, he no doubt learned a thing or two about discrimination—Weill is widely believed to be Augusta National's first Jewish member. Throughout his corporate life Weill had cultivated such an outsider's vibe that his biography was entitled *Tearing Down the Walls*. No wonder he couldn't resist Burk's come-ons.

Though Weill's public break was one of the biggest coups of Burk's nearly three-month campaign against Augusta National, she wasn't about to stop circling now, not with blood in the water. Instead of congratulating Weill, she was critical of his statement. "The most disturbing thing is he doesn't specifically address a timeline for working from within the club and whether he's prepared to resign if he's not successful," Burk said, though she did allow that, "I am encouraged by this. I think others will follow Mr. Weill's lead."

It took exactly a day for the next domino to fall, as Harold "Red" Poling, the former CEO of Ford Motor Company, told the AP, "I think there will be [a woman member] at some time in the future. I have a lot of faith in Hootie. Everyone would like to see issues such as this resolved."

Suddenly, the Augusta National membership controversy was important enough to reach the White House. One name of note on *USA Today*'s membership list was William Farish, the U.S. Ambassador to Great Britain. In the October 7 issue of *USA Today*, White House deputy press secretary Scott McClellan acknowledged that Farish was a member but said only that, "Ambassador Farish is highly respected and well qualified for the post. He's doing an outstanding job."

The growing pressure for members to publicly stake out a position on the membership controversy was best illustrated by the machinations of Lloyd Ward. During the last week of September, Ward had blown off *The New York Times*, responding to their request for comment by having a United States Olympic Committee spokesman, Mike Moran, e-mail the paper a boilerplate dismissal. Moran wrote that Ward felt "the momentum for change was best served by working within the system and not in full view of the public." A week later, in the wake of Weill's public statement (through his corporate mouthpiece), Ward couldn't fax his letter to Burk fast enough, and he obviously heeded her criticism of Weill's generalities, writing that he was "committed to breaking down barriers which exclude women from membership at Augusta in the weeks and months ahead. I am working with others who are members of Augusta National Golf Club who share the belief that the organization should include women in its membership ranks. It is my intent to aggressively work for that reform."

On October 8, a day after Ward's letter surfaced, American Express CEO Ken Chenault felt compelled to weigh in. He had not received one of Burk's feared letters, but Chenault was keenly aware that many expected a certain moral stewardship from him. When a succession plan was announced in 1999 that Chenault would take over the top spot at AmEx, he was in line to become the first African American CEO of a publicly traded Fortune 500 company. (Ward wound up nipping him by a few months, at a much lower-profile company, Maytag.) In the business community Chenault has been likened to Jackie Robinson, though he dismisses such talk. "I think it is unfortunate that we live in a society where race becomes so defining," Chenault once said. "I'm very proud of who I am, but the reason I got this job was my performance. And that's what I think should be focused on." It's a noble ideal, but clearly the sense of Other was driving the early October defections. Red Poling is a white-bread midwesterner, but the other three members who spoke out were two blacks and a Jew.

True to his personality, Chenault's statement was straightforward: "I believe women should be admitted as members of the Augusta National Golf Club. I have made my views known within the club because I believe that is the most effective and appropriate way to bring about a change in membership policy."

Four members in five days wasn't yet a tipping point, but the notion that an internal rebellion might produce a female member was gaining currency. Following Chenault's announcement, the front page of Sports in *The Atlanta Journal-Constitution* carried the headline "Women Building Augusta Support." A day later, *The Dallas Morning News* got in on the action, in an editorial that called for Representative Houghton and Ambassador Farish to resign from the club. "Public officials have the same right as any other citizen to freely associate," the paper wrote. "But they have to be more careful than most in deciding with whom to associate. They have to avoid even the appearance that they are condoning practices that are unfair or unconstitutional. If they want to be part of the Foreign Service, or serve in Congress, they should forsake any organizations that discriminate."

The public servants in golf circles were also under scrutiny, as the *USA Today* membership list had made it clear just how incestuous the relationship was between Augusta National and the United States Golf Association.

For most of 2002 the blue coats at the USGA had been basking in the good vibes that had come with their self-styled role as champions of that most downtrodden of sportsman, the muni golfer. In June the USGA had staged the first U.S. Open on a municipal course, and it was one of the most rousing tournaments in golf history. Tiger Woods dusted Phil Mickelson during a taut final round, but the real star was the course, a refurbished Bethpage Black, and the rabble that called it home. For decades Bethpage had amassed such a loyal following that plumbers and fireman and other blue-collar hackers would sleep in the parking lot to secure a tee time for the next day, and this kind of ardor could be felt in the raucous gallery that defined what became known as "the People's Open." The USGA scored more bonus points a couple of months later when it made official what had long been rumored, awarding the 2008 Open to another public facility, Torrey Pines in San Diego, while also announcing that the Open would return to Bethpage in 2009. In a posting on the USGA Web site, Fred Ridley, then chairman of the Championship Committee, tipped his hat to "the People's Open," writing, ". . . it symbolized the game's evolution into a predominantly public game," and then, with a nod to the 2008 and '09 Opens, Ridley wrote, "Public golf represents the past, present and future of the game. We're pleased that the Association has stamped itself as a defender—and promoter—of public golf through the U.S. Open site selection process."

But the notion of the USGA as a beacon of public access was muddled by the USA Today membership list, which revealed that three of the fifteen members of the USGA executive committee were members of Augusta National, including Ridley, a Tampa lawyer, and his fellow USGA vice president Walter Driver, an Atlanta lawyer. (James Reinhart, an executive in a Milwaukee investment firm, was the third.) USGA executive committee members, including the president and vice presidents, are chosen by a nominating committee that is always chaired by a past USGA president; Augusta National has rewarded a healthy number of outgoing USGA presidents with a membership (Bill Battle, 1989–90; Harry Easterly, 1976–77; Will Nicholson, 1980–81; and Buzz Taylor, 1998–99). USA Today's roll call also revealed other green jackets who had served on the USGA executive committee and were still active on various committees; this list included Howard Clark, D. Ronald Daniel, Jim Gabrielsen, Eugene Howerdd, and John Reynolds.

There have always been formal relations between the USGA and Augusta National. Top USGA officials work as rules officials at the Masters, the field of which is populated with the winners of USGA events. The Masters grants a five-year exemption to the winner of the U.S. Open, while annually inviting the winners of the Senior Open, Public

Links Championship, and Mid-Amateur Championship, as well as the two finalists from the U.S. Amateur.

In the wake of Shoal Creek, the USGA adopted the same nondiscrimination policy as the PGA Tour in determining the sites of its championships, and the USGA has followed it to the letter. But for its top leadership to hang out at all-male clubs was considered hypocritical long before Martha Burk made the scene. In 2000 the USGA's executive director, David Fay, sent ripples through the golf community by resigning in protest from Pine Valley. "As a hired hand of the USGA, which seeks to be inclusive, I thought it sent out a mixed message for me to belong to a U.S. club that admits only men," Fay says. Predictably, he showed little sympathy for Augusta National when the membership controversy broke. "They are both a club and a major golf organization," Fay says. "I defend the right of free association, but I think that right is altered if you have a very public and very profitable event once a year."

It didn't take long for Martha Burk to point out the contradiction between the USGA's public policies and private practices. "I think they have been strangely silent, given their own standards," Burk said. "As a ruling body of golf, I think they have a responsibility to speak out. They are ducking the issue in much the same way the PGA Tour is."

Eventually, USGA president Reed Mackenzie was forced to articulate a position, which turned out to be that the USGA did not have a position at all. "Historically, we do not comment on membership policies of clubs like Augusta National," Mackenzie said. "Augusta National has been a long friend of golf and the USGA. Beyond that, they have never asked us for advice, and we have never offered advice."

Mackenzie, a personal injury lawyer from Chaska, Minnesota, took some heat for his nonstatement. His presumed successor, the green-jacketed Ridley, was an even easier target. Ridley has had a love affair with Augusta National ever since he played in the 1976 Masters. It is a tradition to pair the U.S. Amateur titleholder with the reigning Masters champ in the first round, which is how Ridley earned a tee time with a fella by the name of Nicklaus. Ridley, a Florida undergrad at the time, shot a 77 in the presence of the Golden Bear, though he is quick to point out he played sixteen of the holes in even par, his score smudged by a triple-bogey on the devilish 12th hole and double on 14th. Ridley would play in two more Masters, but his middling success on powerhouse Florida teams convinced him to give up his dreams of a pro career in favor of law school. He remained active in amateur golf, and in 1993 he was asked to join the USGA executive committee by Will Nicholson, who happens to be one of the most influential Augusta National members. "It's not a position you seek," Ridley says, speaking by phone from the offices of the law firm Foley & Lardner in Tampa, where he is a partner overseeing the real estate division. "They come to you and ask if you are interested." He could, of course, be describing Augusta National membership.

Smart and self-effacing, Ridley quickly became a standout at the USGA, and inside and outside the organization it was considered a done deal that he would secede Mackenzie as president in 2004. Of course, that was before Martha Burk began poking around following the printing of the USA Today list. Of Ridley, she said, "I don't see how a person who is openly flouting the USGA standards can be elevated to the presidency."

Ridley seemed to have already mastered the art of USGA double-speak. "If you're asking me to put on my USGA hat, so to speak, then I am going to defer to Reed Mackenzie, our spokesman on the Augusta issue," he said in the summer of 2003. "If I'm speaking as a member [of Augusta National], than I won't talk about this issue. I was asked to be a member of an organization and I agreed to its type of governance and I'm going to respect that. I'm not trying to split hairs or be cute or anything, but both organizations have made their positions clear, and I'm not comfortable speaking for either one."

THROUGHOUT THE TUMULTUOUS FALL of 2002, Ridley could take comfort, sort of, that other members were facing even greater problems because of their Augusta National affiliations.

Barely more than a week after Lloyd Ward's letter to Burk surfaced, Sports Illustrated, in its October 21 issue, reported that Ward was losing support within the United States Olympic Committee. Herb Perez, a member of the USOC executive committee, was quoted as saying, "We are believers in Title IX, in women in sport, in women leadership. I like Lloyd, but he cannot change [Augusta National] from the inside. I don't think he would join the Klan and try to change it from the inside."

USOC president Marty Mankamyer added, "Lloyd Ward's membership at Augusta is not a minor issue. I intend to have it on the [executive committee] agenda as soon as I can."

The next meeting was scheduled for November 1, and in the interim Mankamyer continued to bash Ward, whom she had supported for the CEO position in October 2001. "I would have liked to have known [about his Augusta National membership]. I certainly would have had some questions, but we simply did not know." Mankamyer intimated that she might not have been in favor of offering Ward the job had he disclosed his membership. "I can't predict what other people would have done, but . . . I have very definite ideas on what a person who represents and speaks for the USOC should be."

Ward was used to having the details of his life celebrated, not denigrated. His incredible rags-to-riches story has been told countless times, from the cover of *BusinessWeek* to the front page of *The Des Moines Register*. It never fails to inspire. He grew up in a largely segregated suburb of Detroit, the son of a Baptist preacher who worked two jobs to support five kids. Rupert Ward built by hand, out of scrap lumber, the family's twenty-by-twenty-foot house, which had no running water. From his father, Lloyd picked up the value of work, and from his mother, Sadie, he learned the importance of education. (At fifty, she earned her bachelor's degree, followed by a master's in social work.) Lloyd was the first African American captain of the Romulus High School football team, but he wasn't allowed to crown the homecoming queen and get the kiss that came with it, per tradition, because, he says, the town was not ready for such a public display of affection between a black man and white woman.

Athletically, Ward had enough heart to earn a basketball scholarship to Michigan State, despite being only five feet eleven inches. Coaches tried to steer Ward into easy course loads, but he resisted, earning a degree in mechanical engineering. In 1970 he took his first job, at Proctor & Gamble, becoming one of just eight black engineers in a department of 1,200. By 1984 he was a lead engineer, redesigning from top to bottom the Ivory soap manufacturing plant.

In December 1988, Ward jumped to Pepsi, as vice president of operations, and by 1995 he had been named executive of the year by *Black Enterprise*. The following year he was recruited to Maytag, where he became the company's first black executive, toting the titles vice president of the corporation and president of Maytag Appliances. Ward was lured by the promise of one day earning the CEO title, a lifelong ambition.

He was an immediate smash at the company, thanks to his championing of the Neptune washing machine, which cost double the price of most competitors but became a top seller because Ward crafted an eco-friendly sales strategy focusing on how much water it saved. In 1999, he was named CEO, the first black man to hold that lofty title of a publicly traded Fortune 500 company. (He nipped Chenault by a few months.) Ward preferred not to dwell on the color of his skin, allowing only that, "It's a wonderful opportunity and an awesome responsibility." But within Ward's first few months as CEO at Maytag the company issued a disastrous earnings report and the stock price fell 25 percent in a day. A scant fifteen months after his historic appointment, Ward was ousted. A Maytag statement cited a difference in "strategic outlook and direction."

During his brief tenure at Maytag, Ward got to enjoy one of the spoils of his success—his first visit to Augusta National as a member, for the Masters. Sadly, his first time playing the course was on the Monday following the tournament, when he had to dodge the hordes of media hacks, corporate schmos, and various other riffraff that ritually defile the Cathedral in the Pines the day after the tournament. To date, this is Ward's only trip to Augusta National. That a virtual stranger to his fellow green jackets would dive into the membership controversy years later is a bitter irony that has been noted around the club. How can you change from within when you remain an outsider?

At the November 1, 2002, USOC executive committee meeting, Ward's Augusta National membership was hotly debated, but in the end the executive committee rallied around its embattled CEO, releasing a terse statement following the meeting: "In light of Lloyd's principled position on the issue, and his commitment to the inclusion of women, the executive committee has commended him and expressed strong support."

After the meeting, an emotional Ward spoke publicly about Augusta

National for the first time in more than six months. "If you take a look at Augusta not too long ago, it excluded people of color, and I am part of a small, select group of individuals that have broken the color barrier," he said. "My life has been about a lot of firsts, not because I'm special, but because the world has limits and boundaries and dimensions that exclude certain people and include others. So I've been first in a lot of things and I've always used the idea of being first to try to open the door wider for those who might follow me."

Then, in the next breath, he confirmed what many had suspected all along, that the notion of change from within was just a smoke screen. "I can't change Augusta—Augusta has to change itself," Ward said. "But as an individual you have an opportunity to stand up for what you believe in, and that's what I have done. That's what I have done my whole life and that's what I am doing now."

Asked why he hadn't disclosed his membership while interviewing with the USOC, Ward said, "I had no perspective on why that would be important. It just was not an issue."

Martha Burk picked up on this comment when asked about Ward. "If we've succeeded in anything, we've succeeded in raising the consciousness of business executives about sex discrimination," she said. "I imagine it just wasn't on [Ward's] radar screen the way racial discrimination was. If he were asked to join the club today, knowing that it excluded women, he probably would not do it."

No doubt. Ward had been granted a momentary reprieve, but the woes that had come with his green jacket were far from over.

ANOTHER MEMBER who couldn't escape the vortex of the Augusta National membership controversy was Tiger Woods. (Every winner of the Masters is granted an honorary membership that lasts until the following year's tournament.) Since his first, hotly debated comments at the British Open, Woods had been grilled at every turn. He had become such an easy target that eventually even Martha Burk began to feel sorry for him, and she backed off on her criticism, saying, "Tiger Woods cannot single-handedly change the policies at Augusta. We do not believe that Tiger Woods should be the only golfer speaking out in favor of fairness. We call on others, including those on the PGA Tour and the Senior Tour, to follow Tiger's lead and lend their voices to this call for an end to the sex discrimination." On October 16, at a ho-hum pretournament press conference for the PGA Tour's Disney Classic, Woods was put on the spot again.

Question: "Can you believe the shelf life of Augusta?"

Woods: "The Augusta thing is unique because something a little different transpires all the time. Whether it's a company supporting Ms. Burk, or other members supporting Hootie, something's always coming out. I think that's what perpetuates the argument going both ways."

"There are those that feel that Tiger is obligated to say something about it."

"I already did. I said it a long time ago and I stick by what I said. Everybody has a right to do what they want. Is it unfair? Yes. Do I want to see a female member? Yes. But it's our right to have any club set up the way we want to."

"The Augusta issue, is that a no-win situation for you?"

"Hootie is right and Martha is right. That's the problem. They are both right but are going about it the wrong way. If they both sat down and talked about it, it would be resolved a lot better than what is going on right now."

"Rather than making a public spectacle out of it?"

"There's no substitute in sitting down and having a face-to-face long conversation about it. There's no substitute for looking someone in the eye."

Woods's most expansive comments to date were used as a jumping-off point for an A1 story in *The New York Times* four days later under the headline "Debate on Women at Augusta Catches Woods Off Balance." In an exclusive interview with the paper, Woods voiced his mounting exasperation at the Augusta-related criticism that was now going on three months and counting. "I didn't see it coming to this degree," he said. "Yes, I've always wanted to impact lives in a positive way. But I like to pick my own causes, and not be forced into having to do something."

Woods also rejected the suggestion that he steers clear of political controversy for fear it will harm his corporate interests or affect his income from endorsements. "There's no validity to that at all," he said. "I'll say what I believe, but I'll choose when. I have the feeling that sometimes I can't say anything, because I'm going to get criticized. And what's unfair about that is, people always ask my opinion and then sometimes when I give it to them, they don't respect what I have to say. If that's the case, then don't ask."

ON DECEMBER 30, 2002, Lloyd Ward's troubles at the USOC intensified when the *Los Angeles Times* broke the news that he was facing an internal investigation for potential ethical violations. The paper reported that Ward was alleged to have "directed USOC staff to help his brother's company in its bid to procure a potentially lucrative deal to provide power generators" for the 2003 Pan American Games, which are funded by the USOC.

In the ensuing uproar, an executive committee meeting was scheduled for January 13, with Ward's conduct the sole item on the agenda. As always, the embattled CEO's controversial ties to Augusta National were part of the backstory. As the *L.A. Times* reported in one of its numerous follow-up pieces to its original scoop, "One of the central issues confronting Ward now is how much political capital he has expended over the Augusta issue."

At the January 13 meeting, the USOC's executive committee concluded that its CEO had made an "error in judgment," in the words of vice president Bill Stapleton, but Ward escaped formal censure, a controversial decision that intensified the internal strife. Within days, the USOC's ethics compliance officer and a member of the ethics oversight committee quit in protest, to much fanfare. The feuding throughout the organization had grown so unseemly, and so embarrassingly public, that Ward and the rest of the USOC leadership were called into the principal's office, in this case the Senate Commerce Committee, which oversees the USOC.

Ward appeared on Capitol Hill on January 28, absorbing brutal criticism from a host of outraged senators. Ben Nighthorse Campbell (R-Colorado) scolded Ward for creating an "Olympic-sized food fight." He saved some of his most stinging criticism for Ward's Augusta National membership. "I don't know what kind of example you're setting," said

Campbell, who is of Native American descent. "A lot of us believe that any organization that discriminates doesn't need me to be a part of it. I wouldn't belong to a place like that for a minute." He called for Ward to immediately resign from the club.

"While your sensibility and others' might be to show your displeasure by resigning, that is not my sensibility," Ward shot back. "My sensibility is to take the responsibility to try to open the door wider for those that would follow."

Of course, this was the same guy who two months earlier had declared that he couldn't change Augusta National. Clearly the majority of his fellow members had been dismissive all along of his calls for a woman member, and back on Capitol Hill, Senator Campbell tweaked Ward for lack of fight in trying to change Augusta National. "I would have liked to have seen some cages rattled and doors kicked in," he said.

By the end of the bruising hearing it was clear that Ward would have to resign either from Augusta National or the USOC, two organizations that had become mutually exclusive.

THE AUGUSTA NATIONAL MEMBERSHIP'S spate of scandalous news coverage included one other bit of business, courtesy of Sandy Weill. For most of his public life, he had been known as, in the words of *The New Yorker,* "the most successful financier of his generation." On November 14, 2002, he gained everlasting fame of a different sort, starring in yet another A1 story in *The New York Times,* this with the headline "Wall St. and the Nursery School: A New York Story." The piece broke the news of a Manhattan high society scandal that even Woody Allen couldn't have dreamed up: Weill was under investigation by the New York attorney general for allegedly having asked, in 1999, a soon-to-be disgraced Wall Street buddy, Jack Grubman, to upgrade his rating of AT&T stock so Weill could gain the support of Michael Armstrong, the chairman of AT&T and a director at Citigroup, in a bloody board-room battle. (No charges were filed by the attorney general.) In exchange for the favor, Weill donated $1 million of Citigroup's money to the exclusive, $15,000 a year preschool at the 92nd Street Y, where Grubman was desperately trying to enroll his twin two-year-olds. (Surprise, surprise: After Weill put in a good word for the Grubman kids, they were accepted to the school, which has been home to the progeny of Sting, Michael J. Fox, Connie Chung, Kevin Kline, and, yes, Woody Allen.)

The details of the scandal were so delicious that the *Times* played it on a front page three days running—beginning with the A1 story, and then on valuable real estate of the Metro and Business sections. The paper's hard-charging executive editor, Howell Raines, had a pet phrase for this kind of coverage, in which the *Times* dominated stories and overwhelmed the competition: "flooding the zone." Under Raines, the newspaper of record had expanded its influence and its ability to set the agenda for other media outlets.

Within days of the Weill contretemps, the *Times* would begin flooding the zone on Augusta National, leading to sharp criticism of its excesses and larger questions about how the press was handling a story that was growing ever larger and more explosive.

SIX

The Press

IN LATE SEPTEMBER, while Hootie Johnson was at home in South Carolina recuperating from heart surgery, Augusta National entertained two important guests. They were flown in to play hardball, not golf. The two men, who visited separately, were public relations flacks auditioning for a job.

With the exception of two very public statements by the chairman, Augusta National had been stubbornly silent throughout the first contentious months of the membership controversy. The impenetrable privacy that for so long defined the club had become a liability. From the beginning, Augusta National's defenders howled that the press coverage of the membership controversy was one-sided, but that's because only one side was talking. Martha Burk estimates that from "the point of a bayonet" through the 2003 Masters, she averaged forty hours a week dealing with the press and working on Augusta-related business. "If the coverage is more favorable to us . . . it's no accident," she says. "When you make yourself accessible, it is more likely that your words will be printed."

The brutal press that followed the dropping of the Masters' sponsors on August 30, replete with personal attacks on Hootie, finally convinced

Augusta National that it had to change the rules of engagement. But the club's indecision on how to proceed was apparent in the clashing ideologies of the two spin doctors who were brought in for interviews.

One was Jim McCarthy, who ran a boutique firm in Washington, D.C., specializing in the subset of PR known as crisis management. McCarthy's personal politics are libertarian, but he was all over the map professionally. He had represented more than a dozen Native American tribes on issues ranging from gaming rights to the decriminalization of peyote for religious ceremonies. His pro bono work included publicizing the plight of Sudanese refugees. But McCarthy had also done plenty of corporate work, with an emphasis on heavy manufacturing and the biotech industry. (Convincing the public of the safety of genetically modified foods was one of his tastier projects.) McCarthy had also been on the front lines of the gender wars, helping the College Sports Council, an umbrella organization of coaches, craft an assault on Title IX. All of McCarthy's disparate causes—from championing out-of-work wrestling coaches to defending pumped-up tomatoes—are informed by a "core philosophy" of taking on clients who have run afoul of what McCarthy calls "the media/activist industrial complex," whose party members "see the world in a very specific way and try to impose their views on the society at large. I like to take on causes that other firms might avoid. My clients appreciate that I like to get in the arena, take off the gloves and throw down."

McCarthy, thirty-six, radiates the passion of a true believer, and his hyper-aggressive style has made for some hot copy. In 1999, he enflamed a touchy situation in which Kevin Gover, the head of the Bureau of Indian Affairs, was questioning the legitimacy of tribal elections among the prosperous Saginaw Chippewas of Michigan, who had retained McCarthy's services (for a reported $280,000). *The Washington Post* got ahold of a memo outlining McCarthy's plans to plant stories in the press in order to "bring increasing pressure on Assistant Secretary Gover's administration." When Gover's top aide, Rex Hackler, denounced McCarthy's "smear campaign" as "shameful and unethical," McCarthy shot back, "I say to Mr. Hackler, welcome to the Beltway." Gover, now in private practice at the Washington, D.C., law firm Steptoe & Johnson, provides a biting scouting report on McCarthy: "He's ambitious, unscrupulous, he likes the limelight, and he seems to be attracted to unsavory clients. Sounds to me like a perfect fit for Augusta."

McCarthy's competition for the Augusta National account would speak for this book only on the condition that his name, and that of his firm, remain confidential, befitting their polished, low-key profile. He is a partner for a leading New York public relations outfit that deals with some of the biggest corporations in the world, specifically on messy financial issues. Getting recommended for the Augusta National job wasn't difficult. "Many of our clients are members," he says.

The two men hailed not only from different cities, but from competing PR theories. New York firms, with their emphasis on commerce, deal in conciliation and compromise, hoping to head off hostilities and minimize damage to brands and institutions. The ethos of Washington is far more cutthroat. In the political arena, you win or you go home, and playing dirty is part of the fun. "Public relations and crisis management require different skill sets," says Eric Dezenhall, whose firm, Nichols Dezenhall, is one of the leading practitioners of the latter. "PR is about spinning pretty lies; crisis management is about telling ugly truths."

Both McCarthy and the other consultant met with two key members of Augusta National's paid staff—General Manager Jim Armstrong and Director of Communications Glenn Greenspan—and a few influential members who were standing in for the recuperating Johnson. McCarthy obviously provided the hawkish point of view, that the club had the Constitution on its side and should fight on, while his competition was flown in to be a dove, offering Augusta National a way to compromise and end the public untidiness. "They were very serious meetings," says the New Yorker. "The representatives of the club had really done their homework, and they asked a lot of good questions. They were pros—I was very impressed." His message was that adding a woman member was inevitable, and he could help the club do so on its terms. "It was a moment in history for these guys. Hootie had a chance to go down as a great figure in the game. If they wanted to go a certain route, then we could have gotten behind them in a big way. It could have been handled in an elegant and dignified manner."

McCarthy espoused a more pugnacious philosophy. "The worst thing you can do when dealing with an attack activist like Martha Burk is compromise," he says. "To survive, you have to go on the attack—investigate the activist, hold them accountable for their track record and their ideological inconsistencies. You have to take on the press that is often conspiring to give the activists a platform to espouse their views. It's like the argument of appeasement versus aggression in geo-politics—and we all know how Neville Chamberlain fared."

Needless to say, this kind of militancy appealed to the man who had introduced the bayonet into the golf lexicon, and McCarthy got the Augusta National job. Says the consultant who didn't, "It was made very clear that Hootie wanted a strategy to fight back. That wasn't us."

McCarthy went to work for the club before September was out. The days of Augusta National playing defense were now over.

As McCarthy spent October formulating the club's media counteroffensive, Burk's ubiquity was, to him, the most troubling aspect of the press coverage. "The total absence of balance was shocking. It was scandalous," he says. "Every day Martha Burk was telling her friends in the press that Augusta is engaged in sex discrimination. That's an opinion, not a fact. Basic journalistic ethics would demand that reporters present the opinions of those on the other side of the issue, which, I hasten to add, shouldn't have been difficult, because many if not most Americans agreed with the position of the club. Good grief, whatever happened to telling both sides of the story? Whatever happened to fairness?"

"My answer is, McCarthy's not a newspaperman," says *The Washington Post*'s Len Shapiro, the president of the Golf Writers Association of America. "He doesn't understand that nobody wants to read what an extraneous third party from a Washington, D.C., think tank has to say. You go to the source. On this story, Martha Burk and Hootie Johnson were the source of the news. Simple as that."

If McCarthy has an idealized view of reporters, it comes from his old man. For more than three decades, beginning in 1968, Colman McCarthy was a mainstay of *The Washington Post*'s editorial page, as both an editor and a writer. (His column was nationally syndicated in 1978.) Colman became one of the most eloquent voices of the left and, in particular, pacifism, famously writing, "I am a journalist for one reason—to use whatever skills I have to ease suffering in the world."

Fighting for social justice was Colman's passion; golf was his favorite pastime. He grew up on the north shore of Long Island, and as a kid he would ride his bike to any of the dozen or so excellent courses nearby to work as a caddie. McCarthy was a standout player, twice winning the club championship at Sands Point, where he often teed it up with Herbert Warren Wind, the *New Yorker* stalwart who is regarded as golf's preeminent historian. At Spring Hill College in Alabama, McCarthy had a flashy 69.5 scoring average as a junior, and after graduation he couldn't resist the siren song of professional golf. He had little success during a brief cameo on the PGA Tour, but more luck writing about the game. In 1977, he published *The Pleasures of the Game*, a high-brow meditation on golf's enduring appeal. Arthur Schopenhauer, J. F. Powers, Antoine de Saint-Exupery, and T. S. Eliot all make cameos in the course of the narrative, and the allusions include the battle at Yorktown, Papini's *Life of Christ*, and Milton Berle. In the book, Colman identifies his eldest son, Jim, as one of his favorite playing partners, noting that the kid is a "130s shooter."

If little Jimmy's precocity did not extend to athletics, he made up for it with an outsized intellect. Like Martha Burk, he graduated from high school at sixteen, and before enrolling at Notre Dame he took a year off to work as an elevator boy in the House of Representatives. "Every day he was given a sheet of what the congressmen would vote on," says Colman. "A month into the job, Jimmy called home and said, 'Not only are the congressmen asking me what they're voting on, they're asking me how they should vote. Dad, I'm running the country.'"

While in college McCarthy took a year off from his government major to study literature at the National University of Ireland. While over there, he hoisted the Kildare Cup, becoming the first American to win Ireland's informal national championship in debating. McCarthy could work both sides of an issue, because, as his father says, "We always said around the house that a good thinker can argue round, or he can argue square."

When it came to Augusta National, Jim knew that the only way to round out the media coverage was to have Hootie Johnson clarify and amplify the club's position, and he convinced the chairman to go public as part of a three-pronged media offensive in early November. It all began on November 4, the day after the Tour Championship ended at the course where Bobby Jones learned the game, East Lake Golf Club in Atlanta. Five reporters were granted one-on-one interviews with Johnson in his Augusta National office, under President Eisenhower's portrait of Emperor Jones. McCarthy had hand-selected the five media outlets: the *Augusta Chronicle*, *The New York Times*, the *Los Angeles Times*, Associated Press, and *Sports Illustrated*.

Some of America's most important news organizations were denied access to Johnson, blowback from their aggressive coverage. McCarthy gleefully snubbed *The Atlanta Journal-Constitution* because, he says, its Augusta National reporting had to that point been "beyond the pale." (In a September 4 editorial, the *Journal-Constitution* rebuked Johnson as Augusta National's "No. 1 good old boy" and scolded him for the "grave damage he is doing to the sport, the club and the tournament he loves"; eleven days later Cynthia Tucker, the editorial-page editor, ripped Johnson again in a bylined column that credited the chairman with "the most spectacularly ruinous public relations performance since George Wallace stood in the schoolhouse door.") *USA Today* also got the back of the hairbrush, punishment for having outed the membership. While *The Washington Post* had printed in McCarthy's estimation "the single most objectionable piece of pseudo-journalism in this whole episode"—a September Burk profile in the Style section that repeatedly made sport of Johnson's southern-fried persona—the paper was offered first crack at an op-ed piece to be authored by Hootie. But when the *Post* pushed for a touchy-feely spin about how it felt to be at the center of a media controversy, McCarthy went with the more compliant *Wall Street Journal*, which was happy to provide space for a forceful manifesto of the club's position. The *Post* was left with nada. ESPN was also denied, even though the self-styled broadcast leader in sports had been beseeching Augusta National for an interview with Johnson for months. McCarthy felt that the network's coverage to that point had been unduly slanted against the club. "Their idea of research is reading the cartoons that come with Bazooka Joe chewing gum," he says. "Instead of pretending to be journalists, those bozos should stick to something they're good at—like playing catch in the hallway."

The interview with Johnson was so coveted that the chosen media outlets compromised their integrity by agreeing to a club-mandated embargo on the stories until nine P.M. PST on November 11, meaning that they would have to hold off on reporting the news for a full week. (For *Sports Illustrated*, the only weekly in the bunch, the delay was a blessing, ensuring that its piece would not be moldy by the time it appeared.) The embargo was designed so the publication of the stories would coincide with the other two thrusts of the club's offensive—the *Journal* op-ed that was slated for November 12, and the release a day later of a public opinion poll that the club had conducted.

Says McCarthy, "The way the embargo played out was very unfortunate. We were penalized for trying to be nice guys. All of the golf press was in Atlanta for the Tour Championship, so we thought we would save them a return trip to Georgia. However, the timing wasn't quite right with the other things we were working on, so we asked that they hold off on publication. We were accused of some sort of evil manipulation of the journalistic process, and I know reporters love to sniff out conspiracies, but it was much more innocent than that."

The club had one more condition: that the stories appear in a question-and-answer format. Says McCarthy, "We wanted the coverage to be fair, and we wanted our views to get out in an unvarnished way."

"For reputable news organizations to agree to stifle breaking news on a major story like that is really unprecedented," says Len Shapiro. "It's very surprising those news organizations would agree to do that. Letting a subject of a news story dictate the content, and even when it will be published, raises a lot of very troubling questions."

On the appointed day, Johnson greeted each of his five interviewers by reading the same prepared statement: "There has been so much speculation about when we are going to add a woman member. First of all, I'd like to say we have no timetable. Second, our membership has enjoyed camaraderie and a kindred spirit that we think is the heart and soul of our club. It's difficult for us to change something that has worked so well. I've said before and I'll say again that a woman may very well become a member of Augusta. But that is sometime out in the future. In the meantime, we hold dear our tradition and our constitutional right to choose."

Throughout each of the one-hour interviews the chairman hammered his talking points like a politician, staying on message with carefully chosen and rehearsed language.

Doug Ferguson of the AP began by asking, "Would you ever consider canceling the Masters?"

"No."

"Under any circumstances?"

"No. There will always be a Masters."

"Even if you felt this debate had reached a point that it was starting to tarnish the image of the Masters or the club?"

"I don't see that happening. The majority of Americans are with us on this issue. I want you to know that."

"How do you know that?"

"I just know it. I know it by the response I get here. [Here Johnson pointed to one of his conspicuous props, a clipping from a Lancaster, Pennsylvania, newspaper, in which 90 percent of respondents in a poll of 624 people said Augusta National should not have to admit a female.] And I also know it because we're right. You know, some of the media tries to portray us—or this woman portrays us—as being discriminatory and being bigots, and we're not. We're a private club"—here Johnson slipped into a spiel that would be repeated in every interview—"and [single-gender] organizations are good. The Boy Scouts. The Girl Scouts. Junior League. Sororities. Fraternities. Are these immoral? But they're trying to portray us as being discriminatory and being bigots. We will prevail because we're right."

With other interviewers, he added Smith College or Spellman College to the list of single-sex organizations, but the Boy Scouts and Girl Scouts were his favorite points of comparison. To Cliff Brown of *The New York Times*, Johnson said, "I think Augusta National makes a huge contribution to the game of golf. We present a tournament that is world class. One hundred fifty million people watch it. It's the harbinger of spring. I think what we do is good, and I think most people recognize that. Now, are you going to penalize us for doing something good? Are you going to penalize the Girl Scouts for selling cookies?"

Johnson's temper flared a few times, including a spiky exchange with Ferguson: "You did say in April you had no exclusionary policies," Ferguson said. "But you also haven't had a woman here since 1933. How does that square with the other?"

"It squares that we haven't felt a need to invite one, or that we wanted to."

"That almost makes it sound like a woman has nothing to offer to the club."

"You're really trying to bait me now," Hootie huffed. "Do you think girls have anything to offer the Boy Scouts? Do men have anything to offer to the Junior League? No. We're a private club. We have a right to choose and associate with whom we please."

Johnson was also prickly on the subject of Shoal Creek, the ghost of which hovered over the interviews. When Ferguson tried to draw a parallel between Augusta National's tardiness in adding a black member and its resistance to inviting a woman, the chairman cut him off. "Shoal Creek has got nothing to do with this," Johnson said. "Nothing. . . . Racial discrimination and gender are two different things. Do you know of any constitutional lawyer that's ever said they were the same? Do you know any civil rights activists that have said it was the same? Do you? It's not relevant. Nobody accepts them as being the same." Martha Burk would use these comments as ammo for months to come. Indeed, she was an almost tangible presence throughout the interviews, and nothing irritated the chairman quite like the mention of his nemesis. Brown began his interview by saying, "You've already said there's no timetable for when you will invite a woman. Is it possible that you would add a woman before next year's Masters?"

"No. I said sometime off in the future, which wouldn't suggest that it's on the horizon."

"Martha Burk has stated that if Augusta indicated that it was going to add a woman . . ."

Johnson recoiled as if the mention of that name had somehow tainted the sanctity of the chairman's office, interrupting Brown and saying, "Ms. Burk has nothing to do with this club."

Brown, an easygoing character under most circumstances, was unyielding: "I understand that. But she's a part of this issue. So as I was saying, she has stated that if Augusta indicated a willingness to add a woman in a reasonable period of time, she would back off from protests, or whatever."

"Her threats mean nothing to me. We have no timetable."

"Why did you decide to respond so publicly and strongly to Martha Burk's letter?"

"She threatened the club, and I didn't like it. And she's done everything that I predicted she would."

"Wouldn't it have been better just to write her back and state your position, without doing it so publicly?"

"You're splitting hairs with me. What's done is done. The point is, let's not think about my response. Let's think about her threat. I'm not saying it couldn't have been handled better."

John Boyette, the sports editor of the *Augusta Chronicle*, also probed Johnson on Burk, with interesting results. "What was your initial reaction when you received Dr. Burk's letter in June?" Boyette asked.

"Well, I was surprised. Surprised to receive a threatening letter, threatening the club, threatening the tournament, threatening our sponsors."

"After you received her letter, do you think if you responded privately . . ."

"How do you respond privately to someone who threatens you?"

"You could pick up the phone, send her a letter?"

"Well, that's what we did."

Of course, Johnson also sent out a sharply worded, three-page press release. To *Sports Illustrated*'s Steve Rushin, the chairman expressed a modicum of contrition.

"We thought we were doing the right thing. We probably should have toned it down. But we'd been attacked. And she threatened us. And she threatened our sponsors. So there was a little anger there."

"Can one woman really threaten the rich and powerful men of Augusta National?" Rushin asked.

"She threatened us, but she was not a threat. She is not a threat. Do you follow what I'm saying? It's been an irritation."

"Why was Augusta singled out among the nation's single-gender organizations?"

"It's obvious, for the reasons we just touched on a moment ago. We're high-profile, and very successful, and if [Burk] can pull us down, that's a lot more important than pulling down—with all due respect—say, the Junior League."

"But women played one thousand–plus rounds at Augusta last year . . ."

"And I've been asked, 'Well, if you have so many women down here, why do you object to having a woman member?' And I say, 'That does beg the question, but . . . ' We have four member parties, and they're all men, that's what our private club is all about. That's what this club was founded on by Bobby Jones: friends, getting together and playing golf, and just . . . *being men.*"

This remark begot the most interesting exchange of Hootie's media day.

"What do you think of political correctness?" Rushin asked.

"To tell you the truth, I hear that term all the time, but tell me, what does that mean?"

"It means you can't risk, in words or actions, giving offense to others."

"Are we a victim of that? If that's your question, I guess so."

All of these interview transcripts came online during the late afternoon of November 11; the ruffians at ESPN.com broke the embargo hours early by posting the AP interview, and *Sports Illustrated, The New York Times,* and the *Augusta Chronicle* quickly answered with their own transcripts. But Shapiro and *The Washington Post* had the last laugh. It was early on November 11 when Shapiro first caught wind of Johnson's media day, and the snubbing of the *Post*. "I just thought, Screw it, I'm going to call Hootie at home," Shapiro says. "I had been sitting on the number for months, out of respect for his privacy, and because I was told he was recuperating from surgery. He answered the phone, and he was very gracious. He answered all of my questions." Shapiro's story appeared on the front page of Sports the next day, but the *Post* slammed it onto its Web site by the middle of the afternoon on the eleventh, thus allowing Shapiro to brag near the top of the story that Johnson's quotes were "his first public comments on the issue since July 9."

The New York Times and *Augusta Chronicle* played Hootie on A1, with old-fashioned news stories. (Both papers printed partial Q&As elsewhere, while *Sports Illustrated* and the AP both offered the Q&A format preceded by an explanatory introduction.) Only the *L.A. Times* balked at the format, working out a last-minute agreement with Johnson that let Tommy Bonk write for the front page of the Sports section a fluid account of Augusta's hardening position. As for the other delicate details of McCarthy's demands, neither the *Chronicle* nor the AP mentioned the embargo, while the other three outlets made references of varying specificity to the required time lag.

None of the stories was as perfectly controlled as the op-ed that ran in *The Wall Street Journal*, carrying Hootie Johnson's byline. It is an interesting document that illustrates how much more statesmanlike Johnson had become since the "point of the bayonet" press release. "For men of all backgrounds to seek a place and time for camaraderie with other men is as constitutionally and morally proper as it is for women to seek the same with women," Johnson wrote. "Men and women have always occasionally sought out single-sex spheres in certain corners of their social lives, a habit that has always been a positive trapping of civil society. Women gather in book groups to study literature, in investment clubs to discuss the markets, or in fitness clubs to exercise. That they are able to make those choices is a fundamental freedom that most Americans believe is proper and important. That standard goes both ways—that men seek the companionship of other men through sports and other leisure pursuits is equally desirable. The fact that Augusta National presents the Masters, a tournament admired worldwide, does not mean that the right to do so should be abandoned, let alone scorned."

The scrappy former fullback flared only once, writing, "The notion that Augusta National is an enclave of sexist good old boys is ludicrous. Women regularly play the course, with no restrictions. All guests are treated the same whether they are here to play golf or as patrons of the tournament. It is also incorrect to believe that Ms. Burk speaks for all women on this subject. She does not."

In conclusion, Johnson wrote, "How long Ms. Burk and her agenda will be given a voice is up to the media. But how long the public will pay attention is another question. Perhaps this kind of coercion is simply the way by which some political groups try to increase their own membership. It is for others to decide, from where they stand, whether threat-based tactics are appropriate. But from here, it feels like some things are worth defending, and sometimes that means taking a stand. In my mind and in my heart, I know this is one of them."

THE CHAIRMAN'S MESSAGE that the club would not cave to outside pressure got an unexpected boost the very next day, when *The New York Times* ran yet another Augusta National piece, this one on the front page of Sports under the headline "Members of Club Who Favor Change Told to Back Off." The story reported that, "Several Augusta National Golf Club members who say they favor inviting a woman to join the all-male membership said yesterday that they were not at all surprised that William Johnson, the club's chairman, had adamantly affirmed his stance against admitting a woman. The members who said they had expressed their views directly to Johnson or his allies at the club in recent weeks were civilly told to back off on the issue, that their opinions were out of touch with the rest of the membership. 'In no uncertain terms, what I was told and what others who broached the subject were told is that this is the way it's going to be, and it won't change,' said one member, who, like others in the small group interviewed, spoke only on the condition that he not be identified. 'It was put to me that the rest of the membership is united and feels strongly about making a stand on this issue. A few of us were made to feel like we should keep to ourselves on this subject, or maybe consider whether we belonged at Augusta National.' Another member said, 'I was told that maybe I did not understand the history and tradition of Augusta National as well as I should.' "

McCarthy's carefully crafted media assault couldn't have been going any better, or so it seemed, but the momentum was blunted when the results of the public opinion poll were released on November 13, the same day as the *Times* story appeared.

McCarthy had commissioned the poll because, he says, "It was time to have a scientific measure of how the public really felt on this issue. The only polling that had been going on to that point was happening around the watercooler at *The New York Times*."

In fact, there had been numerous mini-surveys done on the membership controversy, but the vast majority had been conducted through golf Web sites or newspaper sports pages. The high level of support for Johnson and Augusta National found in these polls was easily dismissed by the club's detractors because of the very specific, self-selecting audience that was expressing its views. To conduct its poll, Augusta National employed a Washington, D.C., research and consulting firm, WomanTrend, which is an arm of the polling company, inc. Despite a disdain for capital letters, the polling company came with solid credentials, having done surveys for Major League Baseball, the Department of Labor, and Microsoft, among others. The forty-eight-question poll was conducted from October 30 to November 4 on eight hundred randomly selected Americans, a population that turned out to be 51 percent female and 78 percent white. Only 20 percent of the respondents were golfers, while 40 percent identified themselves as "conservative" versus 27 percent who went with "liberal."

The poll began with a reading of the First Amendment. The first sixteen questions contained nary a mention of Augusta National or the Masters, generic offerings like, "In your opinion, what is the most important issue facing women today?"

Though Kellyanne Conway, president of the polling company, would later say, "I'm not going to risk my reputation to have this poll come out a certain way because a client wants a certain result," many critics detected a whiff of editorializing in the questions. Respondents were asked to agree or disagree with a series of statements, including:

"Martha Burk did not really care if the Augusta National Golf Club began allowing women members, she was more concerned with attracting media attention for herself and her organization." (48 percent of men and 40 percent of women agreed.)

"In a way, Ms. Burk's actions are insulting to women because it makes it seem that getting admitted to a golf club is a big priority to all women." (51 percent of men and 55 percent of women agreed.)

"Private clubs like the Augusta National Golf Club whose members share a common interest or characteristic are simply a harmless way for like-minded individuals to get together and associate with each other." (77 percent of men and 75 percent of women agreed.)

In a press release announcing the poll results Hootie Johnson said, "It is enormously gratifying to see that a majority of Americans feel as we do."

McCarthy held a press conference at the Mayflower Hotel in Washington, D.C., to trumpet the results, and its trappings betrayed his roots as a self-described "Beltway flack." In addition to announcing the numbers, McCarthy imported two Augusta natives—caterer Vera Stewart and hospitality consultant Elaine Clark-Smith—to fillet Burk. Also asked to speak was the kind of conservative public policy wonk that McCarthy loves to cite, Kimberly Schuld, the author of *A Guide to Feminist Organizations*.

Burk effortlessly rebutted McCarthy's opinion poll. She dismissed the survey to a number of reporters as a "push poll," helpfully explaining to the *L.A. Times* what that meant: "You push the respondent to a certain answer by the way the question is worded. It's often used in political campaigns. It's considered a highly unethical practice." The *Times* gave big play to questioning the poll's legitimacy, but the most damaging critique to its credibility came from Shapiro. The *Post's* golf scribe was one of the few reporters who attended the press conference at the Mayflower, and McCarthy says, "He was openly hostile to our speakers." Shapiro laughs at the mention of the Mayflower Hotel. "Ah, the infamous press conference," he says. "They lured reporters there under the pretense of the release of this public opinion poll. Fine. But then McCarthy trots out all these women to attack Burk. This goes on for like half an hour, and it really didn't sit well with me. Wasn't this supposed to be about the opinion of the public, not Jim McCarthy's cronies? I told him exactly how I felt after the press conference. That was the beginning of a very strained relationship."

Shapiro exacted his revenge in the next day's *Post*. Under the headline "Poll Favoring Augusta Is Called 'One-Sided'" he quoted Burk as saying, "It's ridiculous on its face that 70 percent of Americans support sex discrimination. It was predesigned to get a certain result, and the result they've gotten has totally destroyed their credibility."

Shapiro also quoted Tom Smith, identifying him "as a nationally known pollster at the University of Chicago." Smith hadn't seen the poll when Shapiro rang, so the reporter read a sampling of the questions to the pollster. Smith deemed the queries "not high quality" and "one-sided," adding that, "some of the questions are seriously flawed and may have a clear slant to them. It is very unusual to personalize so many questions in terms of one person, Martha Burk."

ESPN also got its revenge on McCarthy, devoting a long segment on *SportsCenter* to debunking the poll. This included an on-camera interview with the CEO of the polling company Merketicture, who said, "The questions were so clearly leading the witness, it really shouldn't be referred to as a poll." That was fair enough, but ESPN's Karl Ravich then introduced a ludicrous skit by his fellow *SportsCenter* anchor Rich Eisen, a one-time standup comic masquerading as a journalist. Images of azaleas then filled the screen, accompanied by the strains of insipid piano music. Eisen's voice-over: "Masters Polling Moments, a tradition unlike any other." Cut to Eisen, showily smoking a pipe and seated in a chair wearing a green jacket, with his legs swaddled in a wooly blankie. With mock seriousness, Eisen then read seven of the real poll questions. As this excruciating skit wound down, azaleas again filled the screen, and another voice-over announced: "The Masters Polling Moments has been brought to you by, well, uh, we don't have any sponsors." *Bah-duh-boom!*

Watching at home, McCarthy was aghast. "It was not just a mockery of the poll, but a mockery of journalism," he says. "Those yahoos at ESPN, along with Shapiro, soiled the whole thing. You expect your adversaries to question the validity of a poll. That's a given. What I was shocked by was how the press went after it so viciously. It felt like a personal attack."

It was a fitting end to Augusta National's first PR salvo. Johnson had gotten his point across, but the bad blood was just beginning between McCarthy and the media.

TWO DAYS AFTER the poll was released, the Reverend Jesse Jackson rode into the membership controversy with guns blazing. On November 15, Jackson told the AP that if Augusta National did not welcome a woman member by the time of the Masters, five months hence, he would organize a protest at the tournament. "We support strongly the movement to end the gender apartheid at Augusta National Golf Club," Jackson said.

"The gender bigotry is as offensive as racial bigotry or religious bigotry. . . . If the matter has not been resolved, the Rainbow/PUSH Coalition will join others in active protest at the next Masters tournament." According to the AP, this included "a picket line in front of the club."

There had been rumblings for months about a potential protest at the Masters—Hootie Johnson had predicted as much in his first press release—and in October Burk had woofed to the *Fort Worth Star-Telegram*, "I'm getting e-mails and calls from women . . . saying they're thinking about scheduling their vacation so they can go there and picket. College groups are telling me this would be a fine activity for spring break. Skip Florida this year and go to Augusta. We could put some women there in green burkas. It has potential to be quite a circus down there."

Just a couple of days before Jackson spoke out, Martha Burk had forecast that a demonstration was "more likely than ever." Jackson's entry made these words more ominous, as his Rainbow/PUSH Coalition packed a lot more firepower than the NCWO. Its involvement also evoked the civil rights era that had torn apart southern towns like Augusta. A little golf story was increasingly taking on the scope of a larger struggle.

Three days after Jackson's bombshell, *The New York Times* thrust itself into the debate with a grandstanding editorial. Under the headline "America's All-Male Golfing Society," the paper called Johnson a "poster boy for a particularly regressive branch of the golfing set" and opined that the "Masters magic is based on discrimination that Citigroup, American Express, CBS and other modern corporations vowed to eradicate decades ago. Mr. Weill and Mr. Chenault should lead the way by resigning from the club and encouraging other CEOs to do the same. CBS Sports, which seems to think this issue is no big deal, needs to think again.

"Tiger Woods, who has won the Masters three times, could simply choose to stay home in April. The absence of golf's best player would put a dreaded asterisk by the name of next year's winner. And a tournament without Mr. Woods would send a powerful message that discrimination isn't good for the golfing business. Of course, if Mr. Woods took that view, the club might suddenly find room for a few female members. Justice Sandra Day O'Connor, for example, is said to be a very good golfer."

That the most important newspaper in the world had called out the planet's most famous athlete predictably made international news. (That was the purpose of the editorial, no?) The *Times*'s chutzpah was discussed everywhere from *ABC World News Tonight* to Phil Donahue's talk show to the front page of London's *Daily Telegraph*. It didn't take long for word to reach Japan, where Woods was scooping up a reported $2 million appearance fee to play in the Dunlop Phoenix tournament. "It's frustrating, because I'm the only player they are asking," Woods told reporters. "They're asking me to give up an opportunity [to do something] no one ever has—win the Masters three years in a row."

Throughout the first four months of the Augusta National membership controversy, the media coverage had been an enduring background issue, but the *Times* editorial brought the debate out into the open. Colman McCarthy was a thoughtful voice among those who were becoming increasingly dismayed reading their morning newspaper. Though he has left *The Washington Post*, McCarthy writes sharp-tongued media critiques for *The Progressive* and other publications, and his jaundiced eye has informed his son Jim's worldview. In an interview, Colman says, "The real story with Augusta is elitism, not sex discrimination. The Boston–New York–Washington media axis thought, Oh boy, we caught these southern good ol' boys doing some mischief. It became the Northeast pseudo-liberals piling on white southerners, which is the last group you can mock and deride with little fear of being seen as biased."

Interesting choice of words, that last one. The Augusta National membership controversy had erupted just in time to be part of the media bias zeitgeist. In December 2001, Bernard Goldberg published the book *Bias: A CBS Insider Exposes How the Media Distort the News*. It was an instant phenomenon, spending twenty weeks on the *New York Times* bestseller list, including seven at number one. Goldberg's core argument was that the sophisticates who manufacture and package the news in New York have little understanding of the people and beliefs in the "red states" that George W. Bush carried. Goldberg posits that an entire generation of left-leaning young men and women, outraged about Vietnam and inspired by *The Washington Post*'s work on Watergate, became reporters hoping to save the world. Those folks are now running all the important media institutions, and their biases are being foisted on a large segment of the public that sees the world differently.

Goldberg's polemic captured the mainstream reader and made him a darling of the brand-name conservatives who rule talk radio, but his critique had even more resonance because it echoed a similar dissatisfaction that had been gurgling up from the World Wide Web. In an era when *The Village Voice* is owned in part by Goldman Sachs, the turn of the century had ushered in a radical new alternative media, the Web log. Blogs offers a broad spectrum of political bents, but one thing is clear: Liberalism is as rare in the blogosphere as it is on the PGA Tour. "It is a fundamentally conservative/Libertarian medium because liberals already have their own media outlets," says Clay Waters, the founder of the blog TimesWatch, which is dedicated to "documenting and exposing the liberal political agenda of *The New York Times*" at timeswatch.org. "They have the networks, CNN, *The New York Times*. They don't need any more platforms. Conservatives have to create their own, whether it's Fox News or blogs."

Media criticism is increasingly the specialty of blogging's biggest stars. Jim Romenesko (poynter.org), Glenn Reynolds (Insta Pundit.com), Mickey Kaus (Kausfiles.com), and Andrew Sullivan (andrewsullivan. com), among others, have commanded the attention of the journalism world simply by monitoring what is being written and offering spiky commentary along with the links. They also serve as an outlet for the leaking of juicy information. As the *Columbia Journalism Review* put it recently, "More than just A. J. Liebling–style press criticism, journalists finally have something approaching real peer review, in all its brutality."

A Web junkie who requires hourly fixes, Jim McCarthy knew instinctively that blogging could have a profound effect on moving public opinion about Augusta National. "Media crit through blogging has become so cutting-edge, the only analogies I can think of are military," he says. "It's like secondary shrapnel. It's like blowback. Because of the viral nature of linking, one story, one idea, can spread to thousands of Web sites in a matter of hours. As far as crisis management PR goes, there are a lot of implications. It's a great way to set the record straight and get your point of view on record in an immediate way. It is a hyper-effective way to defend clients in the face of a media onslaught. It won't work for everyone. I don't think Martha Stewart or Jeff Skilling would have much luck. Those cases are built on facts and numbers. Augusta National is about ideas and opinions, which is the fuel that powers blogs. There is an old maxim that you don't get into a fight with people who buy ink by the barrel. Well, the Internet is equivalent to thousands of barrels of ink."

From virtually the moment he was hired by Augusta National in September, McCarthy began "steering information and planting ideas" with "about a dozen" bloggers and online media critics, including Romenesko and Kaus. "I recognized that the mainstream golf press was going to be resistant," he says. "Certainly there was a core group of writers who were openly hostile to the club's views. Blogs opened up an entire new front. It was a process of germination. The plan was to construct ideas with the media that would act as a filter so they would read subsequent pieces of information with the lens that you created."

McCarthy had no trouble picking out his first target (though he says "I like to think it was a defense, not an attack"). "Stopping *The New York Times* dead in their tracks was critical to the overall effort, because the *Times* sets the agenda for the broader media world," he says. "The knuckleheads in the ESPN newsroom—if you can call it that—stop playing Nerf basketball only long enough to read, it seems, comic books and the *Times*. They're just one of the many of lesser media outlets that float like a flotilla in the wake of the *Times*."

An added bonus was that much of the blogosphere is openly contemptuous of the Gray Lady. "There has always been a low roar about Howell Raines and the *Times*," says TimesWatch's Clay Waters.

Raines took over as the paper's top dog, executive editor, on September 5, 2001, following a steady march up the masthead. For the previous eight years he had run the editorial page, earning the wrath of Democrats for his stinging criticisms of Bill Clinton and enraging the right with what was otherwise perceived as a hard-core liberal agenda. Though the average newspaper reader is blissfully unaware of the personnel machinations at their favorite fish wrap, Raines's promotion led to a certain amount of chagrin among media critics. "It raises eyebrows any time an editorial-page editor moves to the news side, especially an ideologue like Raines," says TimesWatch's Waters. "Naturally you wonder if they can be fair and objective."

Even within the *Times*, the iconoclastic Raines was viewed with curiosity. He was a swashbuckling character who wore a Panama hat to work, and in a newsroom chock full of Ivy Leaguers he stood out because of his thick drawl and southern roots. In his 1993 memoir, *Fly Fishing through the Midlife Crisis*, Raines writes, "I am a son of the hillbilly tribes of Alabama . . . The blood that beats in me is hillbilly blood, and when I use the words 'hillbilly' or 'redneck' . . . it is with binding affection and due reverence for those who have gone before." Throughout his *Times* career he drew snickers for his constant references to his hero, legendary Alabama football coach Bear Bryant, but Raines was no rube. He quoted Yeats as often as he did the Bear, and he had been deeply affected by the civil rights movement in the South, which he covered as a young newspaper man at the *Birmingham Post-Herald*. Race remains one of his obsessions; in 1991, he won a Pulitzer Prize for the article "Grady's Gift" in the *Times Magazine* about Grady Hutchinson, a black woman who went to work for the Raines household when she was sixteen and Howell was seven. Grady straightened her master's curly hair, read him *The Old Man and the Sea*, and spoke to Raines about, as he would write, "a hidden world about which no one has ever told me, a world as dangerous and foreign, to a white child in a segregated society, as Africa itself." Through Grady's eyes he first saw the "choking shame" of racism, and she taught him "the most valuable lesson a writer can learn, which is to try to see—honestly and down to its very center—the world we live in." It surprised no one that Raines's handpicked number two, managing editor Gerald Boyd, became the highest-ranking African American in *Times* history.

Raines saw himself as an agent of change at a paper that had been around for a century and a half, and his oft-quoted mantra to "raise the competitive metabolism of the paper" rankled some within the *Times* because it implied that they had grown fat and happy. His vision of a more proactive, aggressive paper was quickly put to the ultimate test—the Twin Towers were toppled six days into his reign as executive editor. Standing at the crossroads of history, Raines oversaw some of the best journalism ever committed. He later likened his role to that of Ulysses S. Grant, and the troops he commanded for the September 12, 2001, issue were truly awesome: three hundred reporters and more than fifty photographers produced sixty-seven stories about the attacks of 9/11, a total of 82,500 words that spanned thirty-three pages in all. Raines and the *Times* never relented, producing one staggering edition after the next in the months to come. The reward was a record six Pulitzers for the 9/11 coverage. In trumpeting the awards, Raines told his elated staff that their work "will be studied and taught as long as journalism is studied and taught. We have a right to celebrate these days of legend at *The New York Times*."

Suddenly the toast of a media-obsessed town, Raines used his new-found capital to shake up his staid old paper. Editors and reporters were moved around the paper like chess pieces, and Raines centralized power among himself and a small group of intensely loyal lieutenants. Raines's specific vision of breaking high-impact stories was imposed on every cor-ner of the newspaper, and in the tribal culture of newsrooms, a backlash was inevitable. The Washington bureau began referring to the *Times*'s leadership as "the Taliban" and to Raines as "Mullah Omar." But Raines pressed forward in reinventing the paper. After the smoke cleared on 9/11, he finally had the chance to attack what he perceived as the paper's two weakest sections, Sports and Business. In his mind, the former had a regional emphasis and was forever getting beat on the big stories by the likes of *USA Today*, while the latter had a defeatist attitude trying to compete in the same town with the overwhelming resources of *The Wall Street Journal*. When Enron imploded, Raines told the Business staff that it was their 9/11, and they responded with some of the boldest reporting ever to grace the *Times*'s business page. Raines never made a similar pro-nouncement to Sports vis-a-vis the Augusta National membership con-troversy, but he recognized it was the perfect story for Sports to shed its parochial traditions.

"The *Times*'s future is as a national newspaper, which means it's got to be strong on this kind of story," the ordinarily media-phobic Raines said in an interview for this book. "Augusta National is not a New York story per se, but I think it was important to the national readership. I don't want to get too fancy about this. I like breaking news. And I don't define that as getting to the train wreck first. It is finding stories of such signifi-cance that your competitors have no choice but to follow them, or find-ing stories of such compelling interest that no reasonable reader with the time to spend is going to go past them. And that was the kind of journal-ism we were trying to do.

"My major interest in sports as a journalistic subject runs in a sociological direction. It's such an important part of American life. It's such a force in social standards. It's such a business force. So what I envisioned is a Sports section that was more national in scope, and while you record the events in sports, you write about the world of sports in a serious, journalistic way."

It took a few months for Raines, and by extension his paper, to become fully engaged in the Augusta National membership controversy. In his mind the *Times* got "back in the ball game" with its October 20, A1 exclusive in which Tiger Woods made his most forceful comments to date about the membership controversy. By mid-November, the *Times* was churning out almost daily Augusta National dispatches, many of them given prominent placement. The interview with Hootie Johnson went on A1 on November 12. The next day, Sports carried two stories on the front page: "Members of Club Who Favor Change Told to Back Off" and a column by Selena Roberts that carried the headline "Augusta's Chairman Lives in a Time Warp." Addressing the chairman, Roberts began, "It must be comforting to live inside a vintage Sylvania, cozy in a black-and-white world where June Cleaver is your ideal woman."

The next day, two more stories ran in Sports, one questioning the validity of McCarthy's opinion poll, the other a column by Pulitzer Prize winner Dave Anderson. The usually mild-mannered Anderson ripped Johnson's record as chairman—the bungling of the Masters past champs, the compromising of the golf course, and now the ugly public spat with Burk. "It has become Hootie's tournament, not the tournament that Roberts and other chairmen built into an American sports institution," Anderson wrote. "So much so that maybe the Masters should change its name. Just call it 'the Hootie.' "

Three days later, on November 17, the *Times* devoted as much space to Augusta National as it would during Masters week. In the important National Desk news hole in the front section, there was a long story forecasting the economic (and psychic) impact on the city of Augusta with a tarnished Masters looming. Noting that a number of major corporations had already canceled their lavish entertaining plans, Jeffrey Gettleman wrote, "This spring, Augusta may get a different taste of the Masters, and it may not be so sweet. Instead of Coca-Cola executives showing up along the banks of the Savannah River, it may be angry women in green burkas."

On the editorial page, Maureen Dowd, the spiky White House columnist whom bloggers love to hate, called Saudi Arabia "the Augusta National of Islam, a sand trap where men can hang out and be men." Facing Dowd's column were four letters to the editor about various aspects of the *Times* coverage on Augusta National. In Sports, Robert Lipsyte chimed in with another column, this one declaring, "Hootie, an elderly white Southerner with a good-old-boy nickname, is too easy to mock in New York."

The next day, November 18, the paper dropped its editorial calling for Woods to boycott the Masters. On November 21, the front page of Sports carried a story about Ladies Professional Golf Association commissioner Ty Votaw's breaking ranks with the golf establishment and calling for Augusta National to open up its membership. (The story was also teased on A1.) "It is Augusta's right as a private organization not to admit women," said Votaw. "But it's not the right thing to do. Augusta is . . . perpetuating golf's exclusionary past and the perception that golf is elitist, instead of what we all in the golf industry want it to be, which is inclusive."

Raines was flooding the zone with glee, and some inside and outside the paper were drowning in disbelief. The most visible protest of the paper's coverage could be found in the November 24 edition of the *New York Observer*—the gossipy, snarky bible of Manhattan media circles—which carried an 1,800-word story about the *Times*'s "tactical assault against the Augusta National Golf Club." Writer Sridhar Pappu, the *Observer*'s eagle-eyed media critic, put down on paper a feeling that was beginning to ferment among the bloggers: "*The New York Times* has prodded and pulled the story, refusing to let it slip from the table of conversation. From its front-page features examining Mr. Woods's place in speaking out about the matter to its strongly worded editorials, the paper has made women and Augusta the biggest sports-and-society story of the year."

Pappu made the case that Raines's strident criticism of the club reflected a conflicted, self-loathing southerner, and he theorized that in Hootie Johnson, Raines was eager to tear down a symbol of a South that he had left behind. Intriguingly, Pappu got *Times* staffers to engage in this kind of psychobabble. "It's been Howell's interest that's driven the story," said Jere Longman, who cowrote the October 20 story in which Tiger vented about the membership controversy. "I think it is an important story, but where his interest comes from, I'm not exactly sure. I would guess that, equating the civil-rights movement and the women's movement, he feels the same kind of urgency."

Pappu's piece was prominently displayed in Romenesko's blog, for which McCarthy takes some credit. "I had been sending Romenesko stuff on the *Times* for months," he says, "pushing the idea that its coverage was ideologically driven, that it was a crusade being pushed as part of the paper's larger liberal agenda. Obviously this story supported the thesis."

Five days later, the *Times* gave its critics more fuel by running one of its most controversial Augusta National stories. Stretched across A1 of the November 25 edition was the headline "CBS Staying Silent in Debate on Women Joining Augusta." The story was cowritten by Bill Carter, the brand-name TV writer whose book *The Late Shift* deliciously detailed the late-night television wars involving David Letterman and Jay Leno. The article was supposed to be a probing think piece, but the story was a muddled amalgam of different themes, regurgitating the broad strokes of the membership controversy, awkwardly working in the results of a *Times* opinion poll, and laboring to provide insight into CBS's predicament, even though the story admitted that "no current company executive agreed to comment on the matter, even behind a cloak of anonymity." Given how little the article advanced the narrative of the membership controversy, it was a head-scratcher that it wound up on A1.

It turns out the story had been assigned personally by Raines, an unusual move for an executive editor. "That story was something I've never had occasion to discuss publicly," he says. "I assigned that story because I was interested in this question: Here is a network that was once the iconic network in American broadcasting, that was traditionally, in the years of Cronkite and his predecessors, identified as being on the forefront of social policy reporting and coverage of the civil rights movement. Now it's basically at the mercy of the Masters, and what does that say about what had happened at CBS? What did it say about CBS's relationship with the Masters, and what did it say about CBS's relationship with its sponsors? That was the story that I was pressing to get."

However, Raines was out of the office when the story was filed, edited, and slapped on the front page. (His mother, Bertha, had died two days earlier.) "I would have run the story, but I wouldn't have fronted it," he says. "I'm not backing away from it, but as a matter of news judgment, people were right to question its being on the front page. I don't think it was executed as well as it could have been, but I think the concept of the story was dead on."

The backlash about the *Times*'s coverage on Augusta National that had been building and building suddenly exploded with the publication of "CBS Staying Silent." On the same day the story appeared, Jack Shafer of *Slate*, one of the most influential online media critics, wrote, "At some point, saturation coverage of a story begins to raise more questions about the newspaper's motives than about the story being covered. The *Times* reached—and passed—that point this morning with its 40th-plus news story, column, or editorial (since July!) about the Augusta National Golf Club's refusal to admit female members. Only a five-star general like Raines could have commanded such extravagant coverage as this.

"The headline of today's Page One, above-the-fold story, 'CBS Staying Silent in Debate on Women Joining Augusta'"—here Shafer offered a link to the piece—"is the giveaway that the *Times* is blowing on embers in hopes that the story will reignite. The fact that the network is *still* silent isn't big news today any more than it will be big news tomorrow, even if the *Times* were to contrive a story titled 'CBS Stays Silent: Day 150.' This sort of churning and whisking of yesterday's topic, adding new ingredients in incremental proportions in story after story until you build a 12-foot tall meringue isn't news coverage, it's blogging!"

Jim McCarthy's description of the "viral" nature of blogging was well illustrated in how opinions about the *Times* spread from Web site to Web site, and, ergo, reader to reader. Andrew Sullivan blogged the *Slate* column the next day, writing, "Jack Shafer does an excellent job limning the now almost comical hyping of non-news stories to fit Raines's paleo-liberal agenda, specifically on the Augusta National Golf Club. . . . The Mickster has sharper comments."

That would be Mickey Kaus, whom McCarthy had been pestering for months about the *Times*'s coverage. Earlier on November 26 Kaus had written, "Jack Shafer points out the strained quality"—here a link to the *Slate* story—"of the most recent NYT front-pager"—yet another link to *that* story—"on the Augusta National Golf Club controversy ('CBS Staying Silent in Debate on Women Joining Augusta') which might as well have been headlined 'CBS Fails to Pay Attention to New York Times Crusade.' Shafer, echoing Sridhar Pappu"—here again, another link—"thinks NYT Executive Editor Howell Raines is replaying (as a Guilty Southern White Boy should) the civil rights struggle of the 1960s. The *Times*, Shafer suggests, latched onto 'a story that it could conveniently exploit for months to the smug satisfaction of its liberal readers.'

"Raines is on the verge of a breakthrough reconceptualization of 'news' here, in which 'news' comes to mean the failure of any powerful individual or institution to do what Howell Raines wants them to do. P.S. If the NYT makes a huge fuss about Augusta's refusal to admit women and it turns out that nobody cares ('Readers Stay Silent in Debate on Women Joining Augusta') doesn't that have the effect of ratifying the practices of same-sex private clubs?"

The roar was so loud that the mainstream media could no longer ignore the story. In the December 9 issue of *Newsweek*, Seth Mnookin used the "CBS Staying Silent" backlash in his lead, and he went on to quote Shafer. He came to the same conclusion the bloggers had long ago: "Increasingly, the *Times* is being criticized for ginning up controversies as much as reporting them out." Gee, you think?

EIGHT DAYS AFTER "CBS Staying Silent," the *Times* offered the perfect rebuttal to the criticism of its Augusta National coverage, as its aggressive reporting bagged one of the biggest scoops of the membership controversy: In an exclusive interview with the *Times*, Tom Wyman announced he was resigning in protest from the club. "I am not anxious to make this personal," Wyman said. "But Hootie keeps writing that there has not been a single case of protest in the membership. And he absolutely believes this will all go away. It will not go away and it should not. I know there is a large number of members, at least 50 to 75, who believe it is inevitable that there will be and should be a woman member. There are obviously some redneck, old-boy types down there, but there are a lot of very thoughtful rational people in the membership, and they feel as strongly as I do."

Though Johnson was irate about Wyman's high-profile defection and his unsparing language—in the *Times*'s story the chairman was also described as "pigheaded" by a twenty-five-year member—the club issued only a blandly worded statement to the *Times*: "We are disappointed that Mr. Wyman has chosen to publicize a private matter. While we respect the fact that there are differences of opinion on this issue, we intend to stand firm behind our right to make what are both appropriate and private membership choices."

This was exactly the kind of high-impact story Raines had been lusting after. The scoop was broadcast to the world when Wyman was interviewed in prime time by Connie Chung. Every paper in the country was forced to credit the *Times* a day later, including *USA Today*, which mentioned its competitor three times in its catch-up account while grudgingly admitting that Wyman could not be reached "despite repeated attempts."

Among those who were talking was Tiger Woods, at a news conference from the Target World Championship. "It was his choice and he certainly felt very strongly in doing so," Woods said of Wyman. "You have to admire that. He didn't have to [resign], but he certainly believed that it was the right thing for him."

Martha Burk also chimed in, telling *USA Today*, "I think more are going to have to follow him. It's good that someone in his position is willing to step away from the pack and do the right thing. A lot of them are hiding under their desks." The *USA Today* story was written by Harry Blauvelt, who, on this touchiest of subjects, betrayed none of the insider knowledge that comes with his father's membership at Augusta National.

Though it was expected, Wyman was not thrilled to be used as fodder for Burk. "He was not a fan of hers," says Michael Wyman, Tom's son. "He didn't approve of her rhetoric. He felt like she was an opportunist."

It was Tom Wyman's family that, in the end, convinced him to resign from Augusta National. In February 2002, during a trip to the club, his three sons had voiced their discomfort with its homogeneity. The issue of the old man's membership had been a source of discussion within the family ever since "the point of a bayonet," but the debate intensified in November when the Wymans gathered for Tom's marriage to Deborah Whiting Little. She was an Episcopal priest who ministered to the homeless in Boston, and Rev. Little, with a social consciousness informed by the activism of the 1960s, could not understand her new husband's attachment to a club defined by privilege and exclusivity. At the rehearsal dinner on the eve of the wedding, Wyman produced a draft of a letter he had been stewing on for days. With the hearty encouragement of his family, particularly Tom Jr., Wyman sent it to Hootie Johnson on November 20.

"There is no question it is our right to decide who is invited to join our club," read the letter, a copy of which was provided for this book by the Wyman family. "At the same time it is also our responsibility to protect the interests of the thousands of people around the world who see Augusta as a treasure to be admired for its role in the golf world. The continuing stream of negative publicity surrounding the controversy is damaging our image seriously and it will continue to do so until we realize that protecting our right of choice is only part of our responsibility."

In closing, Wyman sounded an ominous note. "While I hope you will act responsibly and with reason on this issue, I feel obliged to tell you that your failure to do so would cause me to reevaluate my association with an organization that fails to recognize the role of women in our society. While I have, up to this point, respected your request that this issue not be a subject of discussion either with the public or with other members, I feel that continuing the status quo would cause me to make my views known to a broader audience—if only to remove any doubt that I approve of the present policy.

"Hootie, I hope you recognize that I write to you as a friend and a once proud member of Augusta National whose interest is solely in maintaining its high standards and good reputation."

As Martha Burk can attest, Johnson is not the most tender of pen pals. He blew off Wyman in a response dated November 22. "Obviously I was disappointed to receive your letter," Johnson wrote. "Although I respect your right to disagree, I must tell you that the Executive Committee unanimously adopted our present position on membership, and the overwhelming majority of our members are in complete agreement. I want you to also know that there is no timetable for the admission of women into our membership, nor do I expect there to be one in the foreseeable future. If you feel compelled to resign, we will certainly understand. I hope, however, you will continue to respect the rights of the rest of the membership."

Wyman officially quit Augusta National in a response dated November 27. "Hootie, I recognize that it would be useful to you for me to resign quietly with no report of my departure (or the reasons therefore) beyond Augusta. I have decided to share my positions with the world outside in hope that others in and out of the Club will speak up in favor of admitting women soon."

It was a convenient time for Wyman to walk away from Augusta National because, sadly, at seventy-two his health was slipping. Over the preceding five years he had been suffering from a blood disorder that necessitated weekly injections of white blood cells. Fatigue and balance problems were among the side effects. "His playing days were reasonably limited," says Michael Wyman. "I told him, Dad, the decision would be a lot harder if you were fifty years old and had a lot of golf in front of you."

Upon hearing of Wyman's resignation, Wheelock Whitney, his closest friend among the Augusta National membership, also reflected on golf opportunities lost. "When I heard about Tom resigning, my first thought was, Oh, my gosh, his poor sons. I used to throw a father-son tournament at the club, and Tom came with all three boys, must have been ten to fifteen years ago. That was BMB—Before Martha Burk. Anyway, they all loved golf, and we had a ball."

That was exactly the kind of camaraderie and kinship that Hootie Johnson was always extolling, and Whitney was saddened to see his friend end the fun. "I sent him a Christmas card, as I have every year for the last thirty," Whitney says. "I told him I was disappointed that he resigned and that he had gone too far. I told him that I felt this issue would be resolved soon enough."

Did that mean he agreed with Wyman's estimate that up to a quarter of the club favored making the membership coed? "I think it's true," Whitney said in an interview two months after Wyman resigned. "Everybody in the club anticipated that it would happen eventually. I heard it discussed. I think a lot of members feel the way Tom did—but not to resign over."

And what of these other members—how did they take Wyman's desertion, and criticism? "Put it this way," says Whitney, "I'm sure Tom didn't get many other Christmas cards."

HOWELL RAINES and his troops at *The New York Times* had all of one day to revel in the Wyman scoop. On December 4, the *New York Daily News* dropped a bombshell, under the headline "Times Editors Kill 2 Columns in Augusta Rift." Paul Colford's lead had the staccato rhythm of gunfire: "Editors of *The New York Times* killed a column by Pulitzer Prize winner Dave Anderson that disagreed with an editorial about Tiger Woods and Augusta National's refusal to admit women as members. A column by sportswriter Harvey Araton also was zapped, sources said, because it differed with the paper's editorial opinion about the golf club standoff. The moves came amid extensive coverage of the Georgia club under former editorial page editor Howell Raines, who's called for high-impact stories since becoming executive editor last year."

Colford had a key voice in his story—Dave Anderson: " 'That's right, my column didn't run,' Anderson told the *Daily News* last night. 'It was decided by the editors that we should not argue with the editorial page.' The *Times* editors' decisions reinforce a growing sense in journalistic circles that the paper under Raines looks for conformity in its news and opinion columns."

The blogger outrage was immediate, predictable, and entertaining. Mickey Kaus offered condolences for all the poor columnists at the *Times*, whose jobs had been reduced to, he wrote, "voices in Howell's Castrati Chorus, apparatchiks obedient to the party line. . . . It's Orwellian, I tell you." Romenesko's blog nearly melted, so furious was the linking. In the first forty-eight hours after the story broke, he had more than a half-dozen different postings, each directing readers to a wide variety of stories excoriating the *Times*. The best reading was a string of soul-searching articles in industry journals like *MediaNews* and *Editor &*

Publisher that were more or less predicting the end of journalism as we know it.

Observing all of this bloodletting with a smug satisfaction was Jim McCarthy. "For months I've been pushing the idea that the *Times* coverage is biased, that it was reflecting Raines's heavy-handedness, his dictatorial style, his expectation that everything conform to his worldview," he says. "When the story breaks that they've killed the two columns, the feeding frenzy begins. Suddenly the story is no longer Augusta National, it's the paper and its ideology. The story is no longer sex discrimination but journalistic integrity. That is how you help turn down the heat on a crisis, by changing the subject. Would the *Times*'s spiking of the columns have been a big story without all of the groundwork I laid? Of course. But I'd like to think I played a part in the backlash."

The notion of Raines's squashing any challenge to the *Times*'s crusade against Augusta National made for an irresistible story line, but the truth is more complicated, and more interesting. "Yeah, we screwed that up every way possible," says Raines. "And I'll give you the ticktock on that."

The melodrama had begun on November 18, when Harvey Araton submitted a column around five P.M. in which he made the point that, while Burk's battle with Augusta National was getting all the attention, other challenges facing women's sports were being overlooked, particularly the groundswell to roll back Title IX. "There are a whole lot of Hooties out there, and many with the power to inflict far greater damage on women in sports," Araton wrote. Though he made the point that Burk could be a powerful advocate for women in sports, Araton was dismissive of the meaning of the Augusta National membership controversy, writing, "The symbolism of breaking any barrier—and especially one erected by the rich and powerful—is surely important, but no one should pretend that golf as a social institution will ever be more about inclusion than tokenism."

Raines was in Paris when the column came in, helping to oversee a bloody boardroom deal involving the *International Herald Tribune*, in which *The New York Times* was buying out its partner, *The Washington Post*. In his absence, managing editor Gerald Boyd was steering the ship back in New York. Even more than his boss, Boyd was attuned to issues of discrimination. He had grown up in humble circumstances in St. Louis, raised by a grandmother, and first made a name for himself in journalism covering the White House for the hometown *Post-Dispatch,* where he was one of only two minorities on the beat. "That brought me to Reagan's attention," Boyd once said. "I got far more attention than I deserved, and I would always be called on at press conferences by [the president]." Boyd's White House work got him a job at the *Times,* and after becoming an editor in 1990, he began an inexorable climb up the masthead. In 2000, he coedited the series "How Race Is Lived in America," which won a Pulitzer for national reporting, and after being named managing editor by Raines, Boyd said, "I hope tomorrow, when some kid of color picks up *The New York Times* and reads about the new managing editor, that kid will dream a little bigger dream."

Clearly Martha Burk's message of inclusion had resonance for Boyd. "I was told Gerald objected to the [Araton] column on the grounds that it seemed unfair to Burk," says Raines. "And I'm told there were other editors, including some of the women senior editors, who felt the same way. So it was held on that ground."

After filing his column, Araton drove to the Meadowlands for a New Jersey Nets game. Upon arriving, he checked in with sports editor Neil Amdur, who informed Araton that Boyd had some objections to the column and that it wouldn't run the next day. "Harvey was really pissed off," says a *New York Post* writer who was in the pressroom at the time. "I heard him say 'fucking bullshit' at least a hundred times. But then again, someone's always screaming into the phone in the pressroom. To me it was just another day at the office."

Araton rewrote the column for the next day, November 19. By that afternoon Raines had returned from Paris and was back in the office. "Gerald briefed me on the background on Araton's column," says Raines, "and he said that once again he wasn't going to run it. That was my chance to intervene if I wanted to, but I didn't. I did say, You've been involved in it—that's your decision. . . . That was my only involvement in the Araton column."

On November 20, Araton was informed that the column was dead. "It was explained to me that Gerald felt the idea that I was trying to link the two [would] minimize one at the expense of another," Araton says. "I didn't think I was trying to dismiss what was going on at Augusta National, I was just trying to say that there are far greater issues of gender equity in sports." At some point Araton spoke to Boyd, and, says Araton, they "agreed to disagree."

If Araton sounds blasé, there's a reason. The reality is, columns get spiked every day in newsrooms across America. Editors are the gatekeepers of what shows up in print. It's a fact of life that every reporter understands, though the public at large might consider this untidy aspect of the newspaper business to be a low-grade form of censorship. Says Raines, "How we handle our columnists is a subject not well understood outside the *Times*. Our op-ed columnists are not edited at all, except for style. They serve at the pleasure of the publisher. They write what they want to, [and] if he doesn't like what they're writing, he has a right to fire them. Sports columnists and other news columnists do not have a free-fire zone to write anything they want. Clyde Haberman enjoys writing about city hall day to day, but he's not empowered to write, 'So-and-so is a terrible councilman and I want to throw him out.' It's a commentary on the news, in which the writer's opinion comes into play, but it's not a contract that you write it, we publish it. So the idea of holding a column is not a new one, not a revolutionary journalistic development. It's called editing." (Indeed, in 1980, the legendary sportswriter Red Smith, a Pulitzer Prize winner like Anderson, had a column killed by the *Times* in which he urged the United States to boycott the Moscow Olympic Games. Upon hearing the news, Smith sighed, "I guess I'll just write about the infield fly rule.")

When a writer runs afoul, "typically what happens," says Raines, "is that the desk editor will say, 'Gee, this is a little rough. Pull this back.' What was atypical with the Anderson and Araton columns was that Gerald and I were rung in, and I guess it was because of the whole buzz about the Masters."

It was this buzz that inspired Dave Anderson to turn in his column on November 21, a day early. In an interview, he says, "I took my car in for servicing, and while I was waiting, I was reading the paper. All of a sudden I realized, Hey, Harvey's column is not in here. I called the office to find out what had happened. At that point I got fragments of the story. Neil then asked what I was working on. I told him, and he said, That might not fly. So I wrote it a day early, to give him a chance to show it to whoever he needed to show it to."

In the first sentence of the column, Anderson made an explicit reference to the *Times* editorial that had run three days earlier, and then he lamented, "Please, let Tiger Woods just play golf. That's what he does, and does better than anybody else. He's not a social activist. He never has been. And it's doubtful he ever will be. It's not his style.

"Just because Woods is the world's No. 1 golfer, just because he's a mixture of minorities with African-American, American Indian, Thai, Chinese and Caucasian ancestry, he's not obliged to take a sociological stand. It's not his responsibility. If he did boycott, it would be laudatory but it also would be phony. It would not be him."

After filing the column, Anderson got the bad news from Amdur, the sports editor. "Neil told me I wasn't supposed to argue with the editorial page." Anderson's reaction? "I thought back to Red Smith and the infield fly rule," he says. "I thought, hey, I'm moving up in class. I was disappointed they did it. Not angry, but disappointed. They're entitled to do it. I don't think they should, but the top editors are entitled."

In the *New York Observer*, Sridhar Pappu fingered Boyd as the bad guy, but it was Raines who spiked Anderson's column. He offers a long, interesting defense: "Step back a little to the division of the news and editorial pages," says Raines. "There is a long-standing protocol at the paper that they don't take shots at each other. I was acutely aware of this division. And I think Joe Lelyveld"—who was a top newsroom lieutenant while Raines ran the editorial page—"was during the period when there was this succession battle [for executive editor] going on, because neither one of us wanted to appear to be manipulating that process. Joe and I never discussed this, but we were both very careful to respect one another's prerogatives.

"I give you that background because I think I overreacted to Dave's column. Neil Amdur brought the column to me, which is very unusual. I glanced at it, saw that it was using the editorial as a stepping-off point, and said, Let's not run it. I should have stopped, I should have edited out the [reference to the editorial]. It was easily fixable. The fact is, Neil and I did not sit down and go through it carefully. It was a decision I made literally standing up, in a walk-by conversation, not because that's my style of decision making, but because you have to make so many decisions so fast in that job. I booted that one. I should have sent it back to the writer for revisions, which is a standard procedure.

"In retrospect, people often said, 'Why didn't you just take that one line out?' I'm not sure that just taking out the word 'editorial' would've met my concern at that time—that we appeared to be sticking out our thumb in the eye of the editorial page—because the raison d'être for the column was to rebut the editorial. And the word came back through Neil that Dave had said, 'Okay, I'll write about something else.' It was a week or so later when Dave showed up on TV, talking about"—here Raines laughs self-consciously—"censorship."

Once the *Daily News* broke the story of the spiked columns, Anderson was everywhere, doing dozens of interviews, though for a change he was answering, not asking, the questions. "The fact that Anderson was sucked into this was key, because he was this Mr. Chips, a guy whose integrity is beyond reproach," says Paul Colford, who got the scoop for the *News*. "His professionalism is widely known, even among non-sports fans. That he was the victim fueled the outrage among people who really believe in the paper. It was just such thuggish behavior."

Poor Howell Raines was once again in the wrong place at the wrong time: He was back in Paris dealing with the *International Herald Tribune* negotiations when Colford's story hit newsstands on December 4. Outrage and disbelief tore through the newsroom, and Raines received a series of frenzied phone calls. "I had actually forgotten there was a flap over this," he says. "So from Paris I wrote a memo to the masthead saying, Let's just put both columns on the Internet immediately. Sort of like, We shouldn't have held them, and here they are this very day. And of course we would also publish them in the paper, but let's deal with the issue right away.

"There was a very strong feeling on Gerald's part, and others, that that was the wrong thing to do on principle, that in both cases we had acted on reasonable journalistic principles—in one case separation of editorial and news, and the other possible unfairness in the column. And we shouldn't simply reverse ourselves. At that point, I had to face a decision. Do I overrule my masthead—whose authority and confidence I'm trying to increase—from three thousand miles away, or do I wait and get back to meet with them? I chose the latter. I wish I had gone on my initial impulse, but managerially, you can't overrule your six top executives without them having a chance to talk to you."

In the meantime, Boyd wanted to write a staff memo trying to quiet the outrage in the newsroom. Raines gave Boyd his blessing, but he did not see the memo before it went out. Boyd didn't make any allusions to bayonets, but his missive was as big a flop as Hootie Johnson's infamous manifesto. Boyd had barely pressed "send" when the full text showed up on Romenesko, touching off a parallel controversy. The document was so unusual that the Smithsonian Institute later requested a copy. It read,

> First, we are proud of our leadership in covering this story. Our sports staff, with help from many desks, is doing exactly what some "accuse" us of doing: asking questions that no other organization is raising, and pressing energetically for the answers our readers want . . . There is only one word for our vigor in pursuing a story—whether in Afghanistan or Augusta.
>
> Call it journalism.
>
> Recently we spiked two sports columns that touched on the Augusta issue. We were not concerned with which "side" the writers were on. A well-reported, well-reasoned column can come down on any side, with our welcome. One of the columns focused centrally on disputing the *Times*'s editorials about Augusta. Part of our strict separation between the news and editorial pages entails not attacking each other. Intramural quarreling of that kind is unseemly and self-absorbed. Discussion of editorials may arise when we report on an issue; fair enough. But we do not think they should be the issue.
>
> In the case of this column, the writer had previously dealt with the Augusta controversy at least twice, arguing on October 6 against pressuring the golf club to admit women. His freedom to argue that way was not—is not—in question.
>
> The other spiked column tried to draw a connection between the Augusta issue and the elimination of women's softball from the Olympics. The logic did not meet our standards: that would have been true regardless of which "side" the writer had taken on Augusta. The writer was invited to try again, but we did not think the logic improved materially.
>
> At any rate, we hope no member of our staff really needs this assurance that our news columns enforce no "party line."

Boyd's revealing memo was parsed in Talmudic detail. No blogger had more fun with it than Mickey Kaus: "If Boyd's memo is an example of his idea of 'logic,' I *really* want to read the columns he killed because 'the logic did not meet our standards.' " In a posting with the heading "Flood the Zone I" (yes, there would be subsequent FTZ II, III, IV, and V, all in the same day), Kaus wrote, "Alert reader J.L. notices another revealing sentence in that wonderfully awful and defensive Boyd memo: 'Part of our strict separation between the news and editorial pages entails not attacking each other.' A real 'strict separation,' J.L. notes, would 'require that either side be free to say whatever it likes about the other.' How *convenient* that the *Times*'s 'strict' ethical rules always somehow work to prevent criticism of the *Times* itself! But in this case the paper's internal ideology ('Call it journalism') is so strong it unthinkingly perverts the meaning of plain English words: SEPARATION = SUPPRESSION."

Later in the day, Kaus had another thought: "The NYT's idea of damage control: Don't apologize—slime your writers! It's a surefire morale booster!"

Araton admits that he "wasn't thrilled" with having his logic labeled defective so publicly, but "at that point, I got the sense that it was only Day One of the story being out, that something bigger was brewing and that wouldn't be the end of it."

And how. Here Raines picks up the tale: "So I come back from Paris, and I dig into it. I read both columns. We decide to run them. As the writers want them to run. Dave's ran with the voluntary deletion of the mention of the editorial page. I read the first column and I read Harvey's second column. I thought the second column was very good, and should have run. I think Gerald made the wrong decision to hold the second column. That was the decision I approved without reading the piece, so I take the blame for it. That column should have run at the time it was fixed. Harvey had answered to me every reasonable objection that was raised to it, and the objections were reasonable. So I call Harvey up and tell him we're going to run this column. And he says, I think both columns are dated now, and I'd like to take another crack at it. So he filed again, and the third column was the weakest of the three, and that's what we ran! I wish he had chosen the second column, but I had told him it was his call to make."

The columns finally appeared in print on December 8, after four days of fevered debate. There was so much speculation about how the *Times* would clean up its mess that a day before the paper had run a 1,000-word story in the National Desk news hole in the front section under the headline "2 Rejected Columns to Be Printed by the Times."

Golfgate (as Pappu in the *Observer* was referring to the spiked column debacle) set a problematic precedent for the *Times*. This same vicious cycle—errors in judgment, breakdowns in the chain of command, scathing public criticism, internal turmoil, self-flagellation—would repeat itself a few months later, with cataclysmic results for Raines and the *Times*. More immediately, the controversy about the columns destroyed the paper's momentum on Augusta National. The *Times* had helped make it an issue of national importance, and, particularly in the area of the dissatisfaction within the club, the paper had advanced the story significantly. But with four months still to go until the Masters, the Gray Lady would never recapture the same swagger, or relevance.

"The *Times* coverage fell off a cliff," says McCarthy. "It flatlined." Having accomplished his first objective, Augusta National's spin doctor could begin fighting other battles. "It was time to settle some scores," he says.

DESPITE THE DISTRACTION offered by the *Times*, the public image of Augusta National continued to plummet in early December. On December 5, at a party celebrating the one-hundredth birthday of the one-time segregationist Strom Thurmond—Hootie Johnson's old friend—Senate majority leader Trent Lott offered an ill-conceived tribute: "I want to say this about my state: When Strom Thurmond ran for president, we voted for him. We're proud of it. And if the rest of the country had followed our lead, we wouldn't have had all these problems over all these years, either." Lott's remarks touched off weeks of raging controversy and he was eventually compelled to give up his post as Senate majority leader. What does Trent Lott have to do with Augusta National? Nothing, yet in the public imagination he became linked with another southern leader in the news with whom he shared a passing physical resemblance: Hootie Johnson. *Fortune* printed pictures of Lott and Johnson side by side under the headline "Separated at Birth?" The *Late Show with David Letterman* offered the "Top Ten Ways Trent Lott Is Preparing for the Holidays." Number Nine: "Filling out membership form to the Augusta National Golf Club."

On December 9, while Lott was still the butt of endless late-night jokes, John Snow, President Bush's nominee for the secretary of the treasury, became the second member to resign from Augusta National. In a *Late Show* monologue, Letterman again found a way to zing the club. "I think we've got to be careful about Saddam," Dave said. "He seems to be trying to do the nice-guy thing. Last Saturday, he apologized to Kuwait for invading them in 1990. And today he resigned his membership from Augusta National Golf Club." (Why was Letterman, a non-golfer, so tuned in to the membership controversy? Maybe because his head writer, Bill Scheft, is the nephew of Herbert Warren Wind, the preeminent golf writer who coined the phrase "Amen Corner.")

Politically at least, the green jacket had become radioactive. Augusta National boasts four former cabinet secretaries among its membership. A sitting president, Ronald Reagan, had visited in the not-so-distant past, and just a year earlier member William Farrish had been nominated and confirmed to the Court of St. James's without a whiff of controversy. "Augusta National has now become emblematic of sex discrimination," Burk said a day after Snow's resignation. "I've already won. Even if Augusta National never admits a woman, people will never again look at it without thinking, discrimination. If I got off the stage today, the club is already tainted, the tournament is tarnished, and that will remain. Once . . . it comes to the attention of the president of the United States, it's over, folks."

Burk was referring to White House Press Secretary Ari Fleischer's briefing with reporters from the day before, in which the first four questions were about Snow's Augusta National membership. "Why is he resigning from Augusta, specifically?" Fleischer was asked.

"That's an individual decision that he makes. It is not, in the president's judgment, a disqualifying matter in appointment of cabinet secretaries. But these are individual decisions that individual appointees make."

"Even though it's not disqualifying, did the White House suggest or ask or recommend that he resign?"

"No, it's his decision to make."

Snow had been a member at Augusta National since the early 1990s and was one of the club's better players, with a low round there of 78. His favorite playing partner among the green jackets was Tom Usher, the CEO of U.S. Steel. Snow has never discussed his resignation publicly; Rob Nichols, the chief spokesman for the U.S. Treasury Department, provided a circuitous written statement for this book: "John Snow was deeply honored by President Bush's decision to select him as Secretary of the Treasury. Upon accepting the President's request to serve, Snow said he would put all of his energies into the enormous task at hand. This job, Snow said at the time of his nomination, would be his complete focus, and he did not want to add a distraction to this office—as there is already plenty to do. Accordingly, Snow withdrew from Augusta so he could devote 100 percent of his time and attention to the President's agenda and the country's fiscal needs. Snow is aware of the distinction between exercising rights of association as a private citizen and the policy implications that people draw when you do so while holding positions of public trust. But Snow was not a member of Augusta to make public policy—he was a member there so he could golf. Accordingly, Snow withdrew so he could devote his time and attention to strengthening the economy, which, incidentally, is a full-time job."

Even grading on the curve to account for Washington spin, this line of reasoning is dubious. No, Snow wasn't worried that his Augusta National membership could make for thorny questions at his confirmation hearing, nor did he fear picketing on the steps of the Treasury Department. *He resigned from the club simply because he didn't have time to tee it up.* Never mind that Snow was known to visit Augusta National only once or twice a year anyway. Or that these days he is often spotted at Kinloch Golf Club in Richmond, Virginia, a Jack Nicklaus signature design that was named the best new private club in America by *Golf Digest* in 2001.

Around Augusta National, Wyman was considered a traitor, Snow merely a victim. "I don't count Snow," says club member Wheelock Whitney. "That's a different deal. He resigned for the sake of political expedience, not out of some sort of protest." In fact, Whitney intimates that it wouldn't be a surprise to see Snow reinvited to the most private of clubs once his days as a public servant are over. That is, if he can make time. (Wink, wink.)

So, what does Snow really think in the great debate between Hootie and Martha? The chief spokesman of the United States Treasury says of his boss, in eloquent political speak, "He sees merit in both arguments. He is confident the sport will find a fair and proper solution."

THE PRINTING of *The New York Times*'s spiked columns was not the end of the debate on media ethics and responsibility. In fact, it was just the beginning. On December 12, the front page of Sports of *The Washington Post* carried a sprawling 2,500-word piece in which Len Shapiro tried to get his arms around the meaning of the membership controversy. In the weeks to come, the point of view of the story would be at the heart of a noisy controversy, but the initial buzz centered on a passage buried in the middle of the article: "The club appears to get special treatment in the local newspaper, the *Augusta Chronicle*, owned by publisher William 'Billy' Morris III, a longtime Augusta National member. According to sources, Morris recently called his editors and demanded that a long profile of Burk scheduled to appear on a Sunday front page be shoved back to pages 10 and 11. He killed the accompanying Burk question-and-answer sidebar. Morris also refused to run a recent piece by a writer who agreed in principle with Augusta's position but nevertheless urged the club to give in and admit a woman for the good of the game and the tournament. Morris did not return telephone calls seeking response, and his paper's president, general manager and executive editor declined to comment."

The burying of the Burk profile wasn't as recent as Shapiro indicated—Scott Michaux's well-reported, balanced story had run on September 29. But Shapiro nailed all the other details, and his scoop was widely picked up on, leading to the inevitable tsk-tsking. However, there was only a modicum of the outrage that had accompanied similar revelations at *The New York Times*, in part because of Billy Morris's unusual view of journalistic integrity when it comes to his home golf club.

There has long been a rule at the *Augusta Chronicle* that no story involving the National can be printed without being approved personally by Morris, who makes no secret of where his allegiances lie. Despite the inherent conflict of interest, he is a very visible member of the Masters media committee, often moderating interviews with the players, including his good friend Jack Nicklaus. In 1994, *Chronicle* staffers got wind that two local members of Augusta National were asked to resign for having taken money to arrange tee times for non-members. In an effort to preserve the club's pristine reputation, Morris killed the investigation, leaving *Golf World* to break the story. Of course, his staffers are rewarded for their loyalty: Every May, before Augusta National closes down for the summer, two dozen lucky *Chronicle* employees are allowed to play the course, if they meet one requirement: that they have shot 105 or better in one of the various company golf outings held in the preceding year.

Morris almost never speaks publicly about Augusta National, and he stonewalled all inquiries about his editorial decisions on the Burk story, sucking the oxygen out of the scandal. (Memo to Gerald Boyd: That's how you do it.)

What also helped Morris was the timing of Shapiro's scoop. Five days after it appeared, the media had a far sexier target on the issue of media conflicts of interest—Bryant Gumbel. Since 1995, Gumbel has been the host of HBO's *Real Sports*, a sort of *60 Minutes* for jocks in which, as the promos say, "Nothing is out of bounds." In the December 17 episode Gumbel, rather than one of the show's many correspondents, put together a meaty, twelve-minute profile on Burk. It was timed to coincide with a splashy new component to her campaign against "corporate hypocrisy." As Burk announced on *Real Sports* (and in press releases and print interviews), the NCWO was launching a Web site devoted to Augusta National members who were in leadership positions at publicly traded corporations. Augustadiscriminates.org juxtaposed pictures of these green jackets with their company's non-discrimination policy. Also provided on the site was contact information and an e-mail link to the respective companies so surfers could register their complaints. (Burk's Web site earned her a letter of protest from the city of Augusta's mayor, Bob Young, who wrote, "We have a diverse community where discrimination is not practiced or sanctioned as a matter of public policy. The domain name suggests the city of Augusta and the people who live here discriminate. That could not be farther from the truth.")

In the *Real Sports* piece, Gumbel offered a glowing narration of Burk's bio, and then engaged her in a dialogue about the various issues. In a series of spiky exchanges, it was clear that Gumbel was overmatched intellectually.

Of Burk's new Web site, he said, "Isn't this a nice form of extortion?"

"No."

"Why not?"

"Extortion is when you want money."

"But you are risking my money if I am the chairman of XYZ."

"No. You're risking your money by being a member of a club that discriminates against half your customers."

"Those who disagree with you, are they necessarily sexist?"

"Not necessarily. Some of them just need their consciousness raised."

Here Gumbel let out a laugh. Burk continued: "Lots of folks are sexist and don't know it. And part of my job is to let him know it."

"I heard it characterized to me once upon a time, whereas women are arguing about wanting to pay the tab in a restaurant, um, African Americans can't even get in the restaurant. And there's a big difference there."

"Well, women can't even get into Augusta."

"Most Americans can't."

"But not because of an immutable characteristic. At least theoretically, you as a man have the ability to get rich enough, powerful enough, or good enough at golf to get into Augusta. I as a woman do not have that chance. That is the difference. That is the essence of discrimination."

"We're talking about maybe one or two privileged women."

"Yeah, we are. And . . ."

"Why all this hoopla to afford one more privilege to some already privileged women?"

"Would you have asked that question at Shoal Creek, Bryant? For heaven's sake. Would you say, 'Why are we doing this to let one rich African American man who's already got it made in his life into the Shoal Creek Country Club?'"

Gumbel clearly relished his role as devil's advocate, defending Augusta National so as to provoke Burk. He might have been hailed for some stimulating journalism were it not for one inconvenient fact he somehow forgot to mention on the air: He is a member at Burning Tree, which, until Martha Burk made the scene, was the most notorious all-male golf club in the country.

Gumbel's membership was hardly a secret—it had been reported at least as far back as a 1990 story in *U.S. News and World Report,* and ever since had consistently popped up in stories that chronicled his golf addiction. On the same day the *Real Sports* episode was to air, Gumbel was called out on his conflict of interest by Robert B. Bluey, in a scoop on CNSNews.com that was posted on the afternoon of December 17. Bluey reached Burk for his story, and in a juicy revelation she confided that she had admonished Gumbel off camera about his Burning Tree membership: "I told him it was wrong and he shouldn't do it," Burk told Bluey. "He mentioned it to me and I said, 'Bryant, you're wrong to do this. It's the wrong kind of statement to make not only to the public but also to your own daughter. I think you need to reconsider what you're doing in terms of the public statement that it makes.' I don't think a person in Bryant Gumbel's situation ought to bring himself in line for the criticism he will undoubtedly undergo when this becomes a story in the media, and I told him so."

When Bluey pressed Burk as to why she didn't bring this up while the cameras were rolling, Burk said she would have liked to, but "he had control of the interview." Yeah, that rings true—shy, retiring Martha Burk is always so reluctant to speak her mind, especially around TV cameras.

So who threw the skunk in the garden party by tipping off Bluey? Jim McCarthy, of course. "It reeks to high heavens of hypocrisy, on both of their parts, but especially Burk's," McCarthy says. "If she is genuinely outraged by all-male clubs, then why did she let Gumbel off the hook? Good grief, a prime offender in perpetuating what she deems sex discrimination was a couple of feet away. But no, she didn't want to jeopardize her warm, fuzzy close-up, and a chance to shill for that absurd Web site, and he didn't want to smudge his reputation as a serious journalist. Or what's left of it."

Bluey's scoop quickly spread to the mainstream media, and while Gumbel was hiding underneath his desk, his red-faced superiors tried to defend the indefensible. Ross Greenberg, the president of HBO Sports, issued a statement saying, "Bryant delivered a solid and objective piece.

We had the right journalist asking all the relevant questions related to Augusta and Martha Burk's campaign." Greenberg was more forthcoming in follow-up interviews, calling the whole stink "an unbelievable case study in journalism." Greenberg said that his first instinct was to disclose the Burning Tree membership on the air, but that Gumbel and unidentified producers talked him out of it. The concern, Greenberg told the *New York Post*, was that Gumbel's admission "would taint [the interview] to such a degree that everyone would have assumed any question out of Bryant's mouth was a personal-agenda item."

Gumbel declined to be interviewed for this book. A *Real Sports* producer who worked on the Burk segment would speak only anonymously. "It's bullshit that we can't talk out in the open," he said. "We kill people all the time for being afraid to come on the show. What really hurts about this is that we try to do smart TV, for a more sophisticated audience, and at the critical moment we lost faith in our viewers that they could make up their own minds about Bryant's membership."

Gumbel was so chastened by the episode that in March he felt compelled to host another segment about Augusta National. (He did not feel chastened enough to resign from Burning Tree.) Tail between his legs, he offered this introduction: "Good evening and welcome to *Real Sports*, where we begin tonight with a rather sensitive subject of golf clubs that do not admit women as members. It's estimated there are about two dozen clubs in America that are all male, and yes, I'm a member at one of them."

One of Gumbel's featured guests was Jim McCarthy. Like a prizefighter whose opponent is already bleeding, McCarthy mercilessly jabbed Gumbel, further opening the wound.

Gumbel: "You don't think Hootie's response put some of his club members in a terribly awkward position? CEOs of major corporations that depend on women for a large percentage of their business, and now they are a member of a club that discriminates against those women."

McCarthy: "Hold on a second. The club does not discriminate against women. The club has a right to have its private membership, which happens to be single-gender. You know Ms. Burk belongs to single-gender groups. You yourself, Bryant, belong to a men-only golf club."

"Yes, I do," Gumbel said meekly.

"That is no different than what Augusta National is doing. So to stand up for the right to have that membership, there's nothing wrong with that at all. If Ms. Burk is hurling invectives, there's no one to blame but her."

"Those CEOs who are feeling the awkwardness of that position, are you telling me they should blame Martha Burk?"

"Absolutely. Of course."

"For calling attention to a fact?"

"Well, for casting it in this disparaging way."

"By definition the club discriminates against women by having no female members."

"Martha Burk has called that bigoted."

That last remark by McCarthy sent Gumbel around the bend. The host of the show said, "I am not talking about what Martha Burk calls it, and I'm not talking about bigoted. I'm not talking about rednecks, I am not talking about all the other adjectives that have come down the road. I'm talking about plain and simple the definition of discrimination."

"I think the question is whether the definition of discrimination should be characterized as pejorative or bad or evil or nefarious."

"I'm not ascribing a moral interpretation to it."

"I don't think there should be."

"I am trying to find the definition here of what the club engages in and what it does not. And I think any realistic or objective definition would say, that is, by definition, discrimination."

"In the same way that Smith College is, or the same way the Texas Women's Shooting Club is, or the same way that your golf club is."

Gumbel quickly changed the subject.

IN THE NARRATIVE of the Augusta National controversy, Bryant Gumbel is not the only key media figure with ties to an all-male club. The two female reporters who have driven the story—USA Today's Christine Brennan and Golf Digest's Marcia Chambers—both work under men who belong to all-male Pine Valley: Digest editor-in-chief

Jerry Tarde, and Doug McCorkindale, the CEO of Gannett Co., *USA Today*'s parent company.

Tarde is unmoved by the suggestion that, like Gumbel or Billy Morris, his editorial decisions may be colored by where he plays golf. "The magazine speaks for itself," he says. "We have a good record advocating inclusion and covering inclusion."

Actually, he's being modest. Under Tarde, *Digest* has been at the forefront of exposing discriminatory practices in private clubs, and Pine Valley has hardly been spared in the coverage, even as he continues to enjoy its exclusivity. Tarde's split personality can be attributed to the hardscrabble golf course he grew up playing. Juniata was a 5,400-yard, par-63 on the wrong side of Philadelphia that attracted a racially mixed crowd. The diversity Tarde encountered at Juniata helped leave him with a lasting sensitivity to golf's have-nots. He found his muse in Marcia Chambers, a *New York Times* writer whose thoughtful sports pieces were informed by her master's in law from Yale.

In the May and June 1990 issues of *Golf Digest*, Chambers wrote a groundbreaking two-part special report billed as "The Challenge Facing America's Private Clubs." The articles introduced to the public golf's dirty little secrets, gender and racial discrimination at private clubs. Chambers expertly surveyed the gathering forces—judicial, social, and economic—that were laying siege to the private respites of the privileged. (The issues highlighted in the stories differ from Burk's crusade; Chambers focused on discriminatory practices within clubs, like restricted tee times for women and unequal facilities between the sexes. That is where the case law had been built, not on the policies of single-gender clubs.) Trying to penetrate this cloistered world was the "single most difficult reporting job I've ever had," Chambers says—and this is a woman who covered the Son of Sam case and the Patty Hearst kidnapping, and whose home away from home was New York City's criminal courts building on 107th Street.

Tarde and Chambers made for an unlikely pair of crusaders—she became America's leading voice calling for fair play on the fairways, while he was an unrepentant member of Pine Valley. Yet Chambers says of Tarde's membership, "It is not troubling to me. A lot of women have a problem with [all-male clubs]. I don't. I am an ardent believer in the First Amendment right of association. I do believe that when a club takes on a very commercial, public event, it becomes larger than the club itself. It has an obligation to the public and indeed its own tournament to be more inclusive. I would certainly change my thinking about Pine Valley if it started hosting big-time tournaments."

In 2002, Tarde and Chambers teamed up for another look at exclusionary membership practices in private clubs. Tarde wanted a hard-hitting examination of the implications of having two of the four major championships in professional golf run by all-male clubs, what he calls "an anachronism in our times." Over lunch he mentioned his idea to Susan Reed, who was preparing her first issue as the new managing editor of *Golf for Women*, *Digest*'s bimonthly sister publication. Reed was anxious to, in Tarde's words, "make *Golf for Women* a more important magazine." She lobbied for the story to go in *Golf for Women*, and Tarde agreed, putting Reed in touch with Chambers.

The result was "Ladies Need Not Apply" in the May/June 2002 issue, in which Chambers examined the complicated issues surrounding exclusionary private clubs profiting from public events. Tarde expected Chambers's piece to spark another far-reaching discussion on the issue of sex discrimination in golf, but the reaction was muted. "After the piece appeared, I thought it would be a revelation to people," he says. "Our Communications Department tried to pitch the story to other media outlets. It met with no response. The attitude was, We know that. It's not news."

All that changed when *USA Today*'s Christine Brennan read the story, and, after learning that Lloyd Ward was a member at Augusta National, was inspired to call the USOC chief for an explanation. (In the ensuing column, Brennan gave credit where due, writing, "For the last three years, I went to the Masters and wrote about this issue . . . [T]his year I decided that I would move on to another topic and let the good old boys in the green jackets run their tournament in peace. But then I read Marcia Chambers's compelling account of exclusion at Augusta National in the May/June issue of *Golf for Women* . . .") Ward's comments advocating change at Augusta National were read by Martha Burk, and the rest is herstory. Brennan's, that is.

In the opening months of the membership controversy, she wrote regularly on the topic, but in December—amid all the heat from the resignations of Tom Wyman and John Snow and the travails of *The New York Times*—Brennan went into overdrive, pumping out three Augusta-centric pieces in the span of four weeks. In her December 5 dispatch, she wrote, "I have never met Martha Burk and had never heard of her until her name surfaced in July, when Johnson chose to take her private letter public. Burk has told reporters that she got the idea to write that letter after reading a column of mine about Augusta in April."

Reading this column, and others, Chambers began to feel that the story she had owned for more than a decade was being shanghaied by a Janie-come-lately at *USA Today*. In the tug-of-war for credit on who broke the story, *Digest* interjected a little revisionist history to benefit its star writer. In the April 2003 issue, the magazine offered a synopsis of its version of the Augusta National membership controversy: "It all started back in June when, after an exposé in *Golf for Women*, Martha Burk, head of the National Council of Women's Organizations, wrote to William (Hootie) Johnson, chairman of Augusta National, protesting the club's lack of female members. A month later, Johnson responded with a tersely worded letter . . ."

Strictly speaking, this was true—*after* was a wonderfully vague choice of words—but failing to mention that Burk was inspired to write Johnson by *USA Today*, not *Golf for Women*, was a whopping omission.

The rivalry between Chambers and Brennan was stoked by a short Q&A in the *Sports Illustrated*'s Masters preview, which carried a headline billing Brennan as "The *USA Today* columnist who ignited the Augusta debate . . ." After reading this, an apoplectic Chambers fired off a four-page letter (with seven enclosures) to two *Sports Illustrated* staffers detailing her grievances. In the letter she wrote, "There is no doubt that Christine Brennan's column in *USA Today* was the stimulus that led Martha Burk to write to Hootie Johnson. There is also no doubt that in Christine Brennan's own words she was galvanized to write her column because of a story I wrote. . . . An apparently forgetful Ms. Brennan now believes she did indeed start it all. . . . I am simply urging when the topic comes up again, and it will, that you give credit to my work."

Says Brennan, "I went out of my way to credit her by name, and not just the magazine. I'm very proud of that. Marcia Chambers has clearly done more on this subject than any other person, and I was happy to acknowledge her. Having said that, I'm lucky to write for a newspaper that is seen by a lot of people, and Martha Burk was one of the people who saw my column. It wasn't *Golf for Women* that she picked up. I would also add that the interview with Lloyd Ward is what advanced the story."

There is more at stake than just bragging rights. Brennan has sold to Scribners what she calls a "father/daughter/girls in sports book," with a tentative publication date of 2006. Being known as the woman who sparked the biggest golf story since Tiger Woods's emergence has vast commercial appeal. At the 2003 Masters, while Chambers was at home in Connecticut, Brennan estimates that she gave twenty-five interviews—"I'm not gonna say no to my buddies," she says. "I ask people to talk for a living, so how can I say no when someone wants to interview me?"

This high profile has its downside. During the Masters, Robert Bluey—the CNSNews.com writer who had blown the whistle on Bryant Gumbel—created another stir when he reported McCorkindale's Pine Valley membership. (The story didn't mention that McCorkindale is also a Burning Tree man.) Brennan told Bluey that she was unaware of her boss's estrogen-free golf hangout, but in the story she did have some guardedly critical words for McCorkindale. "In this climate and at this time in our sports history, I do believe that is a worthy topic for discussion," she said. "If I were a member of a discriminatory, private club, I would expect that that would be scrutinized by any and all journalists. I would expect it, and I would be disappointed if journalists didn't because this is where we are today in our culture."

Brennan is quick to point out that, like Chambers, she draws a distinction between Augusta National and other all-male clubs, because of the public aspect of the Masters and the corporate money it generates for the club. Fine, but isn't it a little bit troubling that Hootie Johnson's toughest critic works for a man who holds dear the same beliefs and traditions that have brought Augusta National's chairman so much grief, in *USA Today* and elsewhere? "If Mr. McCorkindale is using his membership just to play golf with his friends, I don't think I have a problem with that," Brennan says. "If he's taking male staff members or employees or advertising clients—as I've heard Tarde often does—then that would be a big issue for me."

Brennan said she would be happy to comment further but she first wanted to speak with McCorkindale. "I've heard he's a member, but I don't know for sure," she said. "I don't know if he's in the process of resigning his membership. I've never met him. I've been meaning to get in touch with him and I haven't. It's a very valid question to ask, and I should have an answer, and I don't. Let me call him and get back to you."

Brennan subsequently reported that two phone calls and two e-mails to McCorkindale's office went unreturned. Asked if she will ever write about her boss's membership at exclusionary golf clubs in the pages of *USA Today,* she says "I haven't thought about when I'll write about the issues again. I sure wouldn't avoid [McCorkindale's memberships], if it was germane."

THE TONE and content of the coverage of Augusta National slowly began to change as 2002 faded into a new year. Like the membership controversy itself, the revolution was sparked by a simple letter.

"The press is a great American tradition, which goes all the way back to Tom Paine printing pamphlets. But we need more voices instead of fewer, and that's never been more important than in today's corporate-driven media world."

So says Christopher Rake, a forty-something reporter from the Washington, D.C., area. Actually, Rake is a pseudonym. His identity is a mystery, or, at any rate, a secret. At least it's supposed to be. He agreed to be interviewed for this book only on the condition of anonymity—and then called from his home, revealing his real name via caller ID. James Bond he ain't. Anyway, in February 2002, Rake began a boutique blog called PostWatch (postwatch.blogspot.org), a daily kvetching about *The Washington Post.* "I became so disenchanted only getting one side of every story," Rake says. "I felt like it was my civic duty to balance the distortion and bias of the *Post*'s coverage."

Despite holding down a full-time job writing for industry trade publications, Rake began every day with a "morning blogging constitutional," continued pecking away over long lunches at the office and then picked up the narrative in the evenings from home. Two hours was his minimum PostWatch workday, and he often put in up to six, unpaid. His dream was to "take the Boeing," in the words of his hero, InstaPundit's Glenn Reynolds—which is to say, attract a benefactor and blog full-time. At that point Rake would have shed the phony identity necessitated by his double life as a respectable journalist. Alas, PostWatch never quite took off, and after a little more than a year, the blog was put on long-term hiatus. But during his brief run, Rake found himself squarely in the middle of the Augusta National dispute.

On December 12, Len Shapiro wrote his long piece recapping the turbulent first four months of the membership controversy. It was in that story that he broke the news of Billy Morris's burying the Martha Burk package that his *Augusta Chronicle* sports staff had cooked up. The tone of Shapiro's piece can more or less be summed up by the quote he chose for the kicker: "Everyone's afraid to take [Augusta National] on, and you know the paper won't do it, not with Billy Morris in charge," he quoted local resident Anna Hargis as saying. "You know what most people worry about? That all this stuff might hurt them getting $4,000 to rent their house. The mentality of the town basically is let the rich boys do what they want to do. To me, it's totally sexist. I mean, Hootie Johnson has four daughters. How does he sleep at night?"

Rake blogged the story under the heading "Dog Bites Man" on the day it was printed, writing, "Len Shapiro gets a huge display in the *Post* Sports section for a story, "Trying to Master the Situation," whose apogee is that dreadful headline. It doesn't tell us much that's new about the Augusta membership issue. And unfortunately it continues a one-sided harangue against the club. Here are the main problems with the story:

"1. He cites polls that support Augusta critics but not those that don't.

"2. He quotes people who believe Augusta's gender policy is similar to race discrimination, but not those who don't.

"3. He quotes a local critic who charges that most people in the community are 'afraid' to speak out against the policy. But he can't find any locals to dispute that allegation or defend Augusta. Not one.

"4. He says Hootie Johnson 'isn't sharing' his opinion on the issue, saying Johnson turned down an interview request. But he oddly doesn't mention Johnson's media blitz last month, including a November 12 interview with Shapiro himself. How many times does he want Johnson to repeat himself?

"5. He quotes an anonymous USGA official who disagrees with PGA chief Tim Finchem, but not anyone to defend him.

"6. You'd never know from reading this story that women play at Augusta all the time.

"There are other problems I hope to blog in a bit more detail, but that's it for now."

If Rake's critiques sound familiar, that's because he was largely parroting the ideas of Jim McCarthy. Augusta National's spin doctor had targeted Rake when he began reaching out to the blogging community to plant homegrown media criticism. "When news was breaking, McCarthy and I would often talk two or three times a day, just bouncing ideas off each other," Rake says. McCarthy knew that PostWatch was an easy way to reach his desired audience. "There's probably two hundred people who read that Web site, and they're all in our newsroom," says George Solomon, who, until his retirement in June 2003, oversaw the *Post*'s Augusta National coverage as assistant managing editor for sports.

On December 18, PostWatch offered a "Len Shapiro Update": "The *Washington Post* sportswriter recently ran a long story in the sports section on Augusta; I did not treat it kindly when I blogged it December 12. Now I have a copy of a letter from Jim McCarthy, a public relations consultant who is working for Augusta and has written a long letter to ombudsman Michael Getler identifying a number of problems with the story." Rake ran six text blocks from McCarthy's letter, which essentially amplified the original PostWatch posting, which had been McCarthy's talking points all along.

For months McCarthy had been bombarding Solomon and Getler with critiques of the paper's coverage, and while both took his calls and read his letters, nothing of substance came out of the dialogue. That's why McCarthy turned to the blogosphere. "There has never before been an effective way to correct the abuses of the press," he says. "Letters to the editor and ombudsmen are controlled by the paper you're criticizing. Decisions about them happen in a vacuum and only seem to encourage an institutional aloofness. Now, with blogging, editors and reporters know that the eyes of their colleagues and the eyes of the public are on them."

After McCarthy's letter appeared on PostWatch, it became a hammer in his continuing dialogue with the *Post*. "You start with the reporter," he says. "Shapiro and I had a falling-out pretty quick. Then you go to the editor. The next stop is the ombudsman. All the while you cc all correspondence to the *Columbia Journalism Review*, to Romenesko, to PostWatch, so they know people are watching. Eventually the message gets through. The specter of having this discussion out in the open scares them into acting. There's no question PostWatch had a big impact on helping the *Post* do the right thing."

About a week after McCarthy's letter was posted, Solomon invited him to the Post newsroom for a face-to-face meeting. Before it was over the sports editor made an irresistible offer: "I said, if you're that unhappy, we'll give you twenty inches to print your side," Solomon recalls. This was not an unprecedented move—a couple weeks earlier, Gene Upshaw, the head of the NFL Players Association, had been given space to vent about an unflattering story. Says Solomon, "We're not afraid to have different voices in the paper. It makes us stronger."

On January 19, the *Post* printed 882 words by McCarthy on page 4 of Sports, under the headline "Responding to Augusta Coverage." McCarthy recapped many of the arguments in his PostWatch posting, blasting the paper for "a pattern of unbalanced, opinionated reporting that has been ongoing in more than two dozen news articles and counting."

McCarthy also introduced some new material. "Injecting opinion and slanting coverage has been at the heart of the problem. Mr. Shapiro, for instance, wrote in a 'Golf Notebook' on July 11 that the timetable for Augusta National admitting women 'ought to be now.' On January 1, the *Post* Sports section ran yet another front-page piece by Shapiro titled 'Burk Ponders Strategy; She May Ask Members of Augusta to Resign.' Since when does 'pondering' qualify as a major news story, especially when Burk's resignation demands were reported exhaustively by the *Post* on November 13? Old news is thus repackaged as imminent or even speculative news. That doesn't advance the story. Nor did the *Post's* Style section story mocking the name, accent and demeanor of Augusta National's chairman, Hootie Johnson. The *Post's* news articles have impugned the club's motives and implied that it exerts some nefarious influence. Martha Burk's every utterance, rumination and even her Web site receives prominent attention. But her view is an opinion, not a fact, and one with which many if not most people disagree."

Shapiro took McCarthy's criticism in stride. "I disagreed with a lot of what he wrote, but I absolutely believe we should have run the letter," Shapiro says. "It was the right thing to do."

McCarthy's letter in the *Post* got big play on Robinson Holloway's Daily Dozen, a golf-writers' roundup posted on pgatour.com, which meant that it was subsequently reported, and cited, in dozens of newspapers around the country. "That was big," McCarthy says of the fallout from the *Post* letter. "When the media pack is swarming it seems unstoppable. But you have to systematically attack them one by one. Most writers, and newspapers, want to stay within the safety and protection of the pack. When you can isolate individual editors and writers they become very, very cautious." With *The New York Times*'s Augusta National coverage having slowed and the *Post* on the defensive, McCarthy set his sights on *The Atlanta Journal-Constitution*. "At that point the AJC was the paper carrying the flag of jihad," he says.

After steady correspondence with the *Journal-Constitution* brass, the paper printed a letter from McCarthy on February 13. (Thank you, George Solomon. "The *Post* set a precedent the AJC could follow," says McCarthy.) His letter ran more than seven hundred words on the op-ed page under the headline "Augusta Stories Give Overkill New Meaning." ("His letter got better play than many of our stories," says *Atlanta Journal-Constitution* golf writer Glenn Sheeley. "That was a big news hole.") McCarthy offered what he called "but a sample of the adjectives the *Journal-Constitution* and its columnists have used to describe the club: eccentric, rigid, antediluvian, good ol'boys, ignominious, indefensible, inane, delusional, loopy, dated, oafish, specious, arrogant, baffling, clueless, pigheaded, obstinate, racist, sexist, archaic, Neanderthal, multithumbed and peevish. . . . At some point, can't readers be trusted to develop and maintain their own opinion on a specific story without the vigilant guidance of the *Journal-Constitution?*"

Also: "In recent weeks, it appears that the paper is now attempting to create news on its own. On January 19, a headline read 'Augusta Flap

Drags While Players Chafe' [and carried the subhead] 'Issue frays nerves: Constant questioning over controversy about club's refusal to admit women rankles pros.' The nerve rankling, of course, was caused by none other than sportswriter Glenn Sheeley himself, asking the journalistic equivalent of the backseat perennial, 'Are we there yet?' "

Says Sheeley, "I thought the whole thing was laughable—like now we have to have our stories approved by Augusta National's PR flack? Gimme a break."

Yet two days after McCarthy's letter appeared, *The Atlanta Journal-Constitution* offered a soul-searching rebuttal, in a piece by the paper's ombudsman, Mike King. Under the headline "Augusta National Coverage: News or Crusade?" King wrote, "It is a frequent question—when does reporting on a controversial issue cease to be real news and cross the line into creating news or becoming advocacy? . . . McCarthy's answer to that is predictable. He has a job to do. But some of the points expressed in his op-ed piece are similar to the comments I hear from readers. Since the demand to allow women members of Augusta National first became known last summer, the *AJC* has printed about 100 separate stories, columns and pieces of commentary about it. The commentary has been almost evenly split on the issue, although clearly the newspaper's editorial position is that the club should be open to women.

"[T]he most frequent complaint I hear about the Augusta National story is that most readers don't care. Even our own poll, published in December, indicated that nearly two thirds of Georgians said they thought the issue is a 'waste of time.' From a public relations standpoint, here is where it gets tougher to keep the stories coming. If our readers think it's not worthy of their attention, why continue to write about it? That's a legitimate question, and here's the answer: because we should never let public opinion be the sole barometer for deciding what is news and what isn't. No doubt, it is a useful tool to determine how people feel. But, as history has shown time and again, it is no substitute for private leadership, public judgment or quality journalism.

"This story is far from over."

McCarthy was stewing on a response when he got word through Augusta National that the *Journal-Constitution* had begun calling the daughters of club members, asking for their thoughts on Dad's green jacket. "The club felt this was an outrageous invasion of privacy," he says, "so I called the cub reporter who was making some of the calls and asked her to please stop bothering these private citizens at home. She went crazy, screaming at me. After that we opened another flank through talk radio. We called a couple of the big-name talk show hosts in Atlanta and told them what was going on. They were appalled at the paper's sanctimony, and they started pushing the story on the air. Their listeners, of course, went nuts. I'm told so many called the AJC that the switchboard was overwhelmed."

Apparently, these voices were heard. Two weeks after his first piece defending *The Atlanta Journal-Constitution*'s work, ombudsman Mike King gave an update on the community reaction: "The rationale offered in this space two weeks ago for the newspaper's aggressive coverage of the Augusta National Golf Club controversy over its male-only membership prompted dozens of letters and phone calls commenting on the *Atlanta Journal-Constitution*'s approach. The sentiment expressed by readers was virtually unanimous: Back off.

"A good number of letter writers described as 'sad' or 'pathetic' my point that even though the majority of our readers believe the issue is a nonstory, we don't let polls and surveys alone dictate our coverage decisions. John E. Lagana of Atlanta had the most eloquent rebuttal: 'Your very noble comments regarding the criteria for deciding what is news and what isn't—including private leadership, public judgment or quality journalism—makes good copy for a term paper. In the real world, however, I suspect and contend that the main criteria for newsworthy items are, in fact, a combination of personal philosophy and what will sell. Again, you and your colleagues have the right to state what you will, on whatever topic you choose. Just, please, spare me the sanctimonious hypocrisy. Don't pee on my shoes and tell me it's raining.' "

What effect did all of this dialogue have on the *Journal-Constitution*'s coverage? The change could be felt in two stories that ran within days of each other. Stretched across the front page of Business in the March 16 edition was the headline "A Record on Par." There was the slightest whiff of disappointment in the sub: "Signs of bias by Augusta's corporate titans lacking." The story began, "Some of America's most powerful CEOs have been denounced for their membership in Augusta National

Golf Club, home of the Masters and where women aren't welcome as members. But away from the golf course and back in their corporate suites, those male executives are just as likely to have high-ranking women working around them as the bosses of other Fortune 500 companies, an *Atlanta Journal-Constitution* review shows.

"In three key measurements of gender diversity at 26 publicly traded companies led by Augusta National members—representation of women among directors, corporate officers and top-paid executives—the record of the club's members is on par with the rest of America's corporate giants."

Two days earlier, the *Atlanta Journal-Constitution*'s hotly debated story about the daughters of Augusta National members had been printed on the front page of Sports, under the headline "Augusta National Watch: Daughters Quietly Back Club, Fathers." The paper described this demographic as, "wives, mothers, businesswomen, independent thinkers, and influential in their own rights. But the bonds between father and daughter appear to override any differences when it comes to Augusta National. That point became clear in interviews with daughters of members willing to go on record about the subject."

Ann Naughton, of Colorado Springs, Colorado, and the daughter of former USGA president Will Nicholson, said, "I suppose if they let women into Augusta, it would be like popping the balloon. There is this aura about it. Is [my dad] a male chauvinist? Not in the least. . . . If he gets enjoyment out of [his membership], more power to him."

To recap, in just a few short weeks the public imagination of the archetypal Augusta National member, a knuckle-dragging woman hater who escaped to the club to fart and scratch his Spaldings while plotting ways to slash the pay of female executives, had suddenly become a fair, enlightened corporate leader who was loved and respected by the women in his life. The image rehabilitation of the green jacket continued with two important magazine articles that came out during the *Atlanta Journal-Constitution*'s period of navel gazing. In the February 17–24 double issue of *The New Yorker*, one of the magazine's top writers, Peter J. Boyer, wrote a 6,500-word piece that was largely sympathetic to the club, and the views of its chairman. Boyer poked a little fun at the NCWO, filling in details on everything from its small, shabby offices to the nose ring of the receptionist. He was also dismissive of Burk's member groups, saying that some of them "basically consist of one woman with a laptop and a cause (International Black Women for Wages for Housework suggests itself)."

Boyer, who has often covered military issues for *The New Yorker*, brought a keen Washington analysis to the warring between Burk and Hootie Johnson, comparing it to the Senate confirmation hearings of Clarence Thomas and Robert Bork, which "introduced into politics a new strategy—that of attaching to the opponent such opprobrium that neutral parties, or even those favorably disposed to the subject, come to recognize a position of opposition as being the safest course. In the past six months, the Augusta National Golf Club has been subjected to a 'Borking' of the first order." Boyer also recognized in his piece the changing tone of the media, which he attributed to Jim McCarthy, whose "aggressive policing of news coverage seems to have tempered its tone."

The most revelatory words in the story tumbled out of Burk's mouth, in her discussions of the differences between the genders. "I am a psychologist," she said. "I once heard someone say that men don't actually like women. Men like men, and they tolerate women. I think there's the sort of cult of manhood at work [at Augusta National.]" She also said, "I myself have what I call the 'girls' dinner.' Just some of the women in the women's movement, and we get together for dinner. Women in Congress do it, too. Here's the difference . . . it's just now come to me, pretty clearly. It is because, when men get together, denigrating women is often a part of the social interaction. When women get together, denigrating men is rarely done. It's just not even on the radar screen. Even among the so-called strident feminists of the women's movement. We don't have anything to hide in that way, and men seem to." These comments were widely disparaged for their, well, chauvinism.

The *New Yorker* story was also notable for the eloquent voice of Tom Wyman, who was speaking from the grave. Shortly after being interviewed by Boyer, Wyman had sustained a serious stomach infection, and weakened by his long-standing blood disorder, he died on January 8, 2003, just over a month after having resigned from Augusta National. It was a stunning end to a life lived in the public eye. For all of his accomplishments in the corporate world, it was Wyman's rejection of the green jacket that defined his legacy. *The New York Times*, predictably, mentioned the resignation in the first sentence of its obituary, while *The Boston Globe* played it even more prominently, in the headline "Thomas Wyman: Had Led CBS, Wanted Augusta Open to Women." "It was a bittersweet end to a great life," Tom Wyman Jr. says in an interview. "Augusta National certainly brought into focus what a positive force for change he was. We were all very proud that he had done the principled thing, the right thing."

There is no question that Wyman was a man of conscience, but seven months into the membership controversy, there was a growing reexamination of what constituted "the right thing." The debate reached an apotheosis in the March 2003 issue of *Golf Digest*, which came out about the same time as Boyer's piece, in early February. If *The New Yorker* is the bible of what Burk calls "the thinking class," *Digest* is scripture at America's golf courses, and sprawled across eight pages of the March issue was an essay entitled "The Case for All-Male Golf Clubs." The author was David Owen, who had written *The Making of the Masters*, the authorized history of the tournament and its host club, with the copyright belonging to Augusta National, Inc. Owen is a favored guest of Jerry Tarde's at Pine Valley, where he was able to research the piece in a setting that is unavailable to his colleague, Marcia Chambers. Tarde was quick to point out that, despite appearances, his magazine's bold argument for all-male clubs was not driven by a personal agenda. "If that was the only piece we had done [on the Augusta National membership controversy], it would be troublesome. But I look at David's piece as part of our overall balance of coverage." More generally, he says, "Most smart people had argued in favor of inclusion. There wasn't any literature that I could find arguing the opposite. I knew David came with baggage because he had done the Augusta book, but he celebrated the prejudice in an entertaining way."

Owen mentioned his book near the top of the story, writing, "During my visits to Augusta, I got a rare, extended inside look at the club and the tournament; I even played golf with Hootie Johnson. Did my experience predispose me to seeing Johnson's side in this dispute? Undoubtedly it did. But it also enabled me to do something that the club's most vocal detractors have seemed unable to do, which is to treat the club and the tournament as real things rather than as abstractions. Some of the loudest shouting so far has been done by people who not only don't play golf but also don't watch or care about the Masters."

One by one, Owen effectively knocked down the arguments of the club's critics and the casual assumptions of much of the public. In an elegiac closing, Owen wrote, "You get the feeling, as you read and reread various attacks on Augusta National, that the critics' real grievance is not about sexual inequality but about these particular men—who are rich, and who love a stupid game, and whose club is in the South, and whose chairman uses his childhood nickname and speaks with a Southern accent. Such men are safe, easy targets for derision. (Burk even mocked Johnson's accent for a reporter from *The Washington Post*.) But the real test of all rights, including the right to spend [time] with members of your own sex, doesn't lie in how you apply them to yourself. It lies in how you apply them to people who are different from you—even when they are as different as this."

The rhetoric of the press, and the public debate about its responsibilities and excesses, was finally beginning to cool off. But the conduct of the media would again make headlines during a stormy Masters week in which so many clashing ideologies would be thrown together. By then, however, the membership controversy had generated enough heat to sustain more than one raging controversy. The buildup to the Masters would be dominated not by the press but by an explosive subplot that mixed racial politics, southern cronyism, power, money, and the First Amendment, to say nothing of the Ku Klux Klan.

SEVEN

Protesters

SAY THIS ABOUT RONNIE STRENGTH—he knows how to ring in the new year with a bang. On page A1 of the January 1, 2003, *Augusta Chronicle*, Richmond County's wonderfully named sheriff put a match to the explosive issue of Masters week protests, all but declaring his hostility toward any possible demonstrations. "It will not be on Washington Road in front of the Augusta National because of safety," said Strength, who oversees a seven-hundred-officer consolidated sheriff and police department that is responsible for every aspect of law enforcement in the Augusta area. Noting that in his estimation the walkways are too narrow and the automotive traffic too thick, Strength said, "You can be assured we would not even consider the sidewalks around the Augusta National."

Martha Burk, with a long history of activism, was hardly intimidated by Strength's posturing. "I doubt if it's up to the sheriff to decide this," she told the *Chronicle*. "There are laws about peaceful protest, so we will be investigating those, as well as what our civil rights are."

Almost overnight Strength developed a national profile, a star turn he had been preparing for throughout most of his life. Strength's father, Howard, spent twenty-six years wearing a badge, first as an Augusta police officer and later as a county deputy. As a boy little Ronnie would often ride in the patrol car with his dad. When the old man switched to a motorcycle, Ronnie would wait for him at the end of the driveway of the family home on McDowell Street, and then sit on the handlebars for the short ride into the garage. "He was a great man, respected by everyone in the community," Ronnie Strength says. "There is only one word to describe him: fair. Everything I have done in law enforcement has been influenced by him. I still keep his picture on my desk. Not a day goes by I don't think of him. He meant everything to me."

Howard wanted a better life for his eldest son, and steered him away from law enforcement. At Augusta College Ronnie earned a bachelor of arts in sociology, with a business administration minor, and while still an undergrad he enrolled in management training at J. B. White, an Augusta department store. Upon graduation, Strength was made operations manager. It was at J. B. White that he developed a taste for the flashy clothes that would later help define his image. "I've always liked looking fashionable and dressing nice," he says. At the same time, "Law enforcement was in my blood, and there was no denying that," Strength says. He joined the sheriff's department in 1976 as lowly road deputy and never looked back. In 1978, he was promoted to investigator in the criminal division, and three years later he was running the violent crimes unit. Strength was widely considered a rising star, but those were dark days for the department. In 1980, Sheriff Bill Anderson began a five-year sentence for selling marijuana. His successor, J. B. Dykes, was accused of accepting bribes in exchange for fixing DUI tickets, and in 1983, he pleaded guilty in federal court to two charges of obstructing justice.

Enter Charlie Webster, a self-described "little country boy" who, after taking over from Dykes, cleaned up the department with such a paternal air he became known around Augusta as Uncle Charlie. His barbecues and fish fries dominated the city's political calendar.

In 1989, Webster made Strength his number two—deputy sheriff—with an eye on grooming him as a successor. No one had ever questioned the heir apparent's work ethic—a story about Strength in the *Augusta Chronicle* in 1996 reported, "He works at least 70 hours a week, hasn't had a vacation in ten years and knows he may die on the job, as his father did"—but Strength needed tutoring on baby kissing, back scratching, and the other interpersonal demands of being sheriff. "Only part of this job is putting bad guys in jail," says Strength. "That part I knew and understood. What I was made to realize is that a big part of the job is politics, and people. I didn't like that part of it. Course, that has changed over the years, thanks to all of Charlie's coaching."

Beyond good grooming and a college degree, Strength had another advantage when interacting with Augusta's ruling class—he's a golfer. For the last two decades he has been a member at Forest Hills Golf Club, a sporty Donald Ross design where every weekend he and seven buddies tee it up in a spirited game. Strength's low round at Augusta National is a showy 78. "I've played it many times," he says. "I have friends up there who are members."

When he finally got the chance to run for sheriff, in 2000, Strength raised over $200,000 in campaign contributions, the most ever for an Augusta-area candidate. His haul included $11,300 from five local Augusta National members personally or through their family or business— Clayton P. Boardman III, William Copenhaver, Ed Douglass, Nick W. Evans Jr., and Dessey Kuhlke. Strength's opponent, Lieutenant Leon Garvin, a thirty-two-year vet on the force, raised all of $23,686. Strength collected more than 75 percent of the vote, and one of the spoils of the victory was an invitation to join Augusta Country Club (ACC) in March 2001, making him the rare lawman who can rub elbows with the swells at the local club. ACC also provided valuable networking opportunities with Augusta's leading citizens: Most of the local members at the National also belong to the country club.

The sheriff department's links to Augusta National run deeper than its leader's golf game. Strength and three of his officers—Colonel Gary Powell, Captain Jim Griffin, and Lieutenant Jackie Klaus—are members of the Masters police and parking committee. Their compensation is the most coveted ticket in sports, a complimentary Masters badge, which is transferable to friends or family. It's not just the brass at the sheriff's department that cashes in during Masters week. Each year, Augusta National employs seventy-five to one hundred deputies to work security and parking detail during Masters week. The deputies take vacation time but work in uniform, typically twelve-hour shifts seven days in a row. Their paychecks are cut by Augusta National Inc.; in 2003, the hourly wage was $14, pretty good given that the deputies are also collecting vacation pay for the week.

Considering the close ties between Augusta National and Strength and his troops, it's no surprise that the sheriff's department is protective of the club. In March 2001, five activists from In Defense of Animals, aged seventeen to thirty-three, were arrested on Washington Road in front of Augusta National and charged with disorderly conduct for staging a mini-demonstration in which they held a sign with a picture of a mutilated beagle and a picture of Warren Stephens on which "Puppy Killer" had been scrawled. Stephens, a longtime member whose father Jack was Hootie Johnson's predecessor as chairman, is the president of Stephens, Inc., and at the time of the arrests the investment firm was the largest shareholder in Huntingdon Life Sciences, which IDA claimed killed up to 180,000 animals each year for medical research. The protesters were arrested because, according to the *Augusta Chronicle*, they "did not apply for the required permit but would not have received one if they had because the spot they chose to demonstrate—on the grass near Gate 2, the main entrance—was unsafe for a demonstration, Sheriff Ronnie Strength said." As this book went to press the charges were still pending against the In Defense of Animals five, despite the ACLU's long-standing attempts to have the case dismissed.

The harsh treatment of the animal-rights protesters was surprising given Augusta's record on supporting free speech. On November 15, 1986, about seventy-five members of the Ku Klux Klan paraded through downtown, dressed in robes and carrying Confederate flags. According to the UPI, "The NAACP tried to have the march stopped, but U.S. District Judge Dudley Bowen"—remember that name—"upheld the Klan's First Amendment right to demonstrate, although he said he agreed the white supremacist group is abhorrent."

The city of Augusta has been similarly tolerant in allowing anti-abortion forces to exercise their First Amendment rights. On October 17, 1990, Rev. Mark Ross, then the associate pastor of the local St. Mary on the Hill Catholic Church, led a Rosary on the sidewalk in front of the Planned Parenthood on Broad Street, the busy thoroughfare at the heart of downtown Augusta. The prayers continue to this day, sanctioned by permits to protest doled out to a handful of disparate groups that rotate the days of the week of their gatherings. "They're treated like anybody else, whether it's Martha Burk or Sons of the Confederacy," says Colonel Powell, who handles permitting for sheriff's department. The size of groups allowed under the various permits differs. One group that gathers on a monthly basis is authorized up to two hundred, but each gathering typically attracts ten to twenty protesters on a busy downtown block.

In Augusta's marketplace of ideas there is also room for a little pornography, though it didn't arrive without a tussle. In June 2002, the Augusta Commission rejected the application of a proposed emporium of adult movies and magazines, Video X-Mart, citing zoning laws that were subject to broad interpretation. The X-Mart folks sued, claiming their First Amendment rights were being stifled. Judge Bowen, always the man on the scene, agreed, granting a preliminary injunction against the city. Echoing his ruling on the KKK march of sixteen years earlier, Bowen wrote, "No matter how undesirable the speech, allowing the exercise of First Amendment rights serves the public interest."

So, surveying the last quarter century of free speech in Augusta, the Ku Klux Klan, abortion protesters, and pornographers have all enjoyed their First Amendment rights, while a handful of animal-rights activists were busted for trying to do the same. The situations are all different, but the conclusion is inescapable: Freedom of expression is okay as long as you don't target the hallowed ground of Augusta National, a golf club with friends in high places.

On JANUARY 21, 2003 the Augusta-Richmond County Commission heard a motion to amend Title 3, Chapter 4, Section 11 of the county code, which regulates demonstrations and protest activity. The public hearing was held in the main room of what is known locally as the city-county building, a rectangular space that calls to mind an elongated second-run movie theater. The cushy, upholstered chairs gently rise toward the back of the room, creating a coliseum effect for the ten commissioners, who are seated side by side at the front of the room at a long dais.

The proposed changes to the existing protest ordinance were substantial. Under the amendment any group of five or more would have to apply to the sheriff for a permit to demonstrate; the application would have to be received at least twenty days in advance of the demonstration; the sheriff would be required to respond to the application within seven days; and any application that was denied would automatically to be appealed for judicial review.

The hearing began with opening remarks by the city attorney, Jim Wall, who recapped all the proposed changes to the ordinance, and then said, "All of these things are designed to protect and enhance the rights of someone who wants to protest, whereas I think the general sentiment has been that it is designed to limit."

This was greeted with an immediate skepticism. A motion to deny the ordinance was seconded by Commissioner William H. "Willie" Mays III, who then commanded the floor. Mays has a presence about him, and not just because he's a healthy six foot three inches and has a day job as a mortician. He is second-generation royalty among Augusta's black political elite. His mother, Carrie, was elected to the city council in 1970, becoming, according to the *Chronicle*, the first black woman to hold such a position in the whole of the Southeast. Willie earned a seat of his own on the city council in 1979, at the tender age of twenty-eight, and in the years since he has emerged as a leading voice in Augusta's black community. Turning to Wall, Mays said, "Let's not be coy about the timing of this ordinance. We've had a lot of comment out in some parts of the media as to why this was being done in the first place." Mays is not known for his brevity. When he begins speaking, the shoulders of the other commissioners perceptibly sag. He launched into a long history of local protests that touched on his sit-ins with fellow students at Augusta College in the 1960s as well as the Ku Klux Klan's march through Augusta. "Now, if the ordinance on the books was good enough for the Klan to parade in Augusta, Georgia, and get the protection of law enforcement on a bright, sunny, Sunday afternoon, it's good enough for a peaceful protest." He went on like this for a bit longer, finally ending by urging his fellow commissioners to reject the amendment. The room, which was about two-thirds full, erupted in applause.

Commissioner Lee Beard, a school principal for nearly a quarter of a century, followed up Mays's remarks by saying, "We may be talking about something local here, but I've had calls from New York and a couple more calls from other places wanting to know what this ordinance is all about. And it is becoming a national event. I would hate to be on national TV talking about how we are coming up with something to stop a demonstration that's going to happen in April. This is poor timing. It shouldn't have been brought at this particular time because we all know what the repercussions are going to be."

Here Commissioner Marion Williams, who moonlights as a pastor at the Friendship Baptist Church, spoke up, with the kind of passion that draws *Amens!* from his congregation: "If not for [the right to protest], a lot of them folks on this panel and in them chairs would still be picking cotton today, Jim. If you're going to play ball, Jim Wall, let's play with the same ball all the time. Now right is right and wrong is wrong."

Others commissioners were more concerned with appearances than First Amendment rights. Speaking for the first time, Commissioner William B. Kuhlke Jr., who runs profitable family businesses in real estate and construction, wondered aloud why the city couldn't draft an amendment that more fully *censored* the protesters' free speech. Sounding an ominous note, he said, "You've got two organizations that have said they are going to demonstrate against the Augusta National because of their membership policy, but I think the spin-off effect is going to be devastating to the city of Augusta."

By now the meeting had run for more than an hour, and its fevered pitch had left everyone in the room weary. A vote was called. Five commissioners gave thumbs-up to the amended ordinance: Boyles, Bridges, Fred Cheek (a computer researcher), Stephen Shepard (an attorney), and Kuhlke. No doubt Dessey Kuhlke, the commissioner's brother, was pleased; Dessey happens to be a member at Augusta National. In an interview, Commissioner Kuhlke says, "I never considered not voting, because I didn't see any conflict. I'm not a member [at Augusta National]. This ordinance was not about a particular case but rather a citywide issue of such concern that I felt I had to vote."

Five commissioners voted against the amendment: Beard, Mays, Williams, Richard Colclough (a mental health counselor), and Bobby Hankerson (a retired Georgia state employee now working as a pastor). The Augusta charter grants a vote to the mayor only to create or break a tie, but Bob Young was out of town on this fateful night. With a 5–5 deadlock, the amendment to the protest ordinance was denied, at least until the next commission meeting two weeks hence. Of course, what colored the headlines was not the outcome of the vote so much as the demographics—all five commissioners who supported the revised protest ordinance were white, while all five who opposed it were black, just the latest dustup in Augusta's long history of contentious racial politics.

A CENSUS IN 1790 recorded approximately twenty thousand slaves among the Augusta area's eighty thousand residents. In the hundred years after the Civil War, African Americans enjoyed little mobility in the community, even as the population boomed. (Augusta is now 50 percent black and 45 percent white.) When Augusta's own James Brown integrated Bell Auditorium for the first time, in 1964, the vast majority of the city's black citizens lived in the Terri, local shorthand for the 130-square-block ghetto in the south part of town that was once known as Negro territory. The seething dissatisfaction in the Terri finally exploded in May 1970, when a race riot tore apart the city. The trouble had begun when a sixteen-year-old named Charles Oatman was beaten to death at the Richmond County Prison. The black community believed it to be the work of white prison guards, and a public protest was organized, attracting a crowd into the thousands that turned violent after a confrontation with police. A broad swath of downtown Augusta was looted and torched, and one thousand National Guardsmen were called in to restore order. All six people killed in the riot were black.

The *Augusta Chronicle*'s powerful headline following the riot said it all: "Our City's Trail of Sorrow."

Out of the ashes of the riot emerged an increasingly politicized black community, and it began to affect change at the ballot box, not in the streets. The Mays family was among the first wave of politicians to break the color barrier in Augusta, as was Ed McIntyre, a charismatic figure who in 1981 became the city's first black mayor.

But McIntyre did not bridge the gulf between the races, he widened it. Hizzoner had been in office less than two years when he was indicted by a federal grand jury for demanding payoffs running into six figures from a handful of companies seeking to do business in Augusta. McIntyre was a polarizing figure on whom both races projected their fears and hostilities: In the black community McIntyre was widely considered the victim of a setup, as his two principle accusers were local political figures with whom the mayor had tussled.

In 1984, McIntyre resigned from office after being convicted of bribery and two counts of extortion. He served fourteen months in jail, cementing his martyrdom with Augusta's black community. In 1998, at the age of sixty-six, McIntyre tried to reclaim the mayor's office, cribbing one of Jesse Jackson's slogans for his campaign: "Keep Hope Alive." His opponent was Bob Young, who was making the plunge into politics after twenty-six years as a local media personality, first as a disc jockey at WBBQ, then as a news anchor at WJBF-TV (Channel 6), where he also hosted *The Young Report*, a political talk show.

Young certainly looked like a TV smoothie, with his Bernini ties and blow-dried hair, but he had been a helicopter gunner in Vietnam and wasn't afraid of a fight. He also packed plenty of firepower thanks to the largesse of the business community. Young's $186,916 in campaign contributions was the most for an Augusta-area candidate until it was bested two years later by Ronnie Strength. It included $10,700 from eight local Augusta National members either personally or through family or business—Louis Battey, Clayton P. Boardman III, Ed Douglass, Phil Harison, Boone Knox, Dessey Kuhlke, Claude Nielsen, and Leroy Simkins.

The 1998 mayoral campaign probably set a new low for political discourse in Augusta, which is saying something. According to the *Chronicle*, "During the campaign, the Youngs were targets of a smear campaign via letters sent by e-mail and traditional mail, some of which were sexually explicit."

Young got his revenge when it came time to count the ballots, defeating McIntyre in a runoff. The new mayor promised sweeping change, but by the end of his first term he was singing a familiar tune around Augusta. In his State of the City address in February 2002, Young criticized unnamed county commissioners for being "race-baiting obstructionists" whose "constant bickering" was to blame for government gridlock. He cribbed the same language for a September 2002 mailer soliciting campaign contributions, this time singling out by name black commission members Willie Mays, Marion Williams, and Lee Beard.

Young was still playing the race card after beating McIntyre in a re-match in November 2002's mayoral election. "The racial problems in this city are in government," the mayor said, six weeks before the first vote on the proposed amendment to the protest ordinance. "They are not problems in the community. Until people in government have an attitude adjustment, it's going to be that way." In another shot across the bow to the black commissioners, Young said, "Let them come to the table and express their concerns. But they better have more than just saying, 'It's racist.' Bring me an educated opinion. Don't bring me excuses."

Given this divisive backdrop, there was little question whose side Young was on when he showed up for the county commission meeting on February 3, 2003. On the docket once again was the proposed amendment to the protest ordinance. But a resolution seemed unlikely on this night, because Commissioner Cheek was away. In the bottom-line math of Augusta politics, that left five whites and five blacks.

In the weeks since the first vote, the commission's racial split had become big news, and the full house in the city-county building included reporters from *The Atlanta Journal-Constitution*, Associated Press and *Newsday*. More heated discussion ensued among the commissioners, but when it came time to vote, the score remained 5–5. This second black-white stalemate generated headlines from New York City ("Add Race to Augusta Conflict," in the *Daily News*) to Chattanooga ("Masters Protest Divides Augusta," in the *Times Free Press*.)

Two weeks later the county commission reconvened, this time in full. After all of the fevered buildup, it took less than five minutes for the amended ordinance to be approved, as Mayor Young, the meeting moderator, hurried through the vote, for which he cast the deciding vote.

The tweaking of the protest ordinance predictably got big play in the press, and Burk offered a characteristically sharp critique, telling *USA Today*, "It sounds to me like the mayor is more interested in serving Augusta National Golf Club than the city of Augusta."

*   *   *

It didn't take long for the rubber to meet the road on Augusta's revised protest ordinance. On February 10, two days after the climactic commission meeting, Todd Manzi became the first person to take out an application to protest during Masters week. He had driven 460 miles from his home in Tampa, because the sheriff's department insisted that all permit requests be claimed in person.

Manzi was not a new face to those steeped in the minutiae of the Augusta National membership controversy. He had been making noises since October, when he launched ItTakesBalls.com, which was followed by TheBurkStopsHere.com. The Web sites were a curious mix of commerce and dogma, with Burk the star of both Manzi's rants about the membership controversy and the merchandise he was hawking. He had created a line of apparel embossed with "It Takes Balls to Be a Member," including T-shirts ($16.95), caps ($19.95), and polo shirts ($38.95). Also available were golf balls printed with Martha's mug and the caption DRIVE BURK OUT! ($19.75 a dozen) and anti-Burk buttons ($20 a dozen). Manzi was such an earnest fellow that he had included a "mission statement" on his Web sites: "Our goal is to provide people who feel like we do a way to vent their outrage. Buying our apparel is a form of protesting Dr. Burk and the NCWO. We want to sell enough shirts and hats to make the corporation's story newsworthy. We will use that platform so that Todd Manzi can voice the opinion: As a society, we are tired of groups like the NCWO threatening commerce over frivolous issues."

Manzi, forty-one, was especially attuned to the forces of the economy, having lost his job as an advertising salesman in September 2002. He decided to channel his outrage at Burk into a business opportunity. In short order he had hired a Web designer and a clothing manufacturer, and he even put out a press release announcing the launch of the Web site. His efforts were met with a collective yawn. In the first four months fewer than two hundred orders trickled in, and he was $20,000 in the hole. The apathy toward Manzi's Web sites was all the more painful because he was the family's sole breadwinner. His wife, Barb, was committed to being a stay-at-home mom to their two small children. "I support Todd because he's my husband, and I also support the message, but it's like there's another woman in our marriage," Barb said of Burk. "We haven't had a normal family life because he's always on his computer. The economic strain has also been tough. We're living on credit cards."

Manzi's self-loathing reached a crescendo in an early-winter posting on his Web site: "My wife thinks I am devoting more time and energy to Martha Burk than I am to her. She is right. My neighbors think I am the most boring guy on the planet because this is the only issue I want to talk about. They are right. My friends think I am being irresponsible and that I should get a job and support my family. They are right."

His protest permit application changed everything. Overnight, Manzi became the star of the latest development in the membership controversy, earning front-page treatment in the sports pages of *The Orlando Sentinel* ("Male Augusta Crusader Has View Worth Hearing") and *St. Petersburg Times* ("National Debate Becomes Man's Crusade"). Showing a certain amount of ideological flexibility, he even suspended a boycott of *USA Today* to pose for a whimsical picture in which he was wearing dozens of his anti-Burk buttons.

Though he was an army of one, Manzi requested approval for fifty-six people at his Masters week protest. (He also took out paperwork to become a licensed vendor.) No one was looking forward to exercising his or her First Amendment rights during Masters week more than Manzi. "It is a wonderful chance to get the message out," he said. "Hopefully I can also move some product."

A little more than a week after Manzi submitted his protest application, he was forced to share the spotlight, as Women Against Martha Burk applied for a permit of their own. The group was the brainchild of Allison Greene, twenty-eight, a vivacious lifelong Augustan who manages the Boll Weevil Café, on Ninth Street. Amused by the seriousness of the other would-be demonstrators, Greene said she was planning a "tailgate party slash protest—emphasis on the party."

"You know, with Martha and Todd Manzi, it's gonna be like *West Side Story II*," she said. "I can just see them dancing down Washington Road, snapping at each other. I am not confrontational. You will not see a catfight between me and that freak-a-zoid." For those scoring at home, she meant Martha, not Manzi.

Despite the catchy name of her group, Greene was motivated not so much by a beef with Burk as by her own civic pride. She grew up on

Quaker Springs Road, went to school at St. Mary's on the Hill and St. Thomas Aquinas, and married a local boy whom she had known since grade school. "I love Augusta so much, and it has bothered me like you can't believe to hear Martha Burk talking trash about my city," she says. "And the things she has said about the Augusta National are outrageous. It is an icon in this town."

Greene has in her home a photo of her standing outside the front entrance to the club. "That's mandatory for an Augusta citizen," she says. What's the appeal of a club that for the average Augustan is as unattainable as a spot on Hollywood Boulevard's Walk of Fame? "It just sprinkles a little stardust on the rest of us," Greene says. "It's what makes this town special. When Celine Dion played there a couple of years ago, that was a big deal. There was a crowd waiting outside the gates, hoping to get a glimpse of her when she left."

At the Boll Weevil Café, the tablecloths are the color of a green jacket, and posters from Masters past cover the exposed brick walls of the converted cotton warehouse that dates to the 1850s. As the membership controversy picked up momentum, Greene couldn't tune out the low roar of anger about the Yankee woman who was doing so much harm to Augusta's image and economy. One of the enduring clichés in the press coverage of the membership controversy was the aggrieved Augusta caterer (or real estate broker, or travel agent . . .) who blamed Burk for driving away business during Masters week. By the time Greene had applied for her protest permit, numerous large corporations had scaled back or canceled altogether their hospitality for Masters week, among them a good number whose corporate officers had been targeted by Burk— including Coke, AT&T, and Citigroup. Many local industries were able to absorb the losses, as individual fans or smaller groups snatched up the suddenly available hotel rooms, rental cars, restaurants reservations, and other services. The businesses that served up the big-ticket items, like caterers who supply $100-a-plate dinners, took a whacking. But the real backlash came from the average upper-middle-class Augustans who, for the first time, were unable to rent their homes for up to $10,000 a week for corporate entertaining.

Listening to all of this disenchantment at the Boll Weevil, Greene decided to write to Burk in January. "It was a thoughtful letter, with ten questions," Greene says. "I was trying to figure out how I was supposed to feel. Well, I never heard back from her, and that is just so sad. I'm a woman, I'm from Augusta, and my voice meant nothing to her. I gotta tell you, that pissed me off."

Thus was born Women Against Martha Burk. The scope of the gathering Greene applied for fit her modest ambitions—she requested authorization for twenty-five, ahem, protesters at the quiet corner of Ninth Street and Reynolds on the Sunday before the Masters was to begin, April 6. "I didn't want to interfere with the golf or add to the congestion on Washington Road," says Greene, ever the concerned citizen. "And I thought it would be a good opportunity to bring people downtown."

Her request was so benign that Sheriff Strength okayed the protest on February 24, after taking only a couple of days to review the details. It was the first of the hotly debated permits to be issued. (Manzi's was still under consideration.)

Burk offered a curt tribute to her fellow protester: "It's a free country. This is what a democracy is all about."

A day after Greene's permit was issued, Burk essentially began her campaign of civil disobedience in a story that landed on the front page of sports of *The New York Times*. "To protest, you have to have access to the people that you intend to influence," Burk said. "To prohibit a demonstration anywhere on Washington Road, outside the entrance to the club, is unacceptable. Why are protesters a safety hazard any more than pedestrians are a safety hazard? It sounds like they're already finding ways to turn us down."

She continued to lay out her case the next day, during a public appearance at Bowling Green University on February 26. "We're not planning to do anything illegal. We're not planning to do anything disruptive," Burk said. "If I parachuted onto the first tee, they wouldn't show it. If you want to get on TV, stay outside. That's why I'm staying outside. Our goal is to point out the corporate hypocrisy that surrounds, feeds and creates this event."

Also pushing the message was Rev. Jesse Jackson, who had latched on to the NCWO months earlier. As Burk tells it, Jackson entered the fray more or less uninvited. "Nobody approached anybody," Burk says. "There didn't need to be any communication because we are all on the same page philosophically."

Jackson brought name recognition to the cause and credibility in activist circles, as well as the resources and infrastructure of his Rainbow/PUSH Coalition. But he was also a loose cannon who could easily compromise Burk's message that Augusta National=sex discrimination. With the Masters now on the horizon, Jackson began devoting more time to speaking out on Augusta National. This included a well-publicized trip to Greenville County, South Carolina—Hootie Johnson's ancestral home—in early February, during which Jackson linked the Augusta National's membership practices to the county's decision not to make Martin Luther King Jr.'s birthday a holiday. With Jackson stealing a good deal of the attention, Burk began having second thoughts on their partnership. "I don't want this to be Jesse Jackson's protest," Burk said. "I don't want this to be a partnership, I don't want this to look like a partnership. I want this to be a woman-led thing. He is supposed to be in a supporting role on this, but once you're on the ground you can't control the reverend."

Case in point was Jackson's appearance on *Crossfire* on February 28. The day before, the news had broken that a self-styled member of the Ku Klux Klan had applied for a permit to protest during the Masters supporting Augusta National's freedom of association. It was one of the most incendiary developments in the membership controversy, and Jackson was all too happy to add more fuel to the inferno.

He was introduced on-air by cohost Tucker Carlson: "Mr. Jackson, I want to read you something you said yesterday on an Atlanta radio station AM 680 about the Masters tournament. 'The name does not really come from being the master of golf,' you said. 'You know it really comes from slave masters.' Now that's untrue. Why did you say that?"

"Well, that is its original meaning," Jackson responded. "It was. It's on a plantation. It was about only the masters could play, the white male masters. It was slave masters. And for a long time, they held on to that policy. The secret society of white men."

Carlson: "Mr. Jackson, that's not true. The tournament was called the Augusta Invitational."

"Well, there is evidence that it's true. And my point is that the gender and racial and religious bigotry are on the same moral plane, and we consistently fight those evils."

Cohost Paul Begala: "Reverend, have you heard from Hootie Johnson?"

"Well, we tried to reach Hootie and we couldn't reach Hootie. But Hootie is picking up allies. I mean you look at this kind of locking people out, and one day it's George Bush on Martin King's birthday attacking affirmative action, and now the attack on Title IX. And then there's Trent Lott, and now the KKK is joining them. So they are picking up allies, but on the wrong side of history. The burden is on the Augusta Country Club members. And today, the KKK has developed some kinship with another secret society."

No wonder Burk was growing wary of the reverend. Jackson can be excused for his irritating habit of referring to the home of the Masters as Augusta Country Club, a proud organization that is entirely distinct from Augusta National Golf Club. And laying the challenges to affirmative action and Title IX on Hootie's doorstep feels like a reach, though perhaps this can be chalked up to his brand of hyperbole. But the allegation that the name of the Masters began with slave owners is pure poppycock, not to mention nonsensical—the tournament began seventy years after slavery was abolished. Jackson, in an interview for this book, continued to peddle this half-baked theory. But he was far more persuasive in discussing the larger meaning of the membership controversy. "It is [our] common struggle," Jackson said. "For most of this country's history blacks couldn't vote, and women couldn't vote. Affirmative action, Title IX, these are not women's issues, these are not black issues. These are issues of the minority versus the majority, and women and African Americans are united in the struggle. They try to demean our fight by saying this is about one wealthy, white businesswoman getting into an elite club. They try to marginalize the issue, trivialize it. Why fight for one talented black man to play second base for the Brooklyn Dodgers? Because baseball has a larger meaning, just as the symbolism of Augusta transcends the links. Jackie Robinson opened the door for others of varying talents who were all nonetheless equally deserving of the opportunity.

"The showdown at Augusta will now be as big as the tournament itself. Maybe bigger."

REV. JACKSON was hardly the only observer to gleefully connect the Klan and Augusta National. The previous day's *Atlanta Journal-Constitution* story had reported that, "The Augusta National Golf Club's policy of all-male membership has gained a surprise supporter, the American White Knights of the Ku Klux Klan. J. J. Harper, Imperial Wizard of the Cordele-based KKK group, on Thursday requested an application for a permit from the Richmond County Sheriff's Department to protest during the Masters tournament. 'We are going to stand up for the rights of the Augusta National to choose whomever they want to choose as a member of their club,' Harper said in a telephone interview on Thursday evening. 'I'm sure the Augusta National welcomes the support of the Ku Klux Klan because they seem bent on discriminating against women at any cost,' Burk said. 'Augusta National should not be shocked by the KKK's endorsement. . . . They have behaved in a manner that attracts this type of support.'

"Augusta National also responded—through spokesperson Glenn Greenspan—when told of the KKK's support. 'As a result of the controversy created by political activists, a number of organizations—some of them extreme—have sought to voice their political views. Anyone who knows anything about Augusta National Golf Club or its members knows this is not something that the club would welcome or encourage. For our critics to try to capitalize on this sideshow is utterly reprehensible and has no place in any civilized discourse.' "

The press, which in the preceding weeks had offered its most balanced coverage of the membership controversy, collectively threw its hands in the air and declared defeat for Augusta National, as if the actions of one crackpot could end a complicated national debate. Jim Rome, the wildly popular, nationally syndicated sports radio talk-show host, voiced the conventional wisdom at the time: "Hootie, when the Klan supports you, you've officially lost the argument." Everything from the Civil War to Shoal Creek was now back in play as the media deconstructed the effect on Augusta National of those three inflammatory letters, KKK. Even the most reserved of observers was moved to hyperbole. "It will escalate now—big time," Tiger Woods said. "It's no longer just about a female member. It's going to be an absolute joke, just a zoo." Forever seeking to avoid even a glimpse of controversy, Woods had a novel idea on how he might miss the untidy scene on Washington Road during Masters week. "Maybe I'll just parachute in," he said.

For newspaper columnists everywhere, J. J. Harper was a gift from the golf gods. Ann Killion, in the *San Jose Mercury News*, offered a series of jokes by way of commenting on the news:

"What's the first sign of spring at Augusta? The magnolias bloom and the bedsheets appear.

"How many Augusta members does it take to screw in a lightbulb? None. They just ask the nearest imperial wizard to light a cross."

Killion continued: "If you take an extreme position, as Augusta National has done, you're going to have extremist bedfellows. Sheets and all."

On the editorial page of *The Atlanta Journal-Constitution*, Cynthia Tucker fleshed out the point: "Johnson ought to spend some time considering his new status as KKK hero. The adage you can judge a man by the friends he chooses has a corollary: You can also judge a man by the friends who choose him. Just what does Harper see in Hootie? Why, a man who shares his philosophy of exclusion, of course."

Phil Sheridan, in *The Philadelphia Inquirer*, offered the most over-the-top piece on the Klan and Augusta National, under the headline "Yo, Augusta: K-K-Kiss Your Argument Goodbye." "Everything Johnson says in defense of his club's exclusionary policies could just as easily come from the mouth of some Imperial Wizard somewhere," Sheridan wrote. "You could argue, in fact, that the KKK is more honest than Augusta. The Klan makes no apologies for its racist, anti-Semitic, anti-Catholic, anti-everything-else ideology. The Klan is proud of that. Heck, that's what the Klan is. Johnson, on the other hand, has had to engage in all manner of doublespeak in order to state his case. . . .

"In a world debating war [in Iraq] and coping with the threat of terrorism . . . it's very hard to get worked up about whether Buffy Sue Richlady is playing Augusta as a member or a guest. The Klan changes all of that. Instantly. Even if this splinter group doesn't follow through with its demonstration, the damage is done to Hootie and his blowhards. There is no going back to any reasonable discussion about the issue, nor should there be. . . . Sorry, Mr. Johnson, that's life in the hood."

Actually, it would be nice if the introduction of an extremist element into an intellectual argument caused clear-eyed observers to tone down their own rhetoric rather than ratchet it up. The few pundits who looked beyond the easy punch line discovered that J. J. Harper was just one guy with a flashy title and a colorful Web site. Organizations that monitor hate groups, like the Southern Poverty Law Center (SPLC), dismissed Harper as the sole member of his organization, which led to a catchy new nickname—the One Man Klan. The KKK as the embodiment of evil was seriously undermined by a goofy photo on Harper's Web site, in which he was sitting on a tractor-style lawn mower with two well-groomed poodles on his lap. This image inspired one of the most memorable quotes of the membership controversy, when Joe Roy of the SPLC told the New York *Daily News*, "If he shows up at Augusta with his two poodles, he'll have a protest of three." (It was this kind of dismissive reaction that validated the decision of Jim McCarthy and the Augusta National brass not to comment on Harper beyond the initial statement distancing the club from the controversy. They were convinced that those who used Harper to further their own agenda—whether it was Burk, Jackson, or reporters—would badly overplay their hands, creating an inevitable backlash.)

To the *Daily News*, the SPLC's Roy added, "I don't know that Harper in his wildest dreams imagined he'd ever get this kind of attention." What exactly was Harper hoping for? It was hard to tell in all the press coverage, in which he was a cipher who served mainly as a jumping-off point for the opinions of the writer. It would be necessary to travel two hours to the southwest of Augusta, to rural Cordele, Georgia, in order to understand the Imperial Wizard's world.

HARPER'S ELECTRONICS is a sagging outpost at the end of a downtrodden commercial strip in Cordele, Georgia (population: 12,000). Despite its petite size, the repair shop is hard to miss—just look for the Confederate flag flying from the roof and the fluffy white poodle standing in the doorway. Slog through the dirt parking lot and Tinkerbell offers an enthusiastic hello, as does her master, J. J. Harper, who is turned out not in a starched bedsheet but rather droopy Wranglers, white New Balance tennis shoes, and a black cap emblazoned with U.S. ARMY VETERAN.

Harper, thirty-nine, has a gentle manner, a boyish, gap-toothed grin framed by a wispy mustache, and a high-pitched voice often punctuated by a laugh that can only be described as a squeal. He is a gracious host, offering both his favorite soda (generic brand diet orange) and chewing tobacco, Timberwolf ("when Copenhagen went to three dollars a can they lost me forever"). Polystyrene cups with his viscous, malodorous spittle teeter on every flat surface of his workshop. The place is a riot of dismembered computers and disemboweled VCRs, their innards sharing shelf space with an array of other electronic gadgets in various states of decomposition. Harper ekes out a living bringing these dated machines back to life.

Giving a tour of the detritus, Harper seems as friendly as the Maytag repair man. Then he comes to a back room, where the amplifier to a car stereo is inexplicably hanging from a string near the window. "That's nigger bait," he says casually, explaining that his store has been the target of frequent break-ins. Harper has booby-trapped the place like a downmarket Inspector Gadget: Tug on the dangling amplifier and a makeshift iron maiden—a board with dozens of protruding nails—springs to life. A doorway is wired so a two-by-four on a spring will smash an intruder's ankles. "A man's gotta protect his property," Harper says with a twinkle.

Tour over, he plops down in a beat-up chair, gathers Tinkerbell in his lap, and proceeds to tells his tale, absentmindedly stroking the dog throughout. It turns out the Imperial Wizard was born in Augusta, to an educated family. His brother still lives in the area, working as a registered nurse. His mother is an anesthesiologist in Tifton, Georgia. Little J. J. was a smart, pudgy kid with a keen mechanical bent, but he never quite fit in with his peers. He quit high school after the tenth grade, joining the army in 1984. After doing basic training at New Jersey's Fort Dixon and advanced technical training at Massachusetts's Fort Devin, he was then sent to Augsburg, Germany, for a two-year hitch as a Morse code interceptor. "This ol' redneck has been all over Europe," he says proudly.

Harper thrived in the structured environment of the military. After earning an honorable discharge, he found the real world too messy for his tastes. His political views grew more extreme, and this man who had read so many technical manuals sought how-to advice in a book chock full of it. "The Bible provides clear answers," Harper says. "The real world is nothing but compromises. I guess the easiest way to put it is I just got fed up with so many things in this world."

As his reading ranged further afield, he became enchanted by the history of the Ku Klux Klan. "I support the Klan's beliefs—the original beliefs," he says. "The founders of the Klan were strong Christians, and the organization started as a social group. The founders were high-class people, the top of society, and they stood for something."

The Klan was born in December 1865 in Pulaski, Tennessee, fathered by a Confederate Army general named Nathan Bedford Forrest. All six of the original founders were officers in the Civil War, and college-educated. The name of their group reflected a refined sensibility, as it was drawn from the Greek word for circle, *kuklos*. The Klan was originally just a diversion from the chaotic postwar life. "Their problem was idleness, the purpose amusement," David M. Chalmers writes in the definitive account of the KKK, *Hooded Americanism: The History of the Ku Klux Klan*. "They met in secret places, put on disguises, and had great fun galloping about town after dark. . . . At first there was no thought of violence, but this soon changed."

The Klansmen discovered that their hooded romps through the countryside provoked fear in the populace, especially among the recently freed slaves, whose very presence in turn created so much apprehension in their former masters. Almost overnight, Klan dens began springing up throughout the South, and maintaining a forcible separation between the races became a primary preoccupation.

With the violence quickly spinning out of control, Forrest formally disbanded the Klan in 1869, and by 1871 the Invisible Empire was kaput, but it endured as one of the treasured folk myths of the South. The Klan was brought back to life by D. W. Griffith's *Birth of a Nation*, a two-hour-and-forty-five-minute epic that more or less invented modern cinema, while reinventing the Klan. Beginning in 1915, with the release of *Birth of a Nation*, the Klan began a reign of terror that would last for half a century.

"The modern Klan has abused its power and tarnished the name," says Harper. "All the Klansmen I've met say they're Christians, but from what I've seen they ain't."

Harper's disenchantment crested in January 2003, when he joined seventy-five other Klansmen in Montgomery, Alabama, to march in front of the headquarters of the Southern Poverty Law Center. "I was embarrassed," Harper says. "Every time they yelled 'white power,' I felt it was beneath me."

The American White Knights was an order that had been largely abandoned, its members absorbed into the Aryan Nation brotherhood. In the wake of Montgomery, Harper claimed the name for his own and appointed himself Imperial Wizard (not that there was any competition for the job). Through his Web site he laid out a specific personal ideology. Among the tenets are a fierce patriotism, so-called family values, and a call for personal responsibility, codas informed by a strong dose of Christianity and even a dash of racial tolerance. "What makes me different from every other Klan group is that I believe there are black Christians," the Imperial Wizard says. Likewise, he rates Tiger Woods as his favorite golfer. "Nothing's ever been given to him. He deserves all of the money and the fame, because everything he has, he's worked for. I think he's a very positive role model. Other Klan groups would say, 'You crazy, he's just another nigger.' No, I don't believe that."

Of course, whenever the Imperial Wizard catches himself sounding too broad-minded, he gratuitously turns to racist bile, a conversational tic that makes it seem as if he suffers from a sort of Tourette's syndrome.

"Did you know that blacks are proven to have brains fifteen to twenty-five percent smaller than whites?" he says at one point. "That's a fact. I didn't make it up."

"Did you know," he says, a bit later, "that the night before he was shot, Martin Luther Koon had sex with three white women, and then beat them up?"

One of Harper's many contradictions is that even as he is spewing this kind of corrosive nonsense, he is reflective enough to recognize the split in his personality. "I got a lot of hate in me," he says quietly. "I do. I guess I try to fight it."

No one inflames his passions more than Jesse Jackson, and it was the reverend who pushed Harper into the Augusta National fray. "Jesse Jackson is one of the most ungodly men on earth," the Wizard says. "He's a hypocrite. He lives a so-called Christian life, but he's running around fathering children out of wedlock. It's an insult to all Christians that he calls himself 'reverend.' And now he's gonna come to my state and lecture me? Well, that can't go unchallenged."

Playing the Klan card in his protest application was nothing more than a calculated attempt to get attention. The Imperial Wizard acknowledges the utter cynicism of his position, pushing Christian brotherhood disguised as a world-famous hate group. "My friends tell me, 'J. J., why don't you forget about the Klan and join the American Family Association? You'd be a perfect spokesman.' I say, You're not gittin' it. If the AFA goes to Augusta, it won't even be covered. No cops, no attention, so why bother? But if the Klan goes to Augusta, now that's a big deal. People will say, 'Why would you want that negative attention?' Because it's better than none at all. You can't change the world in one day, and this is where I have to start. They hear the messenger and not the message, but eventually it will sink in. The attention is not for my personal objective, but for people to see what's happening to our country. The power of protest is to open people's eyes."

EMBOLDENED BY the unflattering press that Harper had created for Augusta National, Martha Burk loosed an eye-opening quote on March 3. At a luncheon sponsored by the Pacific Women's Sports Foundation, Burk talked a little Texan, declaring herself a product of the "Lyndon Johnson School of Etiquette," and announcing that, regarding Augusta National, she was ready to "kick some ass and take some names."

Three days later, she finally submitted her application to protest during Masters week, and to poor Ronnie Strength it must've felt like she was wearing steel toes. Attached to the permit request was a letter from Gerald Weber, the legal director for the Georgia branch of the ACLU, who wrote, "The applicants . . . believe that a number of aspects of the recently revised demonstration ordinance present clear violations of the applicants' constitutional rights to peaceably demonstrate on public property. If necessary, the applicants plan to file a lawsuit in federal court outlining their constitutional concerns. . . . However, they remain willing to avert litigation and work with county officials to ensure an orderly and peaceful demonstration where the applicants can communicate their concerns to the participants and attendees of the Masters Golf Tournament at Augusta National Golf Club."

Burk applied for two distinct protest sites, both for Masters Saturday between ten A.M. and three P.M. She asked to place up to two hundred people on Magnolia Drive on the north side of Washington Road, facing the players' and members' entrance to Augusta National. (Magnolia Drive turns into Magnolia Lane on the other side of Washington Road, on Augusta National property.) This would have necessitated closing down Magnolia Drive for the duration of the protest. Burk also asked for an additional twenty-four people to be stationed directly across Washington Road, on both sides of the front gate of the club, at the mouth of Magnolia Lane in the shadow of its famous "Members Only" sign. There is no sidewalk on that side of Washington Road. The protesters would be standing on a grassy, uneven throughway approximately five feet deep, hard against the towering bamboo hedges that thwart outsiders trying to look in, with Washington Road's endless traffic whizzing by.

Burk also filed an exhaustive plan detailing the NCWO's steps to assure, in her words, "a safe, orderly, and nonviolent protest." As Burk told reporters, "Nobody can say this is an outrageous request. A trained facilitator wearing an armband will lead the groups, and a liaison will be assigned to work with the sheriff's department." She also pointed out that the Saturday date was a compromise, a conscientious effort not to affect the climactic final round. "We're making a good-faith effort to not disturb the tournament," she said.

The NCWO had some company at Sheriff Strength's office on March 6, as J. J. Harper also submitted his application, asking for fifteen to twenty-five people to protest "in support of Augusta National and against Rainbow/PUSH's leader Jesse Jackson" at "a location as determined by law enforcement, near the Augusta National Golf Club entrance." Harper kept his options open, requesting any day from April 6 through 13, from nine A.M. to six P.M.

A day after Burk's plans were made public, Todd Manzi amended his application to ensure that he would be able to shadow his nemesis. He asked for fifty-six people "at the main gate of the National, just outside

Magnolia Lane and across the street on Washington Road." He also selected Saturday, April 12, as his desired date, from nine A.M. to four P.M.
Same day as Martha Burk.

On March 10, a new application floated in, from an Atlanta resident
named Dave Walker, a Vietnam vet who requested space for seven to
demonstrate in favor of the war in Iraq.

As if this cast of characters were not eclectic enough, another application was received on March 10, from Deke Wiggins, a twenty-nine-
year-old Augusta grain broker. As Wiggins tells it, two nights earlier he
came up with an irreverent protest idea while watching *Married with
Children*. Over an ensuing dinner at Vallarta's Mexican Restaurant with
some friends, he cooked up something called People Against Ridiculous
Protests (PARP). Manzi and Women Against Martha Burk and the Imperial Wizard had viewpoints, however idiosyncratic; PARP was a protest against the very notion of protesting. With its irresistible name and
irascible stance, PARP became the story du jour for a couple of news cy-
cles. Wiggins fielded so many interviews that he was moved to post a
mock serious press release on his Web site (parp.homestead.com) declaring, "The fact that our group . . . has garnered so much attention and
support proves how ridiculous all of these protests have become."

All of the counter-protesters aligned against Burk could have been
dismissed as a goof, but the combined weight of these groups was having
an effect on Strength's decision making. Burk herself had said that for a
protest to be effective it had to be seen by the intended audience. So if
these groups were demonstrating against Burk, by her logic they had to
be in the same place at the same time as her. PARP, too, had requested to
protest on Masters Saturday from ten A.M. to three P.M., asking for a
whopping 175 demonstrators on Burk's desired spot on Magnolia Drive,
plus an additional eleven across the street on either side of Augusta National's front entrance. Did PARP have any intention of turning out
those kind of numbers? "No, of course not," Wiggins says. "This whole
thing was done for laughs. But I put a big number on the application because I thought it would be a bonus if I created some problems for ol'
Martha."

On March 12, six days after the NCWO's application had been submitted, Rainbow/PUSH applied for three separate sites: one hundred

protesters to join Burk on Magnolia Drive; one hundred more to gather a couple of blocks to the west, at the corner of Washington Road and Berckmans; and one hundred more to be placed a couple of miles to the south at the corner of Highland and Wheeler Roads, a high-volume intersection that was chosen because it is on the edge of a racially mixed neighborhood and thus might inspire more community support.

The clock was ticking for Strength to respond to Burk's March 6 application within the mandated seven-day period. Strength's problem was that the total number of protesters who wanted to hang out in front of Augusta National on Masters Saturday had swollen to a daunting total of 709: 224 for the NCWO, 200 for Rainbow/PUSH (not including the 100 from the distant Highland/Wheeler site), 197 for PARP, 56 for The Burk Stops Here, 25 for the American White Knights of the Ku Klux Klan, and 7 for Dave Walker and his pro-war pals. Strength had declared back in December that the sidewalks and surface streets around Augusta National were not fit for a protest, and that was *before* 709 would-be demonstrators were added to the mix. There was little surprise, then, when Strength made a March 12 announcement banishing Burk and all of the counter-protesters from the front gates of Augusta National. In a letter to Burk that was released publicly, he wrote, "The sheer numbers expected by you, as well as the other applicants for permits, render inadequate the area requested by you. This area is not of a sufficient size that would allow you and the others who have requested to protest/demonstrate at that location to do so without risk of their being in Washington Road, either intentionally or by being pushed. . . . Attempting to accommodate all groups in such limited space would, in my opinion, lead to an unreasonable disturbance of the peace."

By way of a compromise, Strength offered one site on which all the various demonstrators could gather, a 5.1-acre grassy field off Washington Road surrounded by small businesses and the Savannah West apartment complex. The plot of land was four-tenths of a mile to the east of the club entrance. The main artery delivering traffic to Augusta during Masters week is Interstate 20, to the west of the club, meaning that all of those cars would arrive at Augusta National without having to pass the proposed site.

In an interesting twist, the land was owned by Augusta National. It had been purchased a couple of years earlier, during a spending spree in which ten limited-liability corporations controlled by club members or Augusta National's law firms snapped up $23.7 million worth of property around the club, in an effort to stop the tacky commercialization of the area and possibly allow for an expansion of the tournament infrastructure. The county would be leasing the land from the club for the express purpose of the protests.

Burk responded to the news by going on the offensive, saying, "The fact that the site offered is owned and controlled by the Augusta National is quite a statement." Within days she began referring to the proposed sight as "the Pit." (This irked Mayor Young to no end. "Don't call it the Pit," he said in an interview. "That lovely meadow is five prime acres well suited for development.") Burk also sought to undermine Strength's decision by attacking him personally: "I found out that Sheriff Strength is given complimentary tickets to the tournament," she said. "I believe that he does have some loyalty there."

"Would that affect my decision making? Absolutely not," Strength shot back. "I have to make decisions based entirely on what the law is, and also make decisions on public safety to ensure that everyone not only living in this community but every visitor in this community is protected. That decision will be made solely on that. Nothing else."

Suspicions of Strength's motives ran deeper than just a stray Masters badge. Noting that the sheriff's election campaign was managed by David Fields, the vice president and general manager of Radio Cab, which is owned by Augusta National member Ed Douglass, local ACLU attorney Jack Batson says, "Radio Cab controls all the public transportation in Augusta during Masters weeks—those cabs are the only way in and out of the club. And if you look at his statements, what Strength was really afraid of was that the demonstration would impede traffic. You see where I'm going with this?"

THE NCWO and Rainbow/PUSH filed suit in U.S. District Court on March 12, the day of Strength's decision, challenging the constitutionality of Augusta's protest ordinance and how it was applied by the sheriff.

Jack Batson signed the complaint, shining a spotlight on the Atticus Finch of Augusta.

For a quarter century, Batson has been fighting for the civil liberties of Augusta's citizenry, his clients almost always the poor and disenfranchised. He was attracted to the city because, in his mind, it was a microcosm of America, with its divide between the haves and have-nots tinged by race. "I came down here to study the Constitution and democracy, and find out, at a bottom-line level, does it really work, especially where people don't have money," says Batson. "I've found that a lot of blood, sweat, and tears can be exchanged for money. That's what it takes to have your freedom—sacrifice." He knows of what he speaks. "There have been four or five years where my income was zero dollars and zero cents. Literally nothing. But don't make me out to be a saint—I wouldn't be able to do this except for the fact my wife makes a good income. I couldn't accept the standard of living. So I'm kind of chickenshit, too." (Batson's wife, Lisa Krisher, is the director of litigation for the Georgia Legal Services, where she oversees sixty lawyers who represent people below the poverty line.)

Jack had been drawn to the law because, he says, "I wanted to be more American than the flag. I wanted to fight for the democratic ideal." His passion had been forged in Fort Collins, Colorado, where his mother worked in the campus meal service at Colorado State University. Little Jack used to hang out in the cafeteria, where he gravitated toward a group of charismatic athletes. "All these black guys were my heroes," says Batson, although he adds that John F. Kennedy was also an inspiration. "I'd hear the n-word thrown at them, and I couldn't figure it out—these were the coolest guys around. The civil rights movement hit when I was in eighth grade, and I knew which side I wanted to be on."

The other defining event of his politicization was the Vietnam War, and Batson's outrage was fueled by more than just ideology. He had been close friends growing up with a kid named Alan Gunn, before their paths diverged in junior high. While Batson had joined the National Guard to avoid the draft, Gunn became a helicopter pilot in 'Nam. He is still missing in action. "I've often thought, There but for the grace of God goes I," says Batson. He pauses, and suddenly Batson is gasping for air. "This is hard." He begins sobbing softly. "What happened to Alan inspired me to spend my life trying to make the world a fair place." Now the tears are coming in torrents, and he is fighting to get the words out. "I went to . . . law school because . . . I thought . . . I could make a difference."

A consistent critique of Martha Burk's campaign was that it was a frivolous boutique issue that, at best, would affect only a handful of wealthy businesswomen. Down in the trenches, Batson had a far different view. To him, the lawsuit against the protest ordinance was about more than just Burk or Augusta National. "A lot of these issues break down along racial lines because race and money are inextricably linked," Batson says. "To the extent that the county council vote was black and white, it's because the constituents of the black council members are much more likely to have something to protest against in the future. Race is money, money is tied to power, and a lack of power leads to actual oppression in the form of an ordinance that abridges civil rights. Unless you scream about it."

In the case of *Martha Burk v. Richmond County*, that passion was funneled into the March 12 complaint, a collaboration between Batson, the ACLU's Weber, and Sarah Shalf, an attorney at the leading Atlanta firm Bondurant, Mixson & Elmore. The brief referred to Augusta's protest ordinance by its numerical code; *Burk* was challenging its constitutionality: "Section 3-4-11 allows the Sheriff overly broad discretion. It allows the Sheriff to deny an application in whole or in part 'for any reason' if he determines that the plan submitted will raise any 'public safety concerns.'

"For instance, a permit might be denied under this provision if the viewpoint espoused by the applicants is likely to cause a strong reaction among listeners. Subsection (3)(e) allows denial of a permit if the proposed plan 'would present an unreasonable danger' to the public health or safety, while subsection (3)(g) allows denial if the plan 'would lead to an unreasonable disturbance of the peace.' Neither basis for denial defines or even suggests the scope of what might be 'unreasonable.' Further, these subsections do not exclude impermissible considerations, such as the content of the speech. . . ."

What had begun with a simple private letter was now a matter of record for the federal courts. The Honorable Dudley H. Bowen Jr.—the same judge who ruled the Klan could march through downtown Augusta, and who allowed Video X-Mart to open its doors—would determine the fate of Martha Burk's protest. But if the first eight months of the Augusta National membership controversy had taught us anything, it was that this story would devour anything or anyone in its path. So it should come as no surprise that Judge Bowen would soon be ducking Burk's shrapnel because of his ties to Augusta National members, and that his own memberships at exclusionary clubs had long been a source of controversy.

A FOURTH-GENERATION AUGUSTAN, Bowen began practicing law locally in 1965. In 1979, he was nominated as a district judge in Georgia's Southern District by Senator Sam Nunn, the noted Augusta National member. At the time Bowen was a tender thirty-eight years of age, but it wasn't his youth that led to his bruising confirmation process.

Bowen's nomination came against a backdrop of increased scrutiny of the cronyism that had long affected the federal judiciary. In October 1978, President Carter signed the Omnibus Judgeship Act, a new law that allowed for the appointment of 152 federal judges designed to, in Carter's words, "redress a disturbing feature of the federal judiciary: the almost complete absence of women or members of minority groups."

The opposition to Bowen's confirmation was spearheaded by the Southern Regional Council (SRC), a watchdog group dedicated to diversifying federal judgeships. The organization was so outraged by Bowen's nomination—ahead of a prominent black attorney from Augusta, among others—that it produced a case study on the process, writing, "A combination of political patronage and little concern for minorities on the bench has no better illustration than in the recommendation of Dudley Bowen Jr. The nomination demonstrates how one U.S. senator—in this case Sam Nunn of Georgia—allowed politics to override merit."

Bowen's ties to Nunn began with his father-in-law, Dr. John Milton "Pepper" Martin, a lifelong friend of the senator, and the campaign manager in Richmond County for Nunn's first Senate race in 1972. In Nunn's reelection bid, Bowen became a vigorous and generous supporter. According the report by the SRC, Bowen donated $210 to Nunn's campaign in 1977, but that was just a drop in the trough. "An analysis of the contributions to the Sam Nunn for Senate Committee in Augusta suggests that a large proportion of the approximately $14,000 of campaign funds from Augusta was raised among Bowen's colleagues, clients, and the colleagues of his father-in-law," the SRC reported. "Bowen [was] also instrumental in the preparation and success of an 'appreciation dinner' for Nunn in June of 1977. The dinner raised almost $16,000 in unspecified contributions for the senator's campaign." According to the SRC, the approximate $30,000 tied to Bowen represented nearly 25 percent of Nunn's individual contributions in Georgia during 1977 to 1978.

On October 18, 1979, Bowen's confirmation hearing was held in Washington's Dirksen Senate Office Building. Sam Nunn was among the senators presiding over the proceedings. The leading voice of opposition against Bowen was Steve Suitts, the executive director of the SRC. Addressing the senators, Suitts recounted Bowen's controversial journey: "The nominating commission of the Southern District of Georgia recommended five attorneys as the best qualified individuals to be a federal judge. Mr. Bowen was not among those names. Upon request, the nominating commission added three alternates whom they would recommend. Mr. Bowen was not among those names. Only when asked by Georgia's U.S. senators to submit all people qualified in the judgment of the committee as minimally qualified, as one member told us, only then did Mr. Bowen's name appear as a potential nominee.

"This failure [in process] does not constitute simply a harmless error or failure to observe procedural nicety. If Mr. Bowen's nomination is approved under the facts as they are known today, his confirmation will lend credence to the view that the procedures and standards for nominating federal judges under the new act constitute nothing more than a sham."

Senator Nunn's maneuverings were not the only point of contention surrounding Bowen's nomination. In the buildup to the confirmation hearing, it came out that Bowen belonged to five all-white private clubs, including Augusta Country Club. Three different speakers at the Senate hearing railed on Bowen for the segregated company he had been keeping. The most forceful was Roy C. DeLamotte, an Augusta native who doubled as a Methodist minister and professor of Bible ethics. Substitute the appropriate nouns for gender instead of race and Martha Burk could have cribbed the comments twenty-three years later. "What a man does with his leisure, when he is free to express his true character, is often more revealing than what he does when bound by the laws and properties of his daily work," DeLamotte said. "Thus a federal judge, for example, who freely chooses to spend his leisure hours in a segregated private club, is saying to all the world, 'Here I do not have to seem unprejudiced; here I do not have to treat all men as equal; here I do not have to do justice regardless of race or creed.' "

At this point in the hearing one of the senators produced a letter Bowen had written the day before, in which he indicated he had resigned from all five of the clubs in question. A shaken Bowen was finally given the chance to defend himself. After a brief recital of his legal bona fides, he said, "It is true that I have resigned from clubs of which some people have complained. I did that not out of any fear or not because anyone had threatened me or even more than slightly suggested that I should. I did that because I wanted to convince the people that would come here today that I intend to be entirely fair and entirely disassociated with any group that will not apply the law fairly and impartially."

Long after Bowen was confirmed by the Senate, the legacy of his private club affiliations could still be felt. In 1995, Bowen and two other federal judges were charged with the thorny task of redrawing Georgia's congressional districts, which many in the black community saw as an attempt to dilute its political power. The all-white clubs popped up in numerous news accounts, including a story in *The Atlanta Journal-Constitution* that carried the headline "Judges Who'll Draw Lines Have Critics," with a subhead that read, "Strong feelings: Black activists in particular suspect the judges of favoring the white power structure."

So Bowen brought enough baggage for two bellhops to *Martha Burk v. Richmond County*. Martha would later make a big deal about Bowen's ties to the National, saying, "That judge should have recused himself. We understand he's good friends with some of the members."

Bowen refuses to defend himself. In a brief phone conversation, he said, "I've had a career-long commitment to myself that the best way to ensure the dispassionate nature of the court is to not talk about how things happen, or why. I just have this policy, and I believe it is the best way of handling things. It's tempting, you've given me a very nice platform, but I'm going to have to decline in the most cordial manner possible." He did say that Senator Nunn was "a great friend and a fine gentleman."

In a written statement provided for this book, the senator stuck up for his pal: "Judge Bowen and I have not, and would not, discuss a case that is under consideration in his court. To imply that friendship would influence Judge Bowen's decision-making is erroneous and absurd. Judge Bowen grew up in Augusta, his family lives in Augusta, and he knows many people who appear before his court. I have never heard any hint of unfairness about Judge Bowen's decisions or any questions regarding his integrity."

Indeed, around Augusta Bowen's friendship with members of the National is greeted with a shrug. Yes, the judge's annual Masters week party at his home is often dotted with green jackets, including Nunn and Georgia real estate magnate Boone Knox, whose wife, Georgeann, is close friends with the judge's wife, Madeline. But says David Hudson, one of Augusta's most prominent attorneys, "One does not become a federal judge by being obscure. Such a person moves in certain social circles; such a person is active in a certain strata of business and civic life. To rise to the federal bench in Georgia, it would be likely that such a person was friendly with Augusta National members, given the prominent standing of the membership. For a federal judge to come out of Augusta, it's not a likelihood but a certainty that they would be friendly with members."

After a flurry of briefs were filed in late March by both Burk's legal team and Richmond County, Bowen called for a motion hearing on April 2. The Masters has always been known for its dramatic finishes, and the legal proceeding surrounding the 2003 tournament would be no exception. The hearing would be held a scant eight days before the first round was to begin.

THE COURTROOM in Augusta's federal courthouse is so majestic it looks like a Hollywood set. The room boasts soaring twenty-five-foot ceilings, which are adorned with carved dark-wood paneling and illuminated by a gorgeous colored-glass above the center of the room. Judge Bowen cuts a figure equal to the setting, with a rich baritone, ramrod-straight posture, and the regal air of a man who has been wearing the robe for nearly a quarter century. On April 2, the room was packed to capacity for the motion hearing of *Martha Burk v. Richmond County*. Sheriff Strength was the star of the show, and, as usual, he dressed to impress, in a gorgeous gray suit that brought out the silver in his hair, a crisp white shirt showing plenty of cuff, a burgundy tie with subtle striping, and black tassled loafers buffed to reflective shine.

Early on, Richmond County attorney Jim Ellison had a short exchange with Strength that cut to the heart of the matter. "Suppose Ms. Burk's group was the only one who had asked for that particular location. Would that have alleviated all of the concerns that you have expressed concerning that location?"

"It would not," Strength said.

At the conclusion of the hearing, Bowen said, "Counsel, I can't tell you when, but I will get back to you by way of a decision as soon as possible."

Bowen's ruling, whenever it came, would bring to an end an illuminating look into the explosive politics of Augusta. The messy public process had already laid bare the far-reaching influence of the town's famous golf club. At issue was a city ordinance that had been voted in by the brother of an Augusta National member, then signed into law by a mayor and enforced by a sheriff who had pocketed tens of thousands of dollars in campaign contributions from various green jackets, to say nothing of the priceless free badge that the sheriff receives for his work on the Masters parking committee or the many tens of thousands of dollars his men rake in during tournament week in paychecks cut by Augusta National Inc. Strength was all set to banish Burk to the Pit, out of sight of Magnolia Lane; all he needed was the go-ahead from a judge who had been put on the bench by one of the most powerful men in the club.

Welcome to Augusta, Martha.

EIGHT

Pre-Masters Jitters

WHILE THE POLITICAL and legal wrangling in Augusta provided riv-eting theater, elsewhere the run-up to the Masters was chock-full of juicy flare-ups, mini-scandals, and intriguing plot twists.

The Augusta National membership controversy filled its first body bag on March 1, when Lloyd Ward resigned as CEO of the United States Olympic Committee. Up until then, the collective damage had been confined to besmirched reputations—as Bryant Gumbel, Jack Welch, and Tiger Woods could attest—and the tarnishing of august institutions, CBS, the PGA Tour, and *The New York Times* among them. But Ward's was the first head to roll because of Augusta National. The deathwatch had begun the moment Ward was attacked at the Senate hearing con-vened in January to address the USOC's turmoil, in which some of the sharpest criticism was reserved for its CEO's decision to remain a mem-ber of an exclusionary golf club. In the end, Ward jumped before he was pushed, and he played the martyr card on the way out, saying in a state-ment that "competing interests" within the organization have "placed its CEOs in an untenable, if not impossible role." Because he had resigned, Ward forfeited any severance; all he got was a year of medical benefits and a laptop computer.

Clearly the alleged ethical violations were the final, fatal blow in Ward's troubled tenure, but talk to enough people around the USOC and the feeling is that his downfall was largely because of Augusta National. One of Ward's top lieutenants, who would only speak anonymously, says, "Lloyd made his share of mistakes, but he could have survived them had he not burned up so much goodwill over Augusta. His whole job boils down to fund-raising, and you simply can't have your CEO in the newspaper inviting controversy. It's bad for business. His stubbornness [in not resigning from Augusta National] made him a very inviting target for the people here who wanted his head for other reasons."

Three days after Ward bit the dust, there were more Augusta National rumblings in high places, as Georgia Governor Sonny Perdue was quoted in *The Atlanta Journal-Constitution* saying, "From what I'm hearing, they want to do that right thing. They just feel a little trapped right now. I think everyone at some point would like to see [the club admit women]."

The next day Hootie Johnson pulled out the same poison pen he had used to send his letter to Martha Burk, firing off a rebuttal to Perdue that was leaked to the press. Wrote the chairman, "I must tell you that I read in the newspaper with some dismay your remarks about our membership. . . . I can only infer from your comments that your opinion is that single-gender, private clubs such as ours are somehow morally wrong. Allow me to point out, if I may, that ours is hardly the only such group in Georgia. Indeed, if the standard is applied evenly, should Spellman College in Atlanta do the 'right thing' as well by admitting men to their institution? Should the Junior League of Georgia be required to admit men?

"[Georgia] citizens have overwhelmingly voiced support for our position and the important principle of individual freedom that is at stake. I would like to think that the support we enjoy is also a result of our long record of bringing honor and prestige to the State of Georgia.

"For the Governor of our state to suggest that we should capitulate to special interest groups when the Constitution is on our side and we have done nothing wrong is a bit surprising and very disappointing."

From the governor's mansion to the Supreme Court, the membership controversy was a story that continued to touch the powerful. Three days after Johnson typed his letter, *GolfWeek* ran a startling item in the "Forecaddie," a gossip column that is candidly billed as nothing more than "Revelations and Speculations": "The Forecaddie hears, from more than one source, that the Augusta National Golf Club plans to 'announce' the addition of its first female member April 9, the day before the start of this year's Masters. The Chosen One? Supreme Court justice Sandra Day O'Connor."

This was such big news it made the front page of Sports in both the *San Antonio Express-News* and the *Dayton Daily News*, and became a recurrent presence on the bottom-of-the-screen crawl on CNN. This said more about the jumpiness in the press to be on top of the Augusta National news than the quality of *GolfWeek*'s information, because nothing in the "Forecaddie" item rang true. Augusta National always admits its new members in the late summer, so they can partake in the October festivities that accompany the reopening of the club. Beyond that, even if Hootie was to have an inexplicable change of heart and welcome the first woman member, there's no way he would overshadow the Masters with a splashy announcement on the eve of the tournament. Augusta National quickly confirmed the obvious, spokesman Glenn Greenspan saying, "That report is completely erroneous."

A rather defensive *GolfWeek* source says, "We didn't make it up. It had been circulating on the Senior tour for a while. We heard it again from somebody who has been in golf for a long time who is very close with an Augusta National member. That was when we ran with it. What we heard later, from the longtime golf guy, was that it had been offered to O'Connor but she turned it down."

No doubt the *GolfWeek* source had been reading *Golf Digest*. In its January 2003 issue, *Digest* did a feature on O'Connor, simply because for years she had been the default choice among the wishful thinkers and club apologists who wanted to believe Augusta National was forever on the verge of adding a woman member, a notion Johnson would later put the lie to. In fact, O'Connor had long been a sort of urban legend around Augusta. Says Allison Greene, of Women Against Martha Burk, "In January 2002"—months before Burk had ever heard of Hootie Johnson— "the rumor was flying around that Sandra Day O'Connor had become the first woman member. Everyone in town was talking about it. It was daily coffee talk in here [at the Boll Weevil Café]." O'Connor had also been singled out in *The New York Times*'s editorial in November 2002 as a good choice to break the National's sex barrier. In the *Digest* article, she tried to put to rest such loose talk:

"I'm not looking for a new membership anywhere," O'Connor said. "I'll pass on that."

Perhaps her ambivalence could be traced to all the bad vibes emanating from the club. Two days after the O'Connor story broke, Augusta National had a starring role in yet another desultory news cycle. The University of Georgia's basketball coach, Jim Harrick, had been under siege for weeks, as his program was being investigated for academic fraud and other major NCAA violations, which he denied. The situation had grown so dire, and the evidence of wrongdoing so overwhelming, that on March 10, Georgia athletic director Vince Dooley announced that the Bulldogs were canceling the rest of their season. Harrick got the news when Dooley rang his cell phone, and where was Harrick? As would be widely reported, he was playing golf at Augusta National, sullying just a tiny bit more the public image of a once-secretive club that now found itself in scandalous headlines without even trying.

As ALWAYS, March brought the PGA Tour's Florida swing, a four-tournament jig during which the anticipation of the upcoming Masters ordinarily reaches a fever pitch. In 2003, the mood was markedly different among the players. "For people who watch and play golf and can't wait for the springtime and the Masters to come along, it sets the whole tone, and [the membership controversy] has detracted from that," said Mark O'Meara, the 1998 Masters champ. "It's had a pretty major effect."

It was nice of O'Meara to fret about the fans, but pro golfers are independent contractors accustomed to thinking only of themselves, and by and large their views of the membership controversy were shaped by how it affected them. "Oh, Hootie Johnson—he's made a lot of our lives very uncomfortable," said Nick Price.

No doubt because of the endless grief that the membership controversy had caused Tiger Woods, his colleagues had grown gun-shy about expressing their opinions. "If you've got an inkling that you think women shouldn't be there, you better keep your mouth shut," said Hal Sutton. "Because if you say it, you're going to be in Hootie Johnson's situation and they're going to crucify you."

"It's hard to say what's right or wrong these days anymore," said promising young tour pro Charles Howell III, an Augusta native. "I have an opinion. But nothing I say can be right. If I say one thing, well, then half the people argue about it with the other."

This kind of non-response was not good enough for many reporters, who were forever looking for new angles. The players had long since become weary of the endless questioning. "No matter what you say, everyone is going to have to ask you about it again the next day," said Davis Love III. "It's turned into a circus, and we shouldn't even be part of it."

In February, six-time Masters champ Jack Nicklaus had said, "I sort of ride the fence. I try not to offend. I'm a member there, but I also try not to impose my feelings. Am I tired of hearing about it? Yeah. Am I unhappy it's not been resolved? Yes." A month later, after having endured steady questioning, Nicklaus had had enough. "Have you ever seen me duck a question? Well, I'm doing it now," he said. "I'm not going to comment on that. I think I'll be saying a lot more by saying nothing."

Taken as a whole, the PGA Tour membership is an extremely conservative body politic. The 1993 Ryder Cup team had made noises about boycotting a trip to the White House in protest of President Clinton's tax laws, and in 2002, *Sports Illustrated* conducted a poll of seventy Tour players, asking them, among other things, if they had ever voted for a Democrat. Just 25 percent said yes. It was not surprising, then, that many players were dismissive of, or downright hostile to, the NCWO's campaign. "Martha Burk is actually promoting Martha Burk," said Paul Azinger. "It's very self-serving. Whatever woman they eventually make a member at Augusta National will be the most exploited woman in America. And I'm sure Martha Burk is against the exploitation of women."

Amid all the debate, the overriding sentiment among Tour members was that they just wanted the whole mess to go away so they could get back to thinking of nothing but the size of a sixth-place check. "The solution is, give a woman a membership and case closed," said John Daly. "But it's not my call."

"I couldn't care less if they let twenty ladies in there," said 1992 Masters champ Fred Couples.

As the season lurched toward Augusta, all of the players were seeking a little perspective. "There's so much bad blood at this point I think somebody's gonna have to do something to make it right," said ten-year vet Olin Browne, a member of the Tour policy board, alongside two Augusta National members. "It's an unfortunate thing, but I guess this is how social evolution occurs."

IN THE FINAL WEEKS before the Masters, Martha Burk resembled nothing if not a political hopeful on the campaign trail. She spent March crisscrossing the country in a series of public appearances, selling her platform. One of the first stops was on March 8 in McLean, Virginia, where Burk was honored by the Women's Center, a nonprofit group that provides counseling and education services. She got a surprise when she arrived at the hotel that was hosting the conference: about a dozen male demonstrators in homemade sashes carrying signs such as HOORAY FOR HOOTIE and JUST SAY NO TO UNREASONABLE FEMINISTS. As soon as Martha rolled up the chanting began: "Just say no to Burk! Just say no to Burk!" The protest was the work of the National Coalition of Free Men, a Minneapolis-based nonprofit that, according to its Web site, "works to free men and boys from the limits of sex discrimination."

Burk took the showing of opposition in stride. "I admire their pluck," she said. "I understand they've been out there a couple of hours." Told that the protesters were billing themselves as "Duffragettes," Burk said, "They got the 'duh' part right."

It was a great line, and a reminder of Burk's wit and charm. As the membership controversy had dragged on, she had grown increasingly strident, and with the Masters in sight, she seemed to be feeling the pressure. Her contention that Augusta National "welcomes" the support of the Ku Klux Klan was plainly ludicrous, and she had also been unable to resist interjecting some provocative opinions on the racial divide in Augusta politics. In both cases she overplayed her hand, and the cheap attacks on the club were beneath her.

It was a relief, then, when Burk's comments suggested she retained enough perspective to be respectful of the looming war in Iraq. (By mid-March it was a question of when, not if, bombs would begin raining on Baghdad; the timing, in relation to the Masters, moved Dennis Miller to tell MSNBC, "*The New York Times* will decide to support the war as soon as they find out Saddam has opened an all-male golf club in Tikrit.") On March 14, during a visit to Chicago for the Empowerment 2003 conference, Burk said, "We can't get bound up in a march about golf when the nation's mood is on war." Still, for months Burk had found that the best way to get attention was to be provocative, and even in a conciliatory mode she couldn't help playing with fire. In her speech to about two hundred people, she closed by saying of Augusta National's membership practices, "Saddam Hussein is eligible, Margaret Thatcher is not. That shows you how absurd this all is."

In the March 18 *Washington Post,* Burk spelled out her position on the war more clearly. As she told Len Shapiro, "To be down there partying in Augusta when the country is at war is unseemly. If I were organizing [the Masters], I would consider postponing it just for the public image it would put forth.

"If they do not cancel the tournament out of deference to our fighting men and women, we will still be there. The tone will be different than what it might have been. We don't want to marginalize ourselves while the nation's mind is on the war. We need to point out that [the club's membership practices] are wrong. We will still have a presence there if they go on with it. But our methods and our message will be slightly different, depending on national events."

Augusta National spokesman Glenn Greenspan responded in a statement: "Planning continues for this year's Masters Tournament, and just like other major sporting events, we will be evaluating the situation as it unfolds. But for Ms. Burk to use the possibility of war as an opportunity to inject herself into the news again is the lowest form of self-promotion."

They were free to disagree, but Burk's comments seemed to signal the beginning of more civil discourse. Her timing was perfect, as the day after the *Post* story ran the first military strikes began in Iraq. With the nation now at war, surely the inflammatory rhetoric surrounding Augusta National was now over.

The cease-fire lasted all of one day.

On March 20, Augusta National's media consultant, Jim McCarthy, dropped a few metaphorical bombs in the *San Francisco Chronicle*, saying, "Ms. Burk is a specialist in drive-by attacks and outrageous statements. . . . Just because she can craft a pithy quote does not make her a philosopher." Later he defended Hootie Johnson's "point of a bayonet" press release, saying, "There should have been no doubt about the nature of Ms. Burk's threat, so the instinct to confront it was absolutely correct. Just because a drive-by shooter isn't accurate doesn't mean you don't duck when the car comes around the corner."

The next day *The Scotsman* printed quotes from its own interview with McCarthy. He had begun a correspondence with the paper by sending a nasty letter two weeks earlier, calling its coverage "heavy on invective and light on reasoning and accuracy." Given a chance to spout off, McCarthy said of Burk, "She's a bomb-thrower. If you look at her record, it's one of drive-by activism. Even a blind drive-by shotgunner is going to hit a target once in a while."

Back in Washington, Burk was outraged at the fusillade of violent imagery. "When McCarthy started popping off early on, I stayed silent, because I didn't want it recycled nine thousand times. After that garbage came out in the *San Francisco Chronicle*, I had my lawyers fax a letter to the club that day, telling them they need to do the responsible thing and shut this guy up. The next day he popped off again. I sent another emergency letter to the club, letting them know that he was compromising my safety and I would hold them accountable.

"McCarthy crossed the line," Burk continues. "Between TV and that damn talk radio there has been enough overheated rhetoric, but coming from the club, it's out of line. I have been very careful not to introduce any imagery of violence and mayhem into this debate." Burk later repeated these criticisms in *Sports Illustrated,* in which she said McCarthy's remarks would have been "more suitable for an exchange about gang wars than gender wars."

Of course, following Johnson's decision to drop the Masters' sponsors, Burk had been quoted in the *Irish Times* in early October, saying, "We are not out of bullets. There are many options open to us." Two weeks later she told the *Fort Worth Star-Telegram* that, after *USA Today* printed the club's membership list, she felt like, "I had six more bullets."

These were clearly just rhetorical flourishes; McCarthy pleads the same defense, saying, " 'Drive-by activist' is Beltway parlance, it's short-hand for an activist who pops up at the scene of a controversy and shoots from the lip, trying to interject themselves into the debate. It's a well-known phrase around D.C. which I would guarantee Burk was familiar with, and for her to pretend to feel threatened was just another way for her to try to grab attention." No word on the prevalence of "bomb-thrower" and "drive-by shotgunner" as clever PR phrases.

These explosive comments were just a precursor to Burk's most loaded rhetoric yet. On March 26, while the nation was riveted by im-ages of the U.S. military's overwhelming blitzkrieg and on edge because of a host of captured POWs, Burk made the biggest strategic mistake of the membership controversy since Hootie Johnson had launched the whole affair eight months earlier. At a rally/media event on the steps of City Hall in New York City, flanked by a handful of city council members and a sprinkling of activists that she described as "people of conscience," Burk said, "Broadcasting the Masters now and showcasing a club that discriminates against women is an insult to the nearly quarter million women in the U.S. armed forces. It's appalling that the women who are willing to lay down their lives for democratic ideals should be shut out of this club. . . . Democratic ideals do not include discrimination."

Following a strategy that had been fine-tuned in the preceding months, Augusta National responded almost instantly with a spiky state-ment from spokesman Glenn Greenspan: "Ms. Burk will say anything to get publicity. But if she is invoking the troops to draw more attention to herself, only three words apply—shame on you."

Burk's pithy and highly effective remarks early on had set the tone for the Augusta National membership controversy, but as the Masters neared, her shrill remarks about the KKK and Augusta's racial politics were sharply off-key. Still, the reaction they generated was nothing com-pared to the fierce response to her women in the military comments. Writers and pundits teed off on her with a stunning intensity, the outrage betraying the frayed nerves of the post-9/11 world, and also, perhaps, the collective fatigue of her audience. Burk had been front-page news for eight and a half months in a culture with an attention span about as long as an MTV video. After singing her praises for so long, the golf press simply needed something else to write about. Martha as the bad guy was a fresh new angle, and in the aftermath of the military comments it was writ large in the headlines.

The Orlando Sentinel: "Trying to Link Pow, Masters Is Incredibly Offensive Move."

The San Diego Union-Tribune: "Of Bunkum and Busters: Burk Raises Rhetoric on Augusta National."

Tampa Tribune: "Burk Crosses Line by Trying to Equate Golf, War."

Modesto Bee: "Burk Misfires with War Comments."

The prose was equally unforgiving. AP columnist Steve Wilstein's first sentence said it all: "Sorry, Martha Burk, you just lost me."

In the *Chicago Sun-Times*, columnist Jay Mariotti wrote, "More insufferable than ever, Burk is shamelessly using the war hook as a means to further pressure Hootie. Whatever good impressions she had made in battling Augusta National's stone-age attitudes about all-male membership have evaporated amid her ignorance and grandstanding."

In the *New York Daily News*, Mike Lupica wrote, "Martha Burk doesn't just sound desperate, she sounds like a fool. . . . The more Burk talks, at a time when Hootie Johnson of Augusta National doesn't say anything, the more she makes it impossible for people to find any way to root for her.

"Burk should have been the hero. . . . This started out being about what's right, even for private clubs who believe they have the law behind them. Whatever Martha Burk says, she thinks it's about her now. She should have put Hootie away long ago. Now the whole thing has gotten tipped on its head. Now you wouldn't want to join any club that has Martha Burk as a member."

Burk began backpedaling furiously—an AP story a few days after the City Hall press conference carried the headline "Burk Says War Comments Were Misunderstood"—but the damage was done. She would later say, "There did seem to be a backlash and the one regret I have is that I didn't explain in enough detail why we stood up to talk about this important issue. Our groups have advocated for women in the military for many years. We're fighting every day to keep the role of women in the military strong, because the Bush administration is trying to diminish that role. In fact, one of our strongest groups is Women in Military Service to America, the largest women veterans group in this country.

"I didn't give all that background, so people thought we were just jumping into the fray. But I still maintain it's something all Americans should think about—why should women not be equal at home when they're fighting for freedom abroad? I regret people didn't understand the background of the NCWO and the military. Believe me, we've been there and we will be there."

Lost in the furor over the war comments was that the gathering at City Hall in New York was supposed to be a protest against CBS. Some of the officials gathered alongside Burk had worn T-shirts with the CBS logo and the words "Continues to Broadcast Segregation." It was announced during the press conference that eight city council members were sponsoring a resolution condemning Augusta National's membership practices and calling on CBS not to televise the Masters.

Burk continued the campaign against CBS three days later, on March 29, organizing a mini-protest in front of the company's headquarters on West Fifty-second Street in Manhattan. All of five demonstrators showed up to pass out anti-CBS leaflets. Burk was not one of them. Lurking in the shadows was what appeared to be a young paparazzo but was actually one of Jim McCarthy's interns, who was dutifully snapping away pictures with a digital camera. "There's nothing wrong with that, is there?" McCarthy asks, sheepishly. He had sent the cameraman because he wanted to document the lack of support on Fifty-second Street for Burk's cause. He had also done surveillance on the turnout at City Hall, which he claims included only media and support staff from the various groups on hand, and no actual demonstrators.

During the jittery weeks before the Masters, it was becoming increasingly obvious that Burk was having trouble rallying protesters. Though the Honorable Dudley H. Bowen Jr. had yet to rule on where the Masters week demonstration could be held, the date was already etched in stone. Only a couple of weeks out, Burk was still actively recruiting would-be protesters on the home page of the NCWO Web site and at her various public appearances. In interviews Burk was also explicitly downplaying expectations for the protest. The week before the Masters, she told *Newsday*, "I think people may expect a lot more than we plan out there. It is not going to be mass chaos. It is not going to be illegal. It is not going to depend on thousands of people disrupting traffic or disrupting the tournament. It's going to be, as protests go, fairly small. We are going to have an orderly protest that makes our point. And then we're going to go home." None of this would have been necessary had there been an out-pouring of support from the 7 million members of the NCWO, whom Burk so often invoked as a measure of her influence. Even before the divisive comments about the war it appeared that Burk's following was on the wane.

"I would dispute that it was waning," says McCarthy. "The grassroots support was never there in the first place. The reason we took pictures at all of her protests was so there would be irrefutable proof that she simply had nobody standing with her. I didn't want Burk to be able to say that if the Augusta protest fizzled, it was an isolated incident, affected by the local politics or whatever other excuse she could dream up. There was a pattern here. All of her staged media events were designed to produce cookie-cutter stories by a sympathetic press, but at none of them was she able to rally any support from the public. That's why I was confident that Burk would not be able to deliver any numbers in Augusta. I also knew the press would turn on her in the end, because they would feel like they had been duped. I, however, would call it self-delusion. The signs were there all along that her support was a mile wide and an inch deep. All you had to do was take a closer look."

IT'S IRONIC that as Burk was stumbling and bumbling to the finish line in Augusta, she scored what she considers one of her most note-worthy achievements. On March 31, Representatives Carolyn Maloney (D-New York) and John Lewis (D-Georgia) introduced a congressional resolution entitled "Fair Play: Equal Access in Club Membership." The text read, in part:

"Whereas the right of private association among friends, colleagues, and like-minded individuals is a deeply held American value when it is

truly private, but is immorally invoked when it is used as a cover for discrimination;

"Whereas the President, the Vice President, nor [sic] any member of
Congress, justice or judge of the United States, or political appointee in
the executive branch of the Government, by virtue of their public office,
are obligated to adhere to a higher standard of conduct than what is minimally required by law, a standard of conduct that reflect the American
value that discrimination is wrong;

"*Resolved by the House of Representatives (the Senate concurring),*

"It is the sense of the Congress that neither the President, the Vice
President, nor any member of Congress, justice or judge of the United
States, or political appointee in the executive branch of the Government should belong to a club that discriminates on the basis of sex or
race."

Though Augusta National was not named in the bill, the club was repeatedly invoked at a Capitol Hill press conference on March 31, where
Martha Burk was one of the featured speakers. "It is absolutely appropriate that the Congress address this issue," said Burk. "People in Congress
are guardians of the public trust and are obliged to set a standard that citizens can admire and emulate. These individuals are entrusted to assure
freedom from discrimination through our system of national laws and
policies. It should be no less with their personal behavior."

Maloney, whose district comprises mainly the east side of Manhattan,
added, "By saying 'Women, keep out,' Augusta National sends a strong
message to women everywhere: 'you are not our equal partner.' "

Twelve Democratic congressmen signed up as sponsors on the resolution, including presidential hopeful Dick Gephardt. "Our leaders at the
highest levels of the federal government must set the right example on
this important issue," Gephardt said.

However noble the intent, the resolution had almost no chance of
being passed into law; to even reach the floor for a vote it would have to
navigate three committees—Judiciary, Government Reform, and House
Administration—that were all chaired by Republicans considered hostile to the intent of the bill, according to Maloney aide Afshin Mo-
hamadi. Yet Burk was eager to claim a symbolic victory. "Critics have

liked to say from the very beginning that this is a frivolous cause," she says, "but I'm sorry, once Congress gets involved, it is a matter of national importance."

TWO DAYS BEFORE THIS congressional resolution was offered, Hootie Johnson made a stunning public gesture of his own. In an unprecedented showing of contrition, the chairman ended months of acrimony and finally allowed that his controversial retirement policy was wrongheaded and unfair. In finally acknowledging the political realities of the situation, Johnson safeguarded the best interests of the Masters by preventing a messy spectacle that threatened to overshadow his beloved tournament. Said Johnson, "After discussions with Arnold Palmer and Jack Nicklaus, the Club has decided not to implement the past champions qualification next year. Arnold, Jack and I agree that past winners should be able to play as long as they'd like, so long as they feel they can remain competitive. We will count on our champions to know when their playing careers at the Masters have come to an end. I am comfortable that the champions will abide by the spirit and intent of the lifetime exemption."

The misdirection of the announcement was lost on no one. New York's *Newsday* ran the cheeky headline "Augusta Ends a Ban (Not That One)," and by aligning himself with icons of Masters' past exactly two weeks before Martha Burk's protest, Johnson gave more ammo to the cynics in the press. In the *Boston Herald,* Karen Guregian wrote, "Hootie Johnson and his all-boys club . . . are merely using legends Arnold Palmer, Jack Nicklaus, Gary Player, et al as pawns in their battle with Martha Burk. [Johnson] probably thinks he's going to be embraced now by the public for letting Arnie and Jack back. He probably thinks the women's issue is going to disappear, or at least dissipate, because he's made peace with the old-timers and made them feel welcome again on Magnolia Lane . . . Sorry Hootie, this change of heart has a rotten smell."

Party poopers such as Guregian were a distinct minority. Tiger Woods called the decision a "great move." Palmer issued a statement saying,

"Jack and I are grateful to Hootie Johnson for his thoughtful consideration of this issue, and thank him on behalf of all of the past champions
for retaining this important Masters tradition." Palmer, seventy-three at
the time of the announcement, went on to say that he was already looking ahead to 2004, when he would tee it up in his mind-blowing fiftieth
Masters.

Three-time Masters winner Gary Player had been Johnson's most
vociferous critic among the past champs, because had the age limit of
sixty-five been enacted in 2004, as threatened, he would have been
forced out following Martha's Masters (ditto Charles Coody as well as
Tommy Aaron, who was still competitive enough to have made the cut
in 2000 at the age of sixty-three.) In an interview with *Golf Magazine*
in early 2003, Player was asked how Hootie Johnson will be remembered.
His harsh reply: "As a man with good intentions who made countless mistakes and used very poor judgment." Now, in the wake of
Johnson's change of heart, Player was just another member of Hootie's
fan club. "I am delighted with the decision," Player said. "I respect the
fact that Hootie Johnson and his committee have the courage and humility to admit they were wrong and change back to the former tradition." He added that, "I was one of the few players who had been
outspoken on the decision. I'd like to think that it was constructive criticism and I would like to think that this played a small part in changing
their minds."

It was interesting that these most powerful of men could so easily
sway Johnson, yet all of them claimed to be impotent on the subject of
women members. (Recall that in July, Nicklaus, a dues-paying green
jacket, had said, "I'm just a member. The club has its policies, and I'm not
[involved] in the policies of the club.") But the untidy inconsistencies in
the public positions of Nicklaus, Palmer, and Player were overlooked in
the rush of warm and fuzzy goodwill that came with the thought of the
Big Three enjoying more golden moments on the fairways of Augusta
National. And all because of Hootie! His deft recovery on the past-
champs issue completed an image rehabilitation that was months in the
making. The same man who had been called "pigheaded" by a former
member on A1 of *The New York Times*, who had earned the wrath of editorial writers across America, and who had been accused of welcoming

the support of the Ku Klux Klan, was now being lauded for his "thoughtful consideration" and his "courage and humility"—by the giants of the game no less. This last plot twist capped a wild month, packed with developments that would continue to resonate. The stage was now set for the most anticipated golf tournament in history, which promised to be a Masters unlike any other.

NINE

Masters Week

MASTERS WEEK ACTUALLY BEGINS a day early, as the preceding Sunday is when the club opens its doors for competitors to play their first official practice rounds. That Sunday is also one of the busiest days of the year for Augusta National members, who have unrestricted access to the course. Phil Mickelson, Nick Faldo, and Seve Ballesteros were among the fifty or so Masters competitors who had arrived early for the 2003 tournament, but on Sunday they had to share the hallowed grounds with a bunch of bogey golfers. After a rain delay in the morning, club members teed off on the 1st hole in rapid succession for a full hour, topping, shanking, slicing, and pull-hooking a series of drives. It was noted by many of those milling around the 1st tee that five women were among the members' guests.

"I thought the course would be empty, maybe a couple of pros fluttering around and that would be it," veteran Australian pro and Masters rookie Peter Lonard said from the edge of the putting green, taking in the scene. "I didn't have a clue. This was quite a shock to the system."

About the same time Lonard was waxing about the unique "presence" of the Masters, a few miles away Women Against Martha Burk (WAMB) was staging the first protest of the week, though it was cleverly disguised as a tailgate party. The rain had driven the WAMB supporters under the large overhang of a building at the corner of Ninth and Reynolds streets, in downtown Augusta. A green-and-white banner stretching ten feet across proclaimed WE LOVE AUGUSTA. Various hand-made signs adorned the wall of the building, including WOMEN LIKE HAV-ING THEIR OWN CLUBS TOO. Clusters of yellow and green balloons had been attached to four tables, where would-be protesters munched on hamburgers, hot dogs, pizza, potato chips, and lollipops. Nearby a plastic kiddie pool had been filled with ice and drinks. WAMB founder Allison Greene had spent $350 of her own money on the get-together—"three months of baby formula," the new mom said. But despite the rain, nearly one hundred Augustans dropped by to show their support. "The whole day was so much fun—a chance to get together, celebrate the Masters, dish on the Martha Burk thing, and also talk about real issues," said Greene, whose slacks were drenched from the knee down by the rain. "We wanted to show the world that despite what Martha Burk thinks, Augusta is full of good people, and we love our city just how it is. And, yes, a few adult beverages were also consumed."

While Greene fussed over her guests, her husband, Steven, had re-tired to a nearby restaurant to drink beer with a half-dozen male friends. "All the girls were over here and the boys over there," Allison said. "It just proves that Hootie's right—we do need to get away from each other once in a while."

On the same day that Burk was barbecued by WAMB along with the hamburgers and wieners, she left a pair of spicy voicemails for the author of this book. She had been enflamed by a story in *Sports Illustrated*'s Mas-ters preview, which had recently hit subscribers' mailboxes; the piece captured the edginess of the Augusta citizenry, including a disgruntled local who was quoted as saying of Burk, "She oughta be shot." An ac-companying time line of all the plots twists in the saga regurgitated a couple of rhetorical flourishes that Jim McCarthy had loosed in the pre-ceding weeks, during which he called Burk a "bomb-thrower" and a "drive-by shotgunner," among other things. In the first long, rambling voicemail, Burk called *Sports Illustrated*'s use of the quotes "reprehensi-ble," "dangerous," and "potentially actionable."

Reached in Washington, D.C., late Sunday afternoon, Burk continued to vent. "These people are nuts anyway," she said, cryptically. "We don't need to egg them on. That sheriff is putting me in an open air field, on a stage, next to a busy road with an apartment building behind me, and McCarthy is running around talking about drive-by shooters and bomb-throwers. . . . It gives people ideas.

"I'm feeling very vulnerable right now. Maybe you think I'm being paranoid, but the fact is, Augusta has become a very hostile city toward me, and to top it all off, the Klan is going to be there too. I'm sorry, but the Klan is not something to be taken lightly."

THE IMPERIAL WIZARD of the White Knights of the Ku Klux Klan is showing off his gun collection. It's Tuesday of Masters week, but here in rural Cordele, Georgia, two hours' drive southwest of Augusta, the tournament feels a million miles away. The Imperial Wizard lives in a tidy redbrick house, off a quiet country road on the outskirts of town. Stashed in his bedroom closet is a small arsenal, including an AK-47, an assortment of rifles, and a handful of handguns. Underneath his bed are thousands of rounds of ammo. The Imperial Wizard is asked if he likes to hunt. J. J. Harper breaks into a broad, ironic grin. "You mean besides niggers?" he says.

The Imperial Wizard lets out a high-pitched, boyish squeal. He knows how vile the sentiment is, yet he can't resist playing to his audience. It's mostly a show, of course, and not a very convincing one. The house is adorned not with charred crosses but an overflow of his wife, Evelyn's, decorating touches: bowls of potpourri, handmade wall hangings, lacy throw pillows. Three white poodles scamper afoot. The Imperial Wizard often scoops up Tinkerbell and cradles her like a child, cooing mindlessly.

Tonight the Imperial Wizard has welcomed into his home a Jewish reporter from what he calls "the most sin-filled place on Earth"—New York City, natch—because, he says, he is "misunderstood." He has been a punch line in the press for over a month now, and wants the world to know that he has feelings, too. Sitting on his velour couch, in a living room with seventies-style wood paneling, the Imperial Wizard unburdens himself. "All this stuff that's been said about me, it hurts," he says, his voice thick with emotion. "I've lost sleep over this. I've lost weight. I've had to worry about people calling me and my family names. It tears me up. Anything negative the body rejects. Everybody has feelings—some just hide them better than others."

He does indeed look wrung out. The past couple of nights the Imperial Wizard has stayed up till the wee hours hand-painting signs for the Masters protest, which is fast approaching. The day before was an eventful one around Augusta, as a monsoon washed out the practice round. Tens of thousands of fans were turned away at the gates, as the grounds were deemed too wet and treacherous to accommodate spectators. Also on Monday, Judge Dudley H. Bowen Jr. issued a pair of rulings, upholding the constitutionality of Richmond county's amended protest laws and siding with Sheriff Strength in banishing Burk from the front gates of the club to the Pit with the rest of the protesters. The latter ruling has delighted the Imperial Wizard. "I want to see Martha up close," he says. "I want to get a sniff of her." Seated in a chair in the living room, he suddenly spins around to face his computer, which is stashed in the corner of the room. (Evelyn has her own computer setup, in a den adjacent to the kitchen.) The Imperial Wizard calls up a Web site on which a photograph of Burk is prominently displayed. "She ain't a bad-lookin' woman," he says. "No, sir. I bet in her day ol' Martha drove the boys crazy."

The Imperial Wizard surfs the Web furiously, looking for news stories or other postings in which his name might appear. Eventually he turns his back on his keyboard and picks up his lament about the press. "Newspapers say I'm a redneck, but this skin is white," he says. "They say I'm trailer trash, but as you can see I have a nice, brick home. They think that out here we just got indoor plumbing, but I've seen more countries than most Americans ever will. They say I'm prejudiced? The media have prejudged me, too."

He stops to catch his breath.

"You'd have to be a fool not to expect it to get a little nasty, but that doesn't change the fact that these things still hurt."

Evelyn sits in an armchair on the other side of the room and lights up a cigarette. She has the husky voice of a lifelong smoker. The Imperial Wizard calls her Momma. "I'm not his mother, I'm his wife," she says, by way of explanation. "I wouldn't marry him for three years because of the age difference." Momma doesn't offer her age—she looks to be at least thirty years older than Harper, who is thirty-nine—but she does mention that she has eight grandkids and two great-grandkids. They met at a VFW function, when J. J. asked her to dance. "Every now and then he would surprise me with a different step," Momma says. "I liked that. He was a good dancer."

The Imperial Wizard is a most attentive host, saying at one point, "Hope you're hungry, because we fixed somethin' special for ya." Now dinnertime has arrived—beef stew, creamed corn, buttery biscuits, green salad. Everybody serves themselves in the kitchen and then retires to the living room, to eat in front of the TV news, which is aflame with carnage from Iraq. The Imperial Wizard cleans his plate in a matter of minutes, finishing it off by humming "Hmmmm, hmmmm, hmmmm, that's goooood eeeeeaaaaatin'!"

Momma clears the dishes, and the Imperial Wizard swivels in his chair to check his e-mail. "Ain't this a beauty," he mutters. The Imperial Wizard begins to read aloud a missive from an e-mail buddy he identifies as a Klansman in Alabama. *"I thought your rally was in two weeks, not this Saturday,"* the Imperial Wizard says, his voice full of vinegar. *"I have a family gathering planned but I'll try my best to make it and support the cause."* The Imperial Wizard pauses. "What a fearsome organization the Ku Klux Klan is."

Momma has little interest in the hullabaloo her husband has created. "That's his baby, not mine," she says. "I do my thing and he does his." Arts and crafts are her passion. She produces two bags stuffed with her creations—clever figurines made of beads on safety pins, and cute little pins in the shape of butterflies or hearts or American flags. "I like to do the red, white, and blue," Momma says. "They're real good sellers, especially these days, when everybody is so proud to be an American."

None more so than her husband, whose favorite amendment is clearly the second. Earlier in the evening, while milling around his electronics shop, the Imperial Wizard had casually produced from his waistband a Ruger nine millimeter. Waving the sleek pistol to and fro, he said, "It's like American Express—I never leave home without it." In fact, in recent days he has been engaged in a dialogue with Sheriff Strength about bringing firearms to the Masters protest. The Imperial Wizard knows the ins and outs of his license, which prohibits guns at public gatherings, but he wants the sheriff to know that he is planning to keep some firepower in his truck, for the drive to and from Augusta, and to be accessible from the protest site, just in case.

As the evening draws to a close, the Imperial Wizard grows pensive. "I'm going to this protest, and I've put myself in a very dangerous position," he says, eyeing Momma and her American flags. "My family's at stake. There's always a crackpot out there who will do anything to get his name in the paper."

EARLIER THAT DAY, the Imperial Wizard's favorite golfer, Tiger Woods, had journeyed into the Masters pressroom for a highly anticipated audience with his inquisitors. Predictably, the first question was about the controversy that had engulfed the Masters:

"Tiger, when you came out on Tour, there was a national ad campaign: 'Are you ready for me?' And I remember very early on your being asked about it. And you said . . . I'll read it so you'll know where I'm coming from. And you said, 'The message is that there are still clubs practicing denial of membership and play, not just against minorities, but also women and Jews. So it's just saying that a minority finally has a chance to make an impact.' My question is, you were passionate about it then, are you as passionate today?"

Woods answered in his most wooden tone: "I am."

"Thank you."

"Um-hmm."

This time Woods's deadpan generated spasms of laughter among the reporters. His dogged questioner pressed on.

"It did not come across that way, Tiger. It's not been very evident. Why not?"

"Probably that's just your opinion."

The awkward exchange ended when another reporter broke in to ask Woods about the trifling matter of winning three straight Masters. This pattern would recur throughout the press conference: uninspired banter about the membership controversy interrupted by golf queries.

Question: "Do you feel this week you have an obligation to speak out about the social issues around the sport or an obligation not to speak out about the social issues surrounding this whole thing?"

Woods: "You know, I've already answered that. And I've answered that many times prior to this event, and right now I'm just trying to get myself ready to play on Thursday."

Question: "In your own mind, Tiger, do you categorize women not being allowed to join a golf club as prejudice against a minority?"

Woods: "That's a good question. Never looked at it that way."

Follow-up: "Do you have any gut instinct on the matter?"

Woods: "Oh, everyone here knows my opinion. Should they become members or should they be members? Yes. But you know, I'm . . . I don't really have a vote in how they run this club."

Question: "Given your personal opinion on the membership policy here, if you were a full member rather than an honorary member, how much more do you feel you could have done or would have done to inspire change in that policy?"

Woods: "I think that you would have a lot more say-so. But I think even Jack and Arnold, being members, I don't think they have as much say around here as people think."

Jack and Arnie had the chance to speak for themselves when it was their turn in the pressroom. Each entertained exactly one question on the matter. Palmer was up first: "Arnold, I'm sure you've been through this countless times, but for those of us who haven't heard it, can you tell us what your feelings are about the Masters policy on women members?"

"I'm sorry it's happening—I suppose that's the major thing I have to say about it. And I think about all the things that are happening in the world today, and we have got enough controversy outside this golf tournament and [we] shouldn't be and shouldn't have to be concerning ourselves with things such as this. I think that's all I have to say about it."

No one had the temerity to press the King. Nicklaus was treated with similar deference. Question: "Do you have a position or feeling on women membership at Augusta?"

"I've said all I'm going to say on it," said Nicklaus, who like Woods and Palmer before him had precious little to say at all.

*   *   *

WHILE WOODS was fending off his tormentors on Tuesday, across town Martha Burk and Jack Batson spent the day working the phones, putting the finishing touches on an emergency motion asking the Eleventh Circuit Court of Appeals to suspend the joint rulings Judge Bowen had issued a day earlier. Jerry Weber, legal director of the ACLU's Georgia branch, was providing additional firepower, as was Sarah Shalf, who had stayed up most of the night working on the emergency motion.

In ruling in favor of Richmond County, Bowen had addressed two separate but related issues—the "facial" constitutionality of its recently enacted protest ordinance, and the "as-applied" validity of Burk's being prohibited from demonstrating at Augusta National's front gates. Bowen dealt first with the constitutionality question, in an eighteen-page treatise bulging with dozens of citations from previous First Amendment rulings, many handed down by the Supreme Court. One of the cruxes of Burk's legal challenge was that the ordinance was an unconstitutional "content-based prior restraint on speech" because in its wording it targeted "[a]ny expression of support for, or protest of, any person, issue, political, or other cause or action." Bowen found this argument "unpersuasive," writing, "The ordinance does not discriminate against a particular viewpoint or limit speech to certain subject matters. Instead, it prohibits all protests and demonstrations without prior approval."

The other key component of Burk's complaint was that the ordinance was so broad as to be unconstitutional, because by its very imprecision it gave the sheriff an arbitrary power in silencing protesters. Again Bowen disagreed, writing, "Nearly every standard contained in the protest ordinance upon which the Sheriff can base a denial of a permit has been ruled sufficiently specific and objective by the Supreme Court."

In the second ruling, banishing Burk from the front gates, Bowen speculated what would happen if Burk and her interlopers were allowed to protest at the front gates: "The admixture of the throngs of pedestrians, the protesters, and the profound automotive congestion in the streets presents, at minimum, a realistic, plausible, even probable potential for some accidental injury. Vehicle-to-vehicle contact or vehicle-to-pedestrian contact might foreseeably occur just from the distraction offered by protesters at the requested sites."

Bowen then showed a deep compassion for the businessmen in his hometown, writing, "The level of success of many enterprises in the area depends not upon the activities of weeks of exposure to a constant market that a large metropolis would offer, but upon the fortunes developed over a six-day period in a small city during the Masters. . . . The effective blocking of the thoroughfare for the virtual entirety of one of four tournament days would result in an unreasonable and undue arrogation of Plaintiffs' First Amendment rights, exalting them far above the rights of motorists, pedestrians, and property owners who have an expectation of the orderly flow of traffic in and out of Magnolia Drive and of the benefits which might accrue therefrom."

An interesting twist in Bowen's ruling was that he used the approval of Rainbow/PUSH's secondary protest site as justification to deny Burk the front gates. "The intersection of Wheeler Road and Highland Avenue is enormously busy during tournament days," Bowen wrote. "Highland Avenue is the second major artery that feeds the parking lots of the Augusta National. . . . The fact that the Sheriff has allowed protesters to gather at the Wheeler Road/Highland Avenue intersection buttresses and confirms the conclusion that the Sheriff exercised responsible, professional discretion in his review of all the applications for protest." Bowen's citation would not be the last time the specter of Jesse Jackson would haunt Burk during Masters week.

In his conclusion, Bowen wrote, "Having considered the file, the record, and the evidence adduced at the hearing, I am without doubt that the reasons articulated by the Sheriff are grounded in legitimate concerns for the public safety, and not in the impermissible purposes of preventing embarrassment to the Augusta National or to the city of Augusta."

Burk's emergency motion, as well as Richmond County's rebuttal, was filed with the Eleventh Circuit Court of Appeals fewer than twenty-four hours later. Burk's motion seized on Bowen's concern for the "many enterprises" that accrue their "fortune" along Washington Road—that would be the rabble hawking "The Original Hootie Hat," $500 photos of Tiger Woods, and black-market badges for $3,000 and up, as well as Hooters girls distracting motorists with skimpy deals on chicken wings, and the endless number of enterprising residents with handmade signs who charge $30 a car to park on beautifully manicured front lawns on every side street. As Burk's brief put it, ". . . the business interest in not being inconvenienced does not trump Appellants' First Amendment rights. *Every* protest or demonstration causes some degree of inconvenience, yet our courts have consistently upheld the right to effectively express one's views on a matter of public concern on the public streets."

In conclusion, and by way of offering a solution, Burk's brief pointed to the 2002 Supreme Court decision on public demonstrations that the city of Augusta had used as a model to overhaul its own protest ordinance: "Understanding the need for a practical solution to these protest requests in a short period of time, the Appellants propose that this Court look to *Thomas v. Chicago Park District*. The ordinance at issue there has a first-come, first-served provision. The Appellants propose such a provision be applied here."

Whereas Burk's motion was written in a detached, lawyerly voice, Richmond County's rebuttal had an aroused, even passionate tone, garnished with hyperbolic language. City attorney Jim Wall urged the Eleventh Circuit to uphold Bowen's "meticulous and fact-laden" rulings because "the extraordinary remedy sought by the Appellants is wholly inappropriate" and would lead to "chaos and bedlam."

Wall disputed Burk's contention that she had first dibs on the front gates because her protest application was the first to be received. While the city's time line shows that Burk's application was received first, the application from Rainbow/PUSH, with whom Burk was now inextricably linked, did not trickle in until March 12; in the intervening six days, three other applications came in, making Burk–Rainbow/PUSH effectively fourth in line, according to the city's accounting. Further, "Most applications were pending at the same time," Wall wrote. "The Sheriff was merely trying to treat all applicants equally and fairly. . . . The Sheriff would have been subject to criticism, and rightly so, if he had given Appellants or any other group preferential treatment."

Wall saved his most chiding tone for Burk's claim that a protest in the Pit is not a protest at all: "Appellants claim irreparable injury based solely on the disingenuous argument that the audience at the alternate location 'will be in cars, and the occupants can roll up their windows and ignore the protest.' Appellants do not provide any case law, and there is none, that requires that the Sheriff provide them with a captive audience. Furthermore, a protest that is 'less effective' in Appellants' minds is not the legal equivalent of 'irreparable injury.' "

With the dueling briefs having been filed, the next battleground would be the Eleventh Circuit Court of Appeals, which had been asked to resolve the issue by Friday, a scant three days away. Burk was, typically, steeled for battle. "Of course Bowen's ruling bothered her," said Batson, "but she's basically nonplussed by things going against her. Otherwise she wouldn't be doing what she's doing. She's got a spirit that can't be denied, and she felt very passionately that she had the First Amendment on her side, so she was ready to fight on."

Freedom of speech was also an issue inside the gates at Augusta National. Monday's *Atlanta Journal-Constitution* reported that the club had announced that "in keeping with tradition and long-standing policy, Masters patrons are requested to avoid wearing any apparel, including hats, buttons/pins or similar items expressing an opinion, pro or con, on any social or political issue. These are inappropriate at the Masters and could detract from the Tournament."

It was just as well, because on the eve of the tournament Hootie Johnson was ready to further express his opinions on the social and political issue that he had helped create.

WEDNESDAY'S *Augusta Chronicle*, under the headline "Big Question Lies Ahead for Johnson," set the stage for the chairman's annual pretournament press conference, which would be held at eleven o'clock that morning. "It has been billed as one of the most anticipated question-and-answer sessions in recent Masters Tournament memory," the paper said, underselling the point. Johnson's "state of the union" was shaping up as the media event of the new millennium.

In previous years the chairman had always played to a half-empty house, as droopy-lidded reporters bantered with him about the length of the second cut and other mundane matters. This year promised to be different; it was Johnson's first public appearance since he had bared his bayonet.

With more than nine months of fevered buildup, the pressroom on Wednesday morning of Masters week had the charged atmosphere of a boxing arena in the moments before a heavyweight prizefight. Johnson entered the ring a few minutes ahead of the slated eleven o'clock starting time, looking dapper in a crisp white shirt and striped tie that matched his green jacket. He took his place on the stage at the front of the interview room, flanked by his usual cornermen: Billy Payne, the chairman of the media committee, and Will Nicholson, chairman of the competition committee. Five dozen other members crowded into a room with an advertised capacity of 161, standing shoulder to shoulder along the back wall and filling out rows of chairs. Clad in identical green jackets, these stone-faced men presented a conspicuous show of solidarity, and one without precedent, as the chairman's press conference never attracts more than a handful of stray members. In fact, so many green jackets were taking up space in the interview room that an agitated crowd of reporters spilled out of its double doors into an adjoining breezeway. Late arrivals tried to push their way in like harried commuters squeezing onto a packed subway car, but eventually they were turned away by Pinkertons, forcing a sizable number of reporters to watch Johnson on closed-circuit TV in the main work area, which only blurred the line between news and theater.

Payne opened the proceedings with a short introduction of the chairman. Johnson's posture straightened as he produced a sheet of notes, and then his beautiful voice washed over the assembled audience.

"Before I take your questions, I would like to read a statement: Over the last ten months everything that could possibly be said on the subject of Augusta National and its membership, everything that could be said, has been said. The fact is we are a private club—a group getting together periodically for camaraderie, just as thousands of clubs and organizations do all over America. Just because we host a golf tournament, because some of our members are well known, should not cause us to be viewed differently. I have also stated that there may well come a time when we include women as members of our club, and that remains true. However, I want to emphasize that we have no timetable and our membership is very comfortable with our present status.

"Now, going forward, our club will continue to make its own decisions. And we will continue to make what hopefully is a major contribution to the game of golf and to charity.

"Now I look forward to your questions about the Masters tournament, and golf in general. However, as I said earlier, I will have nothing further to add about our membership or related issues.

"Now, Billy, I'm ready for the first question."

"Yes, sir," Payne boomed into the microphone. "Ladies and gentlemen, questions, please."

There is a pregnant pause that often precedes the first question in a press conference, as reporters each wait for another to speak up. During that split second of silence, many a golfer has been moved to say, "That was easy," and feign getting out of his chair, which always draws a cheap laugh. Predictably, Payne's entreaty was followed by an awkward moment of complete stillness, but then one hand shot up in the dead center of the room.

Christine Brennan.

Interviewed ten days earlier, Brennan had been asked if she feared she might be prevented from asking a question, or simply never be called upon. "I haven't thought about it all," she said. "I kind of fly by the seat of my pants. But I'm definitely not reluctant to [try to] ask a question for fear of being snubbed."

Another second or two ticked by, and Brennan's arm strained ever higher, accompanied by the slightest twirl of the hand, like the smartest girl in the class impatiently waiting for the teacher to call on her yet again. Poor Billy Payne—who had known Brennan for years through their Olympic work—was desperately scanning the room, trying to will another hand into the air. "Oh, we were always gonna call on her," he would say later with a chuckle. "But on the very first question you'd like to have a few more options." Finally Hootie muttered something under his breath. It wasn't projected loud enough to be picked up by the microphone or stenographer, but a rabbit-eared reporter sitting in the front row, John Riegger of *The Orange County Register*, heard Johnson say, "Let her go." Payne dutifully followed orders, immediately pointing at Brennan. Her voice filled the room.

"Mr. Johnson, with all due respect to your comment, I'm curious if you're comfortable with this environment for your tournament, i.e., all of the attention, all of the questions, all of the controversy that's surrounding it. Does it make you comfortable that your tournament is being treated in the way that you would hope it be would be treated? Thank you."

"I think we'll present a great tournament, Christine," Hootie began. Brennan was intently nodding her head, but she couldn't contain the slightest smile. For Johnson, something as subtle as using his adversary's first name had a disarming effect, and not only on Brennan. "And I don't think that this issue is going to be a major issue. It's not a major issue. We have been talking about it for ten months and I've made my statement."

Next question: "Is there any consideration to lift, clean, and place for the tournament?" Laughter swept through the room. In this overheated atmosphere, a straight golf question seemed absurd. Hootie deferred to Nicholson, who indicated that the field would be playing the ball as it lies. Ed Sherman, of the *Chicago Tribune*, followed with the next query, igniting one of the key exchanges of the press conference.

"Mr. Johnson, many of us have not had a chance to question you about this [membership] issue. If you're comfortable and you feel you're in the right on this issue, why won't you take any questions from us?"

"Because we have talked about this for ten months, as I said."

"You've only given—" Here Johnson cut him off.

"What question do you have?" he asked, with a touch of exasperation.

"We have lots of questions."

"Is the question why I won't answer a question? I mean, go ahead. What is your question?"

"I mean we have lots—" Cut off again, and this time the chairman had steel in his voice:

"Well, what is your question?"

"Just people in this room have lots of questions," Sherman continued, and now there was an audible rustling in the room, and awkward glances were being exchanged among other reporters, "and you're coming in here saying that you're not going to take any questions on this issue. We have talked about this for ten months. You have not talked about this for ten months." Still no question.

"I've made my statement," the chairman said. "We are here to have the Masters Tournament. I just told you if you have a question, I'll answer it, but don't lecture to me."

Pow! For nine months Johnson had been endlessly pilloried by the press, portrayed as a hapless, doddering rube, among other things. He had absorbed this abuse while uttering only sparing words in his own defense. Johnson may have acted like a southern gentleman to the lady who asked the press conference's first question, but all of a sudden here was the smashmouth football player, the scrapper who more than once had been kicked off the field for fighting. Three questions into the most freighted press conference in Masters history, he landed a knockout punch.

Of course, in dispatching Sherman, Johnson had indicated a willingness to address the membership controversy, contrary to his opening statement. Fifteen of the next sixteen questions would focus not on the golf tournament at hand but rather the meta-story, beginning with, "Mr. Johnson, does the Augusta National intend to take any responsibility for the loss of revenue from local businesses as a direct result of this controversy? Martha Burk has said, Don't blame me, blame Augusta National."

"I think the city of Augusta has done very well with the Masters Tournament for a long, long time. And I think they support us in the convictions that we have, about being a private club. The city of Augusta, the people of Augusta, are totally behind us."

This broad assertion went unchallenged, as Doug Ferguson of the AP spoke up with a question. "Do you think you'll have television sponsors next year?"

"We haven't really pursued that, but I think there's a good chance that we will."

With a little extra relish Payne pointed to the back right portion of the room, barking, "Furman!" *The Atlanta Journal-Constitution*'s Bisher, Augusta National's loyal defender, now had the stage: "Did your career as a blocking back prepare you for a controversy such as this?"

It was not a question so much as a cue, and Johnson hit his mark. "I don't think I have experienced anything quite like this assault," the chairman said, and Bisher, at the back of the room, let out a belly laugh.

The humanization of Hootie continued. Next question: "I've noticed at least four businesses up and down Washington Road that are selling pro-Hootie merchandise and at least two businesses that have had some sort of sign either pro Hootie or saying, Martha go home. Have you seen those? And if so, what do they do for you?"

"Well, we all like to be supported," was Johnson's answer.

After the chairman deflected a pair of unfocused questions, Brian Murphy of the *San Francisco Chronicle* spoke up. "You often cite Clifford Roberts as your inspiration for running the tournament. Have you drawn on any conversations you had with him when he was alive or readings that you've done from his writings on how to handle the situation that has come upon you in the last ten months? And as a follow-up, are you concerned at all that the tournament that he wanted to be the best in the country has been at all impugned or maligned by what's happened?"

"Well, it's been maligned, but I don't think it's been damaged," Johnson said, showing an impressive precision with the language. ("Maligned Not Damaged" would be the headline in the following day's *Los Angeles Times*.) "And I think that the Masters will continue to be one of the great sporting events of the world, next year and the year after and the year after and the year after."

Murphy reminded Johnson of the first part of his question: "Any conversations that you had with Mr. Roberts?"

"No, I haven't had any conversations with him lately."

It was a good line, considering Roberts had been dead for twenty-six years. But the thunderous laughter it provoked was not quite commensurate with the quality of the joke. Much of the chuckling seemed to be a release, fueled by the giddy discovery that ol' Hootie actually had a sense of humor. The mood in the room was perceptibly shifting, from adversarial to almost affectionate.

Next question: "Given the furor that's ensued, if you had a chance to do this thing all over again and respond to Martha Burk's letter, would you do it the same way?"

"You know, I'm not going to rehash this thing for ten months. I mean, if I had something to do over again or somebody else did something else. We are here and we're presenting the Masters Tournament. I've made my statement. You understand that, I believe."

Glenn Sheeley, whose work in *The Atlanta Journal-Constitution* had been described as "nerve-rankling" by Jim McCarthy in his letter to the editor, had been waving his hand for a stretch, and now Payne finally called on him, at what turned out to be an inopportune time. "I was going to ask that," Sheeley muttered. He plowed ahead, simply rephrasing the previous question. "I know Martha Burk has said that there are some wordings she might have done a little differently. What I was wondering is if you would have worded anything differently?"

"I'm not going to address anything that I said or did, or she said or did, or anything about this issue. I'm not going to do it."

After a pair of uneventful questions, Thomas Boswell, the earnest columnist for *The Washington Post*, raised a hand. "I don't know if this will give it more of a historical perspective, but nobody has a better perspective of the sweep of the Masters, the history of the Masters [than you do]. When you look out twenty years from now, do you think Augusta will have women members then, and do you have any views in the long term whether it should or not?"

Johnson was unimpressed by the fancy invocation of the historical perspective, and he wasted no time in blowing off Boswell, just as he had Sheeley. "Well, I really can't speculate on what might happen twenty years out," Johnson said. "I'm sorry." Boswell frowned and scribbled a couple of notes. For those scoring at home, it was now Hootie 2, *Washington Post/Atlanta Journal-Constitution* 0. Asked later if Johnson had purposely snubbed two of his prime tormenters, McCarthy was unable to swallow a chuckle. "Let's just say Hootie is much more sophisticated in dealing with the media than anybody knows."

Next question for the chairman: "Could you elaborate on the decision to rescind the age-limit policy?"

"Yes, I could. I've been looking for that question, as opposed to the woman issue." That awkward last phrase, and Johnson's stilted delivery, earned another laugh from the reporters. ("The woman issue" also echoed Bill Clinton's famous dismissal of Monica Lewinsky as "that woman.") Johnson smiled, soaking up the reporters' mirth. "I guess you might say that I overfixed our problem," he continued, adding another new word to the lexicon. "And we did have a problem, the tournament had a problem. And I overfixed it. First Arnold wrote me a letter and expressed his displeasure and discomfort, and a few days later I got a letter from Jack expressing similar sentiments. And I asked the two of them to come to Augusta and visit with me. And they did. And I told them that I thought I had a solution." This was an impressive anecdote on a couple of levels. Johnson, so rigid and resolute on his so-called woman issue, was admitting a mistake, which is like the Catholic Church issuing a press release announcing that the Pope is in fact fallible. Also, to casually convene an audience with Palmer and Nicklaus is a sign of ultimate power in golf. Johnson continued:

"I told them that it was my belief that Mr. Roberts and Bobby Jones, that their belief about the lifetime exemption was for a champion who believed that he would be competitive and would play thirty-six holes to try to make the cut. And that I believed that was the spirit and intent of the lifetime exemption. And they were in agreement with that. And I think that was essentially what was in the press release that went out to you folks. And I also talked to Raymond Floyd, and I also talked to Tom Watson and I also talked to Byron Nelson on this same issue"—Johnson was now clearly enjoying name-dropping golf's immortals—"and they all seemed to be in agreement with that philosophy. And with that, we rescinded the new qualifications that were to go into effect in 2004. I hope that answers your question."

Mark Cannizzaro of the *New York Post* was up next. "Speaking of Jack and Arnold, have either of those gentlemen expressed any opinion regarding the woman issue at Augusta? And does the opinion of any of your past champions and honorary members regard—" Johnson cut him off:

"That's two questions. Let me answer the first one. The first one is that I don't discuss membership matters. And they are members." The press conference may have been the unveiling of a kinder, gentler Hootie, but this piquant response was a reminder that he was still the chairman of Augusta National, and as such could act like a crank in defending the members' privacy. "Now, the second part of the question?"

"Past champions. Their public opinion on whether . . . for example, Tiger's on record as saying that he believes that there should be women members here."

"Well . . ." Johnson sputtered, and Cannizzaro pressed the point.

"Does that have any influence on you at all?

"I won't tell Tiger how to play golf if he doesn't tell us how to run our private club."

Pow! Another haymaker, and this one brought smiles to the faces of a number of the green jackets in the room. Along the far right wall of the interview room was a green-jacketed Fred Ridley, the presumed president-in-waiting of the USGA. Johnson's press conference was a primer for Ridley on how to handle hostile reporters, and hearing the chairman punk Tiger, Ridley growled, "Good answer, Hootie!" just loud enough to be heard by a reporter standing behind him.

The ebb and flow of the Q&A continued. A dozen questions later Johnson was asked, "Do you plan to remain indefinitely as chairman of Augusta National?"

The question drew a few chuckles, but Johnson's answer brought down the house: "You're not going to get rid of me any time soon." It was the biggest laugh of a surprisingly loosey-goosey session, but it contained a powerful message of defiance.

Next question: "Your record in the past in South Carolina as supporting a lot of progressive causes, are you concerned that to the general public, when they hear your name, it's associated with this particular issue, considering all the support you've given to other issues in your political life and your business life?"

"Well, historically I do have a reputation for fighting against discrimination. And I have a good record and I'm proud of it. But our private club does not discriminate. Single gender is an important fabric on the American scene. There are thousands and thousands [of such organizations] all across America. Both genders. Health clubs, sewing circles"—titters swept through the room at that cliché of 1950s Americana—"Junior League, Shriners, and we should not and we are not discriminating. And we resent it very much when that accusation is made against us."

Three questions later Karen Crouse of *The Palm Beach Post* was given the floor. "I was wondering what your daughters have said to you about this issue?"

This brought a smile from the chairman. "What my daughters say? Well, I think I relayed this story to John Steinbreder a couple of weeks ago." This was a reference to the *GolfWeek* senior writer, more name-dropping. Nothing flatters the press like the public recognition of their brethren. "I have four daughters," Johnson continued, "and the other day my wife had a birthday. And we have this place on the lake, and my wife and the four daughters wanted to go to the lake to celebrate her birthday. And they let me know that they really didn't want me to come along with them."

More laughter. Johnson was about to drive home his point about the natural inclination of the sexes to seek companionship with one another, but instead of coming off as a misogynist, he had skillfully offered a charming anecdote to which the (overwhelmingly male) press corps could relate.

"And they didn't want their husbands to come along. We congregate there all the time, but they were going to do their thing. It's just a natural thing. And I don't know how to articulate that or how to explain it. But it's just been going on for centuries and centuries that men like to get together with men every now and then and women like to get together with women every now and then. And that's just a simple fact of life in America."

By now Johnson had been on stage for close to half an hour, and the press conference was beginning to wind down. Payne made an announcement that the chairman would take only a couple more questions. Near the back of the room Len Shapiro began waving his arm. Payne made *The Washington Post*'s golf writer wait two more questions before acknowledging him.

Shapiro: "There's been a resolution introduced in Congress asking that any members of federal government, from the Congress to the federal bureaucracies and the ambassador ranks, not be allowed to join the ranks of private clubs that do not allow both genders." (As Shapiro spoke, the USGA's Ridley muttered, "If that's not an abuse of Congress I don't know what is.") Shapiro plugged away. "I wonder if you have any comment on that and do you think that has a chance of passing?" That last bit—"chance of passing"—was a tactical mistake, as it allowed Johnson to focus not on the merits of the resolution but its viability.

"Well, that's what I was going to ask you," he said. "Has it passed?"

"It was just introduced last week," Shapiro said.

"Well, you know anybody can introduce something. We'll have to wait and see what happens to the resolution before I would have a comment on that."

Payne broke in. "Ladies and gentlemen, thank you." It was a weak ending to what had been an encounter of high drama. Luckily, Dave Anderson rode to the rescue. *The New York Times*'s Pulitzer winner was, as always, in the right place at the right time. "Normally I just sit wherever," Anderson would later say, "but for this press conference I didn't want to miss a thing, so I sat in the front row, right in the center." He waved for Johnson's attention, and the chairman acknowledged the esteemed columnist. Anderson approached his topic with typical delicacy:

"The issue of your tenure here, shall we say?"

Johnson was delighted. "Oh, that's . . . that's good."

Anderson clarified his question. "Is it your decision to step down, or is there a board that could ask you to step down or do you stay as chairman as long as you wish?"

"Well, that's a membership matter. And . . ." Johnson was interrupted by more laughter. Discretion is one thing, but this was ridiculous—he had made a point of entertaining Anderson's question, and now he was dismissing it. Johnson gathered himself. "I do want to make one point, though. If I drop dead right now, our position will not change on this issue," he said, punctuating the point with manly downward jabs of his index finger. "It's not my issue alone. And I promise you what I'm saying is, if I drop dead this second, our position will not change."

Payne, with a renewed sense of theater, immediately dropped the curtain, all but shouting, "Thank you, ladies and gentlemen." He thus preserved one of the all-time walk-off quotes, ensuring that Hootie's final, defiant words would be ringing in the reporters' ears as they charged back to their laptops.

Back in Washington, D.C., Martha Burk did not watch the live telecast of Johnson's press conference on the Golf Channel, but moments after its conclusion her phone began to melt. For weeks Burk had been nurturing a new strategy to shift the focus from Johnson and Augusta National to the larger issues of what she calls "corporate hypocrisy." Burk was delighted to get reports that Johnson had explicitly stated that the entire membership was united behind him. "Hootie has changed the rules," Burk said. "He has publicly said that the membership supports him, so there's no way that any of those guys can continue to say they're trying to change from within. We wanted to be reasonable and give them the opportunity to affect change, but clearly that time has passed. I expected more of those guys to be courageous. You know what CEO oughta stand for? Chicken Executive Officer."

That zinger was just a warm-up, and Burk ratcheted up the rhetoric as reporter after reporter tracked her down in her office. "He certainly has fallen on his sword for the cause," Burk told *USA Today*. "I'm disappointed that he is so firmly entrenched in an old and antiquated policy that discriminates against women and damages the image of golf."

Hammering the theme that Johnson had made explicit that he had all of the members' support, Burk told the *Augusta Chronicle*, "[The other members] should come forward and . . . hold their own news conference affirming their support for sex discrimination."

To *The Washington Post*, Burk said, "I find it astounding that a man with Mr. Johnson's record and stature has unfortunately stated that he's willing to die for the cause of continuing to discriminate against women."

Burk's tone was unwavering, even late in the day when she fielded a second round of calls after the Eleventh Circuit Court of Appeals, in Atlanta, declined to review Judge Bowen's joint orders in a one-sentence pronouncement. The long, bitter legal battle was over, and Burk was now resigned to staging her protest in the Pit. "This was our last shot," she said of the Eleventh Circuit. "I'm disappointed that the wall of discrimination is so high down there that local authorities, and even the judges, are willing to conspire with the club, the mayor, and the city commission to deny us our free-speech rights."

THE HEAVENS OPENED AGAIN on Thursday morning, washing out the first round of the Masters, the first time a full round had been lost to weather since 1983, and the first opening round to be postponed since 1939. In the absence of any tournament action, all of the buzz centered on Hootie and Martha. Masters week was now half over, and to this point it had been a disaster for Burk. Two federal courts had denied her a dream of holding a protest outside Augusta National's front gate. She was now relegated to what promised to be a chaotic grassy field full of competing demonstrators and clashing messages. The three Masters competitors who mattered the most on the membership issue—Woods, Palmer, and Nicklaus—had been dismissive of its importance, and a weary press corps had been unable to engage them. Burk suffered another setback Thursday morning, when, in a conference call with reporters, Jesse Jackson made official what had long been suspected, announcing that he would be AWOL at Saturday's protest, because he wanted "women of color [to be] projected in the leadership role." Jackson indicated that Janice Mathis, an Atlanta lawyer and vice president of Rainbow/PUSH, would be his public face.

Burk was secretly relieved not to have to share the stage with Jackson, but his defection was a high-profile indication of her waning momentum. Jackson is a political animal, with an almost unrivaled knack for attracting attention. A vitriolic letter to the editor that the *Augusta Chronicle* printed during Masters week decried him for chasing "every hurricane, labor dispute, burning building, environmental disaster or news event to seek cheap photo opportunities." For Jackson to bail on the protest was the strongest sign yet that those close to Burk had the feeling that the event might fizzle. Yet in his conference call, Jackson paradoxically continued to raise expectations that something dramatic might happen. While Burk had spent the preceding weeks carefully downplaying expectations for the protest, Jackson shot from the hip in talking with reporters, and some of what he said was patently false. "Plan B is arrest if Plan A is violated," Jackson said, though Burk had previously indicated in public and private that this course of action was never seriously considered. "If it's so isolated that women can't be heard, and I have talked with Martha about this, women are ready to face arrest." Jackson's comments created a stir as far away as Europe, where Agence France's wire story carried the headline "Arrests Possible in Masters Protest Showdown." But closer to home, Jackson was treated appropriately by the press, as a peripheral character. For all the nuance of the issues and the layers to the debate, Masters week was being boiled down to its essence: Hootie versus Martha. With the first round washed out, all anybody could talk about on Thursday morning was Johnson's bravura press conference. The sound bite that had lit up TV screens the night before was his memorable "if I drop dead" declaration, and now Thursday's papers arrived with their verdicts. The consensus was that Hootie had hit a home run, and the story was writ large in the headlines. "Hootie Doesn't Declare Win, But Close," from the *Gainesville Sun*.

"Hootie Won't Bend—Even to Bitter End," from *The Arizona Republic*.

"Hootie Handles the Heat," from *The New York Times*.

"Johnson to Burk: Forget It," from the *Augusta Chronicle*.

Depending on which fish wrap you were reading, Johnson was "defiant . . . and witty" (*Forth Worth Star-Telegram*), "resounding, often defiant, occasionally humorous" (*The Atlanta Journal-Constitution*), "a sharp cookie" (*San Francisco Chronicle*), "[t]ough, firm and serious but with a twinkle or a smile now and then" (*The New York Times*), "stubborn, Southern, no-nonsense, stubborn, courtly, unwavering, stubborn—and right" (*Philadelphia Daily News*).

In the pages of *The Atlanta Journal-Constitution*, Furman Bisher, Johnson's important ally, compared the chairman to Noah and the press to locusts, adding, "The general conclusion was that Hootie had prevailed. He had met the enemy, and the enemy was us, and us had left dragging our tails behind us."

Johnson had also impressed two high-profile tastemakers. The *Augusta Chronicle* may have a circulation of only about seventy-three thousand, but during Masters week it is what everyone in the golf world reads. The paper's lead golf columnist, Scott Michaux, had struggled from the very beginning to stake out a position on the hometown controversy. Nine months earlier, Michaux's first, reflexive reaction was to support the club, like a good company man. After journeying to Washington, D.C., and spending time with Burk, however, he became sympathetic to her views, and it was his spirited interview with Burk that the paper's owner, an Augusta National member, banished from the front page to a lonely corner of the Sports section. But in the weeks leading up to the Masters, Michaux had been turned off by Burk's increasingly desperate rhetoric, and he had begun to wander back into the club's embrace. Johnson's press conference crystallized Michaux's support for Augusta National, and he produced a passionate, polemic column.

"Talk about dropping a curtain on a controversy," he wrote. "Burk will rant at the Martin Luther King Memorial in Atlanta today and chant dissent across Washington Road on Saturday. It will all fall on deaf ears here. . . . The message is very clear: Augusta National will not back down. Like a government that steadfastly refuses to negotiate with terrorists, the club will not yield to the will of activists. . . . While certain folks will surely not let this issue fade away, it's settled with me. Hootie wins in a dead heat . . . The sooner Burk and her cronies withdraw from the debate, the sooner the club might consider change."

Tim Dahlberg of the AP came on just as strong, writing a column that appeared in countless newspapers across the country. Dahlberg's kicker: "No, Johnson didn't come out and declare victory for the club. He doesn't need to. Barring the unexpected on Saturday, though, it might be time for Burk to finally admit defeat."

Of course, Johnson had his detractors. Many reporters picked up on his reference to sewing circles as a sign of his outdated thinking. "Hootie, while you're driving that Edsel, can you drop us at the quilting bee?" Selena Roberts wrote in *The New York Times*.

Even Johnson's critics were conceding that the cause was all but dead. In a caustic column in *USA Today*, Brennan wrote, "Ten years before there's a woman in a green jacket? Make it 20. How about forever? (Now that I think about it, forever might be a little optimistic.)" She joked that the press would now have to work "to obtain the name of the still unborn baby girl who will someday grow up to become the first female member of Augusta National."

In her harsh critique of Johnson, Brennan was a lonely voice, just as she had been four years earlier when she began writing about Augusta National's lack of women members. As contentious as the issue had become since, it seemed as if the press had now collectively made up its mind, falling in line with the numerous opinion polls that showed the majority of the American public supported Augusta National's stance. It would take all of Burk's considerable tenacity to wage an effective counteroffensive.

*   *   *

BURK BEGAN HER MARCH on Augusta by walking in the footprints of Martin Luther King. Her Thursday afternoon press conference was held at Atlanta's Martin Luther King Jr. National Historic Site, across the street from the King Center. Burk's podium was set up in a courtyard near the World Peace Rose Garden and the Historic Ebenezer Baptist Church, facing King's crypt, in the shadow of a statue of Mahatma Gandhi. Behind Burk, in the visitor center, an endless loop of King's stirring speech "The Drum Major Instinct" played. (*"Yes, if you want to say that I was a drum major, say that I was a drum major for justice. Say that I was a drum major for peace. That I was a drum major for righteousness. And all of the other shallow things will not matter."*) All of this was very powerful symbolically, but holding the press conference 130 miles from Augusta had its practical limitations.

Virtually none of the golf press was willing to leave their posts at the Masters to cover Burk's big moment. While hundreds of reporters had been on hand for Johnson's star turn, only three dozen turned out for Burk's. Attendance at the outdoor event was not helped by the weather—the same storm that washed out the first round of the Masters hit Atlanta, and it was a raw, drizzly, windy day, with temperatures in the forties.

Burk began Thursday morning with a four-thirty wake-up call at home in Washington, D.C. A radio station was calling, hoping to set up an interview. "Are you crazy?" Burk asked the caller. The ensuing journey to Atlanta was a bumpy one, and Burk arrived at the King site just a few minutes before the one-thirty press conference was set to begin. Her husband, Ralph Estes, admits that his and his wife's instinct is to "dress Texan," but Burk was clearly ready for her close-up. She had dressed for the cameras and was turned out in alligator skin loafers, a beautiful navy suit, a lime-green blouse, and off-red lipstick. Since her short letter to the chairman of Augusta National had gone public, she had conducted innumerable interviews and made countless public appearances, but this was her most important moment. For Burk's small entourage, it was their first exposure to the magnitude of the story they were at the center of. Burk's young assistant, Rebecca Menso, said with wonderment, on more than one occasion, "It's amazing—everyone knows my name!"

Nine African American supporters were arranged behind the podium, many of them members of Rainbow/PUSH. Standing just over Burk's shoulder, in prime view for the cameras, was Martin Luther King III. On the periphery were young (white) women holding protest signs at chest level: WOMEN PAY WHILE CEOS PLAY, DISCRIMINATION IS NOT A GAME, DIGNITY RESPECT FAIRNESS. Burk leaned into the bouquet of a dozen microphones and began her speech in the measured tone of a parent trying to explain to her child a very complicated family matter.

> Almost a year ago the National Council of Women's Organizations wrote a simple, private letter to Augusta National Golf Club urging them to open their doors to women. At that time we believed the club was on track to change its sex discriminatory policies and that our private request would hasten their process. We never believed the wall of sex discrimination at Augusta National would be so high. Or that the host of the premiere golf tournament in the United States would be so unwilling to make a change. Or that we would be accused by club spokesmen of being the forces of political correctness because we dare to advocate for values that Americans believe in: the absence of discrimination and simple fairness . . .
>
> In the past year we have been asked many times about the rights of individuals to come together and form clubs with folks they choose to associate with. And we have answered that that right to free association is a deeply held American value, and a value that the National Council of Women's Organizations believes in and defends. But when private association is not truly private, when it is indeed invoked as a cover for practicing discrimination, then it is immoral and it's contrary to another deeply held American value: that discrimination is wrong. . . .
>
> The National Council of Women's Organizations will no longer debate whether Augusta National is a small, private club of friends getting together to socialize and enjoy each other's company. It is not such a place. Augusta National Incorporated is a Georgia corporation classified and registered as a for-profit corporation. Augusta National Incorporated owns the brand names Augusta National Golf Club and Masters Golf Tournament and is registered to do business under these brand names. The emphasis needs to be on that word *business*. Augusta National Incorporated's main activity is a very large, for-profit golf tournament. . . .
>
> [Its] member stakeholders are the chief executive operating officers

and chairs of the board of other for-profit corporations. Household names like IBM, Microsoft, U.S. Steel, General Electric, Motorola, United Technologies, and Bechtel. This particular group holds up to a billion dollars in government and military contracts, meaning tax dollars fill their coffers, and some of those dollars wind their way into Augusta National, through dues reimbursement, travel expenses, and entertainment expenses. Yet these corporate leaders maintain memberships in an organization that shuts out half the taxpayers who are footing the bill. Other CEO members of Augusta National Incorporated head consumer companies like AT&T, Coors, Hormel Foods, ExxonMobil, Ford Motor Company, SBC, Basset Furniture, and Berkshire-Hathaway, parent company of Benjamin Moore Paints, Geico and Dairy Queen. Let's not leave out the financial sectors. CEOs and senior officers of Prudential, J. P. Morgan Chase, Bank of America, American Express, Citigroup, and Franklin Investments.

These companies all claim to value women's labor and to be in favor of diversity and against discrimination. They certainly seek women consumers' dollars and stockholders' investments. But these leaders support and belong to a club that shuts out these same women whose purchases allow them to get to Augusta National in private jets and entertain clients with $100 a plate dinners, open bars and exotic entertainment. . . .

As Americans tune into the Masters this week, we hope you will remember the colleagues and coworkers who have been laid off or had rightful pensions denied by corporate titans who will be partying behind the scenes. The free flow of liquor and money, limousines and lavish parties, and all-night entertainment during the Masters will be out of view of the TV cameras, but we hope these excesses will not be out of the consciousness of those who are paying the price so corporate CEOs can live the high life.

Beginning today our campaign moves to a new phase. We are not going to rebut Augusta National's paid media consultant or its chairman about the sex discrimination they're engaging in. We're going to concentrate on the stakeholders, the corporate CEOs who have the power as members. Chairman Hootie Johnson said these CEOs are solidly behind the sex-discriminatory policy. If they believe Augusta National has the right to continue excluding women, I challenge them to hold a news conference and tell us so publicly. Come out and tell us. [Here Burk received her first cheer from the small crowd of supporters stationed behind her, who up to that point had been inanimate. Suddenly she, too, came to life, punching her words with gusto.] You believe this is right, Mr. CEO, then come out and tell us. Does Bank of America stand behind this? Does Citigroup? American Express? Hormel Foods? Coors beer? Just come out and tell us. Hold a news conference. We've got one here and I'm sure all these folks would be happy to attend. If these corporate leaders don't agree with this policy then they need to resign their memberships. [More cheering: "AY-men . . . Hear, hear."] The chairman of Augusta National Incorporated has made it clear that working from within to change the membership policy is going to do no good. The choice is to stand up and support Hootie and support sex discrimination or stand down and resign the membership. I don't see any other alternative. . . .

I hope we will see all of you in Augusta on Saturday. We've had a couple of setbacks down there. The members of the city commission, the mayor of Augusta, and the county sheriff have all gotten together to severely limit our First Amendment rights. They're going to let us be there down the road, down in the Pit, where no one can see or hear us—except you. Last time I looked we still had freedom of the press in the United States of America, even if our free-speech rights are constrained. So please come to the Pit on Saturday in Augusta. Join us. We're going to be making a very powerful statement about the CEOs who party as we speak and support the discrimination at Augusta National Incorporated. Thank you.

BURK HAD DISPLAYED none of the wit or charisma that Johnson had in his press conference, but hers was an impressive argument, as tightly written and well-thought-out as a thesis. Unfortunately, the press conference did not end with those remarks. After the applause had died down, the first thing out of Burk's mouth was, "I was hoping when I stepped up to the podium that we would be joined by Eleanor Smeal, who, as you all know, is the president of the Feminist Majority, and C. Dolores Tucker. I got a call on the way over saying that Eleanor's plane is delayed because of weather. I imagine that Dr. Tucker, who is the president of the National Congress of Black Women, is also delayed, so we will hope that they will join us before the news conference is over."

Another day, another snafu.

Burk then introduced Kim Gandy, the president of the National Organization for Women, who offered a few brief remarks and then introduced Martin Luther King III. He displayed none of his father's oratory skills, and among his jittery mannerisms during his speech was an almost reflexive need to look at the text of his remarks on an 8 1/2-by-11-inch sheet of paper. The only time King seemed comfortable in front of the cameras was when he borrowed his father's words: "I say to the men who are members of Augusta National and the golfers who are participating in the Masters, I say to them what my father said to Bull Conner and supporters of Jim Crow in the sixties. That is, the ultimate measure of a man is not where he stands in times of comfort and convenience but where he stands in times of challenge and of controversy. And at this challenging and controversial time, I ask them, how will you be measured? It is in the spirit of Martin Luther King Jr. that I join with the National Council of Women's Organizations and all progressive-thinking people in America who challenge the status quo. We will protest until women of all races have access to America's promise. Until this club permits wives, daughters, and mothers in relation to admittance, all men and corporations of goodwill should stand firm and not support this archaic tradition."

Jesse Jackson's designated representative then took the mike. Janice Mathis is a tiny woman who was barely visible behind the thicket of microphones, but she had the biggest presence of any of the speakers. In a folksy, engaging manner, she said, "You know, I'm forty-eight years old and I've been a black woman all that time, and I can't tell the difference when I'm being discriminated against because I'm black or because I'm female. They both feel the same. If Rainbow/PUSH is going to have any credibility on race discrimination, then we sure are going to join the battle when gender discrimination rears its ugly head."

C. Dolores Tucker, straight from the airport, was the next speaker. Burk introduced her as a woman "who I marched with outside of Tower Records opposing rap music that denigrates women." This was a surprising admission, given Burk's unrelenting criticism of the Augusta city officials for abridging her First Amendment rights. Don't musicians share those same rights?

Tucker was turned out in a purple dress, a purple head covering, and a necklace and matching earrings made of pearls the size of Titleists. "I'm honored to be here with my sister Martha Burk in this noble campaign for gender justice," she began. Tucker then reached out and put an arm around Burk's shoulders and drew her near. "How dare we fly across the world, denouncing and defeating regimes like the Taliban specifically for their callous treatment of women, while here in our front yards we tolerate pockets of female discrimination such as Augusta National Golf Club," Tucker said, putting a unique spin on the war in Afghanistan. "How dare we invite our women to share with our men the shedding of blood for and against notoriously antiwoman regimes abroad when we cannot invite them to share equally with men the facilities and amenities of better living at home." Burk, who had spent the previous weeks backpedaling from her original comments linking Augusta National and women in the military, finally broke away from Tucker, edging out of view of the cameras. She offered a halfhearted clap, but her face looked tight, and her jaw clenched. Clearly she was uncomfortable with having the war card played again.

Once Tucker was finished, Burk returned to the podium to offer what sounded like closing remarks. "I just want to echo [something Hootie has said], that discrimination based on race is one thing and discrimination based on gender is another. I think this group today, the women and men standing together here, shows us that that is not true. We do all stand together. I will take questions, but before I do I want to show you one of our props." She then introduced the Feminist Majority's Alice Cohan, who was handling all of the logistics for the protest in the Pit. Whereas all of the previous speakers were elegantly dressed, Cohan was wearing an ugly green polo shirt.

"We are unveiling, for the first time, right here, the shirt for Augusta 2003," Cohan said. "It says on it, DISCRIMINATION IS NOT A GAME. It's in a nice Masters green. The logo is the woman symbol with a golf ball on it. And I know that you're all gonna want one. Heidi Hartman, the vice chair of the council, is going to be over on Jackson Street selling them in every size you might need. They are for you a special today—$30. They are to help cover the cost of the demonstration. The CEOs of the big corporations don't help cover the cost."

It was on this grossly capitalistic note that the speeches and presentations ended. Burk then entertained questions. Her best line was in response to a query about the first round of the Masters having been rained out. "We think the Goddess is watching and maybe she's not too happy," Burk said.

As Burk continued to speak with a small cluster of reporters, her husband, Ralph Estes, sneaked up behind her. Earlier he had cast a glance at the sky and fretted, "She should be wearing a coat." Now, like a concerned parent, he engulfed her with a jacket. Burk never looked back or broke rhythm while speaking.

After the last reporter had been satisfied, Burk and her entourage visited the CNN Center in downtown Atlanta, to tape an interview for CNNfn. Afterward, it was finally time to journey to Augusta. Burk's three-car caravan arrived in Augusta in the late afternoon. She was staying at a Super 8 motel on the outskirts of town, not far from Fort Gordon. The sign in front of the motel said HAIR DRYER AND IRONING BOARD IN EVERY ROOM. This only fueled the running we're-in-the-South-now jokes that had begun almost as soon as the D.C. crew left Atlanta city limits.

Burk was sharing the motel with dozens of Masters fans. While she was still loitering around the check-in counter, she exchanged cordial greetings with a pair of beefy, middle-aged white guys with cigars dangling from their lips and American flags on the lapels of their brand-new Masters polo shirts. Moments later she was introduced to Jeff Julian, the PGA Tour veteran who was waging a courageous battle against Lou Gehrig's disease. Julian was not participating in the Masters but was on hand to pick up the Ben Hogan Award for courage from the Golf Writers Association of America. Burk, unwittingly, was getting close to the heart of golf.

Throughout the day, and into the evening, Burk's assistant Rebecca Menso continued working the phones to coordinate dozens of interviews that were scheduled for the next day. At the last minute Jack Batson had offered his expansive house to Burk as a makeshift war room, and she was thrilled not to have to entertain reporters at her motel. This may have been partly vanity—*Martha holed up at the Super 8?*—but her husband cited more visceral reasons. "She's got it in her head that if some crazy finds out where she's staying they will shoot her dead on the spot," Estes said, one more of the day's echoes of Martin Luther King Jr. "I'm completely serious. That's her mind-set."

BY LATE THURSDAY AFTERNOON, as Burk was settling in at the Super 8, Augusta National was all but deserted. Washington Road should have been bumper-to-bumper with departing Masters fans, but traffic was zipping along at a good clip as bored sheriff's deputies took cover in their cars. The only evidence of the hustle and bustle of Masters week was the cluster of tents on the corners of the major intersections near the club, and the merchant doing the best business on this dreary day was selling "The Original Hootie Hat." This green baseball cap had HOOTIE on the front in bold yellow stitching, MARTHA BURK encircled and crossed out in red on one side, and STRONG SUPPORT 2003 on the adjustable Velcro strap in the back. The hat was the brainchild of Cliff Hopkins, a real estate entrepreneur and home builder from Hilton Head Island. Hopkins would sell about five thousand hats during Masters week, at $20 per, a price that included a free bumper sticker. "I never expected to get rich off this," said Hopkins. "I just wanted to show my support for Mr. Johnson and the club. The money is just a bonus."

Personally or through his Web site, Hopkins shipped hats during Masters week to "Ireland, Japan, Kuwait, a batch of fifty to Park Avenue, and one to a destroyer off the coast of Turkey," he says. Wayne Sluman, brother of former PGA Championship winner Jeff Sluman, bought four dozen hats, saying they were for some players and their agents, and then came back for seconds and thirds. The Hootie Hat was also a big hit with Richmond County sheriff's deputies. Says Hopkins, "I was walking down the street one afternoon, early in the week, and a deputy hollered across the road, 'Stay right there!'

"I'm thinking, what have I done? He comes over and says, 'You're that Hootie Hat guy, right?'

"We get to talking, and I can kinda see where this is going. I say, Can I make you a present of one of the hats? He turns and hollers across the street to another deputy. 'He's gonna give me a hat—do you want one, too?' Well, before I know it, twenty sheriff's deputies arrive at the booth, plus a handful of state troopers. Sheriff Strength never came in person, but he definitely got a hat. Probably about ten of them. Virtually every single deputy would say, 'I gotta get one for Ronnie. He'll love this.' "

In fact, the Hootie Hat created so much buzz during Masters week that shortly thereafter Hopkins would be approached by a large national retail chain about creating a Hootie clothing line. Hopkins declines to name the company but does say that it has 540 stores nationwide. "A Hootie golf shirt makes more sense than Tommy Hilfiger," Hopkins says. "No one knows who that guy is. But Mr. Johnson has emerged as an icon. He's an old-school kind of leader, a fearless, man-the-torpedoes type. He's like John Wayne, only bigger."

And what of the original Hootie? How did Johnson pass the time on a rainy Thursday at the Masters? The chairman held a series of meetings with fellow tournament officials, as the czars of the Masters scrambled to overcome the rainout. The forecast for the rest of the week was favorable, but in an effort to cram four rounds into three days the decision was made to send players off both the 1st and 10th tees on Friday, beginning at seven-thirty A.M. It would be a wild, dawn-to-dusk golf marathon.

THE MASTERS finally got under way early on Friday, but Sheriff Ronnie Strength was not about to cede the spotlight. He had called a mid-morning walk-through in the Pit for all the would-be demonstrators and interested media. As usual, he looked as if he had just come from his old job at the department store, as he was decked out in a starched white shirt, a patriotic red-white-and-blue tie knotted tight to the top button, a well-cut, summer-weight navy blazer, and the coup de grâce, tassled loafers.

More than three dozen reporters were on hand, in large part the same crowd that had covered Burk's press conference the day before, plus a handful of the golf press who had wandered down Washington Road. Representing Burk was Alice Cohan, the director of national programs for the Washington, D.C.–based Feminist Majority Foundation, who is regarded as one of the country's best protest planners. Jack Batson was also there, providing support. There was much disappointment among the reporters that the Imperial Wizard, J. J. Harper, didn't make the trip up from Cordele, but the lunatic fringe was well accounted for, including Dave Walker, who would be demonstrating in support of the war in Iraq, Todd Manzi of The Burk Stops Here, and Deke Wiggins of People Against Ridiculous Protests.

The festivities began with a soliloquy by Strength, during which he laid down the law for the next day's protests, hamming up his southern accent for the cameras. "I want to make sure we're all singing from the same sheet of music, folks," he said. "There are certain things we are not going to tolerate. For example, demonstrators cannot walk from group to group. If you want to get your viewpoints across to people passing by, that is fine. But we are not going to let groups holler and shout at each other and cause problems among themselves. Y'all are not going to harass them, and they are not going to harass y'all. . . . Let's leave this place clean. . . . There will be no selling of merchandise. . . . Breaking up in groups and going across the street to the front gate at the Augusta National or any of these sidewalks up here that are heavily traveled would be a violation. The applications have been approved for this site. To break up into groups at the Augusta National would be a violation. . . . We don't want to arrest anyone. We don't think the groups want to be arrested. But if any law is violated or any ordinance is violated, we will take that person or persons into custody." Strength also unveiled a well-thought-out plan in which Burk would be given the western end of the Pit while the counterprotesters would be placed a couple hundred yards away, separated by a stand of trees and the sloping terrain of the grassy field.

Dozens of people were huddled around Strength in a lazy half-circle, each wearing their particular mask, from the stern-faced sheriff's deputies hiding behind mirrored sunglasses to the Dockered reporters earnestly scribbling notes. Batson had the most penetrating analysis of the assembled humanity: "Strength is so slick. He'll say whatever needs to be said at that moment to make the sheriff's office look good. There he was, looking like a damn Wall Street trader. He even had a little tablet, like the guys carry on the floor of the stock exchange"—here Batson's voice turns frantic—"*Buy, sell, buy, buy, arrest, handcuff!*

"Jim Wall, the city attorney, now that was a sight. He was the guy in a plaid shirt, duck boots, and corduroy pants, all of it looking like it had come straight from the dry cleaners. There he was, the gentleman hunter.

"Then there's Alice Cohan, professional feminist, God love her. She's short, balding, chunky, she's got that problem where one of her eyes doesn't focus quite right"—to this list Batson could have mentioned her New Agey outfit, which including beaded earrings and a shawl that looked Mexican in origin. "She is absolutely the antithesis of physical beauty, but what a calming influence, what an inspiration."

Had Batson turned his withering gaze upon himself, he would have seen a resident of the Hill, Augusta's prestigious old-money neighborhood, modeling the latest in Greenpeace couture: a hootenanny rain hat and a slicker taped together at the seams. Everybody else in the Pit was happy to play their role, too.

There was Walker, an African American Vietnam vet, who wore a hat embroidered with GIVE WAR A CHANCE and had an American flag on a stick poking out of his jacket pocket. He was candid about having no interest in the Augusta National membership controversy. "I'm here in support of the president and in support of the war," he said. He seemed to be trying hard to project a Huey Newton Lite vibe. At one point he was offered a cup of coffee and asked how he takes it.

"Strictly black," he said with a scowl.

Wiggins was a cocky kid with a big, fishy grin who looked like he had just rolled out of bed after a late-night frat party. Previewing PARP's plans for the following morning, he said, "We're going to put up a big sign and then not show up. That's kind of the whole point, anyway. I've got better things to do."

Manzi was stomping around the Pit radiating a frightening intensity. He kept badgering Cohan, trying to engage her in a debate that nobody but he wanted to hear.

"I just want you to know you don't speak for all women," Manzi said in a voice that Sally Jenkins described in *The Washington Post* as sounding like "the backup warning beep on a tractor."

"And who do you speak for?" Cohan shot back in a voice "that had the tonal quality of an electronic smoke detector," according to Jenkins.

Cohan ended the mini-confrontation by snapping, "I'm not going to debate you because I don't want to embarrass you."

To his credit, Strength let all of the assembled protesters ask questions and speak their piece. He would nod politely, vacantly, and when the sheer boredom became too overwhelming, he would cut them off and ignore anything that was said. The only time he seemed truly engaged was when he entertained questions from the press. As reporters broke into packs and engulfed the various walk-through protagonists, a primary line of questioning centered on the possibility for civil disobedience, stoked, of course, by Jesse Jackson's inflammatory remarks of the day before. "As a lawyer I'm not going to tell somebody to get arrested," Batson said in a comment that was widely circulated. "My job is to lay down the parameters to my client. I'm not going to tell someone to get arrested. That's a personal decision that each individual will have to make. On the other hand, I'm not going to say to you, 'Don't do that.' "

Said Cohan, "I can only speak for myself, and I'm not here to get arrested. I'm hear to participate in a peaceful, non-violent demonstration. But I can't speak for anybody else. People need to feel like they have a real exercise of their free speech."

Asked if Burk would turn out the two hundred protesters she had been permitted for, Cohan followed the recent party line in trying to play down expectations for the protest. "We're not sure about that," Cohan said. "The weather is not the most inviting. And people are focused on other issues, such as the war."

The weather?

At a fair remove from the mass of protesters and reporters, Captain Ray Meyers, the point man for the county sheriff's office, took in the scene and said with a sigh, "This is going to be the most eventful non-event of the year."

Batson, who has spent his life fighting for ideals, had a different take on the walk-through. "That was unique. That was funny. I enjoyed it. Within a five-foot circle there were all the elements in discord, yet nobody was beating anyone over the head with a club. I guess that proves that free speech can exist. It was the best America has to offer."

FOLLOWING THE WALK-THROUGH, a handful of newspaperwomen convened for a late breakfast at a nearby IHOP. Sally Jenkins of *The*

Washington Post, Johnette Howard and Laura Price-Brown of New York's *Newsday,* Teri Thompson of the New York *Daily News,* and Nicole Benjivino of *The New York Times* had more than a century of combined experience in journalism, predominantly in sports, and over breakfast their conversation veered into a sharing of war stories that have come with being women in an overwhelmingly male world.

Thompson recalled that during her stint at the *Rocky Mountain News* in the 1980s, organizers of a local billiards tournament beseeched the paper for coverage, but when she grudgingly showed up to do a story, she was barred from entering the all-male Denver Athletic Club. Howard remembered covering an awards dinner for the Detroit Tigers at the Detroit Country Club, which at the time was an all-white, all-male enclave. After searching in vain for a women's restroom she was told that there wasn't one on the property. Others pitched in with their own tales of woe. "I don't want to give the impression that all women sportswriters do is sit around and bitch about sexism, because that's hardly the case," says Jenkins, but during the Masters week it was top of mind for a lot of them.

Robinson Holloway, the originator of the influential golf-writers blog What They're Writing, says, "At one point in the mid-nineties I remember counting thirteen women in the pressroom at the Masters, and I was blown away. That was such progress from 1989, when I had started covering golf. Now there's exactly one woman golf beat writer—Lewaine Mair [from Britain's *The Daily Telegraph*]. It's so sad, but it also tells you what a hostile environment golf can be for women." (Of course, some of these women now enjoy more high-profile positions as general columnists, like Jenkins and Howard.)

The dynamics of Masters week only heightened the divide between the sexes. To protect against charges of favoritism, or worse, tournament officials scrupulously gave each news organization exactly the same number of credentials that they had in years past. So, for example, *The New York Times* got its usual two, for columnist Dave Anderson and golf writer Cliff Brown, while columnist Selena Roberts, who was on the Hootie and Martha beat, was unable to get into the tournament.

Ever since the membership controversy had erupted nine months earlier, women had written a disproportionately high number of the stories. Some cared passionately about the issues, others were doing what

Jenkins describes dismissively as "playing on the home team. There is this homer attitude where on every issue, women sportswriters feel compelled to espouse the feminist viewpoint, no matter what, and if you don't you're a traitor to the cause. I've always rejected that kind of thinking, but other people lose their way."

Christine Brennan sees it much differently, pointing out that personal experience inevitably affects a reporter's worldview. Asked why it has been female reporters who have driven the debate on the Augusta National membership controversy, she says, "Could it be because a lot of male golf writers have played at clubs that don't allow women and they're beyond the point of questioning propriety? I am really reluctant to say a woman's perspective is different in sports journalism. I've certainly never felt that covering football or baseball or any of the other major sports. I don't want to sound as if I'm indicting the golf media, because I adore the guys on the beat—in fact, I've dated a couple of them. I adore the guys on the golf beat. I don't want to sound like I'm criticizing them in any way . . . but maybe in this case it did take a female perspective."

As the nation's newspapers sent their women writers to Augusta to continue chasing the story, Jenkins and Brennan were among the precious few who held credentials to the Masters. The rest of this disenfranchised band of reporters were left on the outside looking in. Says Howard, "There was a lot of joking about how we couldn't get into Augusta National, either."

One effect of having so many uncredentialed women writing from Augusta was that Burk's was the only story they could tell. This left the papers' (male) golf scribes inside the gates to cover Hootie and the club's machinations. Thus, the chairman of Augusta National jousting with the golf writers received big play in sports pages across the country, while women writing about a perceived women's issue were much easier to marginalize. This, too, was talked about over pancakes at IHOP, and the proof could be found in Friday's newspapers, and the coverage of Burk's Atlanta press conference. Johnette Howard's story had been banished to the 9th page of the *Newsday* Sports section. Diane Pucin's story was buried on page 16 of the *L.A. Times*. Linda Robertson landed on page 3 of the *The Miami Herald*. (Jenkins wound up on page 1 of the *Post* Sports, but typical of her just-one-of-the-guys bent, she had written a spiky column from Augusta that was dismissive of Burk.) Some newspapers found it easier to ignore Burk altogether: The voice of the nation's fourth-largest city, the *Houston Chronicle*, gave her press conference 226 words of wire service copy on page 11.

To be sure, Burk got big play in the papers that had been championing her from the beginning. *The New York Times*, *The Washington Post*, and *The Atlanta Journal-Constitution* all played the protest on the front page of Sports. The *Times* ran no fewer than three Burk-centric stories on the first Sports section page, plus a large photo from the press conference, with a resolute-looking Burk standing next to one of the DISCRIMINATION IS NOT A GAME placards from her protest. Selena Roberts's column was ostensibly about Burk, but it was informed by a personal exile as well: "In Hootie's secret society of the biased, equality is based on location, location, location. . . ."

BURK HAD SKIPPED Strength's walk-through in the Pit in favor of an all-day media blitz, recognizing that this was her last chance to sell her ideas heading into the protest. Beginning with an eight A.M. spot on a local ABC affiliate, her day was broken into half-hour bits that included interviews with, in order, the *Chicago Tribune*, *The Atlanta Journal-Constitution*, Channel 6 in Augusta, Associated Press, *USA Today*, CNNfn, the Golf Channel, *The Boston Globe*, *The Miami Herald*, *The Orlando Sentinel*, *Dallas Morning News*, *Los Angeles Times*, *San Francisco Chronicle*, *Macon Telegraph*, CBC (Canadian Radio), *The Philadelphia Inquirer*, ESPN, and *Newsday*.

Burk was holed up at Batson's home on the Hill. At first glance the place looked a shambles. The towering exterior had been stripped to the wood, awaiting a fresh coat of paint, and the ribs of the scaffolding were in place on the immense porch. But on the inside the house was a picture of gracious southern living, with an ornate, hand-carved wooden mantel, a vertiginous winding staircase, and a warm decor overgrown with floral prints. Burk was floating between the cozy living room, where she conducted most of the print interviews, and the large, formal dining room, where the TV crews would set up their lights and cameras. She was trying to keep her energy up by working her way through a box of Krispy Kremes.

On the porch a rotating cast of reporters was standing vigil, waiting to be summoned for their exclusive interviews or simply soaking up the scene for color pieces. They relieved the boredom by gossiping with one another, chatting on cell phones, shooting hoops in the driveway, smoking cigarettes, drinking coffee, and reading one another's work in the various newspapers that were scattered about. At Burk HQ the schism between the golf press and those on the Burk beat was thrown into sharp relief. While the dimpleheads were hoofing up and down Augusta National's hills earnestly recording the details of Tiger Woods's stunning 76 in the morning round, the gang on the Hill seemed to have only passing interest in the tournament. (The TV in the Batson's living room was dark until nearly five o'clock, when a visiting sportswriter finally turned on the Masters telecast.) Greeting Burk in the living room of an ACLU attorney, many of the reporters assigned to interview Burk gave off a palpable sense that they were on her side. When *Philadelphia Inquirer* writer Monica Yant Kinney arrived—she was on loan from the City & Region section, where, according the *Inquirer* Web site, she writes about "suburban trends, Philadelphia City Hall, welfare reform and city news"—one of the first things she said to Burk was, "I just talked to that guy Manzi in the Pit. He's so scary."

"That guy is pathetic," said Burk, completing the bonding experience. "I'm not out there selling Todd Manzi T-shirts."

One reporter who was traveling on two passports was Christine Brennan, who left the pressroom at Augusta National to journey to the Hill to interview Burk. They had spoken on the phone a handful of times but, surprisingly, had never met, and upon Brennan's arrival she and Burk hugged like long-lost sorority sisters.

"Do you realize what today is?" Brennan asked Burk, breathlessly.

"What is it?"

"It was a year ago today the column ran."

That would be Brennan's column calling out Lloyd Ward, which had inspired Burk to write her letter to Hootie Johnson.

Though Burk was surrounded by supporters, even in Batson's living room there was evidence of the backlash she had created. One handy example was folded on the couch. The front of this crudely designed T-shirt read IF MARTHA HAD BALLS . . . The back: . . . SHE COULD JOIN THE CLUB. At one point Burk spied one of the shirts, gleefully examined it, and then folded it up with the precision of origami, kicking her foot out with a flourish when she was done. "My parents owned a clothing shop in Texas and I worked there as a schoolgirl," she said.

The origin of the T-shirts was soon revealed: Jack Batson had mentioned that his son was spending the day selling Masters T's, but left unsaid was that Martha was the star of the shirt. Suddenly, sixteen-year-old William Batson burst in. He was a good-looking, tow-headed kid, with a deep tan from his hours in the sun. "There's my son," said Jack, "the shameless capitalist."

"I just sold thirty-six T-shirts in like an hour," said William, who was making a $5 commission on every $20 shirt.

Someone remarked that this was supposed to be a slow economy.

"Not when you're selling anti–Martha Burk stuff," William said. He produced from a bag a handful of the offending T-shirts, which left his old man with a slightly pinched expression.

Here Martha Burk's husband couldn't resist a dig. "Say, how much of your profit are you contributing to fighting gender discrimination?" Ralph Estes asked.

"I don't know," William said. "But I gotta do something with all this money—my pocket is getting pretty heavy."

"Well, I'm just glad to see you spelled her name right," Estes said.

Moments later he was handed a Hootie Hat, and he replaced his fedora with it. "Is it me?" Estes asked demurely. Asked if the selling of all the Burk memorabilia bothered him, he said, "Oh sure, you hate to see others profit from this, but it isn't money we lost, so . . ." His voice trailed off dreamily.

For all the levity, there was business to be discussed. In a quiet moment Burk announced that "we canceled the bus out of Washington. We were only permitted for two hundred, so why worry about the logistics of D.C. when we have Atlanta and Columbia so close? The resources of the activist community are already strained, because tomorrow there is a peace march and a demonstration at the World Bank."

She also dropped the first details of what would mushroom into a juicy story, saying that her people had just become aware of a putative plot by the D.C.-based Heritage Foundation, which bills itself as a "conservative think tank that promotes free market ideals," to sabotage the protest. According to Burk, she had been forwarded an e-mail that was going around, in which the Heritage Foundation was offering to pay women $75 to sign up for the protest bus out of Atlanta and then not show up, in a devious attempt to reduce the numbers at the demonstration. Neither Burk nor her staffers had a copy of the e-mail on hand, but she promised to make it available upon returning to Washington. "That's abortion politics, for God's sake," Burk said. "It's shocking they would stoop to something like this over golf."

That was just a taste of the antipathy that was lurking in Augusta. Sitting on the couch, while his wife conducted a TV interview in the comfortable confines of the adjacent dining room, Estes said, "Yes, I am worried about her safety. We have hired two private security guards who are going to be next to her at all times, but if somebody wants to do something . . . uh . . . weird, well . . ." Once again his voice trailed off.

The topic changed to the relentless media attention on his wife, and Estes was quick to say, "We are not jaded. As Martha says, 'It's the goddam *New York Times*.' It's amazing. It's still a thrill when the *Wichita Eagle-Beacon* calls up. But then again, when she was on the *Today* show [two days earlier], I didn't get up to watch it. I can only compliment her so many times."

Estes was interrupted by the arrival of a van full of undergrads who had driven down from D.C. for the protest and to help with the preparation. His introduction: "I'm Ralph Estes, Martha's husband. She let me keep my last name."

The young woman he was talking to looked at him vacantly, and giggled nervously.

"You don't get the joke, do you?"

More awkward laughter.

"Never mind, you girls must be tired from the drive. Come in, there's plenty for you to do."

Not long after, Burk emerged from the dining room, having conducted her final interview of the day. She was mellow with fatigue, and she plopped down on the sofa and idly eyed the Masters telecast. "Is that

Mickelson?" she said, guessing correctly as Phil's figure filled the screen. "My sons don't like him—they think he's a whiner. And they're so tired of [wife] A-myyyyyyyy always being in front of the camera." Smash cut to Tiger Woods, looking grim as he labored to recover from his opening 76. Burk immediately began ruminating on Woods. "I hope he wins so much. I do admire him. He just works and works and works, and nothing really bothers him—not the course, not the weather, not all of this stuff. I admire so much the way he has handled himself through this.

"The only things I really know about golf I learned from my sons, and one thing I was told about Tiger really resonates very strongly with me: Tiger is the standard. No matter what he does this week or next week or the week after, he is still the standard." Burk is right about that, but Friday at the Masters had been a struggle for the two-time defending champ. When darkness stopped him ten holes into his second round, Woods was two over par, languishing in a nine-way tie for twenty-third. Worse still, he had been shown up by his playing partner, U.S. Amateur champion Ricky Barnes, whose swagger, bulging pecs, and violent swing called to mind a young Palmer. Barnes was one of only four players under par on a soggy course that was playing murderously long. The eclectic crew in red numbers was led by Canadian lefty Mike Weir and included cigar-smoking, Ferrari-driving Ulsterman Darren Clarke, and Mickelson.

On Saturday morning the players would resume their second rounds, meaning much of the field would be fighting to make the cut just as the protest would be getting under way.

FRIDAY NIGHT, as weary Masters competitors slumbered in their rented homes, People Against Ridiculous Protests hosted a raucous hoedown at a dance hall not far from downtown. PARP's spiritual leader, Deke Wiggins, had said all along that the protest was just a good excuse for a party, and he delivered on the promise. The crowd of a few hundred people—which skewed toward toothsome U of G grads—was treated to a tight bluegrass band, mounds of tasty BBQ, and a bottomless supply of adult beverages. The party raged until one A.M., at which point a smaller group of revelers moved to the bar at Partridge Inn. Wiggins stumbled home after two A.M., and at that unlikely hour was inspired to redo the PARP protest sign, which he was due to plant in the Pit in a few hours.

AT SIX-FIFTY-SEVEN on Saturday morning, two big, white Adventure buses wheeled into the Avondale MARTA station in Atlanta, where a handful of protesters, reporters, and photographers were awaiting a ride to Augusta. In bold lettering on the side of one of the buses was EXPLORING GOD'S CREATION. Would-be protesters had been trickling into the parking lot since five-thirty, and it was clear by the low turnout that the second bus would not be needed.

By seven-fifty A.M. the lone bus was on the move, carrying two dozen protesters. Says its driver, Larry Bloodworth, "From what I gathered, they were expecting more people. The mood on the bus was pretty quiet. I would say they were disappointed." As Bloodworth wheeled out of the parking lot he noticed an understated escort. "Two police cars followed us to the Interstate, and then a couple of state patrolmen tailed us on the Interstate for a while, to make sure we got off okay."

It was an eclectic crew on board. By day's end the message of the protest would be largely obscured, but these bleary-eyed activists gave the issues a beating heart. Lee DeCesare, a seventy-year-old former teacher and cofounder of the Tampa chapter of NOW, had driven eight hours to get to Atlanta in time to catch her freedom ride. "I've been in the women's movement for thirty-five years," said DeCesare, who has four grown children. "I've marched with Betty Friedan. I helped open up the fire and police department in Tampa to women. I call these women in Augusta who support Hootie 'hyenas in petticoats.' " The feisty DeCesare had brought with her a sign affixed to a golf club belonging to her husband, Tom, the mayor of Madeira Beach, Florida: HOOTIE PATOOTIE, SHAME ON YOUTIE. "My husband plays golf. He said, 'What are you Valkyries going to do? You're going to ruin the golf match.' I said, 'I hope we will, dear. That's what we're planning.' "

Sitting near DeCesare were three college kids—Amarknkthia Torres of Berry College in Rome, Georgia, and Sara Myers and Dana Burmeister of Georgia State. They were a giggly lot, making liberal use of the soda and snacks on board, and they whispered that they thought it would be kinda cool to get arrested. This echoed the buttons that were being passed around the bus, adorned with a quote from the late feminist Anita Borg: "Well-behaved women rarely make history." Another rider, Clare Michaud, a third-year law student at Emory, confided that she was anxious to avoid trouble with the law, as she would be sitting for the Georgia bar in a matter of months. Michaud had brought along a sign that read COLLEGE: $80,000. LAW SCHOOL: $124,000. BUSTING UP THE OLD BOYS: PRICELESS.

All the young women were slightly in awe of three distinguished African American gents from the Southern Christian Leadership Conference who sat in the back of the bus reading their Bibles. Ralph Worrell, seventy-four, Fred D. Taylor, sixty, and Frederick Moore, fifty-two, had more than one hundred years of activism among them and, by their reckoning, in excess of fifty arrests for civil disobedience. Worrell recalled standing in the shadow of the Lincoln Memorial in Washington, D.C., in 1963, and hearing Martin Luther King Jr. deliver his "I Have a Dream" speech. Taylor talked about growing up in Montgomery, Alabama, during the era of the bus boycotts. "I remember the white and colored drinking fountains, too," he said. He was journeying to Augusta because, "I think discrimination in any form is wrong. Sadly, we still have a long way to go."

The most confounding protester on board, David McIntyre, had made a 550-mile drive from Englewood, Florida, to catch the bus. McIntyre was a handsome, sixtyish man with a movie star's silver mien, and he was turned out in a beautifully tailored black tuxedo. He had solid activist credentials, having taught in the Peace Corps and for the last five years holding membership with NOW. Yet McIntyre was surprised when it was pointed out that his tux and his sardonic sign FORMAL PROTEST might be construed as making light of Burk's message. "I have two daughters and a son, and I want my daughters to have the same choices in life as my son," he said earnestly. Then why the tux? "I thought it would help attract attention to our positions."

With the interstate wide open, the bus made good time, except for an emergency pit stop twenty-five miles into the trip. "I got real bad cramps in my stomach, I guess is a polite way of saying it," says Bloodworth. "I'm pretty sure it was because of bad fruit salad from the Mrs. I pulled over to use the restroom, because if you use the one on the bus too much, it'll come back to haunt you. After a while the girls came to check on me to see if I was okay. That was real nice."

BACK AT THE PIT, Major Ken Autry of the Richmond County Sheriff's Department had been the first to arrive, at six-thirty A.M. half an hour before sunrise. (Around the same time, the first players were pulling up to Augusta National to get ready for the completion of their second rounds.) At eight the parade began—nearly 120 officers from Richmond County, Columbia County, and the Georgia State Patrol rumbled into Augusta. The vast majority parked in the Pit, while a couple dozen men in uniform reported to the second protest site for Rainbow/PUSH at Highland and Wheeler. In the Pit, squad cars were strategically parked to act as buffers between the various protesters. Two oversized vehicles also rolled up—a paddy wagon the size of a school bus, and an RV converted into a mobile command post. Strength had elected not to make an appearance at the Pit. "I didn't want to be any kind of distraction," he says. But from the sheriff's outpost at Augusta National he kept in constant contact with the troops via radio.

By ten o'clock the Pit was beginning to fill up, though there was no sign of either Martha or the Atlanta bus. Signs had sprouted like weeds on the edge of the Washington Road:

—HONK FOR HOOTIE

—CBS: CONSTANTLY BROADCASTING SEXISM

—LEAVE THE SOUTH ALONE

—DISCRIMINATION IS NOT A GAME

—STOP BURK AND JACKSON'S SHAKEDOWN OF AMERICA

—FAIR PLAY ON THE FAIRWAYS

—HOOTIE, THANKS FOR STANDING UP TO A BULLY

—CEO'S PLAY WHILE WOMEN PAY

—HEY MARTHA, PROTEST THIS!

—DISGUSTA NATIONAL

—BURK IS A JERK

—THE ONLY WOMAN MARTHA BURK HAS HELPED IS MARTHA BURK

—FEMINISTS ARE THE MAJORITY

—BURK DOESN'T SPEAK FOR ME

—THE RIGHT TO PROTEST IS CRUCIAL EVEN WHEN THE CAUSE IS INANE
AND A BLATANT PUBLICITY STUNT

—SUPPORT AUGUSTA'S RIGHT TO CHOOSE

—THE WORST PAIRING IN MASTERS HISTORY:
MARTHA BURK AND JESSE JACKSON

—WILL TRADE PROTEST FOR MASTERS TICKET

— WILL KISS MARTHA BURK FOR MASTERS TICKET

On the east side of the Pit, home to the so-called counterprotesters, silliness was beginning to reign. Deke Wiggins of People Against Ridiculous Protests had dragged himself out of bed and hastily planted his large banner, which looked to be a hand-painted bedsheet. It read: LOOK AT ALL THE RIDICULOUS PEOPLE. A smaller sign bragged: WE DON'T GIVE A PARP. After putting up the sign, Wiggins beat a hasty retreat, saying he was going to watch some golf.

The Imperial Wizard of the White Knights of the Ku Klux Klan, J. J. Harper, was daintily gluing frilly pink ribbon to his large wooden sign, on which he had scrawled what was supposed to be a spoof of a warning label for the menopause drug medroxyprogesterone. It read, in part, "Treats lack of estrogen and progestin [sic] in your body caused by menopause or the removal of the ovaries. Also helps prevent osteoporosis and the urge to protest against golf clubs. . . . If you miss a dose, take the second dose ASAP. Do not request a permit to protest golf clubs during this time!"

As Harper explained, "Martha wants to be a man so badly, but I don't think that's healthy. She needs to get rid of some of that testosterone."

Next to Harper was Dave Walker, identified by a sheriff's placard that said, simply, PRO IRAQ POLICY. Walker, an African American, seemed tickled by his proximity to the One Man Klan. "I don't agree with what he says, but I support his right to say it," said Walker. But the permitted protesters were by now known commodities. Drawing far more interest from the ever-increasing number of reporters and onlookers were the day-trippers who had simply shown up unannounced.

Not far from Harper, a pair of afternoon deejays from the North Augusta station Eagle 102 suddenly materialized. They looked like a couple of wayward Hogettes who had wandered over from the Washington Redskins' end zone. Dale Thomas and Big Robb Tomas were very large men dressed in drag, adorned with bunny ears and volleyballs stuffed into their dresses in lieu of breasts. Each was waving an American flag. Their producer Kevin James was also on hand, turned out in a purple velour suit and an oversized fake gold necklace with a huge medallion in the shape of a dollar sign. "Pimpin' ain't easy," he said. "I'm just trying to get my ladies into Augusta." These jokesters earned endless honks of approval from the Washington Road traffic, which had slowed to a crawl to take in the spectacle.

Standing in the shade a few steps away was a fellow named Alan Ditmore, who looked like he had blown in with the tumbleweed from a lonely corner of Humboldt County. (In fact, Ditmore, thirty-eight, was from Asheville, North Carolina, where he said he worked "as a cowboy. That is, I work with cows.") Ditmore had torn jeans, dusty shoes, and scraggly, greasy hair. His white T-shirt was yellow around the edges, and it was scrawled with black ink. On the front: ALL GOLF'S VILE. On the back: GOLF DESTROYES HOUSEING, FARMS AND FORESTS. He also carried a small sign that said ONLY BIRTH CONTROL CAN SAVE THE WORLD.

When it was pointed out to Ditmore that he had misspelled, consecutively, both "destroys" and "housing," he said, "Damn, I'm a terrible speller. I misspelled 'apartheid' at protests all through the eighties." As for the connection between the membership practices of Augusta National and the destruction of farmland, Ditmore said, "I interpreted this broadly as an antigolf protest."

As interesting as Ditmore may have been, he was no match for Elvis. The King strutted into the Pit around ten-thirty A.M., looking iconic in a sparkly white jumpsuit, chrome sunglasses, and a jet-black wig sculpted into a gravity-defying pompadour, with shaggy sideburns. Underneath it all was Mac Gaddy, a church deacon, investment adviser, and amateur

Elvis impersonator from Charlotte. Said Elvis, "It sounded like it was going to be a zoo. I knew what they needed was an Elvis sighting. I wanted to add to the circus atmosphere." He also admitted that he was hoping a sympathetic onlooker might slide him a badge so he could watch a little golf.

Elvis entertained a broadening circle of reporters with a showman's panache. "I'm thinking of going after Arnold Palmer for calling himself 'the King' all these years," he said. When an attractive young woman strolled by, he jumped in front of her, hurried through a series of wild pelvic gyrations, and said in the smarmiest possible voice, "Hey baby, it's now or never." Naturally, the adoring press corps wanted to know where Elvis stood on the Augusta National membership controversy. "One thing about Elvis—he always supported women."

Amazingly, Elvis was upstaged, by one Georgina Z. Bush, who was either an ornate mime, a man in drag, or some unholy union thereof. Georgina's face was painted a ghostly white with red and blue accents, and it wore red tights, a red American flag cape, and black suede cowboy boots, and carried an umbrella adorned with small American flags. Georgina passed out cards that on one side billed itself as a "queer kissing cousin to George W. Bush" and on the other carried a quote from Hermann Goering.

Georgina created a stir among the residents who lived on the other side of Washington Road, facing the Pit. Many had pulled up chairs or blankets and were watching the spectacle, slack-jawed. One cluster included Ricky Smith, his wife, Duchess, and their friend Paul Willis, who were nursing beverages and passing around a pair of binoculars. "We needed some excitement around here," Ricky said.

By now it was nearing eleven o'clock, and more and more reporters were pouring into the Pit. Their bleating cell phones made for an annoying sound track. Many were getting regular updates on the progress of Tiger Woods, who at that very moment was making a mess of the remnants of his second round and was on the precipice of missing his first cut in nearly five years. No one felt more torn than the *Chicago Tribune's* Ed Sherman; while other major papers had multiple writers splitting up responsibilities of covering the golf and Hootie-Martha news, Sherman was a one-man gang trying to do both at the same time. "Oh, great,"

Sherman said at one point, "Tiger is going to miss the cut and we're half a mile away hanging out with a bunch of crazies."

Not every reporter shared his angst. Christine Brennan was wandering around the Pit with giddy enthusiasm, repeating to herself and anyone within earshot, "This is great! This is America! This is great!"

One of the most unexpected displays of free speech was a black man holding a sign that said RAINBOW/PUSH IS KLAN WITH A TAN. This was the handiwork of the Reverend Jesse Lee Peterson, the founder/president of Brotherhood Organization of a New Destiny. BOND is a conservative African American group based in Los Angeles, dedicated, it seems, mainly to tweaking Rev. Jackson and Rainbow/PUSH. "One mistake we've made is to allow people like Martha Burk and Jesse Jackson to use blacks in any way they want for their agenda," said Rev. Peterson, an eloquent, dignified presence who was standing a stone's throw from a hip-swiveling Elvis. "And because we haven't come forward, people assume we're always in agreement.

"Augusta has a right to exist as a private club. This is America. If we continue to allow people like Jesse Jackson and Martha Burk to intimidate them, where will it stop? The linking of this issue with racism is a slap in the face to blacks."

Rev. Peterson was in mid-soliloquy when nine representatives of Rainbow/PUSH, all of them African American and boasting their affiliation with signs and T-shirts, arrived at the southeastern corner of the Pit. On their way to Burk's patch of earth they strode silently pass the KKK outpost and its racist caricatures of Jesse Jackson. That kind of free speech they were used to. But in front of the KLAN WITH A TAN sign, the procession ground to a halt. The Rainbow/PUSH crew muttered among themselves. Rev. Peterson didn't say a word, but he stared down the group with a defiant gaze. One Rainbow/PUSH staffer finally whipped out a cell phone and pounded a number. His message was brief but direct. "Send some more people down," he growled into the phone. "There's some crazy motherfuckers running around here."

MEANWHILE, the protest bus was inching its way up Washington Road, past the sports bar with the HOOTIE FOR PRESIDENT sign, and the

Days Inn with a cheeky message on its marquee: ROOMS AVAILABLE—
WOMEN ALLOWED. Upon arriving in Augusta, the NCWO's Holder
passed out green NCWO T-shirts adorned with DISCRIMINATION IS NOT A
GAME and then commandeered the bus's PA system to give a pep talk.
"Make sure you have your T-shirts on when we get off at our lowly five-
acre vista. They ID us as being with Martha Burk. We're with other
groups, which includes the KKK, which as far as we know is one sad little
man. The most important thing to remember is that the day is about us.
Do not respond to the other protesters. Do not look at them. The last
thing we want is for the KKK to get all the attention. There'll be volun-
teer workers in purple sashes. If you have a problem, go to one of them. If
anyone tries to physically touch you, get someone with a purple sash. Ignore people who try to talk to you. The workers will help guide you on
the chants. Join in and enjoy yourself. As you get off the bus, grab a sign,
take it with you. Be an impressive and loud group—if we are, we don't
have to come back next year, 'cause Hootie will damn sure let a chick
in." The crowd on board let out a little cheer.

Abruptly the bus stopped on Washington Road, in front of the Pit.
The doors opened and a dozen solemn women in green T-shirts popped
out, followed by a distinguished gentleman in a black tux. He was followed by another burst of green T-shirts, and then . . . nothing. No more
protesters were forthcoming.

A buzz went through the crowd of reporters, onlookers, and law enforcement officers who had gathered in front of the bus. Finally, a state
trooper yelled at the driver, "Is that it?" That was it.

With the arrival of the bus, two dozen lethargic cops snapped to attention and strode toward the roadway. They fanned out in the direction
of the stage, standing shoulder to shoulder, a thin blue line offering the
protesters safe passage to the stage. The demonstrators unloaded picket
signs from the belly of the bus—DISCRIMINATION IS NOT A GAME and CEOS
PLAY WHILE WOMEN PAY—and made a beeline for the stage.

For the preceding twenty minutes music had been playing at a sheriff-
approved volume. Helen Reddy's "I Am Woman" had kicked off the set,
followed by Tom Jones's "She's a Lady," Cindy Lauper's "Girls Just Want
to Have Fun," and Shania Twain's "Man! I Feel Like a Woman." ("I Hear
You Knockin' but You Can't Come In" was a glaring omission.) Now a

dozen of the women from the protest bus gathered in front of the stage and added their voices to the chorus. In unison they began to chant.

"What do we want? Equality! When do we want it? Now!"

"What do we want? Equality! When do we want it? Now!"

A new rallying call went up.

"Two, four, six, eight/Augusta does discriminate!"

"Two, four, six, eight/Augusta does discriminate!"

"Break it down, break it down! The glass ceiling is coming down!"

"Break it down, break it down! The glass ceiling is coming down!"

This brought to mind *The New York Times*'s most recent editorial board scolding, which had run five days earlier under the headline "No Hush for Masters." In forecasting Burk's protest, the paper had written, hopefully, "Perhaps some golfer will flub his backswing after he's disturbed by hearing the chants of angry protesters." (Where is Dave Anderson when you need him most? In golf parlance, you might *flub* a chip, but nobody ever flubs a backswing.)

With all the protesters now on the scene, every reporter in the Pit was trying to come up with a head count. It was easy enough to count up the affiliated T-shirts, whether they were the green of the bus riders, the red of the Feminist Majority, the pink of the college kids, or the white of Rainbow/PUSH. There were about forty protesters in these simple uniforms. But there were also more than a hundred other onlookers—local residents, wayward Masters fans, reporters, and passersby of every stripe. These group affiliations were less obvious, and more subject to interpretation. In the end, the number of "protesters" would fluctuate wildly, depending on who was doing the counting.

"What do we want? Equality!"

"When do we wa . . ."

Suddenly the music died, and with it the chanting, and Alice Cohan scurried to the mike and quickly began to stage-manage the photo op. She directed shorter protesters to stand in front of the stage and banished taller ones to the periphery. "Keep your signs at chest level," she boomed. "Do not raise them over your head and block the cameras."

Cohan then turned her attention to the fifteen camera crews that had set up in a crescent about fifty feet from the stage. "You media folks happy?" she asked. "Can you get a good shot . . . no, not a shot . . . a view?" Here Cohan let out a rueful laugh. "One of the kind police officers and I were talking and he asked me not to say *shot*."

This drew a few chuckles, but for the first time all day there was an undercurrent of tension. The protesters were here, the counterprotesters were here, but where was Martha? Even her husband was on the scene. Ralph Estes wandered over to get a view of the stage, and absentmindedly stepped in front of one of the cameras, which was rolling. A news reader with lacquered hair tried to nudge him out of the way, but Estes batted his arm away and said in low, feral voice, "Don't touch me!" Coming from Ralphie, this naked aggression was a shock.

"I'm trying to help you," the stunned broadcaster said.

"I'm her husband," Ralphie snarled. "Don't grab me again."

The confrontation was defused by a flurry of movement in the northwestern corner of the Pit. Reporters and cameramen were dashing toward a cluster of women who were slowly making their way to the stage. Martha had finally arrived. She was flanked by Congresswoman Carolyn Maloney and Eleanor Smeal, the founder of the Feminist Majority. Behind this trio were a squadron of young women in hot-pink T-shirts with a dictionary-style definition of feminism: THE POLICY, PRACTICE OF ADVOCACY OF POLITICAL, ECONOMIC AND SOCIAL EQUALITY FOR WOMEN. Burk was walking slowly, deliberately. She looked drained, even a tad unsteady. The chic threads she had worn two days earlier at the King Center had been traded in for one of the ill-fitting, chintzy, made-in-China golf shirts the NCWO was selling for $30 a pop.

Her long walk to the stage was chaotic. TV reporters were walking backward and screaming questions, while onlookers hurled invective. The man waiving the WILL KISS MARTHA BURK FOR MASTERS TICKET sign shouted, "No politics, we just want to get into the Masters."

"So do we," Burk shot back.

Finally, Burk made it to the stage, which was framed by an American flag and a large sign that read DISCRIMINATION IS NOT AN AMERICAN VALUE.

The women in front of the stage burst into another chant.

"One, two, three, four/Discrimination no more!"

"One, two, three, four/Discrimination no more!"

"One, two, thr . . ."

They were quieted by Heidi Hartman, the NCWO vice chair who introduced Burk. Martha was greeted by a sharp mix of cheers and boos, catcalls and clapping. Her opening comment was a doozy. "I just want to welcome you on behalf of the fifty-one states of the United States of America," she said. "We've got the lower forty-eight, we've got Alaska, we've got Hawaii, and we've got the police state of Augusta, Georgia. Welcome."

Whereas two days earlier, in Atlanta, Burk's manner had been restrained and clinical, here, in this contentious climate, she came to life, oozing energy and charisma. "We're down here in the Pit, and we're so glad the press came down and found us. We're a long way from that front gate, where those boys are in there doing their sewing in the sewing circle." With that zinger, Burk let out one of her mischievous giggles.

"This is the fourth protest that I've attended since January. Let me tell you where we've been and why. We have been on the steps of the United States Supreme Court, defending a woman's right to have control over her own body. We have been outside the president's commission on Title IX, defending the rights of girls and women to participate in sports. The commission is one block from the White House. And most recently we have been in front of the White House to talk about domestic priorities today in the United States, and why we don't have child care, why we don't have health care. Now, don't ya find it a little ironic that we can be on the front steps of the Supreme Court and we can march in groups larger than four in front of the White House, but"—here Burk revved up her voice and motioned over her shoulder, across Washington Road—"we can't get in front of Augusta National Incorporated? What's wrong with this picture, folks? What are those boys afraid of? Even President Bush lets us come talk to him closer than half a mile away."

Burk then said that she wanted to share the day with a coalition of other women, and she introduced Congresswoman Maloney, saying, "She took a midnight train to Georgia to be here." Maloney's rambling speech was notable for one claim: "Of all the hundreds of organizations that are supporting Martha Burk and women of America working for equality, there is only one organization supporting Hootie, and that is the Ku Klux Klan. It speaks volumes about where he stands and where

Augusta is, and it's time they came into the twenty-first century." There's nothing wrong with a little hyperbole, but clearly Augusta National enjoyed more support than just the Ku Klux Klan. Maloney's reach produced one of the day's loudest jeers. Her other comments were more on point.

"What is at stake here is keeping women out of halls of power," she said. "It's stigmatizing and fosters an environment that creates the pay gap, the pension gap, and the glass ceiling. This is not about getting women into a few fancy clubs. This is fundamentally about achieving the American ideal of an even playing field in which merit and talent determine success, not sex or race."

Late in Maloney's speech an unexpected guest made an appearance. Moving through the crowd was a cardboard Klansman on a stick, eight or nine feet tall, with an oversized Augusta National logo drawn on its chest. This seemed a little over-the-top, but as props would go, it was just the beginning. After Maloney was done speaking, Burk pointed to the two-dimensional Klansman caricature and said, "We are so happy to have some of the club's main supporters in the crowd today. He's got the club symbol on his chest. We're so glad to know who's supporting the boys behind the gates."

Burk then introduced the next speaker, Ramona Wright, the vice president of the National Congress of Black Women. She was an enthusiastic young woman who articulately denounced Augusta National's "discriminatory practices, or so-called tradition." But Wright lost the crowd when she said, "Bear with me, this is going to be a little history lesson," and then proceeded to recap the town of Augusta's development going back to 1735.

Smeal followed Wright to the stage. She was introduced by Burk as "the woman who taught us all how to do it." Smeal spoke with such passion that deafening feedback occasionally poured out of the speakers. "We have been on the front lines now for three and a half decades," she said. "We have knocked on the door of the Duquesne Club, which was the elite corporate interest of Pittsburgh, and we knocked until they admitted women. We knocked on the door of the Cosmos Club, in downtown D.C., which represents scientists and intellectuals and writers, which said there was no woman qualified, and we kept knocking on that door until they admitted women. We knocked on the door of every University Club in this country which originally excluded women, and which now, almost without exception, admit women. We knocked on the door of Harvard University, which excluded women, and by the way, its treasurer is still a member of Augusta. They just appointed a woman dean to a law school we couldn't go to just a few short years ago. We knocked on the door at West Point, the Naval Academy, and the Air Force Academy. Back then they could say we were not fit to serve, and right now we are overseas defending America.

"We are going to keep on knocking at the door of Augusta National Golf Club for one reason. The glass ceiling exists, because where the deals are made, where the CEOs of this nation gather, at too many of these places women are still not allowed. And we're not here just for elite women. Let there be no mistake about it. The deals they make at the golf club affect the secretaries, affect the clerks, affect the fact that we still don't have child care in this country and we don't have paid family leave. The CEOs can come here on the big jets, but the little woman back in the office doesn't have paid family leave."

After a smattering of applause from the crowd, Smeal gathered herself for the finale. "Augusta, open the doors, or we'll be back, we'll be back, we'll be back," she said, shouting at top volume. "I guarantee you they will take a woman. It's only a matter of time."

Burk again reclaimed the mike, and giggling at her friend's intensity, said, "Does anyone doubt it after that?"

Burk then shifted gears. "I'd like to ask Sheriff Strength, if he's within earshot, about something: Sheriff, the abortion clinic here in Augusta is protested against regularly. Are you going to send the antiabortion forces a half-mile away from the clinic? Fair is fair. Put 'em where they cannot be seen and they cannot be heard. Oh, and have they ever applied for a permit? We have been identified as an illegal group if there are two or more of us in front of the club. I challenge Ronnie Strength to apply that standard to the protesters who show up regularly to curtail women's rights at the clinic here in Augusta."

Just as Burk finished that sentence, a man elbowed his way to the middle of the crowd in front of the stage and began shouting "Wooooo-hooooooo!" He was waving a large, bright orange sign that read MAKE ME

DINNER on one side and IRON MY SHIRT on the other. Soon he began yelling the slogans on his sign, plus the utterly confounding "Oprah rules!"

For a moment Burk tried to ignore the disruption. Finally, she looked at him and said, "Do my dishes!" a pretty snappy comeback, all things considered. In short order a sheriff's deputy put a hand on the man's shoulder and led him to the periphery of the crowd, where a pack of two dozen reporters encircled him. He said his name was Heywood "HA-Blowm," the first syllable of his last name pronounced with a hard, guttural inflection. ("I gave it a little Hebrew accent," the man would later tell me. "I don't know where I was going with that.") Reporters asked the spelling and he obliged: H-E-Y-W-O-O-D J-A-B-L-O-M-E. Upon seeing the name in writing, some of the scribes smirked and rolled their eyes. This was an old school-yard prank; naughty boys pronounce the name "Hey wouldja blow me?"

However, not every reporter in the Pit seemed in on the joke, and there was little time to press Heywood on his bio. After only a couple of questions, Richmond County deputy sheriff Danny Clark broke through the circle of reporters and growled, "I asked you nicely already. Let's go. Now." Clark grabbed the man by the elbow and escorted him to the other side of the Pit, where the counterprotesters had been banished. Heywood briskly marched across the Pit and disappeared from sight. Puffed up like a peacock, Deputy Clark then fielded a few questions. "Freedom of speech is nice, but you have to do it where it's appropriate," he said, perfectly distilling the Strength doctrine. "If he wants to express himself, he can go over there with the rest of them."

Back on stage, Burk was saying, "Very shortly we're going to be joined by a very special representative of Augusta National Incorporated. He's right here behind us, and I'm sure he'll be glad to grant interviews."

She then introduced Janice Mathers, the feisty Rainbow/PUSH representative who had also spoken in Atlanta. "This fight is not really about Augusta National as such," Mathers said. "It's really about power, prestige, influence and money in America and who gets access to it and who doesn't." As she continued to speak, there was a flurry of activity behind the stage. Behind Mathers a huge inflatable pink pig was beginning to rise, in the manner of the Sta-Puff Marshmallow Man. The pig, on loan from Ralph Nader, reached for the heavens, ultimately rising to a height of about twenty feet.

Ushering Mathers off the stage, Burk said, "My, my, my, those male chauvinist pigs of the seventies grew up to be the corporate pigs of today. And they're here to join us today. This is Augusta's representative today at the rally. We're so glad he could take time out from the sewing circle down the street." Plastered on the side of the pig were dozens of corporate logos. Burk began to tick them off: "CBS, Motorola, Coors, IBM, GE, Coca-Cola. . . . Speaking of Coca-Cola, I understand Judge Dudley Bowen is having a little party this morning. He had some guests over at his house, including a member of Coca-Cola's board of directors, former Georgia senator Sam Nunn, who also happens to be a member at Augusta National. From what I'm told Senator Nunn isn't the only member there, either. The judge is feeding them and he's talking to them. How about that?"

At this point Burk turned over the mike to Heidi Hartman, who was shouting over the strains of a piece of unidentifiable rap music. Hartman introduced what she called a battle between "the forces of good and evil." The KKK caricature had reappeared, and now there was a new prop, which looked like it had been sprung from a low-budget float in the Macy's Thanksgiving Day Parade. This was a fifteen-foot-tall puppet, made to look like a woman in an army uniform. Its arms were operated by the people hidden within. In short order the mega-puppet lumbered over to the KKK cutout and engaged in a mock fistfight, which, predictably, left the Klansman flat on its back. Hartman then shoved the microphone into the midsection of the army puppet and asked if it had anything to say.

"Just do it."

The crowd was mute. After all the headlines and hyperbole, had a great national debate really come to this? A sad little puppet show? The mind reeled.

After the Klan-on-a-stick was hauled off, Burk reemerged on stage to close the rally. She offered the Cliff Notes of her Atlanta speech, calling on CEOs who belonged to Augusta National to either declare their allegiance to sex discrimination or resign from the club. Pointing in the direction of Augusta National's front gates, she said, "They will open those doors up there to women. They know it and we all know it, because we are right, and we will prevail."

A protest nine months in the making finally came to an end.

The assembled reporters, who had grown docile with more than an hour of speeches under a hot, muggy sun, stormed the back of the stage to ask Burk questions, off microphone. One of the first queries was what she made of the crowd.

"I think the turnout is great given that we learned at the last minute that our opposition had actually paid people to sign up for our buses and then be no-shows," she said, provocatively. "They laid out thousands of dollars—we did the math—and you would be astounded at how much they spent to suppress our turnout. We know the people of America are with us. Thank god Ronnie Strength did not suppress the numbers of the press. We still have freedom of the press, and we're really glad to have you here.

"Will I walk in front of the club today? No. I will walk in front of the club when I can enter the front gate as an equal and not until then."

As Burk continued to field questions, Allison Greene swung into action. The founder of Women Against Martha Burk had endured all the speech making from a corner of the Pit, where she stood cradling a thick stack of petitions, wrapped with a satin bow. Greene had gathered nearly two thousand signatures on her petition denouncing Burk. Some had written comments in the margins, such as "Get a real job, Martha!" One social worker invited Burk to "follow me around for a day to see the real issues facing women today."

Greene cut to the back of the stage to confront Burk. "Martha was talking to reporters, as always, and I kind of snuck up next to her," Greene says. "I caught her eye and said, 'Here, these are for you.' She was hesitant. She didn't really know what was happening. I kinda shoved the petitions at her and said, 'Take this.' She said, kinda icy, 'I'll take it later.' I mean, it was just a stack of papers. It wasn't a bomb or anything. But her security guard had her by the arm, and he turned her body away from me. Now I'm getting upset. I yelled, 'Martha, you owe it to me and the women of Augusta to take these petitions.' She just gave me an eat-shit-and-die look. Then she was whisked away by security and I was just left standing there.

"Some scraggly old guy came up to me and introduced himself as her husband and said, 'Why don't you explain your petition to me.' I started telling him and he cut me off with some B.S. rambling about how I didn't really understand the issues and that I was oppressed and didn't even know it. I will tell you, now I was getting pretty upset. Then that Alice [Cohan] woman came up to see what was going on. I just kind of shoved the petitions at her and said, 'Take this.' I said, 'You say you speak for women, but you're afraid to even hear what we have to say.' She took the petitions, but I was watching her closely, and a couple of minutes later she threw our petitions onto a stack of their protest signs, which were being piled onto the bus. On one hand, I was outraged that she thought so little of the women of Augusta. But I also want to believe that someone, somewhere took the time to read through the petitions, and that somehow our voices were heard."

After bidding adieu to the reporters, Burk was escorted to her SUV with a beefy security guard on each elbow. A dozen or more camera crews and print reporters followed. It looked like a youth soccer game—a clump of people moving en masse in a circle, occasionally kicking each other. Clearly the sexiest story to come out of the rally was Burk's nebulous allegations of chicanery involving the Atlanta bus, and throughout the walk across the Pit and while fielding questions from the passenger-side window of her SUV, she was pressed to provide more details. Asked how many people had been bumped from the bus, she said, "We have no idea. But we had quite a few more people booked for the bus than actually showed up."

Was Augusta National behind the subterfuge?

"We know who it was—it was the Heritage Foundation in Washington, D.C. They're related, we think. We know philosophically that they're related through the club's consultant, Jim McCarthy."

At that very moment, McCarthy was skulking around the periphery of the Pit, cutting a distinctive figure in chunky white tennis shoes, baggy beige slacks, a blue blazer, and dark sunglasses. Moments after Burk drove away, he convened an impromptu press conference for a dozen reporters under an oak tree behind Burk's stage. McCarthy introduced himself as a consultant to Augusta National and then launched into a monologue, declaring the protest "nothing short of an embarrassment.

The numbers speak for themselves. For months Martha Burk has been threatening thousands of protesters, and yet she was outnumbered eight to one by the media. When it came time for America to show their support, apparently there was none." McCarthy was radiating a kinetic energy, his hand shaking furiously in his pocket. "Where's the motorcycle gang she promised? Where's the hordes of coeds on spring break? Where are the burkas?"

When he stopped to catch his breath, the first question was about the plot to undermine attendance on the Atlanta buses.

"I have no idea what she's talking about," McCarthy sniffed. "I'm not going to dignify that with a response."

Bob Kravitz of *The Indianapolis Star* then asked a blunt question: "Why are you even here?"

"Because you're here," McCarthy said. "It obviously deserves a response."

Perhaps sensing a building antagonism, McCarthy abruptly cut off the press conference and walked away, chased by an assistant.

This was the first time the vast majority of the reporters had met McCarthy face-to-face, including the diehards who had been tracking the story for months. Kravitz's description in the *Star*: ". . . he looked like he came from Central Casting. Remember the Martin Short character, the paranoid, chain-smoking corporate spokesman from *Saturday Night Live*? McCarthy would have been more believable if he'd been the Iraqi minister." Teri Thompson of the *Daily News* immediately dubbed McCarthy "Poindexter," while *The Atlanta Journal-Constitution*'s Glenn Sheeley, still smarting from McCarthy's nasty fan mail months earlier, said, "He looked like Bill Buckley's illegitimate son. Talk about a super-dweeb."

McCarthy, circling the Pit, was immune to the put-downs from his adversaries, and moments after breaking away from the first batch of reporters, he stopped to speak to a couple of TV news crews.

"It has been obvious from the very start that the American public regards this as a frivolous smear campaign and not a serious issue. The American public's disinterest, and in fact their hostility to Burk, has come across in polls, in letters to the editor, and in watercooler talk. People simply don't respond to this issue, and that's obvious today."

After that sound bite he again abruptly cut off the interview. He walked away with a purpose, but no destination. He kept traversing the Pit, apparently waiting for an opportune moment, or the right mix of reporters, to field more questions. Eventually McCarthy slowed a few paces from Washington Road, and a third scrum occurred. Again he was asked to explain his presence.

"The club felt that it was important that it has its views represented as well," he said. "Martha Burk's not the only one who has First Amendment rights."

Asked to comment on the crowd in the Pit, McCarthy loosed a memorable epigram. "Martha Burk created a media circus, so it's no surprise a few clowns were attracted to the spotlight."

As assorted volunteers began breaking down Burk's stage and gathering the related detritus (to the strains of Aretha Franklin's "Respect"), most of the remaining reporters migrated to the far end of the Pit to take another pass at the counterprotesters. Unsurprisingly, the Imperial Wizard drew the best crowd.

Earlier in the day the One Man Klan had actually attracted two helpers, a man and a woman who roared up on a Harley and sat behind the Wizard's makeshift booth, passing out flyers. Now they were long gone. ("I had never seen those people before in my life," the Wizard said later. "They seemed to enjoy having their picture taken, but I find it curious that I haven't heard from them since.") Throughout the day reporters had been baiting the Wizard, fueled by a palpable disappointment that he was in jeans and not a white robe. At one point he had been asked by the *Boston Herald*'s George Kimball, "So, when are you going to suit up?"

Now the Wizard was fending off the *Chicago Sun-Times*'s top columnist, Rick Telander. "Where's the white sheet," Telander asked.

"Would that make a difference?" the Wizard shot back.

Absolutely, Telander said, expressing his disappointment that the Wizard hadn't gone all the way with his accoutrements.

"You would look at the messenger and not the message," the Wizard said.

Telander rebutted that he had been waiting so long to see a real Klan outfit, and felt cheated. On that subject, he asked the Wizard where he gets his pointy-headed outfits.

Clearly the Wizard was being suckered, and yet he couldn't resist living down to Telander's expectations. "We make 'em ourselves," he said. This, of course, was poppycock. The Wizard did not have any silly white outfits, and in more reflective moments he had disparaged any Klansmen who would don this outdated costume. Now, in the Pit, with Telander bearing down on him, the Wizard turned to his dinner guest of four nights earlier—that is, an onlooker who knew the truth—and said, helplessly, "Don't say a word."

The Wizard's trial by fire was not yet over. Hard on Telander's heels came *Sports Illustrated*'s Rick Reilly, who writes a hugely popular column on the magazine's back page. Reilly continued the smirking line of questioning, until he was overcome by a moment of clarity.

Offended by one of the Wizard's homemade signs, which claimed that African Americans are responsible for 90 percent of the shoplifting in Georgia, Reilly asked the Wizard to supply evidence backing up the claim. The Wizard offered a sarcastic and somewhat nonsensical response, saying that if Reilly didn't understand the sign he oughta look up its meaning in a dictionary. This touched off a round of insults, and the air was alive with machismo. Says photographer Craig Jones, who witnessed the exchange, "Riles must've gotten a testosterone surge, because he was pumping his jewels the whole time. Had a notebook in one hand and his balls in the other, and he was just workin' it up and down and back and forth. I'm sure he didn't even know he was doing it, but it was hilarious."

As Reilly would write of the exchange, "I insinuated that [Harper's] IQ divided by his shoe size would equal one. He suggested I shut up. I told him I was glad to have met him, in that you don't often get to see the depths humans can achieve."

At this point the Wizard tried a little diplomacy.

"You wanna shake my hand?" he asked.

"No, but I'd like to spit in it," Reilly said.

"If you do, they'll have to get the law over here to pull me off you."

"Then you better pack a lunch, motherfucker, 'cause it'll take you all day."

A couple of Reilly's colleagues stepped in between him and the Wizard, and the confrontation fizzled.

Among onlookers there was a strong sense of disappointment that the day's only dustup had amounted to little more than a few sophomoric taunts. Says Chris Stanford, a cameraman on assignment for *Golf World* who witnessed the set to, "When I heard, 'Pack a lunch, motherfucker,' I got my camera ready. I'm thinking, big-time sportswriter, KKK, this picture could come in handy. It's too bad they didn't wind up rolling around in the dirt. I would have had the whole thing on film."

Moments after the showdown an edgy Reilly was pacing along Washington Road—though, it must be said, he was no longer clutching his genitals. "That was a mistake," said the eight-time national sportswriter of the year. "That shouldn't have happened. You can't let your personal feelings get in the way of the story. Even if you're interviewing Adolf Hitler you have to be professional. You can't become the story." (He would have a change of heart in front of his laptop.)

Asked later about the incident, Harper says, "I had no idea who that guy was. But I get that kind of stuff all the time. It's typical for somebody to lash out at the Klan. In this business you have to keep your cool, otherwise you wind up in jail. That's why I was trying to smooth things over. That's why I stuck out my hand."

Was he scared by Reilly's menacing tone?

"That cross-eyed, bug-eyed, pencil-necked, big-foreheaded, no-good chickenshit sonofabitch? Sheeee-it. I wish he had thrown the first punch. That woulda made my day."

It was after one o'clock when the Wizard had his dustup with Reilly. The Pit was nearly deserted, save for the law. Even the last stragglers among the reporters were drifting away. It was a funny time for the Wizard to decide to finally read the speech he had prepared. He was about two sentences in when he gave up. He sat down on his chair with a harrumph, done for the day. Within an hour the Imperial Wizard would be packed up and in his truck on the way back to Cordele, with three handguns for company. Later he would say, "I was having trouble with my bullhorn, which wouldn't stop squawking. Regardless, I said what I wanted to say. Whether people listened, that's up to them. It was certainly a unique day. Really, it was a circus. I always knew it would be. I was even going to bring cotton candy, but it was too much trouble. The thing is, the sillier it all was, the more it took away from what Martha was trying to do. So in that regard it was a success."

By two o'clock the Pit was empty, but the protests weren't over. A dozen representatives of Rainbow/PUSH were gathered at the intersection of Highland and Wheeler, standing on a small patch of dirt on the corner of the intersection. All that was separating them from an adjacent graveyard was a rusting chain-link fence. Kitty-corner from the protest site was the Wife Saver, the politically incorrect takeout restaurant that is an Augusta landmark.

The protest was purposefully low-key, consisting solely of this small band of dedicated demonstrators holding up signs for the passing motorists. Fronting the group was the Reverend Alexander Smith, a local religious leader and past president of the Augusta chapter of the NAACP. He looked less like a man of the cloth than a member of Parliament Funkadelic. Rev. Smith was turned out in a bright red jacket and a black wide-brimmed hat, and he was adorned with gold-rimmed glasses, gold-capped teeth, and a gold cane. From start to finish the protest lasted about half an hour, and afterward, while walking to his car, Rev. Smith said, "It was absolutely a success, because our voice has been heard in the struggle. Our feeling is that a threat to freedom anywhere is a threat to freedom everywhere. Whether one person stands up to say it is wrong or a million do, that is a victory."

Rainbow/PUSH's Janice Mathers was also on the scene, and she said, "It was important to bring this fight to a different segment of the community. As you can see, this is a residential area, a much more diverse part of town. Because it's quieter here, we were able to have some one-on-one interaction with the people of Augusta. We have talked to a handful of residents here who said they wanted to go to the other protest but they felt personally intimidated by the police presence. So it was important that we came to their community and let them know that we were here fighting on their behalf."

That statement had been made without any TV cameras, puppet shows, or absurdist counterprotesters. It's too bad almost no one saw the quiet dignity of the protest, but maybe that was the point. Burk's critics have charged that she is a media creation forever spoiling for attention. Far from the Pit, at the lonely intersection of Highland and Wheeler, a few dedicated protesters were happy to exercise their First Amendment rights without all the fuss. As he drove away Rev. Smith offered a two-finger salute—the peace sign—to the dozen or so cops who had gathered around the protest site.

LATE SATURDAY AFTERNOON, about the time the leaders at the Masters were descending into Amen Corner, Burk was reached on her cell phone. She immediately began spinning like a Phil Mickelson wedge shot. "We pretty much hit our number," she said. "We had 138 people, by our count. We had negotiated down to 150 with Sheriff Strength in order to get a better sound system. So we turned out exactly what we were permitted, give or take a dozen. How many did Todd Manzi have? A half-dozen? He was permitted for five hundred! How about the KKK? Only three! Well, shit, they lost a couple of zeroes. They were permitted for three hundred! Anyway, I never said that victory would be measured in numbers. We brought our message to Augusta, we have been heard all over the country."

Asked about McCarthy's pithy recap of who hadn't shown up, Burk said, "Some of our groups quietly made it known that they felt the green burkas would be an inappropriate symbol, given the war and the plight of women in Afghanistan, so we discouraged it. Motorcycle gangs? I have no idea what he's talking about. Oh, wait, Ralph is saying something here. . . . Apparently one of our members said something about a group of bikers many months ago, but it wasn't somebody we recruited. That's something kind of trivial from eight months ago. You know what, I don't care what McCarthy thinks. We delivered what we promised."

What about Elvis and the other silliness in the Pit—how will it effect how the protest is viewed?

"It depends on how you guys play it. Sideshows can be fun for a couple of sentences, but they shouldn't obscure the larger story. That's why I didn't walk down to the KKK. I didn't want our message to be compromised. That's why we did not march to the club gates. My getting arrested would have only muddled the message. As angry as I was about the civil liberties situation, it wasn't worth it."

So what's next? "We're going to take a deep breath, enjoy our victory here, and then maybe next week we'll have a board meeting and decide the next step in applying pressure on the membership."

THE LEADERBOARD was as glittering as usual heading into the final round of the Masters. Jeff Maggert was in the lead, at -5, but no one considered this overachieving veteran a serious threat to win, not with the superstars who were nipping at his heels: Mike Weir at -3, Vijay Singh and David Toms at -2, and Tiger Woods, Phil Mickelson, and Jose Maria Olazabal at -1. (Saturday morning Woods had pulled off a dramatic, scrambling par on his 36th hole to make the cut without a shot to spare, then stormed into contention with a dazzling third round 66 that leapfrogged him over thirty-eight players.)

But Sunday morning, the red numbers of the leaderboard were not the only scores being tallied. In newspapers across America, writers had weighed in on the protest, and a revealing little tidbit in the coverage was the number of demonstrators cited. Two of Burk's staunchest supporters came in with the highest estimates. Diane Pucin of the *L.A. Times* put the crowd at "about 100," while Johnette Howard in *Newsday* wrote that it was "no more than 90."

As Howard says in an interview, "I had been on the story for a while, so I knew who was who. For a lot of the reporters coming from the Augusta National pressroom, this was their first exposure to Burk and her people, so they might not have been able to tell the protesters from the onlookers. At the same time, I think people's biases came out in the coverage. To see some of my colleagues let their feelings on a particular issue affect something like a number was shocking to me."

The overwhelming majority of the reporters on the scene estimated the crowd of protesters to be around forty or fifty, or, as Tim Cowlishaw wrote in *The Dallas Morning News*, "This was the Million Woman March, give or take 999,950." Even among writers and news outlets who had been chasing Burk for months, the *Augusta Chronicle* cited "about 50" protesters, *The Washington Post* "roughly 40," and *The New York*

Times "about 40." The Associated Press opined that "even by the most generous accounts, [Burk] had 50 supporters," while *USA Today* said, "The 100-plus officers from the Richmond County Sheriff's Office ended up outnumbering Burk and her protesters by about 2 to 1."

No one took seriously Burk's claim of 138 protesters, or, for that matter, Jim McCarthy's estimate of eight reporters for every protester. (In scanning five dozen newspaper accounts, the consensus was that seventy-five to a hundred reporters had turned out.)

The significance of the actual number of demonstrators can be debated—Burk and McCarthy would do so for months—but its prominent placement in so many news accounts spoke to the effects of having sportswriters covering a story that had more to do with politics and sociology than golf. Scribes from the Metro desk are used to covering nuanced issues with outcomes that are difficult to quantify. Sportswriters reflexively need to report a score; the corollary is that there is always a winner and a loser on the sports page. Instead of seeing Burk's protest as just one component of a long campaign, it was treated by and large as a final, defining contest that had been preceded by nine months of buildup. It was, in other words, covered like the Super Bowl. It was easy for many reporters to decide who won the big game, especially with the protest juxtaposed against Hootie's impressive press conference of a few days earlier. In *The Kansas City Star*, Joe Posnanski wrote that Burk's protest was ". . . too pathetic to take seriously, too sad to mock, too poorly attended to call news, too screwy to ignore. . . . When the circus ended, everybody knew who had won. Nobody needed a scoreboard. It was a ridiculous afternoon. . . . It was a sad death for a cause. There is a very reasonable case to be made that Augusta National, as one of the beacons of golf, as a club that professes to be about the right things, should have women members. There is a very reasonable case to be made that the host of the Masters, golf's premier event, should not discriminate against more than 50 percent of the American population. This wasn't that case. This was a freak show."

In *The Washington Post*, Burk's hometown paper, Sally Jenkins wrote in her column, "Unsolicited advice for Burk: Rather than bemoan the cruel fact that you just can't make some folks invite you into their club, maybe the thing to do is simply get on with putting together the shattered pieces of your life." Ouch.

Burk had returned home to Washington by Sunday, and she was incredulous at much of the news coverage. "Everyone was so focused on the numbers," she says. "Augusta National spun it that the protest failed, therefore the issues weren't relevant. They're nuts. The protest was a footnote. It has no relationship to the larger story, to the issues. If all we cared about was getting numbers, then we could have sold this as an anti-war rally and hundreds of people would have turned up. But we didn't do that, because it was never about the numbers.

"From day one we said we wanted twelve people on either side of the entrance. That was what we really cared about. The two hundred that we were permitted for across the street were a bonus. People would like for me to feel like the protest was the apex of our efforts, but it was really just a footnote."

One of the few newspapers that displayed a broad perspective was *The New York Times*. However overzealous some of its previous coverage may have been, this time the self-styled paper of record offered a restrained, reflective take. Bill Pennington, who had been on the membership controversy story since the beginning, treated the protest not as a sideshow but as a legitimate news story, writing at the top of his piece, "Martha Burk—occasionally booed and jeered—vowed today to wage an unrelenting campaign to pressure Augusta National Golf Club to admit a woman as a member." He went on to quote the best and feistiest passages of Burk's speech making, while also acknowledging, but not wallowing in, what he called "an eclectic mix, including an Elvis impersonator."

The vast majority of other accounts treated Burk and her message as a novelty and the other characters in the Pit as the real show. Writers employed an endless variety of turns of phrase to convey the day's vibe, from *The Orlando Sentinel*'s description of the "Monty Pythonesque parade," to the musings of Manuel Roig-Franzia, the *Washington Post* reporter charged with writing the paper's news account, who called the protest an "often loony display with an acid edge."

The dominant imagery invoked to describe the protest was that of the circus and its scruffier cousins, the county fair and the carnival.

"Burk's Protest Has It All—Except a Bearded Lady" chortled the Cleveland *Plain-Dealer* in a headline.

"It was a counter-cultural county fair, except without the elephant ears and the kiddie rides," reported *The Indianapolis Star*.

"The only thing missing were clowns on stilts, dancing bears and elephants able to stand on small platforms," said *Florida Today*.

" . . . one Incredible Shrinking Head short of a carnival," was Selena Roberts's verdict in *The New York Times*.

"Missing was a cotton candy booth and a large group of supporters for Martha Burk," said the *Chicago Tribune*.

"The scene had everything except a trapeze, a ringmaster—and Burk supporters, for that matter," said the *South Florida Sun-Sentinel*.

One of the most interesting aspects of the coverage was the self-loathing that crept into some newspapers. So many reporters had invested so much time and energy telling Burk's side of the story that they seemed to feel betrayed by the sparse turnout and the silly props she had introduced. Ian O'Connor, the columnist for the *Journal News* in Westchester County, New York, had for months been a boisterous honk for Burk, and a handful of his diatribes had been picked up by *USA Today*. In the wake of the protest O'Connor inverted a line that Jimmy Cannon had once used to describe Joe Louis: "Never have I been more embarrassed by my race," O'Connor wrote. "The human race."

Bill Livingston, in *The Plain Dealer*, wrote, "Let's get this upfront: If we in the media are going to cover events like this and thereby legitimize them, we ought to have the decency to say we're sorry we did. . . ."

Another thread that ran through the patchwork of stories was incredulity toward Burk's accusations of sabotage. Kansas City's Posnanski wrote, "Martha Burk had assured everyone that there would be hundreds of protestors. Twenty walked off the bus from Atlanta. Maybe there were 30 others. Maybe. All this led an embarrassed Burk to charge, somewhat pathetically, that the right-wing organization The Heritage Foundation had played some dirty tricks. 'I understand Mrs. Burk had a bad day,' said Chris Kennedy, a spokesman for THF. 'I understand that when it all didn't go like she thought she immediately turned to the vast right-wing conspiracy theory. . . . Sadly, I cannot say we had anything to do with the problems she had.' "

In the *Journal News*, Heritage Foundation spokeswoman Khristine Bershers said of the allegations, "That's absolutely ridiculous. Nobody here has ever heard of Jim McCarthy. Does Martha Burk even know what we do? We're focusing on the war effort right now."

In the end the Heritage affair was an intriguing subplot that was never satisfactorily resolved. Burk's allegations were printed without her offering any evidence, the foundation issued blanket denials, and reporters simply let the story die. The truth may have been out there, but no one bothered to seek it out.

Careless reporting also led to some embarrassment regarding one Heywood Jablome. In Sunday's *Charleston Post and Courier*, James Scott had filed a 1,100-word story about the protest, which appeared on page 9C. Near the bottom of the piece, 200,000 readers were told, "At no point did the protest turn violent, though officers escorted Heywood Jablome away after he held up a sign directly in front of Burk that read 'Make me dinner' before shouting 'Oprah rules.' " Within days, scores of scolding reader e-mails and letters would begin pouring in. A Nexis sweep of every newspaper in America reveals that over one hundred papers mentioned the incident, but Scott was the only reporter who used the obviously fictitious name of the jokester holding the sign. (A few accounts called him simply "Heywood.")

The only thing that spared *USA Today* a full-blown Jablome incident was its lack of a weekend edition. Michael McCarthy produced a long piece for the paper's Web site, which posted late Saturday night. Sunday morning is always a sleepy time around the Augusta National pressroom, as heavy-lidded reporters are just getting settled in for the long, stressful day ahead. Many of the scribes had started their workday by surfing the Web, reading one another's work on the protest. Deep in McCarthy's story he wrote, "Heywood Joblome [sic], a resident of Atlanta, jumped up and down with a sign reading MAKE MY DINNER on one side and IRON MY SHIRT on the other, while gleefully yelling, 'Whooh-hooh!' The police escorted him away. . . ." That Heywood Jablome was gracing the Web site of the country's largest newspaper produced giddy disbelief in the Augusta National pressroom. Reporters were shouting across the aisles to their buddies to check out the gaffe, and some scrambled to print out a copy of the story for posterity. Word got back to *USA Today* in a hurry, and by one-thirteen P.M. the story had been updated, with Heywood's name being replaced by "a man." Still, Jablome jokes would ripple through the pressroom for the rest of the day and night. (In the wee hours, a prankster commandeered the PA system and announced that any available USA Today reporter should report to the front desk to receive a guest—Mr. Heywood Jablome, of course.)

Sunday at the Masters, Rick Reilly batted out his column for Sports Illustrated, referring with some embarrassment to his "misadventure" in confronting J. J. Harper. "Nobody was arrested," Reilly wrote of the protest. "In fact, there was only one near fight, and that involved the knucklehead pictured at the top of this page. . . ." The sharpest comments in his piece were reserved for CBS. The Tiffany Network offered more than four hours of coverage on both Saturday and Sunday but, as expected, didn't provide a single word or image on the protest that had occurred across the street. As Reilly wrote, "What's amazing is that CBS still didn't find time to cover a protest featuring an Elvis impersonator . . . the KKK and a 20-foot tall inflated pink pig, all of it happening on Saturday not 100 yards from the network's compound of trailers and production trucks. Maybe CBS had consulted Iraqi Minister of Information Saeed al-Sahhaf. Protest? There is no protest going on!"

The folks at CBS read an endless number of these kind of critiques, but in the aftermath of Burk's protest they were feeling vindicated, not that they could publicly crow about it. "We were accused of ostrichism and a lot worse, but maybe the rest of the media had their heads in the sand," said one of the network's top on-air talents, who would not speak for attribution. "Maybe we had it right from the very beginning, treating this like the non-issue that it turned out to be. I mean, the number of protesters was in single digits. In the end, I think the events of Masters week brought vindication that CBS did the responsible thing. This entire thing from start to finish was an amazing case study on a media feeding frenzy, and I'm proud that we did not participate in the spectacle."

BY THE TIME the leaders teed off near three o'clock on Sunday, a sense of relief could be felt around Augusta National. The golf could now take center stage at the most anticipated Masters in history.

As the action had moved to the back nine, the Masters had become a two-man play, between lovable, late-blooming veteran Len Mattiace and scrappy Canuck Mike Weir. Mattiace, who had earned the first two victories of his career in 2002 at the ripe age of thirty-five, began the day at even par, five strokes off the lead and three behind Weir, and he went out and played the round of his life. He birdied two early holes to tiptoe into contention, but it was on the 8th hole that it became clear something magical was happening. Mattiace made a mess of this straightforward par-5, and after three shots he was still stuck in the left rough, about sixty yards short of the green, with towering mounds blocking his view of the pin. Mattiace somehow holed out this impossible pitch for a birdie, and thereafter he floated around Augusta National wearing an endearing perma-smile. When he rolled in a sixty-foot bomb on the 10th hole for another birdie, the crowd was his, and the rousing support propelled him into Amen Corner. On the par-5 13th he stiffed a four-wood for an eagle that gave him the lead, and then followed with back-to-back birdies on the watery 15th and 16th holes, where so many Masters have been lost.

So Mike Weir was three down playing Amen Corner, but he never stopped fighting, not surprising for a kid who had grown up a hard-nosed hockey player in Ontario. Like Mattiace, he had taken a circuitous route to success, having survived five trips to the PGA Tour's Qualifying Tournament. Throughout his struggles, and even more so during the success that followed, Weir had displayed an uncommon grace dealing with the burden that comes with being "Canada's Tiger Woods," as heavy-breathing newspapermen like to call him. Handsome, well-spoken, a dedicated family man, he was on the verge of becoming a star below the forty-fifth parallel. All he needed was one big win, and he took a step in that direction by holing a must-make fifteen-footer for birdie on the testy 13th hole to draw within two strokes of Mattiace, who by that point had reached the 18th tee.

One last birdie would almost surely secure the green jacket for Mattiace, but for the first time all day he seemed to flinch at the magnitude of what he was trying to achieve. He spun out of his final drive and lost it to the right, into the trees. His only play was to punch back into the fairway. From there he flushed his approach shot over the green, stubbed the ensuing chip, then wiggled a frightening downhill ten-footer into the side of the cup. His lone bogey left him with a 65 and a one-stroke advantage on Weir, who was playing the par-5 15th, his last good birdie chance. From ninety-one yards he played a brilliant shot, spinning a sand wedge to within four feet. Birdie. Tie ball game.

Now all Weir had to do was play the final three holes knowing that one lone mistake could cost him the Masters. He looked like he might give it away on the 18th, when a tentative approach left him a forty-five-foot birdie putt. If he made it the green jacket was his, but all Weir really wanted was a two-putt to force a playoff. He left his lag a knee-knocking six feet short. "I wouldn't wish that last putt on anybody," he said later. "That's as nerve-wracking as it gets." He willed it into the hole.

The sudden-death playoff was anticlimactic. Mattiace pounded a perfect drive on the 10th hole, but found his ball in a hook lie on the sloping fairway and badly pulled his approach to the left of the green, where it skittered behind a tree. When Weir stuck his second shot on the green in perfect position below the hole, it was all over but the shouting. Mattiace still had a four-footer for a 6 when Weir tapped in for his 5.

After a long, sloppy hug with his wife on the 10th green, Weir was directed to a golf cart that would take him up the hill to receive his green jacket. Sitting in the cart, he finally let the emotion of the day pour out. He looked up and said, "Unbelievable," and then buried his face in his hands. He began to sob, and he clenched his teeth to stop it from happening again. Weir's father, Rich, wrapped his arms around his son from the backseat. "That's all right, Mike," his father said. "Let it all out. It's okay."

Later, in his champions press conference, Weir said, "It was just a gut-wrenching day. It was an incredible day. I can't ask for anything more. Once it all soaks in I'll realize how special it is."

Weir wasn't the only one overcome with emotion. Following the final round Mattiace tried to address reporters, but he began bawling so violently that his wife materialized to comfort him. "If you care and you really want it . . . it goes to your heart," Mattiace said. "The emotions come out. Today was by far a different feeling than [my previous] wins. The wins are great, don't get me wrong, but this was the most special I've ever felt."

Somehow, despite the rain and a noisy challenge to its very identity, the Masters had delivered once again. Sunday was riveting theater, featuring golf played at the highest level by two of the good guys of sport. (During their final rounds, Weir and Mattiace combined to make ten birdies, one eagle, and only one bogey.) Nearly 35 million Americans tuned in for the drama, making Sunday the third-most-watched telecast in Masters history. During the playoff, CBS commanded a robust 12.4 rating, meaning one in every eight TV viewers in America was transported to Augusta National.

At the end of a crazy, contentious, historic, and histrionic week, it was left to the newest Masters champion to provide a little perspective. "It's obviously been a little odd with a bunch of things going on outside the gates," Weir said, with typical understatement. "And with the weather and everything, it's just been a little bit of a hectic week. But I didn't pay much attention to that. I was here to play a golf tournament."

THERE ARE TWO green-jacket ceremonies at the Masters. Viewers at home must endure the painfully awkward presentation in the Butler Cabin, with its funeral home decor and claustrophobic vibe. Far more majestic is the ceremony that follows, a pleasure reserved only for those at Augusta National. Thousands of fans gather around the practice putting green above the 18th hole, and in the magic hour before sunset, the light is always golden and the long shadows make for an evocative setting. Rows of chairs are set up on the practice green for assorted golf dignitaries, oh so dapper in their crested blazers. The crowd is always five deep on the veranda, while scores of members gather on the edge of the putting green. The brand-new champion and the man who preceded him are also on hand, as is the low amateur. In a tip of the hat to Bobby Jones, the amateur is celebrated with a nice-sized trophy.

The chairman of Augusta National always presides over the ceremony. With the sun fading on the 2003 Masters, he stepped to the microphone. "I'm Hootie Johnson, chairman of Augusta National Golf Cl—"

He never got to complete his sentence. Johnson's rich drawl was drowned out by a roar that would build and build into a deafening crescendo, lasting the better part of a minute. After nine months of being fussed about and too often demeaned, the people of Augusta finally had a chance to voice their support, and there was a visceral quality to all the shouting and clapping. Johnson couldn't swallow his grin, but when the hooting and hollering finally died down he betrayed no self-satisfaction, simply plowing on with his stultifying introductions of the dozens of officials on hand. Eventually Woods presented Weir with his green 42 regular, and then the new champ offered his heartfelt thanks to the fans for all of their support, and the club for its hospitality. With that, the sixty-seventh Masters was finally over.

One by one the assembled members of Augusta National headed home, passing beneath the celebrated back porch and through the iconic, antebellum clubhouse. Upstairs on the veranda, discreetly placed next to the door leading into the grillroom, there had been a brass plaque that for as long as anyone can remember carried a message so iconic it inspired a book of the same name: GENTLEMEN ONLY. For the 2003 Masters the plaque had been reworded with something more inclusive, proof that things change even at Augusta National. The allusion to gentlemen was long gone. Now the sign said, simply, GRILL ROOM. Martha Burk would have been pleased, had she gotten a glimpse.

TEN
Fallout

AN INCREDIBLE MASTERS WEEK had finally come and gone, but the controversy would continue to linger in the public mind. On April 14, the day after the tournament ended, David Letterman offered the "Top Ten Messages Left on Mike Weir's Answering Machine." Among the items:

"This is the Canadian Golf Hall of Fame. Want to be our first member?"

"This is President Bush. Today you made all of us proud to be Canadian."

"Hootie Johnson here. Victory dinner is on me—but don't bring your wife."

THE FRENETIC PACE of Masters week had left some of the most interesting subplots unresolved, including the intrigue surrounding the Heritage Foundation and the bus that shuttled Martha Burk's freedom riders from Atlanta. Upon returning to Washington, D.C., Burk's assistant, Rebecca Menso, forwarded for further inspection a copy of the e-mail that had tipped off Burk to the subterfuge.

It was dated April 4. At the top of the page, in the e-mail header, the recipient's name and address had been redacted. In both the From and Reply To lines was the name Lisa De Pasquale. (At the bottom of the e-mail she was identified as a staffer of the Clare Booth Luce Policy Institute.) The Subject line read: "April 11 CWN—Paula Dobriansky of the U.S. Dept. of State." The e-mail was an invitation to the Conservative Women's Network monthly luncheon, cohosted by the Luce Policy Institute and the Heritage Foundation. The e-mail contained the details of the get-together: Dobriansky, the Under Secretary for Global Affairs, was to be the featured speaker on April 11, at the Heritage Foundation's headquarters on Massachusetts Avenue. At the bottom of the invitation, below De Pasquale's name, a "special notice" had been pasted:

> *Hi ladies. . . . I'm sure you are familiar with Martha Burk—the shakedown feminist who is going after the Augusta Golf Club. She is putting together a bus convoy to leave from D.C. on April 11th and go on down to Augusta to have a rally at the Augusta National on April 12.*
>
> *I am helping some friends in Georgia deep-six her little project. We need people to send in the attached registration form—and then simply not show up. About the easiest act of sabotage ever.*
>
> *We need all the ladies we can find for this adventure—I have a budget and can pay $75 to everyone who signs up—great opportunity for students, interns or other young ladies—besides ourselves of course.*
>
> *Registration form is right here: [URL cited]*
>
> *Please let me know if someone has sent the form in so that I can send them a check.*
>
> *Thanks so much!*
>
> *Kerri Houston*

Below her name, Houston had included a phone number with a 214 area code, which Burk, as a Texan, would have recognized as the Dallas area. On that voicemail, Houston identifies herself as being with Frontiers of Freedom, a Fairfax, Virgina, nonprofit organization that, according to its Web site, is dedicated to "advancing center-right principles . . . to protect private property rights, secure our national security, and promote sensible public policies critical to our country's liberty." The Heritage Foundation—the big, bad meanies who Burk alleged had ruined her protest—had nothing to do with Houston's plot, and Burk knew it all along.

In an interview shortly after the Masters, Houston said, "No organization was behind this. It was just a circle of friends. The Heritage Foundation had absolutely no connection." (She adds that she had never heard of Jim McCarthy, whom Burk also implicated in the plot.)

Says De Pasquale, "Kerri is a friend, so I just threw her notice on the invitation as a favor."

"Burk knew what was going on," Houston continues, "because one of her little minions called me in disguise after I sent the e-mail around. Right off the bat this woman started asking me about the money, and she asked me a lot of questions about why I was doing the sign-up and who was involved. She asked very specific questions, and I was honest with the answers. I made it clear I was acting on my own, not representing any formal groups. There was just something in her manner that made me suspicious, so while we were talking, I did a reverse phone lookup on her number. She was calling me from Martha's office! These people are just not very smart!"

Burk confirms the broad strokes of Houston's account, saying, "We saw the e-mail, and we had someone verify it by calling the number."

What motivated Houston to perform her mischievous act of civil disobedience? "I disagree with everything that comes out of Martha Burk's mouth," she says. "I just felt like if she has a right to disrupt the Masters, then I had a right to disrupt her rally."

As for the numbers involved, Houston says, "Probably a couple of dozen people signed up from D.C. A handful more from Atlanta. There may have been a few more from other places. I know I only cut seven or eight checks. It wasn't about the money for most of the people, it was about what a buffoon Martha Burk is, and this was a small way to try to shut her up." Houston, a divorced mother of two, paid the seventy-five dollar checks out of her own pocket. "I believe you have to put your money where your mouth is," she says.

Beyond a deep satisfaction, Houston didn't get much bang for her five or six hundred bucks. The thirty or so phantom protesters she rallied had no practical effect on the demonstration, despite Burk's protestations.

It's not as if Burk had turned away would-be demonstrators because she was convinced she wouldn't have space for them. There were thirty empty seats on the protest bus that left from Atlanta, and another bus was sent away that morning when it became clear it would not be needed. In the end, Burk may have actually been helped by Houston's machinations, because she could blame a vast right-wing conspiracy for the low turnout on the demonstration. Then again, Burk ceded any moral high ground by playing fast and loose with the facts.

"What was most interesting about this episode was the abject, outright lie she told to the world at her protest," says Houston. "She blamed the Heritage Foundation, even when she knew through her friend that they were not involved in any way. Obviously it was better for her to blame a high-profile, very respected conservative organization than some little housewife in Dallas."

But this is pure spin too. Houston carries the impressive title of vice president of policy for Frontiers of Freedom, and on its Web site her bio describers her as "an expert in media, marketing, and external relations for public policy institutes." Among her former positions are national field director for the American Conservative Union, executive director of the State Policy Network, and director of external affairs for Dallas's Institute for Policy Innovation. According to the Web site, she is also a columnist for *Investor's Business Daily*, and her op-eds have appeared in *The Wall Street Journal*, *Washington Times*, *The Dallas Morning News*, *Forbes*, and "numerous other print, Internet and institutional publications." She is also said to have been a "frequent guest" on *Politically Incorrect with Bill Maher*. That's a pretty big résumé for a little housewife from Dallas.

Two days after the Masters, another mystery from the Pit was solved when *The Atlanta Journal-Constitution* outed a local shock jock named Rich Shertenlieb as the man who had claimed to be Heywood Jablome. Shertenlieb, it turns out, has built a cult following on the radio station 99X by pulling wonderfully sophomoric pranks while wired with recording equipment. (The *Journal-Constitution* noted that Shertenlieb was "once arrested for pretending to use a display toilet at a Buckhead Home Depot." He was acquitted of all charges.) Both Shertenlieb and his alter ego earned more notoriety a few days later, when James Scott wrote a mea culpa in the *Charleston Post and Courier*. Scott was the reporter who had cluelessly printed Heywood's full name as part of his story on the protest.

In a confessional that ran under the headline "Embarassing Lesson: Duped Reporter Learns the Hard Way," Scott wrote, "Unfortunately, I never actually heard the protester's name pronounced, just caught him spelling it out for other [reporters] and jotted it down in my notepad. I wrote the story for Sunday's paper . . . and blithely went about my life, unaware that this one name was about to make my own name known around the country.

"Proof of my unwanted celebrity lies in the seemingly countless messages—actually, there were 87 as of Friday, some from as far away as Washington state, Indiana and even Canada—that have cluttered my inbox, some simply questioning whether the name was real, others lecturing me and the newspaper for having missed what is, apparently, the oldest joke in the fifth grade."

It was a fitting footnote to the often controversial press coverage on the membership controversy.

Reached at the 99X studios, Shertenlieb was aglow from all the attention he was receiving, with even foreign media outlets such as the *London Sun* and *Irish Times* noting his stunt. All the chuckling over his pseudonym had validated for Shertenlieb the agonizing decision to go with that particular nom de prank; up until the last second, he was also considering Howie Feltersnatch and Jack Mehoff.

Shertenlieb had been inspired to crash the Augusta protest in part by an experience he had enjoyed a couple weeks earlier at another demonstration while on vacation in London with his wife. "We were there right when the war in Iraq broke out," he says. "We heard there was a peace rally in Hyde Park, so we thought we'd check it out. Well, this peace rally was basically an anti-America rally. There were signs of American flags with swastikas, cartoons of George Bush getting sodomized, stuff like that. I was really pretty offended. So I made this big sign that said 'America Rules' and walked right through the middle of the crowd, chanting it over and over.

"This pissed the crowd off pretty good. Some bloke grabbed a big ol' wooden pole and cracked me over the head, hooligan-style. I got knocked to the ground, my head was gushing blood, and my wife runs over, and she's like, Ohmygod, are you okay? I said, Okay? I'm more than okay! I just got the shit beat out of me at a peace rally, and I got it all on tape!" (Because one never knows when opportunities for sophisticated comedy may arise, Shertenlieb always has a tape recorder and mike on his person.)

Though he will surely be remembered as the pioneer who introduced *Jackass*-activism to the political landscape, Shertenlieb is quick to dismiss any suggestions that his stunt in Augusta had a larger meaning. "I guess you could say I was protesting on behalf of Hootie. Kinda. I do believe a private club has a right to be private. But really, I just wanted to mess with Martha. I love messing with people who need to be messed with."

THE MASTERS had been in the books all of two days when Hootie Johnson's diffidence was in the news again. In the April 15 *Atlanta Journal-Constitution*, Johnson was quoted in a Furman Bisher column saying, "There never will be a female member, six months after the Masters, a year, ten years, or ever." Later in the piece, he added, "There never has been, at any time, any consideration of Augusta National taking in women members."

Johnson had dropped these comments during a private get-together in his office toward the end of Masters week. "He asked me to come by so we could sit down and talk," Bisher says in an interview. "I'm well beyond the age of pursuing scoops, but sometimes things just fall into your lap." For Johnson, the noted backroom warrior, this requested coffee talk was hardly idle chatter with an acquaintance. At eighty-four, Bisher is the doyen of golf writers, and throughout the membership controversy he had been a fierce defender of the club. Johnson knew that Bisher would be happy to add an exclamation point to the chairman's perceived victory during Masters week, though only at the right moment. Bisher sat on his scoop for at least two days. "I had no intention of letting Hootie's comments overshadow the tournament itself," he says.

Johnson's remarks created the desired stir, though it was left to club spokesman Glenn Greenspan to try to spin a coherent explanation for Hootie's contradicting what he had said just a week earlier in his press conference, that there may come a day when women would be members at his club. "What the chairman has said all along is that the club will never respond to outside political pressure," Greenspan said. "In that kind of climate, the club will stand firm. I think the chairman's statement clearly underscores that position." Or not so clearly.

Regardless, Johnson's comments were significant, because they squelched forever the concept of "change from within." Those promises, from the likes of Lloyd Ward and Ken Chenault and Sandy Weill, had always seemed like a sham, and now Hootie had provided the confirmation. His declaration also deprived Burk's critics of one of their lamest laments, which had been circulating since the very beginning—that the club had been on the verge of adding women members, and she was actually slowing the timetable. (Justice O'Connor had long been part of that wish fulfillment.)

Burk was inevitably roused to comment on Johnson's comments, and, hard on the heels of her protest in the Pit, she sounded beat-down and defeated, which may have had something to do with an e-mailed death threat that had arrived at her office the same day Bisher's column appeared. As she told Len Shapiro in *The Washington Post*, breaking the sex barrier at Augusta National "didn't happen for a lot of years when there was no pressure, and if it didn't happen with pressure, then maybe it won't happen."

In *The Atlanta Journal-Constitution*, she emphasized that she had no further desire to joust with Johnson and that it was time to take the fight against all-male clubs "from our placards to our pocketbooks." Her goal was to move the issue "off the sports pages and onto the business pages." But even this declaration of resolve was tinged with fatalism. "My fifteen minutes may be up," Burk said, "but these issues are going to go on."

The blowback from Johnson's comments was minor. He was chastised in a few places for his gloating—the headline in the *Pittsburgh Post-Gazette* was "Augusta's Johnson Gets Last (Dumb) Word"—but within a couple of days the tempest had abated.

One of the few noteworthy pieces beyond Bisher's came from George Vecsey, but its placement was indicative of the waning interest, even among the true believers at *The New York Times*. While previous columns on Burk had been staples of the front page of Sports, Vecsey's thoughtful musings were consigned to the inside of the section. "Vox populi says Martha Burk failed because only 40 protesters showed up outside the Masters golf tournament last Saturday," he wrote. "Numbers, however, were never the goal. Burk got people talking. She got under their skin. She connected the dots between the club and its powerful members. That was the point.

"Not to compare one musty old-boy network to the civil rights movement, but back in the early '60s people proclaimed failure every time somebody got doused with ketchup and tossed into the street during a lunch-counter demonstration. What they overlooked was the process. Photographs of the civil rights demonstrations were distributed. The whole world was watching. Before long, Martin Luther King Jr. was preaching to millions at the mall in Washington. Golf is hardly civil rights, but telling a few truths is universal.

"Martha Burk served as a prophet. And we all know that prophets are not necessarily heard or respected in their time. They are seen as loonies or harpies. The public scolds."

In the week after the Masters there was a smattering of similar think pieces that tried to make sense of the disjointed Masters week. In *Golf World*, Ron Sirak offered one of the most cogent (and heavily comma'd) analyses: "Though it might be an overstatement to say Johnson has won his showdown with Burk, he has, for the time being, played her to a draw, and, for now at least, that means things at Augusta National stay the same, which was his goal all along."

As the club shut down in May for its long summer, the world at large seemed to have all but forgotten about Augusta National. Robinson Holloway, awakening with the dawn to scan the globe's newspapers for What They're Writing, says, "The silence was eerie. There were literally no articles for days on end. It was like people had washed their hands of the story entirely. I think it was the cumulative fatigue from having followed the story so closely for so long."

FIVE MONTHS AFTER the furor over the spiked Augusta National columns, *The New York Times* was again the subject—as opposed to the provider—of headlines. On May 2, a twenty-seven-year-old *Times* reporter named Jayson Blair resigned under pressure after a series of plagiarisms had come to light. Like so many of the subplots surrounding Hootie and Martha, the relationship between this singular event and Augusta National was not obvious at first, but the membership controversy would exert a profound influence on how the Blair affair played out.

On May 11, the *Times* produced an epic self-flagellation, having learned from the Augusta National column debacle that the best way to confront internal problems is transparently and head-on. In the case of the National, the only official statement was Gerald Boyd's curious internal memo, which was leaked to Jim Romenesko's blog. For the Blair affair the paper opened a vein on the front page, 7,200 words that sprawled across four broadsheet pages on the inside of section A. In the *Times*'s own account of Blair's misdeeds, executive editor Howell Raines was subtly fingered as the bad guy, for aggressively pushing for his young, unstable reporter to be given bigger, more pressure-packed assignments despite many warning signs.

What made the Blair story so explosive, and pushed it from the realm of journalism into sociology, was that the disgraced reporter was African American, and Raines acknowledged having forgiven his mounting transgressions in a personal act of affirmative action. "Our paper has a commitment to diversity, and by all accounts [Blair] appeared to be a promising young minority reporter," Raines told the newsroom staff in an emotionally charged confessional on May 14. "I believe in aggressively providing hiring and career opportunities for minorities. . . . Does that mean I personally favored Jayson? Not consciously. But you have a right to ask if I, as a white man from Alabama, with those convictions, gave him one chance too many by not stopping his appointment to the sniper team. When I look into my heart for the truth of that, the answer is yes."

The verdict at TimesWatch.org was simple, and brutal: Raines was a "guilty white liberal." Once again, the bloggers were ripping Raines for imposing his personal ideology on the business of the newspaper, with disastrous results. Says Sridhar Pappu, the *New York Observer*'s media writer, "Killing those Augusta columns was still in the minds of people when Jayson Blair came down. That kind of damage doesn't go away. The Augusta National debacle created momentum, where this backlash was building up and building up, and with Blair it just exploded."

Mickey Kaus at Kausfiles.com, Glenn Reynolds of InstaPundit.com, Jim Romenesko at poytner.org, and TimesWatch.org were among the many that led the online wilding. Kaus began calling Raines's embattled number two "Gerald 'Call It Journalism' Boyd," an explicit reference to his ill-fated Augusta National memo. Reynolds, in an interview, says, "9/11 is the world event that launched blogs. The *Times*' self-mutilation is the biggest event that ever happened to the medium."

Newsweek played the Blair affair on the cover of its May 26 issue. In the story it made an explicit connection between Augusta National and Raines's subsequent loss of the newsroom. "[S]taffers felt as if Raines led them on crusades, obsessing about stories—like the ban on women at the Augusta National Golf Club, host to the Masters—in a way that caused the paper to make news instead of break it. (Sources at the paper say Raines nominated the paper's Augusta coverage for a 2002 Pulitzer—which shocked some *Times* staffers, because the paper had come under fire for spiking two sports columns that took issue with the paper's editorial stance on the subject.)"

Three days into the scandal, the publisher of the *Times*, Arthur (Pinch) Sulzberger Jr. assured Raines that his job was safe. (Funny that a paper that made such sport of William Woodward Johnson's nickname is controlled by a guy who goes by Pinch.) But even with that vote of confidence, Raines's travails were far from over.

As MAY WORE ON, Raines and the *Times* remained under siege, riveting the self-obsessed media world, but in golf circles there was another sociological story to grapple with. On May 22, Annika Sorenstam, the LPGA star who ranks among the most dominant female athletes in the world, shot a solid 71 at the Bank of America Colonial, becoming the first woman to play in a PGA Tour event since Babe Didrikson Zaharias teed it up at the L.A. Open fifty-eight years earlier. Sorenstam was competing on a sponsor's exemption from Hootie Johnson's old employer, Bank of America, which had earned a spot in the NCWO's Hall of Hypocrisy because its chief financial officer and vice chair of the board, James H. Hance, is a member at Augusta National, as is Kenneth Lewis, the CEO.

In the year of Martha Burk it was impossible not to see the Colonial as another battle in the gender wars. In *USA Today*, Christine Brennan wrote, "For the masses, this is as good as it gets in sports: the boys against the girl. It's Hootie vs. Martha, only better, because it's not about press conferences and protests. No, this time, we get real competition."

Counterintuitively, Burk was one of Sorenstam's detractors; in the run up to the Colonial, one of Martha's quotes was widely circulated: "For an individual player to challenge herself is an interesting sidebar. But in the broader sense, I am not an advocate of integrating sports. It would destroy women's sports. What's the point of putting women at a natural disadvantage? We're not idiots; we know there are physical differences between men and women."

That was about as heated as the rhetoric had been on Sorenstam, in part because Tiger Woods had set the tone by immediately coming out as a vigorous supporter. (They share the same IMG agent.) There was also something of a post-Masters hangover. After all the shouting about Augusta National's membership, it was hard to summon the same passion for an issue that had fewer shades of gray. But a week before the tournament, the fur started to fly when one of the top players on the PGA Tour, Vijay Singh, was quoted by the AP saying, "I hope she misses the cut. Why? Because she doesn't belong out here." Suddenly the ghosts of the Augusta National membership controversy were stirred. *The Atlanta Journal-Constitution* offered a cute little item: "Today's language lesson: Translated into English, Vijay Singh means Hootie Johnson."

Sorenstam floated above the fray, handling herself with the utmost class and discretion throughout the media frenzy of Colonial week. That she missed cut was irrelevant—Sorenstam's journey to the Tour was the feel-good story of the year in golf, and Burk couldn't resist trying to ride Sorenstam's coattails. On the day of the second round, she put out a statement offering perfunctory congratulations to Sorenstam, and then she got down to business: "It is unacceptable that the Bank of America, which will reap enormous financial benefit from Ms. Sorenstam's participation in the tournament, continues to support sex discrimination through memberships in Augusta National Golf Club held by its top officers and directors. It is clear that these corporate executives are willing to profit from Annika Sorenstam's talent and labor, but their membership send a very public message that they do not consider women their equals. The Bank of America should be ashamed for engaging in this blatant hypocrisy."

The tone of the statement was the wrong pitch for the rest of a giddy week, and most in the golf press were happy to ignore Burk's lament. However, there is some interesting evidence to augment her argument. Bloomberg News estimated at $20 million the value to Bank of America of all the publicity surrounding the Colonial. On the day of the first round, CNBC ran Sorenstam's real-time scores in the corner of the screen along with the fluttering numbers of the stock exchange. Bank of America's numbers were better than hers; the stock rose seventy-five cents a share, worth millions of dollars in market capitalization. The bank also enjoyed a bonanza of corporate schmoozing at the Colonial, as each day one thousand tickets were distributed to clients and employees, while fifty or so VIPs were doted on at a well-stocked skybox on the 13th hole. The day after the tournament forty "high worth" customers were allowed to play Colonial Country Club in its immaculate tournament condition.

One of the few media outlets that pursued the Bank of America–Augusta–Annika connection was *The New York Times*. Reporter Richard Sandomir called the club hoping to get Hootie Johnson's thoughts on the historic moment. "I have no idea if he watched," said club spokesman Glenn Greenspan. "But Annika has played here at least once or twice."

Those rounds were not media spectacles but rather relaxing strolls as the guest of a member. The moral? Women are welcome at Augusta National, so long as there isn't a lot of fuss.

TWO WEEKS AFTER Annika's debut at Colonial, Augusta National Inc. announced that, despite the lack of Masters sponsors and the money it had to shell out for the CBS telecast, it was donating $3.2 million to charity, to go along with $100,000 that had earlier been given to the September 11 Relief Fund. The $3.3 million total was identical to what the club had distributed in 2002. (From 1998 to 2003, Augusta National had donated nearly $19 million to various causes.)

The sexier part of the announcement was that the 2004 Masters telecast would also be commercial-free. "There were many aspects of this year's broadcast that were favorable," Hootie Johnson said in a statement. "The response from our TV viewers about the ability to watch strictly golf was very positive."

Apparently Johnson had meant it when he said during the 2003 Masters that the tournament could go without sponsors "indefinitely." (Though the financial hit trickled down to the fans, as it was announced at year's end that the cost of a four-day Masters badge would jump from $125 to $175 in 2004.) According to club spokesman Glenn Greenspan, Augusta National had unilaterally decided to do without commercials in '04. "We had no discussions with our past sponsors or any potential sponsors," he said. Of course, that's another way of saying that major corporations were still afraid to be associated with what had always been one of the premier events in sport.

Noticeably absent in the press coverage on the club's announcement was Martha Burk. In the two months since the Masters, she had kept a very low profile, save for her peripheral role in the debate surrounding Annika Sorenstam. Those who thought Burk had fallen off the end of the Earth were pretty close to being correct. In its story about the commercial-free Masters, the AP reported that, "Burk could not be reached for comment. A message on her cell phone said she was on vacation in the Galapagos Islands."

By the time the National announced its charitable donations, the city of Augusta had also had the chance to balance its books from Masters week. According to the *Augusta Chronicle*, Richmond County taxpayers would have to kick down $9,889.84 for overtime pay to fifty-three sheriff's deputies who were called in to police Martha Burk's protest. The paper added, "Richmond County picked up the tab for the lunch of every officer, provided water and sodas for them and rented several portable toilets for their use, adding several hundred more dollars to the protest price tag."

Mayor Young didn't seem particularly put out, saying, "What would the cost have been had we done nothing and somebody got hurt? This country has been subsidizing free speech for two hundred years. That we have a bill for this weekend should not come as a surprise to anybody."

The costs to the local economy were harder to calculate. As had been predicted, some sectors flourished, while others wilted. "I heard hotel occupancy was up 20 percent this year. I know there was a lot of activity on the secondary market for badges," the mayor said in an interview, invoking the accepted euphemism for scalping. "We attracted a different type of patron this year—not the big corporations with the $100-a-plate catered dinners, but more people who were coming on their own, or in small groups, maybe for the first time. Put it another way—it was middle managers, not CEOs. I think this was not so much about the protests but rather the state of the economy."

In the end, IBM, J. P. Morgan, Coca-Cola, Citigroup, American Express, and Lucent Technologies were among the large corporations that canceled their entertaining or scaled back significantly. Not surprisingly, top executives from each of these companies are members of Augusta National, and they were no doubt concerned about appearances. Burk was happy to take credit for the downsized corporate spending. "I think the economy only affects this kind of entertainment at the margins," she said. "For them to stay away altogether, I think it's us."

Whether out of stubbornness or because of deeper insight, the local business community was unwilling to concede the point. "It was an economic thing," said Kevin Goldsmith, owner of the Pullman Hall catering services, noting the timing of the war in Iraq as well as a depressed stock market. "I don't think it was Martha Burk at all."

Terry Wick, owner of Events & More, an event-planning company, adds, "Last year was actually a worse drop-off than this year. We had clients that lost people on September 11 who said their company felt like they shouldn't be entertaining."

It has been estimated that Masters week has an economic impact of $100 million on Augusta. The biggest loser this time around dealt in much smaller numbers. Todd Manzi, who had created TheBurkStops Here.com to voice his opposition to Burk's ideology and to push what he calls "backlash merchandise," wound up $25,000 in the red on his enterprise, enough to push his family to the precipice of financial ruin. "I went down in flames," he says. "I crashed and burned."

Two days of rain undoubtedly hurt sales during Masters week, though the market was always iffy for $38.95 polo shirts dedicated to Martha Burk. "I've boxes full of the shirts in my garage," Manzi says. "I don't even know how many. Probably a couple hundred. There are maybe three hundred dozen golf balls stacked up in there, too."

Hey, at least he has a lifetime supply of balls for his personal use, right?

"I don't play golf."

Oh.

"At some point in the weeks before the Masters, it became obvious I was in too deep," Manzi says. "I came to terms with the fact that I was going to take a financial hit. What was far more depressing than losing the money was having the message completely ignored. When I came home, I read Bernard Goldberg's *Bias*, and I finally understood the forces at work against me. Too bad I hadn't read it six months earlier, right? I actually thought about doing a book about my experiences, which I was going to call *Extortion*, but my wife told me I'd have to call a divorce attorney first."

Manzi is candid that his entrepreneurial streak put a tremendous strain on his marriage. "We're still smoothing things over," he said in October 2003, in the same week that his Web sites were finally taken down. "When you put your family through something like this the damage doesn't just go away. Everything will be fine when I get back on my feet."

Despite the upheaval it wrought, TheBurkStopsHere.com is on the résumé Manzi has distributed across Las Vegas, where he moved with his family to pursue a sales job that wound up lasting just seven weeks. "Why not?" he says. "It was an experience, I'll say that. I learned so much that will help me in the future. The only downside is that they were expensive lessons. I got a Ph.D. from the School of Hard Knocks."

Manzi is no longer bitter about his experience on the fringe of the membership controversy. Mostly, he just misses the attention. "As a courtesy, I'm planning to contact some of the reporters in February [2004]," he says. "I'm sure at least a few of them are wondering, *Whatever* happened to the wacko? You know, what is that crazy guy up to these days?"

IT'S TOO BAD Augusta National doesn't use any of its charitable grants for out-of-work journalists; three days after the club gave away $3.2 million, Howell Raines was on the street. He resigned under pressure from the *Times* on June 6, joining Lloyd Ward as the second notable whose downfall could be traced to the Augusta National membership controversy.

Even the official version of events, printed on the front page of the *Times*, made the connection. In tracking how Raines had lost support at the paper, it said, "The *Times* also published dozens of articles, several on the front page, on Augusta National Golf Club's refusal to admit women. Critics accused the paper of lavishing resources on a story it had all but created. That criticism intensified after word got out that two sports columns about the issue had been rejected."

Raines's resignation rocked New York City and the larger media world. No one followed the melodrama more closely than *The Observer*'s Sridhar Pappu. He calls Raines's self-immolation "the biggest New York media story ever. There's nothing even close. You're talking about the most powerful media institution in the world going down in flames before your eyes, with the staff in full mutiny. This wasn't a once-in-a-generation story. It was once in a lifetime."

The bloggers had a high time celebrating their victory. Without them, "Howell Raines would still be running the place," Mickey Kaus crowed. Andrew Sullivan opined, "The blogosphere created a growing chorus of criticism that helped create public awareness of exactly what Raines was up to. . . . We did what journalists are supposed to do—and we did it to journalism itself."

Reading all of the postmortems with smug satisfaction was Jim McCarthy, who had been feeding Raines/Augusta material to high-profile bloggers for nearly a year. He called to gloat on the day Raines resigned. "Oh, I'm loving it," he said. "The piling on is the best part. I mean, this in an epic comeuppance."

"Did I play a part? I'd like to think so."

With so much bad mojo coming his way, Raines went deep under-cover after leaving the *Times*, giving only one interview to his friend Charlie Rose more than a month after the fact. In the late summer he agreed to be interviewed for this book, the second time he had spoken publicly.

Raines lives in a town house on a lovely, tree-lined street in Green-wich Village. A brass plaque next to the front door says "1836"—that's the year the place was built, not the address. His well-chronicled obses-sion with fishing is evident in the sunny front room, which is adorned with numerous depictions of fish in the artwork, in glossy photographs, even in the shape of matching ceramic lamps.

In person, Raines is the picture of southern gentility. He offers an ice water, then, after rooting around in the freezer, returns apologetically moments later with a lukewarm beverage. "We spent almost every day this summer in the country," he says, by way of an explanation. He keeps a house near the Delaware Water Gap, a legendary fishing spot.

So often depicted as a newsroom Napoleon, Raines is cordial and un-guarded in discussing Augusta National, saying at the outset, "Ask me anything you want." He remains unrepentant about the *Times*'s cover-age. Take, for instance, the controversial decision to submit the Augusta National package for Pulitzer consideration, despite the uproar sur-rounding the two spiked columns. "You've got to go with your strongest work," he says. "In that category, I thought the Augusta National cover-age stacked up as stronger on its merits in comparison to other potential entries in the national reporting category. One of the packages that it beat out, thank God, was the [Washington] sniper coverage [to which Jayson Blair was a heavy contributor]. And also, I wanted to make the statement that the *Times* is not in the business of being timorous. Thumbing my nose is too strong a term, but *The New York Times* is a paper that's not afraid to take on contentious subjects of social and eco-nomic significance, and in this case, we're proud that we did because I think a lot of people didn't understand the importance of the story, soci-ologically."

Asked how much the membership controversy coverage contributed to his untimely departure, Raines says, after a long pause, "In one sense, in a job like this, you only get so many mistakes." After another pause, he changes directions. "I went into this job as a change agent. I was trying to build a broader, more sophisticated, more eclectic kind of news report that would appeal to the most sophisticated single readership that's ever been assembled. And that's a risky business. Change is a risky business.

"I think Jayson Blair was a landmine. It was going to blow someone's leg off. Unfortunately, it was mine and Gerald's. But you know, I think the reaction among the staffers—some young and unseasoned, others older and set in their ways—was to the aggressive change of the newspaper. Reactionaries on the staff plus the complacent folks who just didn't like my style seized on the Blair episode as an opportunity to stop progress that, in my view, was essential to the future growth of the *Times*." With time to reflect, Raines remains convinced that the *Times* was fighting the good fight with its coverage on Augusta National, even as he acknowledges the mistakes in spiking the two columns. "I hope that the idea of covering sports beyond the scoreboard will become inculcated in the culture of the *Times*. And I think to some degree, it is. Sports journalism as it is practiced by newspapers has a long way to go. I don't know if [the coverage on Augusta National] pushed it forward or back. It was an attempt to cover sports in as rigorous a way as we would cover a corporate story or a diplomatic story. It's a multifaceted story. It's about money, it's about people, it's about society, it's about fairness."

To that list, he could have added that it also became a referendum on the media. Raines may be loath to admit it, but during his tenure as executive editor, he had a lot more in common with Hootie Johnson than a southern drawl: both were iconoclastic autocrats who ran powerful institutions with a singular vision. The difference is that two months after the most contentious Masters in history, Johnson's position looked more solid than ever, while Raines was gone fishing.

SIX DAYS AFTER the regime change at the *Times*, and three days after Augusta National announced its charitable donations, Congress again addressed the issues brought to the fore by the membership controversy. Along with Representative Brad Sherman of California, Representative Maloney introduced the Ending Tax Deductions for Discrimination Resolution, which was a proposal to prohibit the write-offs of business expenses at any discriminatory private club. It also proposed an end to tax deductions for advertising on broadcasts of events at discriminatory clubs. "This bill sends the message that we are not stopping at Augusta," said Maloney. "It is not about ending sexual discrimination at one club, it's about ending sexual discrimination everywhere."

Martha Burk, back from the Galapagos, was on Capitol Hill for the announcement of the resolution. Despite Maloney's remarks, Burk's focus was still trained on one club. "The recent announcement by Augusta National Golf Club that it has been unable to attract Masters sponsors for the second year in a row clearly indicates that responsible corporations do not want to be associated publicly with clubs that discriminate," Burk said. "But neither should they benefit privately from tax deductions for lavish entertainment expenses incurred by CEOs and their cronies for events at such clubs, which cost the American taxpayer." That cost was calculated by Congress's bipartisan Joint Committee on Taxation; it was estimated that over a ten-year period, beginning hypothetically in 2004, $52 million in tax revenue would be generated should Ending Tax Deductions be passed into law.

Sherman, who has headed the nation's second-largest tax agency, the California Board of Equalization, said, "This bill is modeled after a California statute that has been working since 1987. Business entertainment should not be conducted at clubs which discriminate. In California, a discriminatory club must print on its receipts 'Not Deductible for California Income Tax Purposes.' Surely, federal tax law would not give a deduction when a white male obtains a business advantage by using a business facility not available to his competitors."

The resolution picked up an endorsement in an *Atlanta Journal-Constitution* editorial, but it had its share of naysayers. Augusta National spokesman Glenn Greenspan put out the obligatory statement, saying, "The country has spoken on this issue and the fact is that they have rejected this pointless campaigning." The club got a more spirited defense in the *Journal-Constitution*, which, as a counterweight to the editorial, offered a piece by the writer Walter Reichert, who pointed out that donations made to the NCWO are tax deductible, even though the organization accepts only women's organizations. "Using Burk's flawed logic about tax deductions," Reichert wrote, "we can draw the conclusion that

Hootie Johnson, who is a taxpayer, is essentially paying for the campaign against himself and the policies of Augusta National."

One troubling aspect of the bill was buried in its wording: "There are over 3,000 private country clubs in the U.S. It is currently not known how many of these clubs discriminate against women. At least twenty-four male-only clubs have been identified in the popular press." It's anybody's guess how the law could be enforced when its authors are not even sure which clubs it would affect.

By late fall, the bill was stalled in the Ways and Means Committee. (Its cousin, Fair Play: Equal Access in Memberships, introduced by Maloney in March, was tied up in the Subcommittee on the Constitution within the Judiciary Committee.) Says Dan Maffei, the communications director for Ways and Means, "I can't imagine the Republicans moving that through committee or bringing it on the floor. I'd be very surprised if it moved anywhere."

THOUGH THE BILL'S FUTURE is uncertain at best, infiltrating Congress for a second time was the high point of an otherwise quiet summer for Burk. "I'm glad the frenzy has ended," she said in mid-July. "I can focus on the corporate initiative and not get bogged down in the golf aspect." In May she had sent letters to about fifty Augusta National members—"just the active CEOs" she says—asking them to clarify their support for the club in light of Hootie Johnson's declaration that a woman would "never" wear a green jacket. Two months later, Burk had not received a single reply.

Burk tried to put a positive spin on the post-Masters apathy, noting that she had recently appeared on NBC *Nightly News with Tom Brokaw* to talk about women in the military, and had done a couple of spots about Senator Hillary Clinton when the former first lady's autobiography came out. "It's gratifying that Augusta has raised my profile," Burk said. "It's nice that maybe now I'm in people's Rolodexes and they will call me about other things."

Burk did get some notice in the August 2003 issue of *Esquire*, but the story provided little gratification. Tom Chiarella, *Esquire's* resident golf writer, did a short piece about Cialis, a new competitor to Viagra that is reputed to have its desired effect for an exhausting twenty-four hours. Chiarella took the wonder drug for a test drive, but he picked a most unusual setting. "I timed the dose to peak when I was standing in a grassy field at the edge of the Martha Burk protest, surrounded by women of all sizes and opinions on the matter of male membership," he wrote. "Cialis stood well challenged, as there was no greater buzz kill in the entire nation at that very moment than that very spot. And yet the little yellow pill rose to the occasion: I did feel energized, awakening the priapic fourteen-year-old who still lives inside me. Still, I never got wood, because I simply chose not to. I knew there was nowhere for it to go."

This was the perfect postscript from a press corps that had celebrated Heywood Jablome, and Chiarella's performance served as an apt metaphor for Burk's campaign, which had gone limp in the months after the Masters.

IN LATE SEPTEMBER, Martha's old nemesis J. J. Harper, the Imperial Wizard, was back in the headlines. The One Man Klan was protesting again, and this time he brought a hundred friends—all of them African Americans from Atlanta's House of Prayer Church. This unholy union had joined forces on the courthouse steps in Winder, Georgia, to support the local county commission's decision to keep a framed parchment copy of the Ten Commandments on display in the courthouse, despite a legal challenge from the ACLU. As Harper explains, "I wasn't interested in helping the black people, but Christians have to stand together against oppression by the government."

At the rally, House of Prayer worshipper Trina Allen told the assembled crowd of 250, "I'm so glad the KKK stands for the ideals of our church." A church choir four dozen strong sang while the Imperial Wizard spoke. Waving a Bible, he drew shouts of "Amen!" when he said, "The founding fathers of this nation put the Ten Commandments in the courthouse." An Atlanta news channel covered the spectacle live via a helicopter, and *The Atlanta Journal-Constitution* played the story on the front page of the Metro section, with the cheeky lead, "It could have almost been a scene out of an old Mel Brooks movie."

Harper frequently flashed back to his Augusta experience while organizing the Ten Commandments protest. "Everybody gotta start somewhere," he says. "You learn as you go." After all the ridicule in the Pit, Harper clearly realized he was in need of an image overhaul. In Winder he looked like he had been spiffed up by a fashion consultant. (Does *Queer Eye for the Straight Guy* do hate groups?) Gone were the dumpy Wranglers and tennis shoes, in favor of black military fatigues with impressive-looking patches advertising his KKK and military backgrounds. He was also adorned with a beard and macho sideburns. Besides learning to dress the part, the Imperial Wizard applied some other knowledge gleaned from Augusta. "I found out how easy it is to manipulate the media," he says. "The average citizen complains about something like this Ten Commandments issue, no one listens. The KKK is the one doing the complaining, everybody starts listening. When black people and the Klan stand together, ain't nobody nowhere who don't know nothin' about it."

IN NOVEMBER, Fred Ridley was nominated for the presidency of the USGA, as had long been expected. The voting will take place at the USGA's annual meeting in February 2004, but it is a mere formality; at the end of that get-together Ridley will be sworn in as president of the organization he once called the "defender and promoter of public golf." In an interview for this book in the summer of 2003, Ridley had shied away from discussing the potentially thorny issue of his Augusta National membership, saying, "It's a little premature to talk about any issues surrounding the presidency. I haven't been nominated yet, and I don't want to speak hypothetically. Down the road, if I was to be nominated, then I would have more to say." Hey, no problem, we told Ridley—we'll wait for the nomination.

By the time it came, Ridley had apparently begun to understand how problematic it will be for him to preside over the rules and policies for every female golfer in this country while belonging to a private club that excludes them. Following his nomination, a phone call to Ridley's home was returned the next morning by the USGA's director of communications, Marty Parkes, who indicated that Ridley was now unwilling to talk.

Speaking of both Ridley and his vice president, Augusta National member Walter Driver, Parkes said, "They are both completely behind all of our programs for women, and that's the most important thing. Both have always been very supportive of what we have in place for women."

MARTHA BURK scored one last bit of publicity in the fall of 2003. This time the star of so many front-page exposés in *The New York Times* got barely one hundred words buried in the paper's "Sports Briefing" roundup in a corner of page 7 of the October 1 Sports section, on the occasion of Augusta National member John Reed being nominated as interim CEO at the New York Stock Exchange. In calling for his resignation, Burk told the *Times*, "The New York Stock Exchange appointed Mr. Reed to clean up its image and bring responsible leadership and accountability to the organization. No responsible leader would maintain a membership in a club that discriminates against women."

During Masters week, Burk had said that her goal was to take the membership controversy from the Sports section to the Business section, but it was instructive that the *Times* played its Reed item in Sports, even though it was his place in the business world that had made him newsworthy. Even at the *Times*, Burk's campaign was still seen narrowly as an issue affecting the host club of the Masters, rather than the larger struggle she so often pointed to.

Burk's press release received three sentences in the *Augusta Chronicle*, two in both *USA Today* and the *Los Angeles Times*. Reed was similarly dismissive. At his first press conference as interim CEO on October 2, he blew off the one Augusta National–related question. "It has nothing to do with my job at the exchange," he said.

Though the response was muted, at least Burk could be cheered that the press was still paying attention. She had often made the point that it was the media, not her, that was driving the membership controversy. A month before the Masters, at the height of Martha mania, the *Chicago Tribune* reported, "She has been quoted so extensively she has been accused of courting the media. She strongly denies the charge, maintaining that it was Augusta National's hard-line response to her initial letter that generated so much attention. 'I've never called a single media outlet,' Burk said. 'I'm reacting to the calls I get.' "

With the membership controversy well into its second year, the phones at the NCWO had gone dead, save the occasional query from *The New York Times*. Or so it seemed. "Actually, she called me about Reed," says Richard Sandomir, the *Times* reporter who typed up the Reed item. "She said she wanted to offer us an exclusive."

ELEVEN

Beyond Hootie & Martha

THE SUN WILL SHINE, the flowers will bloom, and the emerald fairways will be as perfectly groomed as a trophy wife—in short, the 2004 Masters will look like all of those that have come before it, though not to Martha Burk. "When people look at those pictures they're not going to be thinking . . . about how wonderful this is and what a great tradition it is and how fabulous this is for golf," she says. "They're going to be thinking this is a club run by a bunch of men who will do anything to keep women out. Until this is resolved, the tournament and the club are tainted. Period."

But is it really that cut and dried? Burk has her opinion, as does every other American. When the Associated Press surveyed 1,004 randomly chosen adults in November 2002, 46 percent said that as host of a very public golf tournament, Augusta National should be compelled to open its membership to women, while the exact same number felt that as a private club, the National was well within its rights to remain men-only.

What makes the membership controversy such a polarizing hot-button issue is that both sides are right. It is a binary argument. Does the Constitution give its blessing to Augusta National's membership practices? Without a doubt, and even Martha Burk concedes the point. As a guiding force in golf, presenting a tournament that is open to the world and broadcast on the public airwaves, in a sport in which every other important professional event in this country is governed by a non-discrimination policy, is Augusta National and its men-only stance anachronistic and old-fashioned and inappropriate? Absolutely.

It may not be possible to assign right and wrong to the two sides of the debate, but a related question is much easier to address: Who won the battle for the soul of Augusta National? The answer is, Everybody lost. The Augusta National membership controversy was a dirty bomb that rocked the golf world, with a toxic fallout that spread far beyond. The story was so big that all three branches of the government became embroiled, as the White House, Congress, and the Eleventh Circuit Court each weighed in. The staggering scope of the membership controversy can be measured by the cast of bold-faced names who were damaged along the way during a nine-month festival of schadenfreude.

The most powerful editor in America, *The New York Times*'s Howell Raines, resigned amid a firestorm of controversy in part because of Augusta National, as did one of this country's most prominent African American business leaders, Lloyd Ward. The world's most famous athlete, Tiger Woods, earned scorn for his dismissal of Augusta National's exclusionary practices, while his hero Jack Nicklaus was also diminished. Nicklaus continually pleaded that he was just another dues-paying green jacket powerless to affect change around Augusta, but when confronted with a matter of profound self-interest—the age limit for Masters champions—he and another iconic member, Arnold Palmer, twisted Hootie Johnson's arm so hard the ordinarily unyielding chairman reversed the policy.

Of course, Nicklaus's and Palmer's disingenuousness on the membership issues was common among the golf establishment. Former debate champion and current PGA Tour commissioner Tim Finchem retreated behind a stone wall of silence, all but acknowledging that the Tour's position—recognizing the Masters as an official tournament even as it flouts the Tour's non-discrimination policy for host clubs—is indefensible. The USGA nominated Augusta National member Fred Ridley president of an organization that has staked its reputation on embracing the public golfer. Should Ridley wish to discuss USGA business from behind the hedges of his private, male-only enclave, he can turn to his vice president, Walter Driver, another green jacket.

The membership controversy also had prime-time repercussions. Bryant Gumbel created a mini-scandal by failing to disclose his membership at all-male Burning Tree Golf Club, the kind of juicy conflict of interest that would make a good exposé on *Real Sports*. CBS—the network of Murrow and Cronkite—failed to mention the biggest golf story in years during its hours and hours of commercial-free coverage at the Masters, an absurd see-no-evil strategy that destroyed CBS's journalistic integrity but ensured that it would be rewarded with another one-year contract from Augusta National.

Did anyone come out a winner? Sheriff Ronald Strength developed a national profile as a rock-ribbed defender of the Augusta way, but his legacy remains in doubt. The emergency motion filed during Masters week by Burk and the ACLU to suspend Judge Bowen's joint rulings on the contested protest ordinance was denied by the Eleventh Circuit Court, but the formal appeal remains alive. Oral arguments were heard in November 2003; law.com's November 10 news story reported that, "During 50 minutes of lively oral arguments on Friday, a three-judge panel of the 11th U.S. Circuit Court of Appeals sounded far more sympathetic to Burk's legal argument than many Augusta National members have been to her women's rights claim. Judges R. Lanier Anderson III and Rosemary Barkett seemed particularly skeptical of the law, with Anderson saying it 'discriminates on the basis of subject matter.' " The court is expected to pass judgment in early 2004 on the constitutionality of the ordinance. Strength did not pass the law, but he came to embody it with his gleeful enforcement. Burk remains embittered about what she thinks was an unlawful censorship of her freedom of speech; if she is vindicated in court, it will be a sharp repudiation of Strength's tactics, and the politics that spawned them. (Of course, if Richmond County's protest ordinance is found to be unconstitutional, it will simply be rewritten, as the safety concerns surrounding Washington Road endure. Burk may win in court, but a protest at the front gates of Augusta National will almost certainly remain out of reach.)

Rich Shertenlieb and J. J. Harper both enjoyed a moment in the sun, however fleeting. But the biggest winner in the Augusta National sweepstakes was the club's public relations consultant Jim McCarthy, whose aggressive work was on display for the many Fortune 500 executives who are green jackets. Business has been so good since the 2003 Masters that McCarthy Communications has added three full-time staff members. "The clients I have picked up have all been keenly interested in the media strategy I did for Augusta National," McCarthy says. "They want to know the nuts and bolts of how I did it. How does the story go from Sandra Day O'Connor becoming a member to Howell Raines resigning in disgrace? They know it's not a coincidence.

"It's the first time I've done this kind of media criticism as part of an overall strategy for a client, and I don't know of any other PR firm that has done it. It's pretty cutting-edge. Big PR firms are like large corporations in that they have always been afraid to take on the press directly, because there is this belief that if you create an adversarial relationship, you will never be treated fairly again. But for a venerable institution like Augusta National to embrace that strategy, well, that has certainly opened some eyes. Now I'm trying to build media-crit-driven crisis management into a stand-alone business. Who knows? Maybe I'll be snapped up by a big, deep-pocketed PR firm."

In a story built on shifting perceptions and evolving public opinion, it is only fitting that a scheming PR flack would be one of the stars. But what about the legacies of the membership controversy's two primary protagonists, Hootie and Martha? Coming out of the 2003 Masters the widespread feeling was that Burk and her cause had been vanquished by the iron-willed chairman. The reality is far more complicated.

TO BE SURE, the tiny turnout at her Masters week protest was demoralizing for Burk, and the overall experience in Augusta has left her gun-shy about returning. In an e-mail from October 2003, she writes, "There are no plans as of yet for 2004. It was such a police state—greatly underreported in favor of Elvis, the KKK, et al—and a repeat would undoubtedly be marked by as much or more intimidation by law enforcement and the citizenry, which detracts from our message about the sex discrimination still blatantly practiced and condoned by the club. That's not to say there won't be plans, but I honestly don't know yet."

Since the 2003 Masters, Burk has struggled to generate any momentum for her campaign against the club. The corporate initiative has gone nowhere, and the NCWO's Web site has the feel of an online ghost town. More than eight months after the fact, the home page still carried a solicitation for protesters to join Burk's "rally for women's equality" at ten A.M. on April 12, 2003. Enjoying a rare lull during a frenetic Masters week, Burk's husband, Ralph Estes, had said, "Augusta National is really the power source here. It's like judo—you take someone else's power and turn it into your own. This really doesn't have much to do with golf and the Masters. It's a larger issue. We know this is gonna pass, and quickly. How do we take this capital and use it for our other issue? That's really the question." Burk had ruminated about trying to line up a television talk show, but for now that dream remains unrealized. In November 2003, she finally signed a book deal, with Scribner, to write *Cult of Power: What the Masters Controversy Means for the Women's Movement,* to be published in the spring of 2005. Burk had been talking about writing a book for over a year. Her agent, Peter Sawyer, deems the advance "substantial," but adds, "It was less than Martha wanted, and less than I wanted." He says the book "is really not going to be about the Masters. She'll touch on some of the details, but really the doorway to the club is symbolic of the ultimate glass ceiling. This is going to be a book about diversity issues. Martha doesn't want to rehash all of the gory details of her experiences in Augusta."

By the time the book is published Burk's future as the NCWO chair will have been resolved. Her term is up in December 2004 and she can seek reelection, but, she writes in an e-mail, "I haven't decided about that either." Post-Masters, there has been some grumbling in the ranks. Bishop Ima Jean Stewart, of the NCWO member group African American Women's Clergy Association, says, "I have always believed there are more meaningful issues, things that matter. Who cares about some little golf club in Georgia? I don't, and neither do the other women in my organization, and neither do a lot of other women [in the NCWO]. Get real. To make such a big fuss and then have none of our members turn out, well, that tells you how deep the support was, doesn't it?"

After attending the NCWO's bimonthly meeting in the early fall of 2003, Stewart said, "I felt some tension in the room. I don't know if

Martha is losing support or not, but there was an edginess there." However, Stewart emphasizes that Burk should have no trouble serving a second term as chair, if she so desires. Says Stewart, "You know the golden rule? She who has the gold makes all the rules? Well, NOW puts the most money into [the NCWO], and Martha gets along real well with those man-haters, so I don't think she has anything to worry about."

Whether or not Burk flies the flag of the NCWO, she will certainly continue her activism. But she will have to be judicious in picking her battles. Burk's inability to rally support on the membership issue may say less about her cause than about the disengaged citizenry. Only a few years ago a candidate for president received fewer votes than his opponent yet was sent to the White House by a state government apparatus run by his brother and a politicized Supreme Court. The electorate barely yawned, let alone rioted in the streets. With this malaise as a backdrop, Burk's experience with Augusta National has been deconstructed by some of our sharpest cultural critics, and the analysis is pessimistic. In the days after the 2003 Masters, Jon Stewart, the acidic host of *The Daily Show*, told *The New York Times*, "Liberals and conservatives are paradigms that mean nothing to anyone other than the media. Liberals were relevant when there was a giant cause to fight for [like] civil rights. They accomplished it so well that the only thing left for them to do now is to get women into Augusta."

In *Golf Digest*, of all places, the contrarian writer Camille Paglia criticized Burk's brand of feminism, writing, "The dragon ladies of the National Council of Women's Organizations . . . pose as rebels [but] they are smooth backstage operators in Washington's bureaucratic establishment. [Burk's] automatic archfeminist tactic of intimidation—humorless, peremptory, patronizing—made negotiation or compromise impossible. . . . As a libertarian Democrat, I oppose creeping encroachments on privacy and detest intrusive social engineering that reduces all human relationships to politics."

Jim McCarthy takes a macro view in critiquing Burk. "The activist community has become increasingly radicalized," he says. "The days of protesters buzzing around in Zodiacs trying to save the occasional whale are over. There are no more posters for baby seals. More and more, activists are not protesting against some minor part of your behavior but rather your fundamental existence. Greenpeace's beef with Exxon isn't about a specific environmental issue, it's antiglobalism, anticapitalism. In this new climate, compromise is utterly impossible. The targets are beginning to understand that the only way to survive is to fight fire with fire. They're becoming as aggressive as the activists, and the activists have very little understanding of how the landscape has changed. Nowhere is this more obvious than among the radical feminists. They are using the same tactics, and the same rhetoric, as they did twenty years ago. Their philosophy hasn't evolved, and they're getting left behind."

Burk remains undeterred by whatever criticism is thrown at her. If anything, it energizes her, because she takes it as proof of her effectiveness. Asked about polling data that questions the depth of her support, Burk says, "If James Meredith had taken a public opinion poll, he never would have walked up the steps of the University of Mississippi. If we did social progress by opinion polls, black people would still be slaves, the South would have seceded, women would not have the vote, and most civil rights laws would not have passed."

As Burk knows, perceptions evolve and legacies are subject to revision on complicated social issues. Case in point is the last great public spectacle that riveted the country on issues of sex, power, and discrimination: the 1991 Senate confirmation hearing of Clarence Thomas. The biggest roadblock on his path to the Supreme Court was the testimony of Anita Hill, who claimed that Thomas had sexually harassed her, charges he vehemently denied. There are interesting similarities between Thomas-Hill and Hootie-Martha. Despite the popular memory of their showdown, Thomas and Hill were never in the same room at the same time during the Senate hearings, just as Hootie and Martha have never met face-to-face. On the surface, both powerful men prevailed in their skirmishes; Clarence Thomas has a lifetime appointment to the nation's highest court, while Hootie Johnson remains enshrined as chairman of a club that is defiantly all-male. But the women in these battles still had a powerful effect, even as their reputations suffered. Over the first six months of 1992, the EEOC registered a 50 percent increase in sexual harassment claims, and it was Hill who overnight had made this an issue of national concern, one that is now felt and acknowledged in every workplace. Whatever Burk's tactical mistakes—suggesting that the Masters move to another course, playing the war card, staging a puppet show at the protest—there is no question that she, too, has single-handedly raised awareness, in this case shining a flashlight into a dark corner of the upper class where the men who literally run the world still feel comfortable gathering in a club that shuts out half of the population. When asked why he hadn't mentioned his Augusta National membership during his job interviews with the USOC, Lloyd Ward said candidly that it simply never occurred to him. Burk has certainly brought greater scrutiny to the propriety of all-male golf clubs in general and Augusta National in particular.

In an interview, Augusta National member Wheelock Whitney makes a joking reference to an event that took place "BMB—Before Martha Burk." She did indeed usher in a new epoch. BMB, Augusta National was among the most coveted status symbols of the ruling class, so elite and exclusive that the richest man in the world couldn't buy his way in, as Bill Gates famously had to lobby for years before he was asked to join. President Eisenhower's club was such a refuge for the powerful that in October 1983, President Ronald Reagan stayed at the club along with Treasury Secretary Donald Regan as guests of green jacket George Shultz, the secretary of state; when they weren't playing golf, Reagan and Shultz planned the invasion of Grenada. Now, because of Burk, the green jacket has been stigmatized to the point that cabinet nominees feel compelled to resign from the club. This is all because of Burk.

Of course, Hootie Johnson played a part too. It's a chicken-egg question: Who really deserves the credit (or blame) for sparking the membership controversy? Was it Martha Burk, who started it all with a short, private letter, or Hootie Johnson, who created so much interest with his very public reaction? Had Johnson not responded to her letter, Burk says, "I would have called and left a message, and I would have kept trying." No doubt, but who would have known? What began with nine sentences on NCWO letterhead became the biggest golf story since Tiger Woods made the scene. She never could have done it without Hootie.

As the whole messy tale has played out, many, if not most, Americans have embraced Johnson as a hero for protecting the sacred values of privacy and freedom of association. But to a significant percentage of the population, Johnson will forever represent intolerance and discrimination. As such, he has tarnished the image of golf along with that of Augusta National. Johnson talks often about making a positive contribution to the game. But as a recreational sport, golf is slowly dying. Participation numbers have flat-lined, despite population growth and the popularity of Woods; numerous courses are in financial distress. If golf is to thrive in this country, it will have to be because of women; presently they make up only 22 percent of the nation's golfers, and thus as a group they offer the greatest potential for growth. But whatever the nuances of its position, Augusta National sent a very noisy message to women in golf: Keep out.

What gives this the sweep of tragedy is that Johnson has harmed the things he loves the most, Augusta National and the game of golf. For three decades it has been a Johnson family tradition to spend Thanksgiving at the club. Hootie fairly glows when talking about it: "The family has gotten so big we've changed the format. Now we send out two foursomes of boys and one foursome of girls. I don't even get to play anymore, because all the grandsons and sons-in-law have elbowed me out. I just ride around and watch, not to heckle, but to cheer them on. It's a wonderful day we all look forward to."

The Johnson family foursome contributes to what Augusta National says is a thousand rounds per year played by women at the club. So if the fair sex is already such a constant presence at Augusta National, an oft-expressed sentiment throughout the membership controversy has been, what's the big deal in formalizing the arrangement and giving a couple of the gals a green jacket? The answer can be found at four club gatherings to which Hootie's daughters are not invited.

Augusta National's kindred spirits (to use Bob Jones's pet term) jet in four times a year for stag parties at which no guests are allowed, including wives. The four big shindigs are the Opening Party in October, the Governors Party in November, the Jamboree in late March, and the Closing Party the third week of May. Each has its own flavor. During the Closing, a BBQ pit is set up next to the Par-3 Course, and members hit shots to the first green while juggling drinks and the stray rib. At the Jamboree, preparations are already in high gear for the Masters, so the members' scores are displayed on the oversized on-course scoreboards. "It's as exciting as heck," says Hootie, who has twice teamed with chairman emeritus

Jack Stephens to win the Jamboree, earning a coveted silver box engraved with the names of every participant. Each of these gatherings, which typically attract a hundred or more far-flung members, feature a modicum of "bourbon, cigars, and ribaldry," to borrow a sneering summary from page A1 of *The New York Times*.

So how would the presence of a woman or three change the vibe? Consider that *Golf Digest* reported in April 2003 that the average age of the Augusta National membership is seventy-eight. (No wonder the club's New Year's Eve countdown is at ten-thirty P.M.) That means the typical green jacket was born in the late 1920s, to a mother who was among the first generation of women to be able to vote in this country. He came of age in the years after World War II, when traditional gender roles were rigidly enforced, and made his way in the corporate world in the 1960s and '70s, when a woman's place in the office was at the coffee-pot, fetching a fresh cup for her boss. A man of this generation, particularly if he is from the South, will stand when a woman enters the room. In her presence, interactions are more formal, and more civil. Would this subtle shift in the vibe cause Augusta National to crumble? Of course not—but it would alter the experience of the members, who go to the club to let down their hair, relax, and be themselves. When Hootie Johnson wrote in his "point of a bayonet" press release that Burk was seeking to "radically change" the membership, he meant it. And that is why he has fought so hard.

Johnson is a voracious reader, particularly of biographies of American leaders, and his friends have come to expect regular care packages as he sends, unsolicited, his latest favorite book. The historical figures who most intrigue him include Thomas Jefferson, John Adams, and Theodore Roosevelt, but when asked to pick one hero he summons two—Lincoln and Truman. "They could both make the tough decisions regardless of the heat," Johnson says.

In March 2003, the chairman sat for an interview with this writer. Swaddled in his green blazer, seated in a leather armchair in his office under President Eisenhower's oil portrait of Bob Jones, Johnson was the picture of vitality. (He is virtually the same weight now as during his college football heyday.) "I don't mean to say it's been fun, but it hasn't taken any kind of toll," Johnson said of the membership controversy. "I can handle it. I don't have any plans about stepping down, if that's what you're asking."

JOHNSON MAY NOT WANT to admit it, but there will be life after Hootie at Augusta National. His predecessor, Jack Stephens, served seven years as chairman. Before him, Hord Hardin lasted for eleven. The 2004 Masters will mark Johnson's sixth as chairman. He will be seventy-three, with a history of heart trouble and eleven grandkids to dote on. It would be surprising if Johnson serves more than another two or three years as chairman. Clearly there will be no change in the membership policy while he's the boss, but what about beyond?

Johnson's expected successor is Joe T. Ford, the club's vice chairman and a familiar figure to Masters fans as the jowly fellow who offers a stiff introduction at the outset of the CBS telecast. When Curt Sampson's *The Masters* was published in 1998, prior to Hootie's ascension, Ford was identified as the "chairman in waiting." That he didn't get the job was largely because of timing. At the time Ford was still the acting CEO at Alltel Corporation, which over the last four decades he built into the sixth-largest telephone company in the country, with more than 10 million customers. Among those Ford has enriched is his friend and fellow Little Rock native Jack Stephens, whose investment firm, Stephens Inc., is Alltel's largest shareholder. The connections run even deeper: Warren Stephens, Jack's son and another green jacket, is on Alltel's board, while Ford and Hootie Johnson are on the board of Stephens Inc.

Ford will be sixty-seven at the time of the 2004 Masters, the same age Johnson was when he became chairman. Having resigned as Alltel's CEO in 2002, Ford now has plenty of time to devote to Augusta National. Given his close ties to Stephens and Johnson, it is exceedingly unlikely that as chairman he would be an agent of change on the defining issue of women members.

So if Hootie sticks around for another two or three years, and Ford serves seven or eight after that, any movement on women members is at least a decade away. By then an entirely different generation will have assumed leadership positions at Augusta National. These will be men who reached adulthood just as feminism and the women's liberation movement were taking hold. They now work alongside powerful women in a business climate informed by the legacy of Anita Hill. If women are ever going to wear the green jacket this is the generation that will get it done.

Billy Payne and Fred Ridley are two members currently in their fifties who are widely considered to be strong candidates for chairman. Even before he was a member, Payne dreamed of bringing women to Augusta National as part of his vision of staging a coed Olympic competition. At the time he made a big deal of the club's post–Shoal Creek desegregation as a symbol of its evolution. "I understand and appreciate historical symbolism," Payne said in 1992, in response to objections over Augusta National as the chosen venue. "However, Augusta is moving forward, and I view [women in the Olympics] as a significant positive step."

Payne and Ridley are both lawyers by trade. Settling divisive cases is part of their job. With their backgrounds in the Olympic movement and the USGA, respectively, they have been conditioned to serve a broad constituency. Of course, Augusta National's traditions can override any personal ideology. Nothing in Hootie Johnson's background suggested that he would take such an emphatic hard-line stance against inclusion.

THANKS TO BOTH BURK and Johnson, the membership issue will continue to simmer, ready to bubble over with every news cycle. This most private of clubs has now entered the public domain. "We maintain many databases, and this is just one of them, like baseball salaries," says USA Today's Julie Ward about the paper's Augusta National membership roster. "We will certainly continue to update it over time. Could printing the membership list become an annual part of our Masters coverage? Absolutely."

Johnson's masterful battlefield strategy of cutting loose the tournament sponsors robbed Burk of important leverage, and clearly the club has the financial resources to remain sponsor-free indefinitely. But there are other potential pressure points for Augusta National, beyond what is sure to be an annual examination by the press. What if things don't work out with the Swedish swimsuit model and Tiger Woods marries a feminist and, à la Tom Wyman, embraces social activism? A boycott by Woods, or any other top player, would be devastating to the Masters. The

PGA Tour's position seems particularly vulnerable. If pressure could be brought to bear on the Tour to no longer recognize the Masters as an official event, that could have serious consequences, stigmatizing the National while adding a constellation of asterisks to the Tour's historical record. As dug in as the club seems to be on remaining all-male, recall that it was only a matter of weeks from Hall Thompson's interview with the *Birmingham Post-Herald* to the welcoming of Augusta National's first black member. Change can take years to ferment, and then happen overnight. It may be a decade or more away, but it is inevitable that the Augusta National membership will someday include a woman, as surely as the Bankers Trust board of directors did, and as inexorably as the color barrier was broken in the South Carolina legislature, both part of Hootie Johnson's lasting legacy. Rather than Lincoln and Truman, perhaps Johnson should look to a different historical figure for precedent, one who happened to be a friend. Back in 1957, while Johnson was serving in the South Carolina state assembly, Senator Strom Thurmond pulled off one of the most famous acts of defiance in American politics. In an effort to stall President Eisenhower's proposed civil rights bill, Thurmond filibustered for more than twenty-four straight hours. So as not to give up the floor, Thurmond never left the dais—not to eat, to use the restroom, or even to sit down. Johnson claims not to remember this iconic act of protest, but he does say of Thurmond, "Over time he turned 180 degrees." It is true that in his last twenty years in office Thurmond became more moderate, but that will not be his legacy. He will always be a symbol of intolerance and discrimination, a man who sought to impose his private prejudices on a divided public. History was not on his side. Eleven days after Thurmond's filibuster, the Civil Rights Act of 1957 became the law of the land.

THROUGHOUT THE AUGUSTA NATIONAL membership controversy, partisans on both sides have said that the fight was not about one golf club but rather about larger issues—the constitutional right of association, discrimination against women, and freedom of speech being the most freighted. During her Masters week rally in the Pit, Burk explicitly invoked the omnipresent abortion protesters at Augusta's Planned Parenthood, challenging Sheriff Strength to apply the same level of scrutiny to their activities as to hers.

Planned Parenthood is one of the NCWO's most important member groups, and it also has ties to Augusta National—it was one of the biggest beneficiaries in Clifford Roberts's will. If the Augusta National controversy really is about something bigger than just the membership practices of a private golf club, then the contested sidewalk in front of Augusta's Planned Parenthood should provide a glimpse of its ripple effect. So how is life after Martha there?

"It's been a mixed blessing," says Mary Beth Pierucci, the executive director of the Augusta Planned Parenthood. "Under the old system, every protest group needed a permit, but they could get one the same day, so we never knew who was going to show up. With the new protest ordinance that went in because of Martha Burk, there is a mandatory waiting period, so we have a better idea of what's coming, and we can plan for it. January 2004 is the thirtieth anniversary of *Roe v. Wade*, and twenty days in advance we'll know who's going to be protesting, and roughly what their numbers are. That's the good part.

"What is problematic is that now, under the Burk ordinance, groups of less than five don't need a permit, so there's a couple of very aggressive protesters who just show up whenever they feel like it. They have become a nuisance. But I will say, the sheriff has become very responsive since all the hoopla surrounding the Masters. The other day a couple of carloads of people showed up, and two or three set up in front, and another handful went around the back. I called Colonel Powell, and he said, 'Oh, no, that's just like Martha Burk, and that's not gonna fly. They're one group, and I'll send a car over to make that clear to them.' And in about thirty seconds a sheriff's deputy pulled up and told them that if they didn't have a permit they could be arrested, and poof, they disappeared. I was like, Thank you, Martha!"

So, in the final analysis, what is Burk's legacy in Augusta? Says Pierucci, "I guess you'd have to say, she did some good, and she did some bad."

Notes

Over two hundred interviews were conducted for this book. Where a quotation is drawn from a published report or transcript and that quote appeared in the same form in several places, I have not tried to guess which was the original media outlet.

5 *"Hootie Johnson, ah'm a-gonna . . ."*: Phil McCombs, *The Washington Post*, September 26, 2002.

5 *"It was such a small deal we . . ."*: Karen Crouse, *The Palm Beach Post*, April 6, 2003.

14 *He had grown up reading . . .* : David Owen, *The Making of the Masters*, p. 44.

15 *Jones and Roberts dreamed of . . .* : Owen, pp. 53, 61.

15 *By 1945, it was time to . . .* : Owen, p. 151.

16 *In 1948, Jones was diagnosed . . .* : Owen, p. 161.

17 *As Roberts recalled in a Columbia . . .* : As quoted in Curt Sampson's *The Masters*, p. 146.

18 *The preeminent golf writer . . .* : Owen, p. 19.

19 *It was also at the Masters . . .* : Steve Eubanks, Augusta, p. 109.

19 *The first Masters telecast in* 1956 . . . : Owen, p. 185.

19 *Reflecting on the success* . . . : Curt Sampson, *The Masters*, p. 67.

21 *A Terri philosopher named* . . . : William Gallo, *Sports Illustrated*, April 22, 1996.

21 *When Roberts was ten* . . . : Owen, p. 229.

21 *Among the green jackets was* . . . : Eubanks, p. 156.

21 *At his peak, Gosden* . . . : Sampson, pp. 119–20.

27 . . . *three of the four sacred corners* . . . : I borrowed this lovely phrase from Michael Bamberger, which he used in a *Sports Illustrated* feature dated September 24, 2001.

30 . . . *at Preston Trail* . . . : *Golf Digest*, March 2003.

33 *"He's by far the most* . . .": Mike Tierney, Cox News Services, September 14, 2002.

Chapter Three

38 . . . *put a roof over her head* . . . : This is an old line but I was reminded of it by a Karen Crouse feature in *The Palm Beach Post* on April 6, 2003.

38 *"She was not your typical grandmother* . . .": Crouse.

38 *"The difference between me and* . . .": McCombs.

38 *"Everybody wanted to be a cheerleader* . . .": David Newton, *The State*, March 30, 2003.

39 *"My first-year roommate's parents* . . .": Robert Dodge, *The Dallas Morning News*, March 2, 2003.

39 *"She was just like any other mother* . . .": McCombs.

39 *"Then men started coming out* . . .": Harry Blauvelt, *USA Today*, October 10, 2002.

39 *"The most radicalizing experience of* . . .": Peter J. Boyer, *The New Yorker*, February 14 and February 17, 2003.

39 *"I found it odd* . . .": McCombs.

40 *In the late seventies she* . . . : McCombs.

40 *She says that her budding* . . . : Betty Cuniberti, *St. Louis Post-Dispatch*, August 27, 2003.

45 *"I won't say I ever had an overt death threat* . . .": Crouse.

45 *"She's good-looking, sexy* . . .": Scott Michaux, *Augusta Chronicle*, September 29, 2003.

45 *"She's the woman of my* . . .": McCombs.

46 *"I can't say it was me or the circumstances* . . .": Michaux.

46 *"If we wanted to be effective* . . .": Bob Cullen, *Golf*, April 2003.

46   *"The idea was that children . . ."*: McCombs.

46   *"I have always believed in . . ."*: Blauvelt.

47   *Burk refurbished the boat . . .* : McCombs.

47   *Paul was an advocate for . . .* : Crouse.

47   *"Actually, it's more like . . ."*: David Casstevens, *Ft. Worth Star-Telegram*, October 27, 2003.

50   *"You get more bang . . ."*: Michaux.

57   *"I think there is a great deal . . ."*: Blaine Newnham, *The Seattle Times*, April 6, 2003.

57   *"I think if the Masters . . ."*: George Willis, *New York Post*, April 14, 2002.

Chapter Four

61   *"Our sponsorship is of the Masters . . ."*: Glenn Sheeley, *The Atlanta Journal-Constitution*, July 11, 2002.

63   *"We are not going to do anything . . ."*: Ron Sirak, *Golf World*, July 19, 2003.

64   *. . . a helicopter that was parked . . .* : I happened to be at the K Club at the same time as Woods and his friends.

65   Washington Post *columnist James K. Glassman . . .* : L. Jon Wertheim, *Sports Illustrated*, April 14, 2003.

69   *. . . a high profile class-action . . .* : Wire services, *The Miami Herald*, November 17, 2000.

71   *In fact, Coke's ties to . . .* : The Woodruff material was informed by Curt Sampson's excellent treatment in *The Masters*.

74   *"He is a person willing to sell . . ."*: Steve Elling, *The Orlando Sentinel*, October 31, 2002.

Chapter Five

83   *. . . Welch's abandoned wife, Jane . . .* : Del Jones, *USA Today*, March 5, 2002.

83   *"We want to know how many . . ."*: Richard Sandomir, *The New York Times*, September 28, 2002.

84   *"It is absolutely the wrong kind . . ."*: Sam Weinman, *The Journal News*, September 15, 2002.

84   *"I'm not going to talk about Augusta . . ."*: Steve Wiseman, *The State*, September 13, 2002.

92   *"In her missive to Ward . . ."*: Sandomir.

99 *"As a hired hand of the USGA . . ."*: Michael Bamberger, *Sports Illustrated,* July 29, 2002.

99 *"I think they have been strangely . . ."*: Joe Logan, *The Philadelphia Inquirer,* November 10, 2002.

99 *"Historically, we do not comment on . . ."*: Tommy Braswell, *Post and Courier,* January 26, 2003.

100 *"I don't see how a person . . ."*: Logan.

101 *"I would have liked to have known . . ."*: John Varlas, *The Commercial Appeal,* October 22, 2001.

102 *"It's a wonderful opportunity . . ."*: Ryberg William, *The Des Moines Register,* August 8, 1999.

103 *"If we've succeeded in anything . . ."*: Steve Wilstein, AP, November 1, 2002.

103 *"Tiger Woods cannot single-handedly . . ."*: Steve Elling, *The Orlando Sentinel,* August 10, 2002.

Chapter Six

109 *". . . smear campaign . . ."*: Associated Press, August 23, 1999.

109 *". . . shameful and unethical . . ."*: William Claiborne, *The Washington Post,* August 16, 1999.

109 *"I say to Mr. Hackler . . ."*: Claiborne.

121 *"I'm not going to risk . . ."*: Leonard Shapiro, *The Washington Post,* November 14, 2002.

128 *Grady straightened her master's curly hair . . .* : Ken Auletta, *The New Yorker,* June 10, 2002.

129 *In trumpeting the awards . . .* : Shelley Emling and Caroline Wilbert, *The Atlanta Journal-Constitution,* July 1, 2003.

129 *The Washington bureau began . . .* : Auletta.

139 *"There are a whole lot of . . ."*: The passage quoted here is from the printed version of Araton's column.

140 *"I got far more attention . . ."*: John M. McGuire, *St. Louis Post-Dispatch,* March 15, 2000.

140 *"I hope tomorrow . . ."*: Harry Levins, *St. Louis Post-Dispatch,* July 27, 2001.

141 *At some point Araton spoke . . .* : Sridhar Pappu, *New York Observer,* December 16, 2002.

145 *"Araton admits that he . . ."*: Pappu.

147 *"Augusta National has now become . . ."*: Peter J. Boyer, *The New Yorker*, February 17 and February 14, 2003.

149 All of the Morris background in this paragraph was extracted from Michael Bamberger's feature in the April 5, 1999, *Sports Illustrated*.

157 *The rivalry between Chambers . . . .* : I conducted the interview with Brennan, and wrote the headline. I was also one of the *Sports Illustrated* staffers who received Chambers's care package.

CHAPTER SEVEN

172 *His haul included $11,300 . . .* : A review of county records reveals the following contributions: Clayton P. Boardman III's family donated $9,300—he personally contributed $2,000, his father, $2,000, his mother Ann, $2,000, his wife Catherine, $2,000, his brother Braye, $1,000, and his cousin Alonzo P. Jr., $300; William Copenhaven, $300; Ed Douglass, $500; Nick Evans $500; Dessey Kuhlke $700—$200 personally, $500 from his brother W. B.

172 *"The sheriff department's links to . . ."*: Mike Wynn and Greg Wickabaugh, *Augusta Chronicle*, March 13, 2003.

173 *The protesters were arrested because . . . .* : Sylvia Cooper, *Augusta Chronicle*, March 17, 2001.

177 *A census in 1790 recorded . . . .* : Curt Sampson, *The Masters*, p. 71.

178 *It included $10,700 from eight . . .* : A review of county records reveals the following contributions: Louis Battey, $200; Clayton P. Boardman III, $5,000—$2,000 personally, $2,000 through his brother Braye, $500 through his mother Ann, $300 through his cousin Alonzo Jr., and $200 through his cousin Harold; Ed Douglass, $500, in the name of Radio Cab; Phil Harison, $2,000, through Harison-Kerzic, Inc., of which he is cofounder; Boone Knox's $600—$400 through his cousin Wyck, $200 through his niece Julia; Dessey Kuhlke, $1,000, from his brother W. B.; Claude Nielsen, $500, through Coca-Cola Bottling, of which he was president and CEO; and Leroy Simkins, $500.

179 *"The racial problems . . ."*: Heidi Coryell Williams, *Augusta Chronicle*, December 1, 2002.

187 *"It will escalate now . . ."*: Glenn Sheeley, *The Atlanta Journal-Constitution*, March 1, 2003.

192 *"Lyndon Johnson School of . . ."*: Tim Sullivan, *The San Diego Union-Tribune*, March 4, 2003.

193 *"Nobody can say this is . . ."*: David A. Markiewicz, *The Atlanta Journal-Constitution*, March 7, 2003.

196 *"I found out that Sheriff Strength . . ."*: Wynn and Wickabaugh.

196 *"Would that affect my . . ."*: Wynn and Wickabaugh.

201 *"That judge should have . . ."*: T. J. Quinn, *New York Daily News*, April 9, 2003.

CHAPTER EIGHT

207 *"For people who watch and . . ."*: Glenn Sheeley, *The Atlanta Journal-Constitution*, January 26, 2003.

207 *"If you've got an inkling . . ."*: Sheeley, January 23, 2003.

208 *"It's hard to say what's right . . ."*: Steve Elling, *The Orlando Sentinel*, March 16, 2003.

208 *"No matter what you say . . ."*: Doug Ferguson, AP, March 20, 2003.

208 *"Have you ever seen me duck . . ."*: Joe Gordon, *Boston Herald*, March 23, 2003.

208 *"Martha Burk is actually promoting . . ."*: Mick Elliott, *The Tampa Tribune*, April 3, 2003.

208 *"The solution is . . ."*: Sheeley, January 23, 2003.

209 *"I couldn't care less . . ."*: Sheeley, *The Atlanta Journal-Constitution*, April 6, 2003.

209 *"There's so much bad blood . . ."*: Sheeley, January 23, 2003.

209 *"I admire their pluck . . ."*: David Markiewicz, *The Atlanta Journal-Constitution*, March 9, 2003.

209 *"They got the 'duh' part . . ."*: Joseph White, AP, March 8, 2003.

210 On *March 14, during a . . .*: Ed Sherman, *Chicago Tribune*, March 15, 2003.

CHAPTER NINE

220 *"I thought the course would be . . ."*: Doug Ferguson, AP, April 7, 2003.

220 *"I didn't have a clue . . ."*: Jim McCabe, *The Boston Globe*, April 7, 2003.

241 *"This was our last shot . . ."*: Paul Newberry, AP, April 9, 2003.

242 *". . . women of color . . ."*: Heidi Coryell Williams, *Augusta Chronicle*, April 11, 2003.

242 *"Plan B is arrest if . . ."*: Jim Slater, Agence France, April 10, 2003.

245 *"Burk began Thursday morning . . ."*: Michael Bamberger, *Sports Illustrated*, April 21, 2003.

256 *"I can only speak for myself . . ."*: Michael Carvell, Cox News Service, April 11, 2003.

256 *"We're not sure about that . . ."*: Patrick Hruby, *The Washington Times*, April 12, 2002.

256 *"This is going to be the . . ."*: The Sports Network, April 11, 2003.

260 *"Do you realize what today . . ."*: Bamberger.

264 *"My husband plays golf . . ."*: Michael Carvell, et al., *The Atlanta Journal-Constitution*, April 12, 2003.

268 *In fact, Ditmore . . . .*: Rick Telander, *Chicago Sun-Times*, April 13, 2003.

268 *"I interpreted this broadly . . ."*: Sally Jenkins, *The Washington Post*, April 13, 2003.

269 *"It sounded like it . . ."*: Josh Katzowitz, *Augusta Chronicle*, April 14, 2003.

269 *"I'm thinking of going after . . ."*: Wes Smith, *The Orlando Sentinel*, April 13, 2003.

269 *One cluster included . . . .* : Jenkins.

270 *"One mistake we've made . . ."*: Sam Weinman, *The Journal News*, April 13, 2003.

270 *"Augusta has a right to . . ."*: Smith.

271 *"I Hear You Knockin' . . ."*: Scott Ostler, *San Francisco Chronicle*, April 13, 2003.

288 *. . . there is always a winner and a loser . . . .* : Beginning in 2002, I wrote a "Winners and Losers" column following every major championship for *Sports Illustrated*'s Golf Plus. In this no-shades-of-gray format, following the '03 Masters I made Hootie Johnson a Winner ("Augusta National's embattled chairman hit a home run in his annual Wednesday press conference, as Johnson was funny, combative and resolute in defending the club. He should have gone on camera months ago.") and Martha Burk a Loser ("She likes to brag of seven million constituents, but Burk could only coax about 30 onto the protest bus. Her new tack is targeting Augusta National's members, an admission that Hootie will not yield.").

294 *Sitting in the cart . . . .* : Scott Price, *Sports Illustrated*, April 21, 2003.

296 *Now the sign said . . . .* : Tara Gavel, golfonline.com, April 13, 2003.

Chapter Ten

308 *Bloomberg News estimated . . . .* : Don McKee, *The Philadelphia Inquirer*, May 25, 2003.

308 *On the day of . . . .* : Shawn Langolis, *CBS Market Watch*, May 23, 2003.

308 *The day after the* . . . : Mark Hyman, *BusinessWeek Online*, May 23, 2003.

310 *"I think the economy* . . .": Chris Isidore, CNN/Money, April 4, 2003.

310 *"Last year was actually* . . .": Isidore.

317 *At the rally* . . . : Beth Hatcher, Morris News Service, September 27, 2003.

319 *"They are both completely behind* . . .": Steve Elling, *The Orlando Sentinel*, November 12, 2003.

319 *"It has nothing to do* . . .": Greg Farrell, *USA Today*, October 3, 2003.

Chapter Eleven

327 *"If James Meredith had* . . .": Robert Dodge, *The Dallas Morning News*, March 2, 2003.

328 *when they weren't playing* . . . : David Owen, *The Making of the Masters*, p. 215.

329 *"It's as exciting as heck* . . .": Ron Sirak, *Golf Digest*, April 2003.

334 . . . *one of the biggest beneficiaries* . . . : Curt Sampson, *The Masters*, p. 196.

Bibliography

Abramson, Jill, and Jane Mayer. *Strange Justice: The Selling of Clarence Thomas*. Boston: Houghton Mifflin, 1994.

Bowen, Ann Herd. *Greenwood County: A History*. Orangeburgh, S.C.: Sandlapper Publishing Co., 1992.

Cash, W. J. *The Mind of the South*. New York: Knopf, 1941.

Chalmers, David Mark. *Hooded Americanism: The History of the Ku Klux Klan*. Durham, N.C.: Duke University Press, 1987.

Chambers, Marcia. *The Unplayable Lie: The Untold Story of Women and Discrimination in American Golf*. New York: Pocket Books, 1996.

Cohodas, Nadine. *Strom Thurmond and the Politics of Southern Change*. Macon, Ga.: Mercer University Press, 1994.

Crouse, Timothy. *The Boys on the Bus*. New York: Random House, 1973.

Diamond, Edwin. *Behind the Times: Inside The New York Times*. New York: Villard Books, 1994.

Edgars, Walter B. *South Carolina: A History*. Columbia, S.C.: University of South Carolina Press, 1998.

Estes, Ralph. *The Tyranny of the Bottom Line: Why Corporations Make Good People Do Bad Things*. San Francisco: Berrett-Koehler Publishing, 1996.

Eubanks, Steve. *Augusta: Home of the Masters Tournament*. Nashville, Tenn.: Rutledge Hill Press, 1997.

Feinstein, John. *Open: Inside the Ropes at Bethpage Black*. Boston: Little, Brown & Co., 2003.

Goldberg, Bernard. *Bias: A CBS Insider Exposes How the Media Distort the News*. Washington, D.C.: Regnery Publishing, 2001.

Jones, Robert T. and O. B. Keeler. *Down the Fairway*. New York: Minton Balch & Co., 1954.

Jones, Robert T. *Golf Is My Game*. Garden City, N.Y.: Doubleday, 1960.

Langely, Monica. *Tearing Down the Walls: How Sandy Weill Fought His Way to the Top of the Financial World . . . and Then Nearly Lost It All*. New York: Free Press, 2002.

MacKenzie, Alister. *The Spirit of St. Andrews*. Chelsea, Mich.: Sleeping Bear Press, 1995.

McCarthy, Colman. *The Pleasures of the Game: The Theory-Free Guide to Golf*. Garden City, N.Y.: Doubleday, 1977.

Owen, David. *The Making of the Masters*. New York: Simon & Schuster, 1999.

Pendergrast, Mark. *For God, Country, and Coca-Cola*. New York: Charles Scribner's Sons, 1993.

Raines, Howell. *Fly Fishing Through the Midlife Crisis*. New York: William Morrow, 1993.

Roberts, Clifford. *The Story of Augusta National Golf Club*. Garden City, N.Y.: Doubleday, 1976.

Sampson, Curt. *The Masters: Golf, Money and Power in Augusta, Georgia*. New York: Villard Books, 1998.

Schaller, Michael. *Present Tense: The United States Since 1945*. Boston: Houghton Mifflin, 1992.

Strege, John. *Tiger*. New York: Broadway Books, 1997.

Talese, Gay. *The Kingdom and the Power*. London: Calder & Boyars, 1971.

Toobin, Jeffrey. *Too Close to Call: The Thirty-Six-Day Battle to Decide the 2000 Election*. New York: Random House, 2001.

Welch, Jack. *Jack: Straight from the Gut*. New York: Warner Books, 2001.

Wilson, Charles Reagan. *Encyclopedia of Southern Culture*. Chapel Hill, N.C.: University of North Carolina Press, 1989.

Wolfe, Tom. *A Man in Full*. New York: Farrar, Straus & Giroux, 1998.

Yockey, Ross. *McColl: The Man with America's Money*. Atlanta, Ga.: Longstreet Press, 1999.

Acknowledgments

THIS BOOK WOULD HAVE HAPPENED without my researcher, Gene Menez, but it probably would not have been published until 2006. A crackerjack writer-reporter at *Sports Illustrated*, Gene was for me equal parts gumshoe, fact-checker, and wet nurse. Thanks again for all the help, pards.

I am also indebted to my editor, Jeff Neuman, for the care and attention he lavished on this project. He improved the manuscript in a hundred different ways (and that's a conservative estimate). I also want to thank my eagle-eyed copy editor, Megan Collins, who literally dotted all of my *i*'s.

Every book is an intersection of art and commerce, and in regards to the latter, I was well taken care of by my agent, David Black, a tireless advocate and good friend. David Rosenthal, the publisher at Simon & Schuster, has been a cheerleader for this project from day one, and he moved heaven and earth to get this book out in time. His colleague Kerri Kolen helped make it happen with her endless hard work and good cheer.

This tale was informed by the generosity of a few of my fellow writers. If there were times when it appeared as if I was in more than one place at the same time during Masters week, that's because I was. My longtime mentor Michael Bamberger shared his notebook with me, along with a number of helpful ruminations. I am also indebted to Teri Thompson, who passed along some great proprietary material. Gary Van Sickle conducted one short but crucial interview on my behalf.

Many, many people worked behind the scenes to help me secure interviews and information. I'd like to recognize three: Glenn Greenspan, who went out on a limb to get me into Hootie Johnson's office; Ann Herd Bowen, who provided a driving tour of Hootie's old hometown as well as invaluable source materials from his youth; and Bob Gillespie in South Carolina, who provided so many key phone numbers.

I couldn't have done this book without the support of my colleagues at *Sports Illustrated*. Golf editor Jim Herre not only helped convince me to take on this challenge, but our endless conversations around the watercooler sharpened many of my ideas, to say nothing of those that I stole outright from him. The magazine's brain trust—David Bauer, Rob Fleder, Mike Bevans and, especially, Terry McDonell—were all extremely encouraging, even though that meant having to share my time and attention. I would also like to recognize *SI* librarians Helen Stauder and Linda Wachtel, who saved my bacon at a couple of crucial junctures.

And a special thanks to Jane Rosenman, for making that phone call.

Index